THE COLLECTED PROSE OF

ROBERT FROST

THE COLLECTED PROSE OF
ROBERT FROST

EDITED BY
MARK RICHARDSON

THE BELKNAP PRESS OF HARVARD UNIVERSITY PRESS

Cambridge, Massachusetts

London, England

2007

"The Prerequisites" is reprinted from Robert Frost, *Aforesaid,* copyright 1954, 1969 by Henry Holt and Company. "Education by Poetry," "The Prerequisites," and "The Figure a Poem Makes" are reprinted from *Selected Prose of Robert Frost,* edited by Hyde Cox and Edward Connery Lathem, copyright 1939, 1966, 1967 by Henry Holt and Company. "Some Observations on Style" is reprinted from *The Letters of Robert Frost to Louis Untermeyer,* compilation copyright 1963 by Louis Untermeyer. All are reprinted by permission of Henry Holt and Company, LLC.

Library of Congress Cataloging-in-Publication Data

Frost, Robert, 1874–1963.
  [Selections. 2007]
  The collected prose of Robert Frost / edited by Mark Richardson.
    p.   cm.
  Includes bibliographical references and index.
  ISBN 978-0-674-02463-2 (cloth : alk paper)
  I. Richardson, Mark, 1963–   II. Title.
  PS3511.R94A6 2007
  811'.52—dc22   2007013210

Contents

Introduction

Upon taking up this edition, the reader may first notice, with some surprise, that a great deal of the prose Robert Frost published had appeared before he ever became widely known as a poet—in fact, some eight years before his first volume of poetry, *A Boy's Will* (London: David Nutt, 1913), had even appeared. His reluctance later in life to publish prose, and to collect it in an edition once published, became a matter of some notoriety among the few scholars and editors who, during the 1930s and after, expressed interest in undertaking editions of his prose. They found Frost peculiarly uncooperative, as had Van Wyck Brooks when, in the summer of 1921, he asked Frost to write an essay, presumably for *The Freeman,* which Brooks then edited. Frost replied: "I am no such Puritan as to enjoy resisting temptation. It is hard for me to refuse you: but I must. I used to say prose after thirty; then in the thirties, prose after forty. Still distrusting myself at forty odd, I now say after fifty. Out of what we don't know and so can't be hurt by, poetry: out of knowledge, prose. Wait til I get wisdom; wait til I sell out and move to 'the place of understanding,' by which Solomon (or was it David?) must have meant Chicago—the Middle West anyway."[1] As it happens, neither Solomon nor David meant Chicago. Surely Frost must have in mind Job's heretofore obscurely prophetic reference to the Middle West: "But where shall wisdom be found? And where is the place of understanding?" (Job 28:12). In any case, and keeping the matter fixed on prose, Frost also said, in a 1933 letter giving advice to his son Carol: "You can say a lot in prose that verse won't let you say, especially rhymed verse. You'll set yourself an example in prose of fullness and straightforwardness that your verse will be the better for having to follow. I haven't published any prose, but I know the prose I have written has made good competition for my verse."[2] He had, of course, published prose by 1933, just not in prominent places. A reader had to go looking for the good competition.

Some readers, in fact, did do precisely that. Robert S. Newdick, a professor of English at Ohio State University and an early biographer of Frost, cobbled together a manuscript of Frost's prose in the late 1930s titled "Prefaces and Parleyings." He was in earnest correspondence with Henry Holt and Company, Frost's American publisher, before Frost caused the edition to be held back. (Never published, the typescript of the edition is held now at the Alderman Library, University of Virginia.) In 1938 Lawrance Thompson—later, the author of a three-volume biography of the poet—was also tentatively working on a collection of his prose in conjunction with Wilbert Snow. At the same time Harvard University Press was still entertaining hopes that Frost would prepare his 1936 Charles Eliot Norton Lectures for publication. None of these projects was ever advanced, and the only transcript of the Norton lectures that Harvard prepared for Frost disappeared while in his possession.[3] He explained in a February 24, 1938, letter to R. P. T. Coffin: "I thought I was about ready to let [the lectures] set when I accepted the Harvard invitation to deliver them in writing after delivering them by word of mouth. Something in me still fights off the written prose" (*SL* 461). When Frost renegotiated his contract with Henry Holt and Company in 1940 he promised to produce a volume of prose by the spring of 1941.[4] A trial table of contents for such a book appears in a manuscript notebook held now at Dartmouth College Library. And it may have been at this time that Frost undertook extensive (though incomplete) revisions to his 1931 essay "Education by Poetry"[5] and also prepared, in manuscript, an essay titled "Vocal Imagination: The Last Refinement of Subject Matter," which sums up ideas expressed much earlier in a remarkable series of letters written to poets and friends in 1913–1915. But his native resistance to publishing his prose, expressed already in the 1921 letter to Brooks, overcame whatever resolve he had in 1940 and 1941. The matter was once again dropped.

For many years, Frost's reluctance to commit his prose to print, or to collect it when printed, seemed oddly to have survived his death. It was almost as if he still oversaw these affairs.[6] Several editions of prose appeared in the 1960s and 1970s, but these preserved only a fraction of what he published and were themselves permitted to go out of print. In 1966 Edward Connery Lathem and Hyde Cox published, with Holt, Rinehart and Winston, a slim volume, *Selected Prose of Robert Frost*. This contains Frost's best essays on poetics, and other items of interest, but the book hardly suggests the full range of Frost's work in prose, and it contains a number of textual inaccuracies. *Selected Prose* was followed in 1972 by *Robert Frost: Poetry and Prose* (New York: Holt, Rinehart and Winston), edited jointly by Lathem and Lawrance Thompson, and later reissued by the same press under the title *A Robert Frost Reader*. This reprints about half of the items included in the earlier volume, together with a number of others—a few items from Frost's high-school journalism, several stories for *Farm-Poultry* and *The Eastern Poultryman*, letters, interviews, talks. The selection is more varied than that given in *Selected Prose*, but it is hardly comprehensive, and the texts remain marred by occasional inaccuracies. Elaine Barry's *Robert Frost on Writing* (Rutgers University Press, 1973) provided a good selection of previously collected essays on writing, and published for the first time several short lectures. But by design

Barry's book wasn't comprehensive, omitting, as it did, essays that address subjects not explicitly related to writing; and once again, the volume was not informed by fresh primary textual research.[7]

These problems were partly remedied when *Robert Frost: Collected Poems, Prose, and Plays* was issued in 1995 by the Library of America (edited by Richard Poirier and myself). The present edition supplements that edition, from which it differs in several important respects. It reprints all of the prose Frost is known to have prepared for print, major and minor items alike, and it provides extensive and detailed notes on Frost's habits of composition, on important textual issues, and on related matters. In addition, reprinted in the notes are extracts from Frost's correspondence with various editors, together with other information that illuminates this seldom-studied phase of the poet's career. I have also included many, often lengthy, extracts from Frost's unpublished talks and readings, and from Lawrance Thompson's unpublished "Notes on Conversations with Robert Frost." These performances and conversations were, for Frost, the workshop in which he refined ideas later developed in his major published prose, and it is instructive to see him playing through those ideas extemporaneously.

In arranging the notes, I had two aims in mind: to allow the reader to consult in one place all information presented in connection with a given item, and to provide a kind of loosely consequential narrative of Frost's total career as a writer of prose—a narrative which, it is hoped, will engage the general reader as well as readers concerned with editorial issues. For example, a reader interested in the introduction to *King Jasper* will find, on consulting the notes, an account of the essay's composition; extracts from a bickering exchange of letters among editors at Macmillan unsatisfied with Frost's political views; a record of Frost's revisions to the first draft of the essay; quotations of passages from Frost's unpublished talks that show him working through ideas expressed more concisely in the published essay; and identification of passages from Robinson's poetry quoted in the essay. A reader interested in "The Figure a Poem Makes" will find in the notes, in addition to textual information, reports of a conversation in which Frost explains the meaning of the preface's title, reports of another in which he draws a provocative analogy between poetry and love-making, and extracts from four addresses—one given in 1927, one in 1931, one in the mid-1940s, and one in 1962—in which he discusses other important themes touched on in the preface. A reader examining the three prose articles Frost published while employed at Pinkerton Academy between 1906 and 1910 will find documents offering a portrait of Frost's work as a teacher in his early years in education. Similar matter is provided for most of Frost's major essays and, again, for many of his minor ones. In total, the notes contain more than sixty typescript pages of previously unpublished material supplementary to the published essays.[8] And I have tried to make these notes more or less consecutively readable, and of interest to persons who might not typically delve into what we often call, in the trade, "the textual apparatus."

The contents of the present edition bear out the accuracy and candor of Frost's remark in a 1941 letter to his daughter Lesley: "Any prose I write will be for the purpose of widening the circle of my poetry and increasing our chances of being remembered" (*FL* 226). In the context of the letter this is a melancholy reflection; Frost seemed to believe that his great work was behind him. But as a comment on the occasions of much of the prose he did publish—in particular the prefaces, articles, and ephemera that are not well known—it is on the mark. In surveying the entire range of Frost's published prose, one cannot escape the fact that the central essays on poetics—the introduction to *King Jasper* (1935), "The Constant Symbol" (1946), "The Figure a Poem Makes" (1939), the "Letter" to *The Amherst Student* (1935), and others— were written by a poet of extraordinary and peculiar popularity. (In 1938, for example, he was invited to contribute to a cookbook cavalierly titled *The Stag at Ease; Being the Culinary Preferences of a Number of Distinguished Male Citizens of the World,* for which see item 25.) He ultimately became a thoroughly public figure, even a celebrity, remembered by many Americans more for his personality than for his poetry.[9] This is not beside the point. In reading Frost's major writings on poetics we begin to see how they reflect his efforts to establish, and then to maintain, a public career as a poet in America during the first half of this century. That is to say, his statements on poetics, even when they address impersonal and more or less timeless questions about craft, record his personal struggles to "socialize" his art. For this reason, it seems to me, it is useful to examine the full range of his prose writings, even though a number of the items he published bear relatively slight interest in themselves. Following is a general overview of the items reprinted in the present edition.

Early Prose

I pointed out that a remarkable amount of Frost's prose was published long before he achieved recognition as a poet—most of it before he was thirty years old. Some suggestion of the value of these early writings is appropriate, particularly in light of Frost's remark in a 1925 preface to an anthology of student poetry: "The poet, as everyone knows, must strike his individual note sometime between the ages of fifteen and twenty-five. He may hold it a long time, or a short time, but it is then he must strike it or never" (13.4). Frost's poetry and prose alike affirm this contention. He certainly had developed a style in youth, which is perhaps why his classmates elected him editor of the Lawrence, Massachusetts, *High School Bulletin* in the spring of 1891. He had previously published two poems in the *Bulletin,* but no prose. Frost assumed his duties in the fall, writing five articles for the paper's September editorial page, and serving as editor of the October, November, and December numbers of the *Bulletin.* His classmates and teachers may well have felt something new was afoot at the *Bulletin* when the editor announced, in his inaugural column: "This chair, when not acting as a weapon of defense, will be devoted to the caprices of its occupant. Properly speaking it will be an easy chair, sufficiently roomy for practicing the divine art, 'abandon.' We find it quite impossible to lay open more of the future than this" (1.5). There is much ambition in this boyish declaration, which manages to be both coy and cocky; we are already dealing with a writer. As it happened, Frost resigned four months later out of frustration with his staff. His sister Jeanie's serious illness in late fall 1891 had required him to remain out of school, and, during his absence, Frost delegated preparation of the December number to subordinates. Upon returning to school he found that nothing had been done toward preparing the issue for the press. He had no choice but to improvise nearly all of the copy for the December *Bulletin* himself. He professed to be angry about it. But he always welcomed a chance to perform, and would often say, later in life: "I only go / When I'm the show" (*CPPP* 547). For the December number, over a variety of pseudonyms, Frost published an essay about the ancient city of Petra, a brief history of the "Charter Oak" of Hartford, Connecticut, a bracing (but likely insincere) exhortation to his comrades to become physically fit, and, among several other items, a whimsical fiction about an artist who plagiarizes a painting only to drop dead when he is discovered. The latter ends with an odd flourish, touched by imagery local to the industrial city of Lawrence: "Fastening his arms rigidly up into the night, [the artist] gave a wild shriek and his spirit fled as the mill laborers leave the mill at the shriek of the great steam whistle. It was all done in three seconds. . . . You don't like this tale? Neither do I! You are a philanthropist? Well, I am. That's a coincidence" (1.85). Frost cryptically signed the story "Kthon," maybe to suggest its origin in the psyche of an underground artist who was himself perpetrating a fraud of sorts in getting up an entire issue of the *Bulletin* from nothing (and from recently published histories of Hartford County, Connecticut). After resigning, Frost filled in as editor of the May 1892 number, supplying four editorials. Later, the *Bulletin* for June 1892 reprinted his high-school valedictory address, "A Monument to After-Thought Unveiled."

Already in the articles written for the *Bulletin* we find some of Frost's characteristic concerns. For example, there is this observation from a November 1891 editorial announcing a literary contest, an observation that anticipates later emphases in his writings on poetics: "It has been said that versifiers are mere slaves of rhyme,—a sure proof of a curtailed vocabulary which can be no better done away with than by the entertaining diversion of verse writing" (1.41). Much later he would assert, against the Imagists and free-verse poets, that great liberties may be taken within even strict poetic forms, and that in any event it is impossible, even undesirable, to escape the pressures of form. For Frost, restrictive form was itself the means to become fully sensible of the liberties he was capable of taking. Or, as he expresses it at this early juncture: slavery to rhyme is best overcome by exercises in rhyme. The only way out is through. Frost would remark some sixty years later, in an appearance at Kenyon College: "Here you are with a bursting emotion and you're limited to a very small vocabulary [t]hat the teachers have tried to stretch but haven't stretched much for you. You're so defiant, you don't give a damn for that, you say, 'I don't give a damn if I haven't got many words. Watch me, watch me take them right out of the air.' The[n] you say, 'Not only that, I'm not scared to limit myself a little more with meter and rhyme.' You see, it tightens the vocabulary a little bit more, but it just shows that you're alive and strong and you know you can do it" (quoted more fully in the notes to 36.15).

Frost worked and reworked these ideas about freedom-in-bondage throughout his long career in poetry, beginning, as we have seen, as early as 1891. And there is in his 1892 valedictory address already some indication of how astonishing were his ambitions for that career. Frost rises to a high romantic pitch, as befitted his Shelleyan disposition at the time: "It is when alone, in converse with their own thoughts so much that they live their conventionalities, forgetful of the world's, that men form those habits called the heroism of genius, and lead the progress of the race." "All this is doubly so," Frost contends, in the "theoretical" and "poetic" arenas, as against the arena of "statesmanship" and "action." For the poet, "the after-thought of long nights beneath the universe, of soul stirrings, of the act of thought itself, is [even] more clearly [than it is for the statesman] a part of the next action—its expression. Events may influence" the sphere of action. But in poetry a man is influenced by "the limits of language alone." The peroration has the courage of conviction: "Unbounded full ambition for the greatest heights yet unattained is not too noble for one human mind. Who or what can bound our aspirations? Will courage fail before a thousand unfavorable comparisons?" (see item 1.112ff.). Frost would suffer not a thousand but anyway a good many "unfavorable comparisons" on the part of more conventional folk in his long effort to realize his ambition as a poet during his years "in neglect" (to borrow a phrase from an early poem). At eighteen he already seemed ready to accept—because he describes it here, as if in prospect, so appealingly—the fertile period of withdrawal that would come for him between 1900 and 1906 on the farm at Derry, New Hampshire, and that would shape the contours of his first collection of poetry, and even of his second and third.[10] Speaking in 1892 about the heroism of a genius developed apart from the world's conventionalities, he would have to wait twenty-one years to see that volume of long after-thoughts, *A Boy's Will,* carried over into print.[11]

However that may be, the article next reprinted in this edition, from the Lawrence, Massachusetts, *Daily American,* finds the young Frost in this his first paid writing job affecting the altogether worldly, somewhat sardonic tone of the journalism associated at the time with his contemporary Stephen Crane (though Frost could hardly have known it). Frost had lately taken a job as reporter for a Lawrence newspaper, to which he contributed, among other things, a kind of general interest column, containing such paragraphs as these:

> I am going to betray a confidence and worse than that a poor man's confidence, but only in the hope of compelling for him your natural if unrighteous sympathy. There are a lot of women and children that have let me see them looting coal in a yard near here. They come with buckets and gather it piece by piece under the coal cars. It is feverish work keeping warm for such people. And the curious part of it is, they will not take the coal otherwise than from off the ground, which necessitates their twice handling it, once from the car to the ground, and again from the ground to the bucket. The moral strain attendant on such work must be excessive, and one suffers to watch them skulking and stooping all day long. (2.4)

I have already said a word about the tone of the article. Its themes remind us that, notwithstanding the agrarian setting of most of Frost's mature poetry, he spent his youth in the heavily industrialized towns of eastern Massachusetts. During the 1890s—those years of Depression and labor unrest—Lawrence was in many respects a representative hard-luck eastern city, and with a reputation, if Frost's remarks in the high-school *Bulletin* are to be trusted, for illiteracy (1.6). The town was, culturally speaking, a long way from Cambridge and Harvard, where Frost would, in two years' time, be studying while moonlighting at a local night school. His remarks in the column, as a whole, indirectly touch on problems of working-class poverty (Lawrence was the site of bitter labor struggles); on the difficulties of Armenian refugees from the conflict in Turkey; on the then-influential nativist organization the American Protective Association—an illiberal manifestation of developments hardly impertinent to Frost's fellow citizens in what came to called the "Immigrant City"; and on the Japanese military victory in China, which marked, it may be, the beginning of the end of European colonialism in Asia, and which caught many American observers, including the prominent one to whom Frost refers in the column, by surprise. In short, the column reprinted here shows us a 21-year-old Frost much engaged by public affairs, and writing about them in the rigorously unsentimental tone to which he would, much later, often have recourse. His prose style in 1895 is already vividly realized. It would change relatively little over the years, all things considered. He dryly remarks, in reference to the Honorable Lewis Wallace (1827–1905), the pro-Turkish former ambassador to Ankara and popular novelist: "The author of Ben Hur, for a long time the fellow-townsman of the Sultan, sends his respects to the Sultan and pronounces the Armenian outrages exaggerated. This is hard luck my friends," Frost concedes to his many Armenian-American readers in Lawrence. "You did not expect to find such authority arrayed against you. But take comfort. You may be right. This sort of man is very inconsequential if only he can advance an idea" (2.2). The manner is as self-assured as it is sibylline; it shows great detachment. In these respects, again, Frost's prose suggests Stephen Crane: it is hard to tell just who has been hit, and exactly how. (Frost would make something of an art of this in his later tributes to Amy Lowell and Percy MacKaye, and in his preface to Sidney Cox's book *A Swinger of Birches,* all reprinted herein.) It is a shame so little of Frost's work during his very brief career as a journalist is recoverable (see the notes to item 2 for a record of what is known about it). Nevertheless, the paragraphs reprinted here add some small measure of depth to the context, in Frost's early years, out of which came such poems on urban and industrial themes as "The Parlor Joke" (1910), "The Mill City" (1905), and "When the Speed Comes" (1906), all of which are gathered in *CPPP*. They give us some intimation of the kind of place Lawrence, Massachusetts, was in the young Frost's eyes.

In reading further into Frost's youthful work, however, we pass from Armenian refugees, impoverished city dwellers, and embittered American "nativists," to the farm and farmers "north of Boston" where he lived from 1900 to 1907, and we find him a married man with children and a farm to keep. First among the documents in this phase included here are a series of stories Frost composed for his own children, in which they figure by name: Lesley, Irma, Carol, and Marjorie (known in the earliest of the stories simply as "Baby"). Also present are the family dog Schneider, and a local menagerie of talking squirrels, woodchucks, and birds of various feather. I'll not offer a judgment as to their merit as what is now called "children's literature." But these little stories have a certain enduring charm and wit. And together with the published short stories that follow them in the present edition they fill out for us the portrait of the Frost family's life in rural New England just after the turn of the twentieth century. What these years of relative seclusion meant to the poet is suggested by a remark he later made in a 1915 letter to William Stanley Braithwaite: "I kept farm, so to speak for nearly ten years [i.e., from 1900 to 1909], but less as a farmer than as a fugitive from the world that seemed to me to 'disallow' me. It was all instinctive, but I can see now that I went away to save myself and fix myself before I measured my strength against all creation. I was never really out of the world for good and all. I liked people even when I believe I detested them" (*CPPP* 684). The short stories altogether bear out that last remark.

With these stories we enter on the financially dismal but literarily profitable poultry-farming phase of his career. And in regard to Frost's writings for two New England poultry journals it must be acknowledged first that they are surely the best poultry-stories written by a modern American poet. They are in fact quite good.[12] In "The Original and Only" Frost works in the monologue form that he would realize fully in *North of Boston* (London: David Nutt, 1914), his second book of poetry. "'You want to hear about our hen,' said the practical poultryman," this story begins, and the rest of the piece is entirely in the poultryman's voice. John Evangelist Walsh has offered an interesting analysis of the bearing these early sketches of farmers and farm life have on the later book, some of whose poems date from the years when Frost was writing for the poultry journals (*IMO* 52–61). In these stories we can hear Frost's increasingly sure and successful efforts to "fasten" his characters' speech to the page, to use a term he later favored in his 1929 preface to his play *A Way Out*: "A dramatic necessity goes deep into the nature of the sentence. Sentences are not different enough to hold the attention unless they are dramatic. No ingenuity of varying structure will do. All that can save them is the speaking tone of voice somehow entangled in the words and fastened to the page for the ear of the imagination. That is all that can save poetry from sing-song, all that can save prose from itself" (16.2).

Several of the comical sketches are worthy of Mark Twain, in particular "Old Welch Goes to the Show." But the communities in these stories show little of the pettiness and meanness described in much of Twain's late small-town fiction. There are no Hadleyburgs here. Quite the contrary. In stories like "The Just Judge" and "The Question of a Feather" there is much comedy, but little satire—and no invective. Frost's stories for the poultry journals, like *North of Boston*, show how sympathetic his ear was to the voices of the rural people he wrote about. In his work they are given a subtlety of speech and humor not found, for example, in the New England novels of Edith Wharton, *Ethan Frome* (1911) and *Summer* (1917)—both set in the time and place of *North of Boston*.¹³ Apparently deaf to these subtleties in his poetry, Van Wyck Brooks and other early critics and reviewers of his work irritated Frost by suggesting that *North of Boston*—like Wharton's two novels, or like the poetry of E. A. Robinson—documented the "degeneration" of rural New England life. Consider Brooks's 1922 essay "The Literary Life in America," of which the following passage is characteristic: "That the soil of our society is arid and impoverished, is indicated by the testimony of our own poets. One has only to consider what George Cabot Lodge wrote in 1904 in one of his letters: 'We are a dying race, as every race must be of which the men are, as men and not accumulators, third-rate'; one has only to consider the writings of Messrs. Frost, Robinson and Masters, in whose presentation of our life, in the West as well as in the East, the individual as a spiritual unit invariably suffers defeat."¹⁴ This sort of thing galled Frost. He was still smarting in 1937 when he remarked, in an informal address delivered at Oberlin College and published in 1938 under the title "What Became of New England?": "Twenty years ago I published a little book that seemed to have something to do with New England. It got praise in a way that cost me some pain. It was described as a book about a decadent and lost society" (*CPPP* 755). And speaking on "Poverty and Poetry" at Haverford College in 1938 he said: "I am often more or less tacitly on the defensive about what I might call 'my people.' That doesn't mean Americans—I never defend America from foreigners. But when I speak of my people, I sort of mean a class, the ordinary folks I belong to. I have written about them entirely in one whole book: I called it *A Book of People*" (*CPPP* 759).¹⁵ Frost refers to *North of Boston,* which he had dedicated to his wife over the heading: "This Book of People." But he might just as well be thinking of the stories he wrote between 1903 and 1905, notwithstanding that they are circumscribed by the unusual necessity of treating poultry themes. The stories constitute a valuable if minor contribution to the turn-of-the-century "local color" fiction of New England, and they ought to be read by students of the genre. We sense the fond regard Frost always had for the men and women who figure in these sketches—among them, particularly, his friends Charlemagne Bricault and John A. Hall, both poultry farmers of the first water, and both named in Frost's engaging article "Three Phases of the Poultry Industry." Bricault, a veterinarian, helped Frost get started in the business. Hall would later become the subject of two of Frost's poems, "The Housekeeper" and "A Blue Ribbon at Amesbury."

In the winter of 1906 Frost took a teaching position at Pinkerton Academy in Derry, New Hampshire, that he would hold through June 1911. This association produced several items reprinted herein: an article for the Pinkerton Academy *Catalogue* for 1906–07, a notice of an ambitious dramatic series that he produced at the school in 1910, and a description of the English curriculum published in the *Catalogue* for 1910–11. These documents tell us much about Frost as a teacher, much that was borne out by the course of his remarkably long career in education. In the article published in the 1906–07 *Catalogue* he writes:

> While moving abreast of the times, the Academy has kept unspoiled by transient theory the educational ideals that are not transient. It would be rated as conservative in avoidance of pedagogic experimentation, though less so by comparison with other secondary schools than with many elementary schools. It undertakes to teach with sense and thoroughness the subjects proper to its curriculum. For the rest, its concern is to aim high enough. Work is methodical without subservience to methods. It is held that, for the instructor, "no method nor discipline can supersede the necessity of being forever on the alert." Much must be left to the inspiration of the class-room and the exigency of the case. The constant appeal is to honor, reason and native energy. Government is less by rule than by suggestion. Pupils are taught to think for themselves, and to do things by having to do them for themselves. (5.5)

Sentences like these offer a good example of Frost's understated style: "For the rest, its concern is to aim high enough." His conversational manner is refreshing in so stuffy a forum as the catalogue of a late-Victorian boys' academy, as is also his unmethodical approach. And both give us some intimation of Frost's classroom demeanor. Clearly he favors an improvisational mode: "Much must be left to the inspiration of the class-room and the exigency of the case." This approach to teaching was novel enough to attract the attention of Henry C. Morrison, then superintendent of the New Hampshire Department of Education. Morrison asked Frost to address several teachers' conventions explaining his methods, thereby incidentally sparking Frost's career as public lecturer.[16] We can deduce more about what these teaching methods were from the English curriculum Frost wrote for the 1910–11 *Catalogue*. He immediately lays stress, for example, on recitation, on the oral performance of poetry and prose: "The general aim of the course in English is twofold: to bring our students under the *influence* of the great books, and to teach them the *satisfaction* of superior speech. . . . Expression in oral reading rather than intelligent comment is made the test of appreciation" (5.11–12). This shows a keen interest in "ear" reading, the better to catch what Frost would later call "the sounds of sense."[17] Quite in keeping with this he favors an unstructured class that approaches the condition of conversation: "Discussion proceeds more and more without the goad of the direct question." He wanted to relax the regimentation of the classroom, giving it over to the libertarian "satisfactions" of conversation, where personality is best unfolded and understood. William Pritchard observes that "to begin the study of English in high school by reading aloud, by performing rather than commenting on a piece of imaginative writing, by reading aloud a paragraph of George Eliot's *Silas Marner*—rather than being asked questions about Silas's character or the author's use of symbolism—this was and still is a most original way for an English course to be conducted."[18] Frost never did abandon the agreeably cavalier bearing he struck in his early years as an educator. He writes much later, in a contribution to a 1944 booklet celebrating the 25th anniversary of the Bread Loaf School of English, where he regularly taught: "In my travels recently I have noticed beside the road now and then a diamond shaped sign with the picture of a run-away boy on it and the legend SLOW SCHOOL. I suppose the boy represents a truant and he is running away from school because it is too slow for him. He is an argument for 'acceleration.' The Bread Loaf School of English has had to accelerate somewhat to keep up with the others, but it is only temporarily, we trust. Education in English is properly a slow process of just staying around in the right company till you can speak of and handle a book in the author's presence without setting his teeth on edge" (33.1).

Later Prose

After leaving Pinkerton Academy in 1911 Frost taught education and psychology for a year at the state Normal School in Plymouth, New Hampshire, before departing for England with his family in 1912. Returning to America three years later, he had published two books of poetry in England, with both due out soon in American editions; and he had won a reputation. At this point the contours of his career assume recognizable dimensions. Beginning with his 1919 speech before the Amherst College Alumni Council the pattern of his published prose reflects these contours: there are lectures, largely before academic audiences; prefaces to poetry anthologies, two of them of student verse; prefaces to his own works, or works by other poets; and "tributes" to contemporaries in the literary and academic worlds.

Many of Frost's lectures, prefaces and essays investigate what it means to the artist to "go to college." In the 1919 speech at Amherst College he said:

I have been a great deal worried about an ancient institution, namely, poverty. . . . I have heard some people say they were going to abolish poverty,

just as they might say, "Let us go up and abolish the Amherst House" because they don't like the looks of it; it is ugly . . . The young scholar, the
young poet, the young painter, the young inventor, the young musician has
always found a Latin Quarter where he could decently live in a garret, or a
Barbizon where he could decently live in a cottage; and go half hungry, and
get along somehow, and wear old clothes until he got the thing done and
could show it to the world. Let poverty be abolished and where will the
young poet, the young scholar, the young painter go then? I only see one
place left for him to go and that is to college. (7.2)

These remarks have a personal bearing. By 1919 Frost had himself settled into
what would become a lifelong affiliation with colleges as a lecturer and
teacher. It was one means to abolish his own poverty. Sales of his poetry
alone were never sufficient. He served three years as Poet in Residence at the
University of Michigan during the 1920s. He taught at Amherst College between 1917 and 1962, in four separate terms ranging from two to thirteen
years; at the Bread Loaf School of English regularly after 1921; at Harvard
from 1939 to 1943; and at Dartmouth College from 1943 to 1949. This was not,
for him, necessarily a satisfactory arrangement, as the diffident tone of the
1919 speech quoted here implies. The college, at least in thought, would remain for Frost something of a last resort or "refuge." He would later write,
in a typescript essay held at Dartmouth College Library: "Caveat poeta. I
don't know where a poet could better mew his youth than in the academic
world as long as he keeps one leg out of the grave. Caveat poeta. Let him
look out for himself. Much goes on in college that is against the spirit" (49.1).
Again speaking of the young writer, this time in a preface to *The Arts Anthology of Dartmouth Verse* (Portland, Maine, 1925), Frost writes: "School and college have been conducted with the almost express purpose of keeping him
busy with something else till the danger of his ever creating anything is past.
Their motto has been, the muses find some mischief still for idle hands to
do" (13.4).

By the mid-1920s Frost had already come to doubt whether refuge from
poverty and from the main currents and abrasions of American life was
something an artist really ought to endure. To his way of thinking, in fact,
shelter from the "crudity" and "rawness" of our "national life" (as he sometimes put it) was at best enervating for the poet, and quite possibly worse.
We must read his 1925 tribute to the poet and dramatist Percy MacKaye in
light of these concerns. MacKaye had been instrumental in securing Frost's
own refuge as Poet in Residence at the University of Michigan in 1921.
MacKaye held such a position himself at Miami University in Oxford, Ohio,
and lobbied University of Michigan President Marion L. Burton to offer Frost

an appointment. In a tribute prepared for a banquet celebrating MacKaye's fiftieth birthday Frost remarked:

> Percy MacKaye has spent precious time trying to make the world an easier place to write poetry in. Everybody knows how he has spread himself over the country, as with two very large wings, to get his fellow poets all fellow-ships at the universities. That is but an incident in the general campaign he is forever on, to hasten the day when our national life, the raw material of poetry, having become less and less raw, shall at last cease to be raw at all, and poetry shall almost write itself without the intervention of the artist. (14.1)

Punning on the congregational and financial meanings of the word "fellow-ship" Frost is saying (in effect) that the "fellowship," here, may really consist of patronage. But it is the subtler implications of his remarks that interest me. He obliquely criticizes the institutional supports for poets and writers that were then beginning to assume the form they have today, even though, as a number of articles reprinted in the present edition attest, these were in-stitutions of which Frost was himself something of an architect. The disturb-ing point is that these new institutions promise to make obsolete the person whom they would support: "Poetry shall almost write itself without the in-tervention of the artist."

It is as if Frost's position *felt* powerful and vital to him only insofar as it remained precarious. In any event, that is the mythology he had developed. His idea is that the poet *must* suffer resistance to his aspirations: linguistic and formal "resistance" in his poems—as Frost's essay "The Constant Symbol" shows—but also social resistance outside of them. That is why he was trou-bled by efforts to circumscribe or protect the society of poets and writers, whether in academia or in writers' colonies. He remarks in "Education by Po-etry," presumably referring to Santa Fe, New Mexico: "I have just been to a city in the West, a city full of poets, a city they have made safe for poets. The whole city is so lovely that you do not have to write it up to make it poetry; it is ready-made for you. But, I don't know—the poetry written in that city might not seem like poetry if read outside of the city. It would be like the jokes made when you were drunk; you have to get drunk again to appreciate them" (18.46). The implication of all this is unmistakable. "Fellowship" holds a peculiar liability for the writer: a society made financially and socially "safe" for poets may well give rise to "ready-made" poetry written for (it is to be as-sumed) a "ready-made" audience or coterie.[19]

Frost's skepticism about the poetry of Santa Fe—together with his affec-tion for the "crudity" of our national life—recalls a remarkable confession

made by William James in "What Makes a Life Significant," an essay originally collected in James's volume *Talks to Teachers,* which Frost assigned his
students at Plymouth Normal School in 1911–12, where he taught briefly after
leaving Pinkerton Academy. James is writing about an especially protected
community established at Chautauqua Lake, New York. The passage is well
known but merits quotation here:

> I went in curiosity for a day. I stayed for a week, held spell-bound by the
> charm and ease of everything, by the middle-class paradise, without a sin,
> without a victim, without a blot, without a tear.
>
> And yet what was my own astonishment, on emerging into the dark and
> wicked world again, to catch myself quite unexpectedly and involuntarily
> saying: 'Ouf! what a relief! Now for something primordial and savage, even
> though it were as bad as an Armenian massacre, to set the balance straight
> again. This order is too tame, this culture too second-rate, this goodness
> too uninspiring. The human drama without a villain or a pang; this com-
> munity so refined that ice-cream soda-water is the utmost offering it can
> make to the brute animal in man; this city simmering in the tepid lakeside
> sun; this atrocious harmlessness of all things,—I cannot abide with them.
> Let me take my chances again in the big outside worldly wilderness with
> all its sins and sufferings. There are the heights and the depths, the preci-
> pices and the steep ideals, the gleams of the awful and the infinite; and
> there is more hope and help a thousand times than in this dead level and
> quintessence of every mediocrity.'[20]

Reading these sentences, I am reminded of an article about New York City
that Joan Didion wrote for *The New York Review of Books.* In it, she chides
those who would eulogize the often extraordinary violence and social tension of the city by referring to its unique "energy," its "vitality," or its "unpre-
dictability." When James says that "intensity and danger" give "the wicked
outer world all its moral style," his argument is precisely the sort of thing
Didion has in mind. The theme is familiar from the foregoing discussion of
Frost's tribute to Percy MacKaye. Men like MacKaye seemed to Frost inevita-
bly to invite a prematurely superannuated life for the artist, or, more generally, for the intellectual (and more generally still, for Americans). Frost appears to believe that power and vitality somehow derive from insecurity and
crudity, never from the "middle-class paradise" of a culturally refined retreat,
with all its "atrocious harmlessness." To Frost and James, American society
seemed increasingly, and regrettably, to hold out to its artists and thinkers
two alternatives. On the one hand lay the "worldly wilderness with all its sins
and sufferings"—a "raw" world largely ignorant of, if not outright hostile to,

the "higher" claims of poetry and philosophy. On the other hand lay the "dead level" mediocrity of the cultural refuge, whether it be an artists' colony, a chautauqua, or a university. Such havens may offer, as James remarks, "all the ideals for which our civilization has been striving: security, intelligence, humanity, and order." But they fail to engage the more abrasive aspects of American society, the real patterns and complexity of American lives. It is easy to imagine what Frost would say about aspirations in our own day to foster and sustain in the university a more or less protected society—a society as free as it can be made of the crudeness of our national life (James's "dark and wicked world"). These aspirations, and the reforms through which they are expressed, find an antecedent in the Chautauqua Lake experiment James describes in "What Makes a Life Significant." And recently one sometimes encounters a Jamesian sort of resistance to the "chautauqua" that the university promises, at times, to become in America. Frost was a long time getting around to college as a poet (though once he landed there, he stayed). He had first to arrive at a sense of his vocation that helped him deal, both practically and intellectually, with even the "rawest" American realities. Poetry, as a vocation and as an art, had little meaning for him except as it worked to "adapt his life" to "reality's whole setting"—to borrow terms from a passage in James's *Pragmatism,* which Frost also read closely. Poetry had to locate him somehow in the dark and wicked American world beyond the academy, where, he felt, poets as such were scoffed at, misunderstood, or simply neglected. That is where the prize had to be won. The belief seems quaint today.

There can be no question that Frost is objecting to MacKaye's "campaign" to "hasten the day when our national life shall at last cease to be raw at all." *Something* must work against the poet, who comes to know his own "will," to feel its power and direction, only as he "braves alien entanglements" and the "harsher discipline from without," as Frost puts it in "The Constant Symbol," his greatest essay on poetics (36.12). These entanglements include even the sometimes impoverishing rawness of our national life, and if we abolish this, or shield the artist from it, there can be no exercise of "will," none of "bravery," none of poetry itself. A world made safe for art is paradoxically a world made inhospitable to artists, whose "interventions" are rendered obsolete. If MacKaye wished poets "a beauty of life that shall be poetry without being worked up into poetry," Frost's hard reply to him is this: too ready a system of "fellowship" (both social and monetary) actually diminishes the power of the poet's performance. The world must remain more dangerous than safe for poetry and poets. Such anyway is the point of Frost's October 26, 1930, letter to the young poet Kimball Flaccus: "You wish the world better than it is, more poetical. You are that kind of poet. I would rate as the other kind. I wouldn't give a cent to see the world, the United States or even New York made better. I want them left just as they are for me to make poetical on paper . . . I don't want the world made safer for poetry or easier. To hell with it. That is its own lookout. Let it stew in its own materialism. No, not to Hell with it. Let it hold its position while I do it in art. My whole anxiety is for myself as a performer. Am I any good? That's what I'd like to know and all I need to know" (*SL* 369).

Apparently there is much peril for the poet in establishment. A little preciously, Frost writes for publication in "Maturity No Object," a preface to a 1957 anthology of verse by younger poets: "As I often say a thousand, two thousand, colleges, town and gown together in the little town they make, give us the best audiences for poetry poetry ever had in all this world" (52.5). But he also writes of these same college towns, in private correspondence to his friend and former student John Bartlett: "Amherst, Dartmouth, Bowdoin and Connecticut Wesleyan are going to give me a living next year for a couple of weeks in each of them. The rest of the time I shall be clear away from the academic . . . The only thing that worries me is that Bennington college coming in on our pastoral scenery. I ran away from two colleges in succession once [Dartmouth and Harvard, both of which Frost attended without taking a degree] and they took revenge by flattering me back to teach in college. Now I am running away again and it looks as if they would come after me. I'll probably end up with one of the ponderous things in bed with me on my chest like an incubus" (*SL* 330). These opposed public and private remarks mark the poles between which Frost wavered in establishing a constituency for his art. He felt gratitude toward the academy for supporting poetry, but could never overcome the suspicion that those means of support would somehow undermine both poet and poetry. The last sentence of the letter to Bartlett farcically suggests that Frost's own eventual establishment as the beloved and hoary "bard" of those "two thousand" colleges "town and gown together" might in the end draw the very life out of him. He may have written many of the articles reprinted here in order "to widen the circle of his poetry" and thereby to get himself established, or provided for. But the major essays (and many of the minor ones) nevertheless make subtle, sometimes maddening, arguments against exactly these efforts of provision, which can, as he puts it in "Provide, Provide," amount to a kind of "boughten friendship" (*CPPP* 280). Frost was certainly aware of the irony of it all. The skepticism that often colors his writings on (and in) academia finds its complement in the essays on poetics as he insists that the poet must work through, on the page, the "harsher discipline from without" imposed by exercises in literary form (36.12). Any assessment of his longtime affiliation with colleges and universities—he used to call it "barding around"—must take into account the basic dubiety of this position. A faithful audience can also be an encumbrance, even if it earns one a living.

The Last Years

Increasingly in the 1950s and early 1960s Frost wrote and published miscellaneous articles that have as much to do with his celebrity, or with public affairs, as with his poetry. These items demonstrate his appeal, and his desire to venture, well beyond the mildly hermetic confines of the literary establishment and the academy. They are also evidence that he hoped to establish poetry's claims on diverse disciplines and endeavors ranging from athletics (as in his 1956 essay on baseball for *Sports Illustrated*) to politics to science. He had embarked on a "campaign" of his own—a campaign not merely to "widen the circle" of his own writing, but to widen the circle of poetry itself. In a 1913 letter to the English poet F. S. Flint, Frost wrote, echoing a passage from *Matthew:* "I have lived for the most part in villages where it were better that a millstone were hanged about your neck than that you should own yourself a minor poet" (*IMO* 86). Such were, at least by his own account, Frost's humble beginnings in villages hardly made safe for poetry. But he managed, well before he appeared at John F. Kennedy's inaugural in 1961, to place himself and poetry in "the councils of the bold," to adapt a phrase he once used in a letter. William Pritchard's assessment is accurate: "The final two decades of [Frost's] life were those of a man whose productions as a poet, for the first time in his career, took a position secondary to his life as a public figure, a pundit, an institution, a cultural emissary" (241). In a brief, never-published essay written on the occasion of his appointment as Consultant in Poetry to the Library of Congress in 1958, Frost remarks: "There came a day when it occurred to someone that labor should be represented in Washington. My small toehold is in danger of rousing the proletariat to feeling the need of a Secretary of Poetry. My office will be merely that of consultant to everybody in general. I suppose even a statesman might consult me about what to do next" (57.4). Never mind that the Library had employed Consultants in Poetry before. Frost's having arrived constitutes a "toehold" for something altogether larger. He did bring a remarkable publicity to the office and, in due course, to poetry itself. In January 1961 he read at John F. Kennedy's inaugural, having also contributed a brief essay, under the title "A New England Tribute," to the official published program of the event (see item 68). During the next two years he testified before the U.S. Senate Sub-Committee on Education, visited the White House as an honored guest, and traveled, under the auspices of the U.S. Department of State, to the Soviet Union, where he met Nikita Khrushchev.[21]

In 1959 Frost appeared on a panel in New York City to discuss "The Future of Man." The occasion was the dedication of the Joseph E. Seagram & Sons Building. Other panelists included Bertrand Russell, the biologist and Nobel laureate Hermann Muller, the anthropologist and social biologist Ashley Montagu, and the biologist Sir Julian Huxley. By 1959 Frost's appearance in this company of scientists and philosophers publicly to discuss a topic like "The Future of Man" seemed quite natural. His appeal and his authority were no longer tied specifically to poetry. He was "a consultant to everybody in general." Yet he was always, in a sense, working on poetry's behalf. Included in the present edition is his published contribution to "The Future of Man" symposium. But I reprint also a longer, alternative version of the same talk that he prepared but did not deliver. Frost's contributions to the informal discussion session that followed the symposium are of great interest as well; these appear in the published record of the symposium, some of which is extensively quoted in the notes to item 64. Together these several documents offer an eloquent defense of the humanities against the disturbing scientism represented, for Frost, by the eugenic evolutionary theories of his fellow panelist Muller, who advocated, in his address to the symposium, "genetic selection and manipulation, unhampered by ancient taboos and superstitions."[22] Later, in the panel discussion session, the newspaper columnist Inez Robb remarked: "I think what we wanted to ask you especially, Mr. Frost, was whether your testament to man was an affirmation that he will need love in the future as he has in the past and in the present" (53). The remarkable, and somewhat bizarre, assumptions underlying this query agitated Frost, and one senses that his reply is as much directed to Muller as to Robb: "Look! Look! Man has come this way. Shakespeare himself says the best children are love children . . . That sinful enough for you?" (53). "Love children" are the best: man has come and will proceed by way of passionate spontaneity and native affection, not by way of the rational "selection and manipulation" of the eugenicist. Frost is even more direct in the unpublished version of his "Future of Man" essay, held now at the Dartmouth College Library and reprinted in full in this volume:

> Now science seems about to ask us what we are going to do about taking
> in hand our own further evolution. This is some left-over business from the
> great Darwinian days. Every school boy knows how amusingly short the
> distance was from monkeys to us. Well it ought not to be much longer

from us to supermen. We have the laboratorians ready and willing to tend to this. We can commission them any day to go ahead messing around with rays on genes for mutations or with sperm on ovules for eugenics till they get us somewhere, make something of us for a board or foundation to approve of. But I am asked to be prophetic. As far into the future as I can see with my eyes shut people are still pairing for love and money, perhaps just superstitious enough to leave their direction to what the mystic Karl Marx called historical necessity but what I like to call passionate preference, to the taste there's no disputing about. I foresee no society where artificial insemination won't be in bad taste. (65.4)

In the context of Muller's contribution to the symposium, Frost's satire is especially ingratiating. It is a chilling thought—and Frost means it to be chilling—that we should "take in hand our further evolution" in order to meet the requirements of "a board or foundation." Also gratifying in this context, it seems to me, is Frost's somewhat proprietary, dilettantish attitude, as a poet, toward the biological sciences. He remarks in the discussion session to "The Future of Man" panel:

I am lost in admiration for science. It's the plunge of the mind, the spirit, into the material universe. It can't go too far or too deep for me. But you have to stop and think who owns it. It's a property. Science says, 'It belongs to me.' No, it's a property of the race. It belongs to us. And who are we? Science can't describe us; it contributes very little to our description, a very little bit in all this newness wonder of science that they talk about—it's very slight. The wonderful description of us is the humanities, the book of the worthies and unworthies through the ages, and anything you talk about in the future must be a projection from that. (52–53)

Science, Frost argues, must ultimately be subordinated to social purposes and ownership, not personal or industrial ones. Notwithstanding the blandishments of eugenicists like Muller, science will never be able adequately to describe—let alone properly to value—the men and women that make it. In pointing this out Frost delicately but firmly marks the outer limits of scientific inquiry. I am reminded of a remark in his 1959 essay "On Emerson": "It was a moment for me when I saw how Shakespeare set bounds to science when he brought in the North Star, 'Whose worth's unknown although his height be taken'" (63.9). In the "Future of Man" papers, Frost records the debts even the "hard sciences" owe to mythology and poetry, and thereby broadens not simply his own domain, as "a consultant to everybody in general," but the dominion of poetry itself. This had, of course, long been his interest, as in the 1931 lecture "Education by Poetry," or as in "The Constant Symbol," where he writes: "Poetry is simply made of metaphor. So also is philosophy—and science, too, for that matter, if it will take the soft impeachment from a friend" (36.3).

In any case, Frost's urbanity, humor and disarmingly plain-spoken sophistication altogether justify the prominent position he held on "The Future of Man" panel. He had succeeded, as few Americans have, in becoming a genuinely public poet. By the time of his death he felt prepared to issue the following statement to be read at the fifty-third annual dinner of the Poetry Society of America: "Here we are again the Poetry Power of America and me sorry to be missing. May we never grow less and may our prizes be more felt over the whole country. For the moment I am in no strength to give you anything more than my blessing. May the country never doubt that poetry is it and it is the country" (76.1). The slight confusion among the pronouns of the latter sentence we may certainly excuse: Frost dictated the remarks to his secretary Kathleen Morrison from his bed in Peter Bent Brigham Hospital in Boston only two weeks before his death on January 29, 1963. But much more than merely excusable is the whimsically Whitmanesque sentiment of this death-bed tribute to "the Poetry Power of America." Having nationalized himself as a public figure, Frost was, in a sense, justified—even if only as an indulgence—in nationalizing poetry as well.

Notes

1. The letter is held at Dartmouth College Library. Frost's reference to the "middle west" is explained by the fact that he was, as he wrote the letter, packing up to move to Ann Arbor to assume his post as Poet in Residence at the University of Michigan.

2. The letter, still unpublished, is held now in the Frost Family Collection at the University of Michigan.

3. Frost had arranged for a stenographer to transcribe the Norton lectures as he delivered them extemporaneously. Harvard University Press subsequently prepared a typescript of the stenographic record for revision by Frost. Neither the original stenographic record nor the typescript has survived.

4. Correspondence regarding these negotiations is held in the Holt Archive at Firestone Library, Princeton University. More light on the episode is shed by Lawrance Thompson's "Notes From Conversations With Robert Frost," held now at the University of Virginia. In an entry dated February 2, 1940, Thompson writes, referring to Frost's editor at Holt, William Sloane: "I must write Sloane and tell him I put on my best act for the prose." Apparently Thompson had promised Sloane that he would urge Frost to assemble a volume of prose, or else to permit Thompson to assemble one for him. Reference to the project oc-

curs again in Thompson's entry for August 8, 1941: "Much to my surprise, he [Frost] said that the agent from Holt, Bill Sloane, had been there and that they had side-tracked the prose in favor of a new volume of poems which Frost had promised to deliver to Holt on November 1. I nearly turned over inside when I heard that because I've had a hope that I might get my book of essays ready to come out with the next book of poems. Later I talked with Frost about that and he seemed to like the idea; at least he said he did. I'm going to see if I can get him or Kay to send a note to Sloane suggesting it. But if it should work out that way I've got to work like hell between now and November 1 to get it done." These remarks suggest that Thompson, who had begun work on an edition of Frost's prose in conjunction with Wilbert Snow, was by this time working alone. However that may be, it appears from this note that, by August 1941, Frost had once again managed to defer indefinitely his contractual obligation to produce a volume of essays. The subject comes up only once more in Thompson's "Notes," this time in an entry dated August 22, 1951: "I went over to have a before-lunch wine with the man who had come up from Holt's to see him [Frost], largely to discuss the matter of the book of prose essays. I forget the man's name. He lives in Stamford, and must be in the trade department at Holt's. He didn't get very far with Frost." The man referred to is Alfred Edwards, who later became Frost's literary executor.

   5. See below for a description of the revision. The trial table of contents for the prose volume, written in Frost's hand on a single leaf of a notebook, includes the following titles: "Letter to Seniors in College" (presumably Frost's 1935 "Letter" to *The Amherst Student*); "Preface to Robinson Grief and Grievance" (Frost's introduction to E. A. Robinson's *King Jasper* [1935]); "Education by Poetry"; "Sound as Subject Matter" (a presentation of Frost's "sound of sense" theories); "The Shape a Poem Takes" (presumably "The Figure a Poem Makes," Frost's preface to his *Collected Poems* [1939]); "Crudity Efficiency and the Rate of Poetry" (the word "speed" is written in above the word "rate" in Frost's hand; he sometimes lectured on the topic "Crudities" [*TYT*, 491, 697]); "Rewards" (apparently, Frost's 1939 speech accepting the Gold Medal of the National Institute of Arts and Letters); "Dark Darker Darkest" (in June 1935 Frost gave a talk in Amherst on the subject "Our Darkest Concern" [*TYT*, 417–18, 666, 700]); "An Equalizer Once in So Often for the Public Health" (some indication of the subject of this essay may be found in Frost's poem "An Equalizer," collected first in *A Witness Tree* [1942]; the association of the proposed essay with the poem circumstantially supports assigning this table of contents to the period 1940–42).

   6. No reliably comprehensive checklist of his published prose appeared until 1996, when *Resources for American Literary Study* published one prepared by the present editor: "Robert Frost's Prose Writings: A Comprehensive Annotated Checklist and Introductory Essay," *RALS* 22.1 (1996): 37–78. A comprehensive descriptive catalogue of Frost's works in all genres has yet to be published. A model of how the job might be done is available in Joan St. C. Crane's excellent *Robert Frost: A Descriptive Catalogue of Books and Manuscripts in the Clifton Waller Barrett Library, University of Virginia* (Charlottesville: University Press of Virginia, 1974). But as its title indicates, this volume describes only those materials held in a single major collection.

   7. Barry explains in her preface to the collection: "These texts of Robert Frost's comments on writing make no pretence to comprehensiveness; with new letters and manuscript material still becoming available, the Frost canon is by no means stable enough or fi-

nal enough for that" (xi). In one respect the canon is still neither stable nor final. No comprehensive census or edition of Frost's informal talks has ever been undertaken.

8. For the most part I avoid quoting material readily available in other published volumes.

9. This general celebrity doubtless contributed to Frost's not being taken seriously enough by the then leading lights in literary criticism and theory, who tended, as Frost felt, to remain fixed in orbit around the difficult and hardly populist "high modernists" T. S. Eliot and Ezra Pound. Frost occasionally sounded notes of resentment along these lines in his prose. See, for example, his remarks in an early version of "The Romantic Chasm" (1948).

10. The farm in Derry and the years of withdrawal figure largely in the Frost mythology. He once remarked in a reading given at Amherst College's Ford Memorial Chapel: "When asked, Are you a real farmer? . . . I always say, I was a real one but a bad one. I did not make much of a living. We had a hard time—that makes it all the more genuine. We lived by farming for 8 1/2 years by actual measure. I was thinking the other day I could tear these books [i.e., his books of poetry], tear the leaves out, and I could lay the poems pretty nearly to cover the little thirty-acre farm. I could find places where every single one of the poems took its rise. I could make a little map of the farm; in fact one of my children made such a map and from her incomplete work could locate as many as twenty to thirty of the poems" (unpublished typescript, Amherst College Library).

11. For further remarks about the world's conventionalities, see below.

12. The stories were a novelty in the poultry journalism of the day. See commentary by the stories' original editors on their content and on the occasion of their appearance in *The Eastern Poultryman* and *Farm-Poultry*. As I indicate there, these editors enjoy the unsought-for distinction of having penned the first published criticism of works by Robert Frost.

13. Without prejudice particularly to Wharton, Frost made the following remarks in a 1934 appearance at Massachusetts State College: "Another reason for being versed in country things is for the understanding of people. I don't think any one understands people unless he has learned from country life that lots of people are smarter than they look. I learned that from farmers. They are more important than they look. And city people are not aware of it. The city person thinks that if a man is a lawyer, he must look like a lawyer. That is the trouble with Hollywood. Hollywood wants everything to look what it is. I am always interested in unpromising looks" (unpublished typescript, Amherst College Library).

14. *Civilization in the United States,* edited by Harold Stearns (New York: Harcourt, Brace and Company, 1922), 184.

15. "What Became of New England?" and "Poverty and Poetry" are omitted from the present edition for reasons explained in the Editorial Principles.

16. *TEY,* 348–49. See also Robert S. Newdick, *Newdick's Season of Frost: An Interrupted Biography of Robert Frost,* edited by William A. Sutton (Albany: State University of New York Press, 1976), for an account of Henry C. Morrison's acquaintance with Frost. An extract from the latter book is given in the notes to the present volume.

17. Frost held to these ideas throughout his career. Nearly sixty years after writing the English curriculum at Pinkerton, he read Longfellow's poem "The Flight from Egypt"— an old favorite of his—at an appearance at Trinity College in Hartford, Connecticut. He

introduced it with a caveat: "I'm not going to praise it. I'm *saying* it to praise it" (unpublished typescript, Watkinson Library, Trinity College). That is the kind of praise he always sought from students of poetry.

18. *Robert Frost: A Literary Life Reconsidered* (Amherst: University of Massachusetts Press, 1993), 60. Subsequent references to this text are given parenthetically.

19. In moments like this, it seems, Frost anticipates Dana Gioia's arguments in *Can Poetry Matter? Essays on Poetry and American Culture* (St. Paul, Minn.: Gray Wolf Press, 1992). See the title essay of the collection.

20. *William James: Writings, 1902–1910*, edited by Bruce Kuklick (New York: Library of America, 1987). Subsequent references to this edition are given parenthetically. Frost would have encountered "What Makes a Life Significant" in James's volume *Talks to Teachers on Psychology and to Students on Some of Life's Ideals*, which he used in a course he taught at Plymouth Normal School in 1911.

21. Frost's testimony before the Senate appears as part of the official published record of the hearings in which he participated: *Providing for a National Academy of Culture; Hearing Before the Subcommittee on Education of the Committee on Labor Public Welfare, United States Senate.* Washington: U.S. Government Printing Office, 1960. For a full account of Frost's meeting with the Soviet premier, see Franklin Reeve, *Robert Frost in Russia* (Boston, 1963), and Frederick B. Adams, Jr., *To Russia With Frost* (Boston, 1963). Reeve and Adams accompanied Frost on the journey.

22. *The Future of Man* (New York: Joseph E. Seagram and Sons, 1959), 36. Subsequent references to this text are given parenthetically.

Abbreviations

CPPP   Robert Frost, *Collected Poems, Prose, and Plays*, ed. Richard Poirier
       and Mark Richardson. New York: Library of America, 1995.

EL   Ralph Waldo Emerson, *Essays and Lectures*, ed. Joel Porte. New
       York: Library of America, 1983.

FL   Robert Frost and Elinor White Frost, *The Family Letters of Robert
       and Elinor Frost*, ed. Arnold Grade. Albany: State University of
       New York Press, 1972.

IMO   John Evangelist Walsh, *Into My Own: The English Years of Robert
       Frost*. New York: Grove Press, 1988.

NOTES Lawrance Thompson, "Notes on Conversation with Robert
       Frost," unpublished typescript. Alderman Library, University of
       Virginia.

NRF   *The Notebooks of Robert Frost*, ed. Robert Faggen. Cambridge,
       Mass.: Harvard University Press, 2006.

RFLU   *The Letters of Robert Frost to Louis Untermeyer*, ed. Louis
       Untermeyer. New York: Holt, Rinehart and Winston, 1963.

SL   *The Selected Letters of Robert Frost*, ed. Lawrance Thompson. New
       York: Holt, Rinehart and Winston, 1964.

SP   *The Selected Prose of Robert Frost*, ed. Edward Connery Lathem
       and Hyde Cox. New York: Holt, Rinehart and Winston, 1966.

TEY   Lawrance Thompson, *Robert Frost: The Early Years*. New York:
       Holt, Rinehart and Winston, 1966.

TYT   Lawrance Thompson, *Robert Frost: The Years of Triumph*. New
       York: Holt, Rinehart, and Winston, 1970.

TLY   Lawrance Thompson and R. H. Winnick, *Robert Frost: The Later
       Years*. New York: Holt, Rinehart, and Winston, 1976.

Unless otherwise indicated, all quotations of Frost's prose in the introduction
and notes to this volume are from the present edition, and are referred to by
item and paragraph number, as explained below in the Notes.

THE COLLECTED PROSE OF

ROBERT FROST

O N E

Articles and Editorials from the Lawrence, Massachusetts,
High School Bulletin (1891–92)

[Five Unsigned Editorials (September 1891)]

1   September, School, Study, with somewhat of that which bears upon no one of these, is our toast for this and the succeeding issues.

.   .   .

2   After a long summer for mental recuperation, we return to our work with a welcome for the whole school—thanks be to our subscription solicitors.

3   By way of introduction, it has been the custom to make a declaration of principles; therefore, although we entertain but vague dreams on this subject at present, we will stumble along in the old rut. So many ideas, we begin, set forth in this department will be implicitly believed by ourselves, that, unless statement is made to the contrary, they may be assumed to be what *we think;* in other words, we speak with the voice of equality, by no means gently suggesting. No doubt we endanger our reputation, but we agree that to Raleigh's words, "Fain would I climb but that I fear to fall," there is an answer better than this motto;—"If thy heart fail thee, why then climb at all."

4   Furthermore, this chair, when not acting as a weapon of defense, will be devoted to the caprices of its occupant. Properly speaking it will be an easy chair, sufficiently roomy for practicing the divine art, "abandon."

5   We find it quite impossible to lay open more of the future than this.

For various reasons (chiefly pecuniary) the literary department of the paper has not been enlarged; but we trust our friends find pleasure in beholding a materialized echo of "quality not quantity."

.   .   .

6   The new school year has begun with more promise than it has shown for many years, if not since its very outset. We refer in particular to the increasing number in the school who aim at a college education,—in the Freshman class of seventy-five there are nineteen who have taken a classical course; and if the Class of '94 may be regarded as an indicator of the strength of purpose

of these (the classical) scholars, it is safe to say that Lawrence will soon possess a name far other than its present illiterate one. In the Sophomore class there are eighteen, only two less than last year, who are pursuing the study of Greek.

7   In looking over the college directories, it is a noticeable fact, and one by no means redounding to the honor of our school, that many familiar names claim as their preparatory school Phillips Academy, and this for but one year's preparation there, while our own school, on account of the narrowness of the courses, has lost all claim to her graduates. But we are on the eve of a marked change, which has been inaugurated by the collegiate examinations of June last, in which we were represented at five colleges, and without exception our scholars acquitted themselves creditably both in preliminaries and finals; and more than this, we are proud to say that several have received honorable mention, especially in French.

8   On the whole we feel obliged to rejoice, and as the most substantial rejoicing, send our best wishes with our friends who leave us for Technology, Tufts, Harvard, and Wellesley.

·   ·   ·

9   Since the Commencement of June last, the faculty of the school has undergone one change. Mr. Norton, our recent sub-master, has vacated the Laboratory to assume duties elsewhere, and has been superseded by Mr. L. H. W. French, a teacher of some several years' experience, having just resigned his principality in the Sandwich High School.

10   All who realize the marked improvements that have been going on in the Laboratory during the past year cannot but regret the loss of the teacher, through whose influence these departures have been set in motion.

11   Again we have an illustration of the necessity of offering inducements (such as the opportunity of devoting time and energy to one department exclusively) to some one for making himself a ruling part of *our* Laboratory.

12   To Mr. French, our new sub-master, we extend a hearty welcome, with the hope that his stay may be long and pleasant.

·   ·   ·

13   Several of the High School Alumni have united in presenting the school with a sum which has enabled the *Bulletin* managers to offer a series of prizes for the best literary work published in the *Bulletin* during this school year.

14   During the twelve years' existence of the paper, no better opportunity than this, for bringing out the writing powers of the school, has been offered. We desire this to be thoroughly understood, as we believe that it is of interest to all.

15   It is well known that the average school composition is, not exactly to

quote from a certain author, as round and perfect as the hole where a star ought to be. Nevertheless, we hesitate to say that the "school girl's composition" must always be a synonym for dryness; and in thinking to better the phrase we suggest *thesis necessitatis,*—it is the best way out of a distasteful subject. That essay writing cannot be made a matter of option, we well know, unless it be in a school modeled after the manner of Tolstoi's, which is out of the question in the New England school of discipline; but that there are those who prefer "for honor" to "by necessity" we also know, and it is for these that this offer is made, in the hope of arousing something more than mere words. Those that have a natural dislike for writing at all, we leave to harass an audience for at least three hours of a June afternoon. In a few words, a chance is here offered to all, for independently displaying their abilities, and we desire all from Freshmen to Seniors to respond. We entertain some fear that the contest in poetry will not be taken up, but this apprehension only bespeaks a better chance for those who have yet to enter the arena. In case the poetry prize is unclaimed, the books will be awarded for the *third best composition—the fanciful to be preferred.*

16　　The question of the judges is still under debate in the Literary Board, but we can confidently assure all that those chosen will be fully competent.

17　　For the benefit of those who have not seen the notice hung in the rooms we subjoin the following:

BULLETIN PRIZES.

Prose.

For the best prose *composition,* $15.

For the second best *composition,* $10.

Poetry.

For the best poem, $5.

18　　Compositions submitted for competition shall be published in the *Bulletin* during the school year Sept. '91 to June '92, the contest being open (from time of notification until May 1, '92) to pupils of the four classes of the L. H. S. only.

19　　The prizes being divided into three classes, each writer shall be limited to three papers in each class or six in all, and no one writer may receive more than one prize in each class.

20　　If in the prose contest three compositions be offered by one person, one of these, at least, shall be a review of some author's work or works.

21　　A prose composition shall consist of no more than 1200 nor less than 800 words. On poetry there is no limitation as regards length.

22　　Every composition shall have subscribed a *nom de plume,* and shall be submitted to the editor together with a sealed envelope disclosing the writer's true character.

23   This letter, to be retained by the editor, shall remain unopened until after May 1, '92.

The judgment on these writings shall be assigned to three competent, disinterested persons, by whom the prizes shall be awarded to the successful compositions, and be transferred to the writers by means of the letters. The judgment shall be passed on printed articles only.

24   The prizes shall be awarded in books selected by the successful competitors.

25   Further information on this subject may be had from the editors.

26   (The word *composition* has been used not in its hackneyed sense, but as being more comprehensive than *essay*.)

[Two Unsigned Editorials (October 1891)]

27   There is a certain muse—if muse she be—who has been invoked in these columns again and again, time out of mind. In consideration of this fact, it would be with many misgivings as to the originality of the muse, that we would surrender our mind to her majesty. Although we offer her several shares in the company, it is necessary that we go into no syballine insensibility.

28   In the stead then of launching into a sea of invective against our *friends*—and we cast no slur upon our predecessors, for the human race before its development gained its desires by war—we will make a small suggestion to the scholars, and if the same meet with approval the office of carrying it out will become ours. In a future number we propose to set forth an alternative.

29   The muse to whom we refer has but one mundane name, which is at all times to be read upon the shingle on her office door: it is the word *Library*.

30   As all are aware of the election of Georgia M. Dame to the office of librarian, we have no instruction to give—merely advice. It is the duty of every scholar in the class to patronize the school library. If it is not, why is it there? Shall we not honor in the least the classes who have made "their last will and testament?" Shall *we*, from inborn inertia, fail to lay claim to that upon which other classes have spent so much valuable time and ink? It is a simple matter; let each one select a book and give his order. Then, if success is wanting we will act in concert. Let not those who are eavesdropping—for we speak only to the class—construe this as a threat. We have regarded the efforts of our predecessors too closely not to appreciate how vain it would be for us to follow in their wake. We repeat, patronize the library immediately!

· · ·

31   If success attend us, it will become necessary at least to consider the plan of leaving our little memorial to the library. It may be well to do this in the shape of books; but, although books are said to be civilizers, we are afraid that it would take a great number to wear off the present barn-like appearance of the room in question.

32   In remedying, we would first clear the place of text books, which act would give almost sufficient space for the present books of any value, and would leave the two larger cases empty.

33   Then leaving the books for a few years, we would proceed to the aspect of the room itself. In doing this we have to keep in mind, size, and limit our improvements accordingly.

34   Carpeting would be the first thing; then a reading-table and two or three comfortable chairs, and last, curtains, to supercede the maps in the window.

35   There are several corners in which busts might be placed: in the window between the curtains a statue would add decorative effect to the outer room. True, in the library there is one bust and one statue, both so heavily draped in dust that it was with difficulty we even imagined their personalities.

36   Above we have only made propositions; but we now speak self evident facts. For instance, it is evident that the room will not accommodate an infinite number of books. For this reason we must be select in our choice. We need books of value, such as are not to be found in our own public library. Time is no question, for there is more pleasure in the execution of an act than there is in the result, however satisfactory the result may be. If the class returns buy but one book, it is all the better, we are surer of its value.

36   There is such a thing as a standard work, and there is also such a thing as a rare book. Standards are becoming countless. Rare books continue scarce or are lost altogether.

37   In selecting books this distinction should be kept in mind. It is not the standards that we desire, but the books of reference of which few issues are extant. The office of choosing a committee capable of selecting suitable books, belongs to the class meeting; but if the business is to be carried out satisfactorily, it is impossible for the selection to lie wholly with undergraduates.

38   But remember that this is mere talk unless it be given a chance of being put into effect.

[Three Unsigned Editorials (November 1891)]

39   Thus far, the manner in which our essayists have entered the prize contest has been far from satisfactory. The only way of accounting for this dilatoriness is in supposing that all fear to take the initiative lest they may be put to

shame by succeeding efforts. Let all be reminded that every essay is subjected before publication, to a test no less severe than that applied to the regular literary work of the month, and that our standard is presumably as high as that of other years.

40   But, lest our penetration be questioned, there are those no doubt who are at present nursing their strength to burst upon us with a volley of three labored essays just as the midnight bell tolls a requiem for May 1st. Now if the school act harmoniously in this respect, it is more than likely that the *Bulletin* be published devoid of these painstaking compositions and the prize fund be allowed to accumulate; for had we desired no contributions until the year's end we would have stated our intention of devoting our last issue entirely to the contest. This class meditates injury to itself also, in that writing three articles hap-hazard and trusting that at least one of them may prove a success, is only one way of destroying one's self-confidence and power of judging his own capabilities. This would be second only to egotism and arrogance. It is far preferable to offer but one composition, provided the writer feels that it is his best; but there are those who never as yet have called into requisition their full powers, and it is for these that the three chances are given,—two as climbing staves, one the staff for the flag of victory.

· · ·

41   Holmes recommends "good, honest" prose as a convoy of thought for those who are not sure that they are possessed of the inborn inspiration of the poetic genius. Let him tremble who questions such wisdom as that of the "good old Doctor"; but let him rather forget it and consider in his forgetfulness the saying of some other *spruch-sprecher*. In our colleges, students of English are advised to make use of verse composition for increasing their general vocabulary, becoming conversant with synonyms and gaining variety and felicity of expression. It has been said that versifiers are mere slaves of rhyme,—a sure proof of a curtailed vocabulary which can be no better done away with than by the entertaining diversion of verse writing. Perhaps we speak too flippantly of our subject; but we are not here to persuade any one that the poets (so-called) of our school journals are all to harp among the nation's bards; far from it. We know that our school is not now made up exclusively of future poets, yet we venture to say that there is not a scholar, who, with some little practice cannot surmount our literary columns with a capital of no mean proportions (mechanically speaking). But there have appeared no debutants in this line for several years, and as a result the poetry of the paper is somewhat narrow in its scope, being the effusion of a few pens only. We need not mention pecuniary inducement to a school so obedient to the call of honor, as is ours; we can only make an appeal—an appeal for verse, seri-

ous or otherwise, and especially the otherwise, which relates to epigrams and
squibs of the characteristic school style.

· · ·

42   The football season is past. Although the games played have not been over
numerous, they have been sufficiently great in number to prove the strength
of the team. The boys have met with no defeat, unless it be the game played
with the college "scrub," which was no more than a practice turn out. The
team has been very well managed, and has only to regret that more opportunities of victory have not been presented. Many of the men have distinguished themselves personally; but the feature of every game has been the
team play.

43   The club disbanded on Monday, the twenty-third, after making their impression on the retina of the photographer's glass eye. The boys and their
deeds should be remembered, (no compliment hinted, only an advertisement,) and all who so desire may possess their combined likenesses for
the sum of fifty cents. Business communications must be directed to Capt.
Sullivan.

Petra and Its Surroundings (December 1891)

44   On the summit of Mt. Hor, nestles a shrine beneath which, the Arabians say,
lie the bones of the priest, Aaron. It is a place of the wildest grandeur—one
worthy the last resting place of the Israelitish orator, overlooking as it does
the mountain fastnesses of the warlike sons of Esau, through whose country
the Jews strove so long in vain to force a passage.

45   Mountains rise on every hand; to the north, to the west as far as the great
desert, and south and east as far as the eye can reach.

46   From Mt. Hor the view is one of magnificent sameness; but not until the
cliffs have towered above, not until the storm has crowded its overwhelming
torrents down the ravines, can the grand sublimity of the situation be felt. In
its unstability, the region is like an ice-flow. Everything is constantly changing; mountains are torn away in storm, and mountains totter and threaten in
calm.

47   But the centre of all, once the busy capital of a thriving nation, now the
"City of Tombs," the capital of ruin and decay, is in the sublimest situation of
the wilderness. To reach it a detour must be made to the south and east to
the city's ancient entrance, now called the Sik, which led up to the old mart.

48   From the confusing accounts of many travelers, one might suppose that
Petra was a city, honey-combed with tombs, rising perpendicularly from the
plain to the height of a thousand feet; but Petra of the Edomites, Jews,

Greeks and Romans, is in a far wilder and romantic location. It lies couched down among the peaks south of Mt. Hor. To it the Sik winds down between mighty red cliffs that tower seven hundred feet above, closing in here and there where the rocks have cracked and slid forward, leaving nothing but a streaking of blue where the cliffs seem to meet.

49   It is summer; a dim light falls down into the chasm. The torrent bed that follows the gorge is parched and almost buried in tamarisk and thickets of oleanders in full bloom. The cliffs are festooned with pale fern; ivy climbs everywhere; and the searching roots of the fig-tree cling to the ravine's walls.

50   As one wanders on over the few chariot-worn flags which once completely paved the way, how strange must be the feeling, as the mind reverts to the cave dwellers whose homes are now mere black squares upon the red crags, and then comes down to the time of the Roman, and sees the chariot hurrying down its last stadia after a weary mountain and desert journey, starting with its echo the eagle from his eerie in the crags above.

51   How dreary must seem this present desolation of which the Hebrew prophet so often prophesied.

52   Here the way narrows again, and over it sweeps a great arch, perhaps the city gate, perhaps triumphal.

53   The Sik winds on, its sides excavated, and marked with Senaitic and Latin inscriptions. Suddenly it widens, turns, and there stand a row of pink columns. It is this strange mixture of decay and preservation,—for these columns which front a Roman structure, or rather excavation, are nearly perfect, while but one other building in the city is standing—barbarism and debased civilization, that give Petra its great, strange wildness.

54   When the road unexpectedly fronts the old theatre, a new characteristic of the city is presented. The seats are of stone alternately red and purple. We have noticed the pink of the columns; the mountains in the distance are white.

55   The colors around are almost countless; there are maroon, scarlet, yellow, purple, pale rose, blue, grey, and many mixtures, for one traveler compares certain cliffs to mahogany, another, the same cliffs to watered silk.

56   So varied are the hues of the city that one wonders that the natives did not call it the Rainbow City instead of the "Red City."

57   Beyond the theatre, which is said to be like that of Tusculum, the road widens, and the city proper spreads out deep in among the mountains. The open ground, whose small rolling hills are covered with ruined foundations, is walled for the most part by sheer precipices, falling for hundreds of feet into the city.

58   What little is known of the history of Petra is of the wildest interest. Never has there been a stronghold as impregnable. What a place for romance where everything is as vague as a rainbow half faded in mid-air. In our society novels the imagination displayed is as it were a flying squirrel's flight from a tree-top downward; here it might take its flight as a bird from a fountain of youth.

59   In the city there are traces of four distinct races. For hundreds of years the Edomites held the city, *in* which they were never really conquered. The Jews were sculptors at the time of their conquest, but their chisel was the sword, and they carved naught but destruction. The Pharos, under Rome, made Petra their capital, and by them were built the pillars in the pass and the one building that still stands in the city. Since those days the Mohammedans have built shrines in the cliff niches and on the summits to which the stone-cut stairways lead.

60   To-day, all is ruin but the tombs that honey-comb the cliffs, and the city is a city of the dead. C. B.

· · ·

Physical Culture (December 1891)

61   I do not wish to speak of physical culture, in an athletic sense, but only so far as it is needed to insure good health and long life.

62   Many people are wont to overlook the fact that a man's body ought to be developed as well as his mind. The body is the dwelling place of the mind, and a man who has a good mind, should also have a sound body.

63   If you were to stand on a street corner, in the business part of our city, at just twelve o'clock, and watch the men and women as they hurry from their places of business, and look at them carefully, you would see that scarcely one in ten is erect and well built. You see some who slouch their shoulders, others who look like the hands of a clock at five minutes of six, some cant to one side, like a close-hauled cat-boat in a gale of wind; here comes the thrifty merchant or banker, whose form seems to have "gone before;" you will see numbers of these men before you see one that walks erect, is well proportioned and is graceful in all his movements.

64   If you should examine those men who stoop and are round-shouldered, you would find that this is either caused by continual bending over, or by lifting, not necessarily heavy lifting, but by a constant strain upon the back; this kind of work develops the back, but it does absolutely nothing for the chest, consequently the man is hollow-chested, or his shoulders are warped.

65   Some of the most noted oarsmen in college have died of consumption;

perhaps you may ask the cause of this; "surely," you say, "this man was well developed;" that is true, but he is developed only in one direction. While he has developed his back, he has neglected his chest, and his lung capacity is too small.

66   The remedy for these evils may be found in a gymnasium, under an instructor, who knows the faults of his pupils, and how to remedy them. Perhaps you have no time to spend in a gymnasium; then fifteen minutes spent every night in some simple dumb-bell drill, in a month or two, will work wonders. Another exercise, which takes no extra time at all, and will be found beneficial, is this. When you start to walk anywhere, say to school, take a long breath, filling the lungs to their fullest capacity, and walk about ten steps, then exhale; do this until you can hold your breath for fifteen or twenty steps. This is a simple exercise, but it broadens the chest and expands the lungs.

67   The city of Lawrence will soon be able to boast one of the finest gymnasiums in the state; I refer to the plans of the new Young Men's Christian Association gymnasium, which will be the finest Y.M.C.A. gymnasium outside of Boston and Worcester.

     Sinon.

The Charter Oak at Hartford (December 1891)

68   When the early New England colonists settled Connecticut, Charles I. granted them a charter, but afterwards sent Sir Edmund Andros to take it away, and act as royal governor for all of New England. Connecticut refused to surrender her charter, and after repeated attempts to recover it, Sir Andros himself came with members of his council and a body guard of sixty soldiers. The assembly was in session, and when he appeared, he demanded the charter. He was about to receive it, when suddenly the lights were put out and total darkness reigned. A light was quickly brought, but the charter was gone. A patriot of those days, named Captain Wadsworth, had concealed it in the hollow of an oak.

69   Even as far back as the colonial days, when settlements were being made in Connecticut, the Indians asked the settlers, who were chopping down trees, to spare this oak, as they had some superstitious feelings concerning it.

70   When Mr. Stuart owned the property where this tree stood, some boys built a fire in it, which enlarged the hollow, but did not destroy the tree. This made the hollow of the tree so large as to enable twenty-seven full grown men to stand in it together. Afterwards, Mr. Stuart had a heavy door made to close the entrance, and took great pains to preserve this valuable relic. Hun-

dreds of people came to see the venerable oak, and took away with them such twigs and small branches as the owner would allow.

71   The tree fell during a severe storm, August 21, 1856. At this time fresh acorns were growing on every part of it. Thousands of mementoes were made from its wood, including nutmegs, and the chair of the presiding officer of the Connecticut senate. Several seedlings from the tree are known to exist at the present time.

72   In the Historical Rooms of the Wadsworth Athenæum in Hartford, there is now preserved a relic of this oak tree. A very comfortable seat or chair has been made from the stump of it. Hung over the chair is a poem about this historical tree, written by George H. Clark, the original manuscript of which, is still preserved. Thousands may now see a portion of the oak.

73   The tree measured thirty-three feet in circumference at the base. A marble tablet now marks the spot where the old tree stood.

A. C. C., '94

M. Bonner, Deceased (December 1891)

74   This "hasty" sketch is a classic modernized,—its influence is bad: forbear to read. I may now proceed for my own amusement.

75   I have but one prefatory remark: For all that may be said to the contrary, there is generally more quartz than gold to be found in a mine. I am not preaching. Don't let me discourage philanthropy. Perhaps I can't. Well, never mind, let's make the best of it.

76   Deceased was formerly of mere local celebrity,—in fact had been since receiving pecuniary encouragement for whitewashing an 8x60 board fence, and not doing it on the installment plan, either. I refer to Rapheal M. Bonner, the artist who has recently sustained so stupendous a loss. M. Bonner was a conscientious man—very.

77   It was Christmas Eve, and the great Art Exhibition of Metrop would close at 12 P.M. It lacked just three seconds of that time, when M. Bonner appeared upon the scene in a dressing gown, his face still distorted by a harrowing dream. Three policeman were leaning over the railing, evidently in profound meditation. These men had been stationed there as a protection to M. Bonner's famous painting. M. Bonner was a cautious man, also. Making a speaking trumpet of his hands, the artist then shrieked without undue preliminaries. Something was wrong—the guards recovered their self-possession.

78   "It is gone!—fled!!—taken wings!!!" was his heart-rending monody, and it was *almost* evident, from sundry incoherent utterances, that this had been the

matter of question in the abstraction on the part of the worthies of the law. All had barely time to observe that the canvas had been cut from its frame, when the lights of the pavilion were extinguished.

79   Some enquired of those who had had the good fortune to have witnessed the skeleton, by what means the picture had been purloined. "Sharp knife," was the invariable reply; although one venturesome spirit, who had admired the heaped on paint from a side view, suggested, "Dimund, more like." M. Bonner's spirit was crushed.

80   The next day was Christmas. The average number of beggars were on the street. It rained, of course. Several people who were either very hungry or in the last stages of consumption, stood looking at a monumental wedding cake in a shop window which was aglow on the satellite principle,—raindrops refracting the light of one smoky lamp. M. Bonner went by with his crushed spirit. His house was at hand. He entered—encountered a parcel. Picking it up he rushed to the curbstone. Under the arc-light he read:—

    "Sir:—

        Do not despair. It is not well. There are three hours. Midnight brings you
    all or naught.

            ———"

81   If it had been a Christmas gift he could not have been more elated. He was now nervous. Artists are always susceptible.

82   Long since had M. Bonner decided that the business had been accomplished by supernatural agency. He reasoned thus: "It was no hour for theft. There was my vigilance committee of three, all mighty men. Thieves always leave a clew—are captured. My despoiler is escaped forever." M. Bonner was morbidly inclined.

83   At precisely three seconds of midnight he heard a rap at the door. He arose from his seat on the dark hall stairs, groped his way to the door, and to his unbounded delight discovered a large frame wrapped in heavy paper. That was not all. He hesitated whether to rush out under the arc-light, or to burn paper on the kitchen stove. He made an attempt to recall his benefactor; benefactors never tarry.

84   M. Bonner stood beneath the street light, intermittently cutting and untying the cord that bound his treasure. It is done! The wrapping paper is in the gutter. He turns the canvas to the light. It is blank! But no! There is a card. It is glued to the centre of the canvas. He looks closer, drops the frame, and peering stealthily about into the darkness, hisses slowly, "I—am—dis—covered." It was the identical Christmas card from which M. Bonner had copied his "original" prize painting. Fastening his arms rigidly up into the night,

he gave a wild shriek and his spirit fled as the mill laborers leave the mill at the shriek of the great steam whistle. It was all done in three seconds, and just then the great light went out, and the hungry people suppressed their Christmas appetite, and went out into the night.

85   You don't like this tale? Neither do I! You are a philanthropist? Well, I am. That's a coincidence.

Kthon.

[Three Unsigned Editorials (December 1891)]

86   A class will commence work in experimental physics, next term, a step forward or rather a mere turn in the right direction. We have to regret that the year is so far advanced before undertaking the task. The experiments are as unconnected as floating ribs which support that by which they are themselves supported, that is to say they are of no value whatever unaccompanied by text books for collateral study, which will require more than double the time that we ordinarily devoted to one study, and it may be well for those who have withdrawn from the text books to make this new departure, to bear in mind that this course means far more work unless they make it the useless make-shift which they regard it, and run the risk of a failure in note book preparation.

. . .

87   We have seriously debated with ourselves whether it would not be advisable to introduce a prize story to these our columns, in the hope that, by the hoax, we might gain a hearing from the school; but advertisers are wont to belittle themselves in this way   and professional men do not advertise. [Let some one sympathizing soul news this abroad and the desired effect will be obtained.]

88   Furthermore we would have headed this article with a wood-cut as a sort of book mark for such future classes as may be possessed of enormous sums of money which they know not how to use, had not time forbade.

89   What the school now wants is a telescope—mighty and far-reaching. In astronomy as in everything else, the practical is the popular. It is needless to say that astronomy is one of the most practical as well as theoretical of sciences. It is a most wonderful teacher of observation and cultivator of the more practical imagination. As for interest, we guarantee that there is no one, who reads at all, who can read the introduction to Mitchel's "Stellar World," and refrain from reading the whole book. One cannot but be interested in this romantic science, whose history is as old as the world and whose future is bounded only by eternity. Its devotees are limited neither by place nor sex.

Today many observatories employ women for the more accurate and exact calculations. But setting all this aside we return to it regarded as a school study. The routine of school life fed entirely on books, is unspeakably monotonous, so monotonous, in fact, that we become so depressed as to be uncertain one day whether or not we know what we learned yesterday; a little real observation would stand out of all this blackness as the moon seems to stand out of the dark when looked at through a telescope; it makes the darkness seem pleasant.

90   Forgetting such things is out of the question—let our object be not forgotten.

· · ·

91   The Debating Union has appointed the time for the mock trial and is now making preparation for giving its audience a royal welcome. The trial is for a breach of promise—somewhat of a venture which was made not without some hesitancy. The parts have been assigned in a manner creditable to the ability in character perception on the part of the society. It is now a matter of push.

92   The society is falling into disrepute of late, and for no other reason than that the members are over anxious to emulate the glory of their elders in displaying their parliamentary knowledge, which is merely another word for personal animosity. But few take part in the debates proper. Chalk, paper, and expressive epithets are the weapons of statesmanship. (And, by the way, henceforth, epithets will be the *only* legal tender). In this trial is a chance for awakening interest both in members and non-members. If it could be done without croaking, we would like to say that this interest is all that is to save the society from speedy dissolution.

L.H.S.D.U. Unofficial Report (December 1891)

93   (Dear Mr. Editor:
I humbly apologize for the following, my candid judgment of the sole society of our school. Its value is in its rarity, and the hazard attendant on its acquisition. My observations were taken from a back seat, and I heard two men say in an undertone, "No Visitors Are Allowed Except On Occasions Publicly Announced." I fully intended going out when the meeting opened; but I couldn't tell when it did, and I just remained until the lights were put out. Somehow or other some one noised it abroad that I was a reporter, and so every time one man got up to call to the president, every one else got up and hollered "Mr. President!" so that I couldn't hear what he answered, but I thought he said some one's name, because the man that got up last generally

smiled and went on speaking, while the others sat down, therefore pardon any defects in spelling or chirography, while I remain

　　Yours truly,

　　H. L. M.

　　P.S.—I hope the visitors, and that tall boy will stop throwing chalk, so that the Seniors won't put us out.)

94　　As nearly as I could make it out, this was an irregular meeting of the L. H. S. D. U.,—for the President wasn't in the chair when the meeting opened, and I understood what one man said, and I never do when I read about it; but probably the secretary condenses it and salts it down into portable form.

95　　There was one "gentleman" who seemed very anxious to speak, and everybody was; only it was not time. The same gentleman at last got a chance to say that there was foul play somewhere; but he seemed unable to say enough, so he said it over again, and re-said his last sentence in a vain attempt to round off his speech, and he knew it, you could see that he was nervous. He called a great big fellow a lawyer, at which the big fellow got up and denounced him or his speech. It was hot work until these two came off the see-saw; and then another Senior (I think,—they all must be Seniors by the way they act) said that he did not care to play the feminine part. I noticed that No.1 (he who first spoke) now began to recover from the invective of No.2, and was giving signs of returning vivacity. They made an amendment to the constitution by which 1 and 3 consulted in an ante-room, and 2; after which the society discussed the womanly qualities of 1 and 3, and then voted that 3 was No.1.

96　　Meanwhile the President had been appointing committees, but I could not tell who they were, because all stuck their fingers into ink wells, and wiped them off on their pants in modest expectation, and they didn't get over it for a long time whether they were chosen or not.

97　　I fell asleep when they were doing some more business, and when I woke up I heard some one say that Daniel Webster was a great and *good* man. I was tempted to say, "Who said he wasn't." Just then the great big fellow got up and from the way he sailed into Daniel Webster I knew that he must be standing up for some little boy who had probably spoken just before my waking. If I should be called upon to express an opinion I should say that fellow was a heroic leader of the masses who spoke right to their hearts. I should like to cultivate his acquaintance. The way he appeals to the assembly is touching.

98　　I wish I were not a reporter—I mean I wish no one knew that I was one. The members would not tell me the names of two of their number, one of whom they said glowed with Celtic eloquence, and was excused on account of business; the other sparkled with wit and telling hits, who carried an English Grammar instead of a Cushing's Manual, and was absent.

99   There is to be an affair in the society before Jan. 1, 1893, but I can't tell what it is. Professional men would call it a mill, I think. Complimentary tickets to all trustworthy characters excepting policemen.

Jan. 8, 1892.

[Four Editorials (May 1892)]

100   We wish to acknowledge our obligation to our audience of the coming commencement. Nevertheless, you are to be congratulated that we are approaching civilization, and are so far advanced that we can appropriate a tenth part of our time for lamenting the fate of those who must listen to essays from a whole class.

· · ·

101   For all the apparent formidableness of the exercise schedule now in use in the school, it might be a candidate for larger praise than it is now capable of receiving. Not only should a broader opportunity in the number of courses from which to elect be offered those whose school life terminates here,—on account of conflicting recitations nearly all are restricted to the bare three recitations daily,—but the classical student also, in view of the greater inducements that are being offered yearly for anticipating college work, should be given encouragement beyond mere requirements. This can be done in one way only—producing more time. Saving is producing.

102   The week, not the day, is the basis of school work. In this is the solution of the problem, if problem exists when no conditions have ever been formulated by the mathematician.

103   In the scientific department, and in the mathematical where board work is much used, preliminaries,—preparing apparatus, moving from place to place, etc.,—consume an hour before business is really begun. Add to this the crazy-quilt arrangement of Thursday, the promiscuous putting on here and cutting off there, and, as far as earnest study or recitation is concerned, things look really hopeless.

104   In the classical department, and this holds good for the scientific also: Mind is not so much unlike matter after all. It has the property of inertia. It may be the through express or the accommodation whose speed hisses away at the little way stations. You have noticed this in reading: It is the last few chapters of the book you read in a day wherein you gain your greatest and evenest speed. In thought speed is the overcoming of self consciousness: Things are forgotten by length of time unbroken by reminders.

105   Longer recitations then—in the classics for mind, in the sciences for mind and matter—are what we need. In any course two recitations a week of two hours each would be more than equivalent to five single hour exercises and there would be the one hour to spare for those ambitious of more than satisfying requirements.

106   Not to dilate further, we repeat, the week, not the day is the basis of school work.

.   .   .

107   School spirit is stirring—we now have three societies, whereas a year ago we had but one. Astronomical, Botanical and Geological outings have become customary, or will have become so.

108   In you, Philotechnic, we take a melancholy interest, in thinking of what might have been. There is something strangely weak and loose in your motions as yet, that we would fain obviate. You remind us of an imbecile chicken which once brought its woes to our household.

109   It had a tendency to spread out after the manner of the original egg (provided it had been cracked.) Incarcerated in the oven on a bed of down it was wont to revive and go out into the world for a space, only to relapse. You must try to arouse your united self dependence, Philo.

.   .   .

110   Question: Can we review an author's thought, retell his story? Yes, if you praise while so doing. Can we review a narrative of travel! No, because that would be a re-review—the traveller re-views God's thoughts (nature) and praises them. Twice told is new—thrice told is old. Herein is a definition of originality (school criterion.) We have, nevertheless, found some difficulty in persuading ourselves to this. If we agree on a definition for imagination, evidently, we can still find praise for nature beyond the first writer's. The only true praise is thought. The only thing that can back-bone an essay is thought. We then have one way of getting an essay. The trouble in the school is that in the dim past essays were entirely statistical. It came about that such were confused with those re-reviews spoken of above. And now when we criticize we always think the following paragraph over to ourselves, fearful of the second class:

111   A custom has its unquestioning followers, its radical enemies, and a class who have generally gone through both these to return to the first in a limited sense,—to follow custom,—not without question, but where it does not conflict with the broader habits of life gained by wanderers among ideas. The second class makes one of the first and third. This is best exemplified in religious thought and controversy. It is the second class that would have "an inquisition to compel liberality."

    R. Frost.

A Monument to After-Thought Unveiled (June 1892)

112   A tribute to the living? We are away beneath the sombre pines, amid a solitude that dreams to the ceaseless monotone of the west wind, the blue sky looking sleepily between the slowly bending boughs, and to, its veil of morning mist, uplifted by the morning breeze, white as pure thought, the monument of monuments.

113   From sun-beat dizzy marts, from grassy lawns, from surging summer trees, rise countless marble columns, wrought as noiselessly as if from snow, and all by the one hand here honored alone in loneliness.

114   Well might this marble be a shrine, this grove, a temple whence devotees might seek the world again, and fame!

115   The God—but wait, that carven silence kneeling at its base, whence it tapers away into the boughs above, writes, and this is what she writes:—

116   There are men—that poet who has left us uniting the battered harp the sea storm cast for him upon the shore, was one of these—who go to death with such grey grandeur that we look back upon their past for some strange sorrow, such as does not fall to others, even though we know sorrow to be the same through all time. They seem like Merlins looking ages from their deep calm eyes. With what awe we stand before the mystery of their persons. Such lives are the growth of the afterthought of the soul—the serene rest after toil, in questioning and answering whence and why misfortune is.

117   This nobility distinguishes personality only in the degree of its development, and the broader future, will give to every soul the opportunity to come into the possession of this, its divine right. Then, when no man's life is a strife from day to day, from year to year, with poverty, will it be an attribute commonality of the world.

118   Aggressive life is two-fold: theory, practice; thought, action: and concretely, poetry, statesmanship; philosophy, socialism—infinitely.

119   Not in the strife of action, is the leader made, nor in the face of crisis, but when all is over, when the mind is swift with keen regret, in the long afterthought. The after-thought of one action is the forethought of the next.

120   It is when alone, in converse with their own thoughts so much that they live their conventionalities, forgetful of the world's, that men form those habits called the heroism of genius, and lead the progress of the race. This, the supreme rise of the individual—not a conflict of consciousness, an effort to oppose, but bland forgetfulness, a life from self for the world—is the aim of existence.

121   All this is doubly so of the theoretical. In it the after-thought of long nights beneath the universe, of soul stirrings, of the act of thought itself, is more

clearly a part of the next action—its expression. Events influence the first class, the limits of language alone the second.

122   The poet's insight is his after-thought. It is of varied heart-beats and converse with nature. And the grandest of his ideas come when the last line is written.

123   Life is an after-thought: how wonderful shall be the world? that is the after-thought of life.

124   But look again, all this is mere shadow sheen upon the white marble. The one word there is: After-thought.

125   Now this dark pool beneath the trees is still. There is a white finger on its lips. Let ripples whisper here no more.

   Robert Frost.

126   And now a last after-thought.

127   To those who fix today a point through which from earlier years they draw a line of life projected far into the future, this hour is of a deep significance. But there is no change here, and he who thinks to rest will rest as in a winter storm, to die.

128   Unbounded full ambition for the greatest heights yet unattained is not too noble for one human mind. Who or what can bound our aspirations? Will courage fail before a thousand unfavorable comparisons? There is a space of time when meteor and rain drop falling side by side may touch the yielding earth with equal force. The lighter outspeeding weight may seem in a space to strike with greater force. But who at last can tell which has the greater influence on the world, the one that bore, as scientists have said, plant life or that which makes it live.

129   Strength and all the personality that we can crowd upon the world are ours to give in obligation. Let hope be limitless for all and let each follow hope as best he may.

130   To all old school associations here we show our purposed way in one bell-toned Farewell!

[The American About and Abroad (1895)]

1   The Armenian who communicated with the *American* a week or two ago, came very near telling what promised to be an interesting story. He got as far as the announcement: "This is my experience." His family was in Asia Minor, he said, where the Turkish garrison enforce laws lawlessly. But at this point he became objective, digressed, and concluded with the experience of some one else. Perhaps we may expect him to try again?

· · ·

2   The author of Ben Hur, for a long time the fellow-townsman of the Sultan, sends his respects to the Sultan and pronounces the Armenian outrages exaggerated. This is hard luck my friends; you did not expect to find such authority arrayed against you. But take comfort. You may be right. This sort of man is very inconsequential if only he can advance an idea. Speaking of authority, the omnific John Brisben Walker prophesied the sudden mobilization of China and the speedy overthrow of Japan a few months ago.

· · ·

3   I enjoyed a distinction this week. A poet favored me with a vocal interpretation of one of his own poems, pronounced by specialists equal, if not superior, to one of James Whitcomb Riley's on the same subject. I regret that owing to the defects of my memory, I am unable to produce it here. The author was no less a man than the late audible Hon. Byron Williams, himself a "specialist," he professes.

· · ·

4   I am going to betray a confidence and worse than that a poor man's confidence, but only in the hope of compelling for him your natural if unrighteous sympathy. There are a lot of women and children that have let me see them looting coal in a yard near here. They come with buckets and gather it piece by piece under the coal cars. It is feverish work keeping warm for such people. And the curious part of it is, they will not take the coal otherwise than from off the ground, which necessitates their twice handling it, once from the car to the ground, and again from the ground to the bucket. The

moral strain attendant on such work must be excessive, and one suffers to watch them skulking and stooping all day long.

· · ·

5   All wide-awake loafers will be found hereafter on the curbstone at the corner of Union and Essex streets. Outside the opera house I know of no place so lively. Every day a little crowd gathers there—the crowd comes first I maintain—and then a sleigh appears and is injured in the car tracks. No person is ever injured, only sleighs, so that witnessed in moderation the episodes will prove a harmless substitute for murders, highly to be recommended.

· · ·

6   What has gone wrong? Here is intelligence truly portentious. Is the A. P. A. defunct? I found what appeared to be a switchman's shanty, in a remote neighborhood, dismantled of its windows, littered with stones and glass within, and with this inscription in white chalk upon the door: "A. P. A.— Nommore!" Two explanations were possible. The structure was a mausoleum or rather a cenotaph, like the grave, wherein reposed the body of Brown

(Lost at sea and never foun')

erected and decorated on the spot with flint implements to the memory of the A. P. A. and in that case the A. P. A. was dead or about to be. Or the A. P. A. was not dead and this was their work; they had maltreated the patient wood until it had transcended itself and miraculously cried out in the tragic orthography: "A. P. A.—Nommore!"

[Children's Stories]

1   One day the baby went up the Berry road and she walked and walked and walked and walked and walked and walked and walked and walked so far she saw a monkey first. And the monkey said, "Hello, here's some nuts." And the baby said, "Those aren't nuts—those are brown eggs—Molly laid them." And the monkey said, "No she didn't." And the baby said, "Ye-e-e-s." And the monkey said, "No-o-o. *You* come with me." And he took the baby's hand and they walked and walked and walked and walked and walked and walked and walked so far they saw a kangaroo. And the kangaroo said, "Come and look in my pocket." And the baby said, "What you got in the pocket? Oh a banana." "No it's a boomerang. The man threw it at the kangaroo and it didn't hit the kangaroo and it fell on the ground and the kangaroo ran and picked it up and put it in the pocket." And the baby said, "No." And the kangaroo said, "Yes. *You* come with me." And he took the baby's hand and they walked and walked and walked and walked and walked so far they saw a bear. And the bear said, "Hello, baby, here's some honey—eat it." And the baby said, "Might get in baby's teeth." And the bear said, "Emma likes it." And the baby said, "No she in't." And the bear said, "Yes. *You* come with me. And he took the baby's hand and they walked and walked and walked and walked and walked and walked so far they saw an alligator. And the alligator snapped his teeth (like this). "What does he want?" He wants some 'bacco. But the baby hasn't got any 'bacco. So the man threw a piece in his mouth and he snapped his teeth (like this). And the man said to the baby, "Where—you—been?" And the baby said,

> "I've been to see the monkey
> And the kangagarangaroo
> I've been to see the poultry show
> And the mulligatawny stew."

"No, that in't aright. What's the marter?"

> "I've been to see the monkey
> And the kangarangaroo

> I've been to see the honey bear
> And the alligator chew."

And the man said to the baby, "*You* come with me." And they walked and walked and walked and walked and walked and walked so far they saw a Mamma. And the Mamma said, "You come here. Where you been?" And the baby said,

> "I've been to see the monkey
> And the kang—"

And the Mamma caught the baby and undressed her and threw her in the crib and covered her over and keessed her.

· · ·

2   A little girl went out to walk from her mama and she came to a cow and got past it and it didn't hurt her and she came to another cow and got past that one too and it didn't hurt her and so another and another, four in all. Then she turned around and came back past the same four. She got past the whole four twice without a hurt and came home and told her mamma and her mamma was so glad she had come through all right that she hugged her. I neglected to say this little girl had her doll Rosa with her and *she's* awfully afraid of cows.

· · ·

3   Schneider was asleep on the piazza and he felt something pull his hair and jumped up and looked but he couldn't see anything. So he lay down again and went to sleep and pretty soon he felt it again. He went right in the house and asked Lesley if she did it. Lesley said, "No," and Schneider couldn't understand. The next time he lay down he only went to sleep with one eye open—this one—no I guess it was the other.

4   In a minute he saw a little bird fly out of the woodpecker tree right at him.

5   It was so near when he jumped up that it got scared and lit on his nose. "Ouch," it said, "Cold!" It flew into the woodbine.

6   "What do you want?" Schneider said.

7   "Hair for a nest."

8   "Why don't you use your own feathers—you're full of them."

9   And the bird said, "Do you mean full like a pillow?"

· · ·

10   Schneider met a squirrel and the squirrel said, "If you don't catch me, I'll show you another squirrel fatter'n I be." And Schneider said, "All right—come on."

11   So the squirrel went squirreling up the road and Schneider followed till they came to a hole and the squirrel said, "There."

12   But Schneider said, "That isn't any squirrel."

13   And the squirrel said, "Well that's the hole the squirrel lives in, and if you can catch him, you can have him."

14   "Well," Schneider said, "well—uh—that don't seem hardly right."

15   And the squirrel ran up a tree and said, "Why don't it?"

·   ·   ·

16   One day Schneider chased a woodchuck down his hole and began digging after him like everything.

17   But the woodchuck had two holes and he came up out of the other one and sat up and said, "I see your tail, Schneider, I see your tail."

18   Schneider ran over and chased him down that hole and began digging there.

19   Then the woodchuck came up out of the first hole and sat up and called again, "I see your tail, Schneider, I see your tail."

20   Schneider was so mad that he gave up and went home.

21   The woodchuck laughed and said, "Goodbye, Schneider. Come again."

22   Schneider said, "Oh stop talking—woodchucks can't talk."

23   And the woodchuck said, "Neither can dogs."

24   That's so, they can't.

·   ·   ·

25   One day Schneider went out to talk to the cow. Schneider barked at the cow and the cow curled up her tail, kicked up her heels, snorted and ran after Schneider.

26   She chased him down the pasture to the bars. Schneider went under them and she crashed through them and ran down the Derry road and went to biting the floor.

27   Schneider ran into the house and hid in the pantry.

28   "Will the cow come in here? Will the cow come in here?" he said.

29   "No," I said, "the cow won't come in the pantry, silly dog."

30   "Perhaps I'd better go up stairs," he said.

31   So he fell up stairs and went under a bed.

"The Lord Protector"

32   Once there were three little girls who were afraid of almost everything when they were away from home, engines and electricians and automobiles and road rollers and bears and giants and cannons. But when they were at home they felt perfectly safe because they had a little brother there just a little bit smaller than they were who was a great hero. He always walked about with his chin close in to his neck and his fists in the pockets of his new trousers.

He kept almost whistling. All about the yard, like bones in front of a lion's den, were scattered the sticks and clubs that none but he could wield and the carts and boxes and things he had broken by not playing with them gently enough. When he heard a wagon coming down the road he would come to the barn door to let people see that he was on guard. As long as they went by it was all right. He had a terrible smile, a terrible smile. He made the three little girls feels perfectly safe even at night.

"Old Stick-in-the-Mud"

33   Irma went wagging her dress out into the big pasture. And one of the fence posts down in the low ground saw her and asked her what she was after.

34   "Checkerberries!"

35   "Are you sure it isn't cranberries? I know where there are some of those, or were last fall."

36   "No, checkerberries!"

37   "Well I guess I can direct you to some of those. Just ahead of you."

38   "I don't see any."

39   "Not there; to your right, to your right. Oh, no, no, no, no. Here, you come here and hold this wire and I'll go and find some for you."

40   So Irma went and unbuttoned the barbed wires from him—there were three of them, and he showed her how she would have to hold them to keep them just the right distance apart so that the cow couldn't get out—one in her mouth and one in each hand. She had to take a very awkward position and the wire in her mouth made it hard for her to talk.

41   The fence post pulled himself out of his hole and set off. He didn't seem to know as well where the checkerberries were as he thought or pretended he did, for he went zigzagging here and there brushing the grass with his foot without once stooping to pick any. Finally he came back to Irma and said:

42   "I just thought: What would I pick into if I happened to find berries."

43   "If you *happened* to find berries! Irma sputtered on account of the wire in her mouth. I thought you said you knew where the berries were. Pick them into your hands. But hurry up. I can't keep these wires spaced right much longer."

44   "But I haven't any hands. Perhaps I'd better go to the house for a can."

45   "*If you do!* Irma sputtered. I'll just drop everything and let the fence fall,"

46   "Don't do that. The cow will get out."

47   "I will—now!"

48   "Oh don't little girl. Well go ahead. I don't care. Drop 'em. It won't be any loss. The cow's yours. And you know how it will be if she gets a taste of ap-

ples; she'll simply go apple crazy and then she'll have to go into the barn for the rest of the season."

49   Irma squeezed a tear out of each eye as the fence post stumped off.

50   On his way to the house he came to a hole in the pine grove where long ago someone had taken out a few loads of dirt and had afterwards dumped rubbish there. In it he spied a very rusty old tomato can (but not much rustier than the wire Irma held in her mouth so faithfully through it all) which he thought would do well enough. He waved it at Irma as he came hurrying back with it.

51   "Just you hold on a minute or two longer in all three places," he laughed.

52   Irma had made up her mind to tell Papa. There were berries as Irma knew very well from having been there before with the other children and presently the fence post found them. He picked and picked and if he had had a corn can instead of a tomato can I believe he would have filled it: as it was he must have picked a pint. Irma began to be afraid that he was tricky and might be planning to go off when he got through and leave her to hold up the fence forever. But presently he came and let her look down into the can of berries.

53   "Oo!" she exclaimed.

54   "Now button the wires on to me," he said, "and go home to Papa. He dropped into his watery hole with a splash.

55   She did as she was told, wiped her mouth on her sleeve, picked up her berries and was about to run for it, when suddenly she remembered that she wasn't going to forgive the fence post no matter how handsomely he treated her in the end. So she put her head on one side, wagged her dress, and said big-lady-silly-ways: "What's your cutey little name, please?"

56   "What, mine? Why my name's Old Stick-in-the-Mud."

57   That was all she wanted and she ran home to tell Papa on him. First she bragged a little about her berries, and then she settled down to cry so that someone would ask her what was the matter. That gave her a chance to tell her story. She told the whole thing, not leaving out the part where the fence post laughed at her.

58   "What fence post was it dear?" Mama asked.

59   "It was Old Stick-in-the-Mud. I got it out of him."

60   "Oh! Old Stick-in-the-Mud," laughed Papa. "He's a nice old fellow. He wouldn't do anything to hurt you. That's just his funny way. He's awfully old—oldest one on the farm—stands in an awfully wet hole too—sort of leans forward. But goodness he likes little girls, likes everybody. He's knotty but not naughty. Remember to say 'Thank you' to him next time you're down that way."

"The Crash"

61   Once the children got on the table with all the dishes and the lamp. They were tickling each other and having a good time when suddenly the whole thing went down, dishes, knives and forks, lamp, children and all—crash! Up jumped President Roosevelt in Washington. "What was that?" he said. His secretaries all came looking in at different doors to see if it was the President; there were the Secretary of Farming and the Secretary of Postage Stamps. "What was that?" he shouted at them. "Good gracious if that happens again." His glasses kept falling off his nose as he put them back on. "Don't let that happen again," said the Secretary of Farming and the Secretary of Postage Stamps both together. "It mustn't," said the President, and rushing to a window he threw it open and shouted louder than ever, "Don't let it happen again!"

62   Don't let it, will you?

. . .

63   Fairies live in juniper bushes—you just have to believe that. Well one day two little fairies peeped over the pasture wall into the orchard and one said to the other, "You go," and the other said, "No, you!" It was October, too early for late apples and almost too late for early. The rows of trees nearest the wall were Baldwin but down over the hill there was a row of Haas and they thought there might be an apple or two left there—on the ground of course and dead ripe and all the better for that. But they were afraid of Carol and they kept arguing, "You go," "No you" till at last one said, "Let's go together," and the other said, "Well, then let's." So they gave one long look down toward the house and then ran for it. They came to the first tree and there was nothing there, to the next and it was just the same. The further they went the more frightened they were to find Carol. They went so fast they wouldn't have seen an apple if there had been one. But just as they were leaving the very last tree one of them stumbled over an apple so big that it knocked him down. It was a beauty, so red it was black. He tried to pick it up but he couldn't. He could lift it but it was smooth and kept getting away from him. So the other fairy took hold too. They started back for the wall with it and when they dropped it they'd roll it away. They were so excited they didn't know what to do. But they thought they were sure of it when suddenly away down by the barn they saw Carol walking backward. They dropped the apple right where they were—it happened to be right under a Baldwin tree— and ran. They didn't go far because they hated to give up the apple, but lay down behind the wall and waited. Pretty soon Carol came along fast as you please and practicing talking so as to learn when no one was near to

listen. He came to the Haas apple. He picked it up and looked at it—not a crow bite in it. Then he looked at the tree. It was Baldwin and he knew it was. There were hard green Baldwins on it. "Huh," he said, "did you do that?" He was speaking to the tree. "I never heard of a Haas apple off a Baldwin tree—I never. I guess Lesley better know about this!" So he began to call her. "Lesley," he screamed. Quick as a flash something said, "Lesley." "Huh," he said, "that's a funny thing, funny as about the apple. Perhaps this is a funny orchard or else this is a funny day!" He didn't call any more but went and got Lesley. When he came back with her the apple was where he left it only it had been turned over, but he didn't notice any difference; Lesley was puzzled too. "It couldn't have rolled here up the hill," she said. "You don't suppose," Carol said, "there's so many trees they've got mixed up about their work." Lesley laughed. "And there's something else I didn't tell you. When I called just now there was something called right afterward. I'm sure sure!" Lesley laughed and told him that was an echo. "An echo? Mightn't the echo have done it?" But Lesley didn't hear that—she was thinking. They sat down in the grass to get low to try to understand. Their backs were to the wall so that when a stone fell off it they were taken by surprise. They hardly turned in time to see two little heads pop out of sight on the pasture side. Carol saw them better than Lesley. "Fairies," he cried. Lesley said, "I can't believe it." "Fairies sure," said Carol. They ran for the wall but only saw a flash of blue and yellow go out in a juniper like a lamp flame. Lesley said, "I might have known. They like them to polish up for looking glasses and they like the smell that's better than flowers. Well my little fairies you shall have your apple." And she went and got it and set it down on the pasture side of the wall. But it was the last fall apple of the year and Carol didn't like giving it away. For a moment there was a queer squeezing sound from his nose and then he opened his mouth and wailed. He kept it up all the way back to the house. Elinor wanted to know what was the matter and Lesley told her. Elinor said, "The poor little fellow's tired—he hasn't had his nap."

· · ·

64   When I went to the raspberry patch to pick berries one day I got on the wrong side of a rabbit. The poor fellow couldn't get home because I was in the way. He had to hide till I got through picking. He cuddled down in a dark place just like a little ball that won't tell you where it is. He trembled as if it was winter but it was only berry time. He had to stay there two quarts.

· · ·

65   One day Leslie met a squirrel in the woods and she said, "Do you live here? Why don't you come and live in the nest in the woodbine on our piazza long a' folks?"

66   And the squirrel said, "Ain't you Schneider's Leslie?"

67   And she said she was,

68   And the squirrel said, "Well I'd like to come but I guess I couldn't."

69   And Leslie said, "I won't let him bark at you."

70   Well if he don't bark perhaps I can stand the rest. I'll come down and see about it."

71   So the squirrel came but when he saw the nest in the woodbine he said, "My, my, whose nest was it?"

72   And Leslie said, "A squirrel's."

73   "Well I'd have to do a lot to it before I could live in it. But if you'll do what you said about Schneider perhaps I'll try."

74   So he went to work bringing grasses in his mouth like reins in Billy's. And when he got through the nest was as big as a pumpkin and he lived in the middle of it somewhere but you couldn't tell whether he was in or out until you called him. And when Leslie wanted to know anything about anything all she had to do was open the window and ask him.

·   ·   ·

75   Two birds sat in a bare ruined tree by a deserted birds' nest filled with snow and talked about it.

76   One said, "Why not clean it out and sleep in it?"

77   The other said, "Nests aren't to sleep in—they're for eggs.

78   And the other said, "Don't it look all lonesome? Let's sing about it."

79   And the other bird said, "Winter birds can't sing—only cheep."

80   "Let's cheep then."

81   So they cheeped.

·   ·   ·

82   The baby went up the Berry road and saw a donkey. And the donkey said, "Boot out. I'm going to kick."

83   And the baby said, "Well kick the other way then."

84   And the donkey said, "I won't."

85   And the baby said, "Well wait a minute."

86   And the donkey said, "I won't wait!" And he gave an awful kick right into the air. But he didn't kick her bonnet off because she ran home. She ran home and told her Mamma. And her Mamma said, "Don't go up there then."

87   And the baby said, "But I wants to."

88   "But you won't."

89   "No, I won't."

90   And the Mamma said, "Hear him snap and click just like a rubber donkey." (rubber donkey!)

·   ·   ·

91   A frog left his brook to find another brook. He started up the road but the day was hot and dusty and he got so dry he could hardly jump. He asked a man how far it was to the next brook. And the man said, "There's a brook right down here at the foot of the hill."

92   And the frog said, "That's the one I came from."

93   "Well you'd better go back to it. You look like it. Its your nearest water.

94   And the frog said, "I can't." He looked like the end of your fingers after a bath.

95   Just then he saw a pail of water in our yard for the hens to drink out of and he went for it so fast that the man laughed.

96   He jumped at the edge of the pail three times and missed and fell back; but at last he got in and the water was cool and the frog felt better.

97   "This is good water," he said. "I wonder where it came from. My mother told me my brook came from the cranberry bog but I didn't know."

98   He lay sprawling on the top and went to sleep.

99   Pretty soon a hen came for a drink and she saw him there. She looked at him first with one eye then with the other. Then she cackled.

100   "Don't," the frog said, "don't tell everybody."

101   But she wouldn't stop and the other hens came to see what was the matter. And they all cackled. The frog said there was nothing the matter—he felt better. "Please don't look at me—it makes me feel funny."

102   He dove down to the bottom to hide in the mud but there wasn't any mud. It was wood and he bumped his nose.

103   He couldn't do anything but wish.*
     *wish that he hadn't come

· · ·

104   Papa didn't see Margery in the yard and came out to ask the other children where she was. "Why where is she," they cried, frightened that they had let her get out of sight when they were supposed to take care of her because she was the youngest. "Margery!" but no answer. "Oh there she is over in the ferns. See her? See her? See the scoop of her bonnet?—sticking up like a rabbit's ears when he thinks he's hiding.

105   "What's she doing over there?" Papa wondered.

106   "Sitting down, just."

107   "Eating something she ought not to very likely: run and see."

108   Papa followed slowly. "What *is* she doing?"

109   "She has a lot of leaves in her lap and she won't tell us."

110   "What is it Margery?"

111   "I'm reading."

112   "Reading what?"

113   "Stories on leaves."

114   She picked up a leaf, frowned at it seriously a moment then laid it aside for another.

115   "What does it say on the leaves?"

116   "Stories."

117   "Different stories? What does it say on the one you have now? Read it to the other children. We'll all sit down here with you on the warm ground and listen to you."

118   "'X, B, A, H, ritmetix.' You mustn't laugh."

119   "But we mean the story, not the letters. Read us that."

120   "It says. It says. I don't want to tell you. It isn't bed story time, is it?"

121   "But you must read it, be a good girl."

122   "It says: A butterfly on a flower. And he had his wings up together. And along came a bee. And the butterfly spread out his wings and covered the flower so the bee couldn't get any. The honey. And the bee said, 'Oh you want it all.' And the butterfly said, 'I came to it first.' And the bee said, 'I thought of it first. I'll sting you.' And the butterfly said, 'I shan't call you my nice little bee anymore then.' And the bee said, 'You're naughty.'' And the butterfly said, 'You're naughty.' And the bee said, 'I'll tell mama.' Have they got any mama?"

123   "Have they?"

124   "I guess they have. And the bee said, 'I'll tell mama,' and so the butterfly had to let him have some. Because he needed it from that flower to make his honey taste right."

125   "That's a fine story. Now read us another."

126   "That's all tonight. But I'll read another if the children are all good children."

"The Wise Men"

127   Carol kissed us all good bye and climbed into the nut tree, going quickly round and round the trunk where the branches were best until he was out of sight. He was out of hearing too before any of us thought to ask him when he would be back, so there was nothing to do but wait and see. He was so long gone with no sign of him, not a falling twig or nut, that we began to wonder, especially as it grew dark. We were afraid that he would not risk climbing down by starlight and we would have to stay under the tree all night.

128   That was the way it turned out. We took turns watching for him and morning came and there was no Carol. The night was perfectly quiet and the

leaves were still in the whole great tree and each of us as he sat alone listened intently for any sound of the little boy. We thought he might have shouted to us some word of what was keeping him. But he seemed to have forgotten us.

129   It was the same all day for the tree seemed as deserted as if it hadn't held so much as a bird's nest. We let everything else go on the farm, the cow un-milked, the weeds unhoed while we stood and talked about the strange thing that had happened to us. The day passed and another night.

130   But toward evening the next day there was the cry, "Here he comes!" Margy had seen him or the nails of his boot-heels feeling for a footing away among thee braches. How strange he looked! He looked changed. First we all ran forward: then we all ran back—three steps. He had touched ground and now he turned toward us blinking—an old grey man. His beard was long and white and pointed and his hat was long and red and pointed and all covered with stars and new moons. He wore a long cloak clear to his feet and carried a big book under his arm. He turned three times round as if he wished to make himself dizzy but it was only to get his bearings. Then without a look to show that he knew we were there he walked straight past us up the little hill into the sweet ferns and tramp tramping away into the woods. Well!

131   We hadn't said a word. We hadn't moved until he was gone. Now we started chattering. Irma said he was as small as Carol, but too old. Lesley said, "To get as old as that he would first have to grow to the size of a man and that might take five years if he eat well and then he would first have to shrink back to his own size and that would take five hundred years because it takes longer to grow small than it does to grow large."

132   Margy was for going after him.

133   Lesley said, "The way he's headed he'll come out in the village if he goes far enough and doesn't climb another tree; and the people will bring him back to us—if they can tell who he is—that's so—they can't can they?"

134   Suddenly Margy and Irma cried out at the same time, "Here he comes again!" and "Here comes another!" We didn't know which was right.

135   This one was exactly like the other, beard, hat, book, cloak and all. He went through the same movements turning slowly three times to get his bearings and then set out for the ferns and the wood in the footsteps of the other. But we were not so surprised as before. We got our voices and managed to speak. We even tried to stop him by putting ourselves in his way though we didn't dare to lay hands on him he was so queer. He brushed past us and out of sight.

136   We all gathered under the tree to look up for the appearance of another one. As we were standing along came Smith and pulled up his horse to talk

about the weather. But you may imagine that we didn't want him there when another of those old men might come down at any minute and then what would people think of our farm? So we tried not to encourage him to talk answering only with yes or no and not saying anything new ourselves. We got rid of him just in time. If he had looked back as he drove away he might have seen as it was, but I think he was a little cross at our bad manners. It was the third of the old men and exactly like the other two. I am sure you would find the number of stars and new moons on the hats of all three precisely the same.

137   The question was: Were they Carol? How could they be? It was a great puzzle.

138   But not for long, for hardly had we lifted our eyes to the tree again when we saw the real Carol coming down in the same clothes he went up in. He came to the ground with a thud.

139   "Have you seen my cap down here?" he said.

140   "No but we saw three old men," we said.

141   "It ought to have come down. I dropped it. Are you sure you didn't see it?"

142   "No but we saw three old men," we said.

143   "Oh those fellows."

144   "Who were they?"

145   "Three old know-it-alls I got acquainted with up there. How long have I been gone? Say it's the strangest thing about that hat. I dropped it for you so you'd know I was all right. It must have been day before yesterday. I don't want to lose that. I'll tell you about the old men some other time. Let's hunt for the hat."

146   "No tell us now. What were they doing in our Nut Tree?"

147   "Trying to find out how high the sky is. When I arrived on top there they sat in a ring looking up in the sky with their hats sticking out behind and their beards in front. Each had a book open in his lap and his finger marking a place on a page. I said hello to them but they were too solemn to notice anything like that, so I tried again with a question.

148   "'What are you doing?'

149   "Every one looked suddenly at me as if I was new, rounding his eyes terribly and opening his mouth. Then they looked at each other. No one spoke.

150   "'What are you doing?' I said again.

151   "'Trying to find out something' they answered in one voice and their heads back again.

152   "'What?' No answer.

153   "'I should think such old men as you would know everything,' I said to tease them.

154   "'We do we do we do. Everything but just one thing and if you had not come and interrupted us we'd have known that in a few minutes.'

155   "'What is it?'

156   "'How high the sky is.'

157   "'Oh, I'll give you something you can tell me if you know everything. What's it going to do tomorrow?'

158   "They all tipped up their faces again.

159   "'What's it going to do tomorrow if you know everything? That's what I'm up here to find out.'

160   "'We don't want to talk to you,' they mumbled without taking their eyes off the sky.

161   "But I stuck to it. 'Tell me what it's going to do tomorrow? That was too much for one of them; I don't know which one for there was no way of telling them apart. He slapped his book shut, got up and went down thee tree.

162   "So I bothered the other two for a while without getting a word out of them though I could tell by the shaking of the little tassel away out on the end of their hats that they were disturbed; until one after the other they left me in a rage. Then I came down. But the funniest thing is about the cap."

Stories for *The Eastern Poultryman* and *Farm-Poultry* (1903–1905)

Trap Nests (February 1903)

1   Aiken had worn the starched collar of servitude to dress long enough; he wished to get back to loose clothes and the country, and he saw in hens a way.

2   He remembered the hens at home in his boyhood as more or less of a nuisance. They had roosted on the rolling stock and scratched behind the live stock in the barn, and what eggs they laid they were careful to conceal where no one could find them until rotten. But from all accounts they had become a different thing. There was easy wealth in them for whoso had the tip.

3   Aiken did not forsake all to go into the hen business, as many have done to their cost. He sat a high stool in the office of Somebody & Co., where the wages were small and the perils to life and limb, dyspepsia and writer's cramp, seemed numerous. But, although he did not like the job, it was his whole-wheat bread and butter, and he was too cautious a man to abandon it for an uncertainty. So he made a preliminary experiment in the hen business on a very small scale in his back yard, through the instrumentality of his wife.

4   He provided Mrs. Aiken with all the literature on hens that he could come at, and told her to go ahead. Only he expected her to make it pay. He had heard of three dollars a year in a hen, and he asked her to bear that in mind.

5   Mrs. Aiken was a practical little woman with an English accent, and as it was to save Aiken from a sedentary life or die herself of married life, she went at the new business with a will. At first she seldom troubled Aiken with her doubts and perplexities. She faced alone the problem of fixing on the only right breed of hen for beauty and use. Unassisted she attacked the large subject of feeding for eggs.

6   First she fed cut clover for a while exclusively, then green cut bone exclusively, and finally, in despair, a balanced ration prescribed by an irresponsible editor. But she fed without results. It is true that the hens did not die; the adult hen is hard to kill except with a weapon. But they did not lay and Mrs. Aiken was at her wit's end.

7   Once more she tried steamed cut clover, which she had the greatest faith in

for its aromatic odor. Then, because she had to, she appealed to Aiken. He had heard that the chief reliance of the new poultryman was green cut bone. But she had fed that, morning, noon, and night, for a week, and it had come nearer sickening the hens than anything else. Aiken told her what she already knew, that he did not wish to be bothered. He told her to feed anything she pleased—all he cared about was results.

8   Mrs. Aiken had been thinking. She could not say that all she cared about was results, but she cared a great deal for results. She would have been glad to consider her hens too, but if they would not let her, was it her fault? Though of a kind heart, she was no sentimentalist to prefer suffering herself to seeing dumb beasts suffer (and when you come to think of it, hens aren't but a dumb little dumber than they are beasts). If the hens wouldn't lay, they should be made to lay—she would have recourse to the barbarous trap nest—they had brought it on themselves—she washed her hands of the responsibility.

9   She had held trap nests in reserve for some time. She brought herself to mention them to her husband. He had heard of them. He entertained some such idea of them as she, namely, that they were intended to catch and hold the hen until she was willing to purchase freedom at the price of an egg—hold her to ransom, so to speak. He would have had no scruple in employing them himself, but for a woman it was different. They really did savor of vivisection and the Inquisition. Mention of them gave him pause.

10   "Heroic measures?" he said with an attempt at lightness.

11   "I hate to do it that bad," she said.

12   "And I won't let you do it," he spoke up like a man. "I'll do it myself. Someone has got to suffer, and I guess it'll be the hens. Buy the nests."

13   "We can make them," she said. "They are like ordinary nests, except that they have doors like a boot-jack hanging on hinges from the top, the points of the inverted 'V' resting on the inside of a sill so that it can only open inward."

14   "Very well, we will make them, and then none of the old maids in the neighborhood will be any the wiser."

15   So the trap nests were installed. The hens took the opposite side of the pen and craned at them with a scandalized cackling, and then forgot them, and went about their business—which was not laying. At that time they were on a diet of quartz and charcoal. They did everything that real hens do, and their little ways interested Mrs. Aiken the livelong day. They scratched, they preened, they went to roost. But they never laid, and, as barren hens, naturally avoided nests, and how much more these suspicious looking nests with closed doors.

16   Every night Aiken said, "Caught anything?" and Mrs. Aiken shook her head disconsolately. Aiken wasn't sorry he had kept his place with Somebody & Co. until he had investigated the hen business for himself.

17   "Say," he said hopefully one evening before he had cast his overcoat, "we forgot to bait those traps."

18   "There," cried Mrs. Aiken. "But what shall we bait them with?"

19   "What are you feeding them now?"

20   "Grit, principally," she said.

21   "Do they take to it?"

22   "They did at first, but I'm afraid they're what is called 'off their feed' again. I might try cheese."

23   "No, starve them a day or two and then try corn."

24   The plan succeeded, and one night Mrs. Aiken had to announce that all the hens were in custody and most of them in one nest.

25   "Probably the first hen in acted as a decoy, and the others followed till there was no more room," he surmised. "Well, they'll keep each other warm."

26   "They are gasping now from the heat."

27   "That's but one inducement the more to make them do as they are asked. They'll know what it is to serve on a jury."

28   "But if one of them should lay an egg, how shall we know which one it is to release her?"

29   "The good will have to suffer with the bad—the Lord will know his own, as the bishop said." Aiken took a growing satisfaction in ruthlessness, for such, he felt, was life.

30   But the hens were obdurate. A week passed and there was not one egg. Aiken began to reconcile himself to the thought of lifelong bookkeeping. He saw nothing for it but to acquire the use of his left hand in writing.

31   "I know they can if they will," he told his wife irritably.

32   "But perhaps they can't will. It seems to me they're too nervous to concentrate on laying or anything else."

33   "I wonder who invented trap nests, anyway. Did you ever hear of their profiting anyone?"

34   "I know they're used. But they seem so cruel. Still, they're no worse than stomach-pumps to feed hens with."

35   "Do they use those?"

36   "Yes, it's called intensive poultry keeping."

37   "Intensive, huh! Well, I'm going to let the farrow song-birds loose, and we'll get out of the business faster than we came in."

38   So said, so done. The doors were opened and the hens staggered forth on their hocks—those that were left. Several lay trampled flat as a pancake. One

of the survivors burst into a meaningless cackle. It was the persistence as well as the quality of the noise that infuriated. If she had been satisfied with a stanza or two in that vein, Aiken might have borne it. But she was a hen, and Aiken was human and a dyspeptic. He kicked that hen through a window and drove the others through the door. Then he shooed them all to the top of the yard fence, where they sang together like the stars at the creation— thence broadcast over the neighborhood.

39   "How unreasonable," said his wife. "You can't get out of the hen business as easy as that. Your chickens will come home to roost."

40   "Will they? I'll stay here and see that they don't."

41   And armed with a broomstick, he stayed.

R. L. F.

A Just Judge (March 1903)

42   There was once a ninety-six point hen, and she was a ninety-six point hen, and she really existed, and this story recounts only facts. The judge that first scored her said to the man beside him who footed up the cuts, "Well, that is the least I can give her." He might have been pardoned for saying, "Well, that is the most I can give her," but that was not that judge's style.

43   She was what is called a chance bird. Not that she did not come of good stock. Her parentage was not altogether obscure. Only there was nothing in her ancestry that quite accounted for her, and she outclassed all her sisters and her cousins and her aunts, some of whom were on exhibition with her at her first show.

44   That judge said privately that he would have been glad to score her a hundred, and it seemed foolish not to, but he had to think of himself. "I made that score card in the sweat of my brow," he was reported as saying. "Well, what were her defects?" someone asked him. "You will have to consult the score card; I don't pretend to remember; the impression she left on me was one of perfection." Which was the making of that pullet.

45   From the time they hung the blue ribbon on her coop, she always had an audience to the end of the show. She was well trained and took it all as a matter of course. She showed herself front, three-quarters, profile, back, almost as regularly as a revolving show case. But she listened to the praise on every hand with composure, the more so as much of it would have made her of another breed entirely.

46   This story is about the confirmation of the first judge's judgment by that of judges that came after him. For No.1 so to call her did not go home to the breeding pens of the man that raised her. She was bought, as it proved, for showing until used up, and sent on her travels. She had a cold winter. She

made her debut early in the season, when the important shows were all to come. She went to them all by express in a draughty shipping coop, and at all of them she won first place, always with special mention from her judges.

47 But if she was worth anything as a breeder or to keep this was not the kind of treatment she was entitled to, and if she liked it herself at first, she soon tired of it. It ceased to console her that she was making one man's reputation. She became a bird acquainted with depot platforms in all sorts of weather. She learned to judge humanity at large by the treatment she had received at the hands of expressmen. She suffered a disillusionment that manifested itself in a change in the carriage of her tail.

48 That was the beginning of the end. Next it was her face paled; then her legs lost their color; her eyes dimmed. And just in time to save herself from being ridiculed as a bird greatly over-estimated at the lesser shows, on the eve of the greatest show of all she collapsed entirely. She lay in her pen a heap of ruffled feathers, such a sorry spectacle as invited only pity. She had made a glorious campaign and this was the upshot. It would have been kinder to her reputation to have spared her a little and given her a chance to win at the only show really worth while.

49 But though she was plainly marked for death, she was not forgotten in her last hours. Experts told her story again over her prostrate form. She had more victories to her credit than any other bird of the season, and what a pity that she should not have been allowed to put the finishing touch to her record by winning here. She must have won, some said. It was doubted and argued. Judges present who had known and scored her were appealed to. With them it was a personal matter. They defended her with spirit. One said, "I firmly believe that pullet was sent into this world especially for this show— and look at her. It's a shame!"

50 A life-sized photograph of her was produced from somewhere, taken when at her best by a committee of some club appointed to revise the standard. Someone had written under it, "Real Perfection as distinguished from Ideal Perfection."

51 All this was vindication enough and more than enough for the opinion of the judge that had brought her out of the obscurity of her first show. But the remarkable part was to follow.

52 It was not generally known that even at the point of death the famous No.1 found a buyer. In the excitement of the close of the show she was not thought of. By those that knew of her sale it was assumed that she was destined for stuffing and mounting. No one ever expected to see her again or hear of her either, after the echoes of her first season's achievements had died away.

53 But that was not the kind of pullet she was. She was bought at a risk by a

man that knew his business and intended to give her a fighting chance—which was all she asked. She was carried far, far from shows and the fear of shows, to a settled life and natural conditions. And she amply repaid everything that was done for her, and came straight back to life, and before spring was well advanced was laying precious eggs, though considering her antecedents, they were probably not nearly as precious as herself.

54   She was lost to the world in the mountains of northern Vermont, where hens being known by the amount of noise and dirt they make, are not distinguished one from another. Her owner was of the quiet kind that prefer to let their belongings as well as their actions speak for themselves. She was not advertised and she had no visitors. She bucked the trap nest at least thrice a week, and as her eggs proved fertile in spite of what she had been through, by the end of the summer a good proportion of the chickens about the place bore the toe marks that related them to her. She tended strictly to business and her work showed that she had two at least of the requisites of a good breeder, she was prolific and fertile. Whether it would turn out that she could transmit her superior qualities was another matter.

55   But it was not merely as a breeder that her owner valued her. He had built somewhat on his hope of winning with her another year; but he did not underestimate the chances he took when he bought her with this in view. The chances were there: first and foremost, she might never recover; then if she recovered, she might never recover her original form; and there was always the chance that like many another wonder, she might not be able to hold her own through the breeding season and the moult. She soon disappointed his fears as to her recovery and her recovery of form, and with the care she had, she approached the moult with everything in her favor.

56   The moult is a trying time to the poultryman. He would gladly cut it out. There is not an object in sight to keep his courage up. The hens are a disgrace, and as for the growing stock, for all that one can tell, they may be all culls. It will be Christmas, it seems, before the youngsters throw the red or the oldsters reclothe themselves against the cold. One poultryman who always displayed the sign "No Admittance" on his houses during the last moult, in a moment of exasperation went and superadded the word "Positively" with his own hand.

57   No.1 was as disheartening as the rest of them in the doldrums. She went to pieces all in one day like a smitten thistle head. She was as ready for a swim as anyone could be without the inclination, and she didn't seem to care how long she stayed so or who saw her. At length she began to grow short quills as if in her second year she intended to be a porcupine, but she took her own time about this even. "Better a porcupine," her owner said, "than that sort of

an undrawn carcass." But finally his patience (what there was of it) was re-warded, and No.1 was in feathers again.

58 And he swore that she was the same old bird. It often happens that fowl are so changed by the moult that their owners do not know them, nor they their owners. But No.1 was the identical bird, or his eyes deceived him. Of course he might be partial—and then again he mightn't be. At any rate he was ready to back her.

59 The shows began. Poor No.1, if she had known what was in store for her, would perhaps have contrived not to clothe her nakedness. She found out when it was too late that she was in for another strenuous winter. She made her first appearance near home; it was a small show but it was bad enough. The babel of roosters in the large hall, the smell of cats, and the uniformity of the coops made her deathly sick. It was like reopening an old wound. She was expected to win there hands down, and she did, and this was the manner of it.

60 It was scoring time, and a group halted before her coop, among them her owner: but the one she noticed particularly, or should have noticed, since if she had but known it, she owed him a grudge, was the judge who had discov-ered her in the first place. There he was again with the same hypercritical look in his eyes or eyebrows. He began an inventory of her faults carelessly enough, but as he proceeded his expression changed. Suddenly he looked up and around him as if for an explanation in the faces of his audience. Finding none, he resumed his task, but with more and more perplexity.

61 "What do you make it?" he said at last.

62 "Four," said his attendant.

63 He took the card and regarded it with open mouth. "I wonder," he said. Then he crumpled it and thrust it into his pocket. "Try again! I must be get-ting so old that I cannot find faults as I used to. Two in two years."

64 The result was the same. "Gentlemen," he said to the company, "who owns this bird and where is he? Unless I am greatly mistaken, she and I have met before. I scored a bird 96 points once and I never intended to score an-other that, if I could help it, and I don't believe I have, for I think she's the same one. Does anyone know if her owner is in the hall?"

65 "Here," said the individual in question.

66 "Do you happen to have any of the score cards this fowl made last year?"

67 "All of them, I think," was the answer. "Right here in my pocket. I bought them with the bird."

68 "Well, the first one has my name on it and I should like to see, and have the rest of you see, how it compares with the one I have just signed. She is the only bird I ever scored ninety-six."

69   The cards were held side by side. The judge beamed. "I said once that I should be glad to score her 100, because I wasn't sure I saw the faults I gave her, but I have found the same ones again, so they must be there, but, by cracky, they were hard to find—they were hard to find."

70   With the rest of her story we are not concerned. She was mercifully preserved from a repetition of her experience of the previous winter by the interference of the judge to secure her for himself. He bought her at a fabulous price, and kept her as a living witness to his own consistency as a judge.

    R. L. F.

A Start in the Fancy (July 1903)

71   The man with the courage of his convictions was home from the Score Card Poultry Show with a ten-dollar pullet, and the fact got into the local papers and his neighbors dropped in to condole with him.

72   "Can you see that much money in a hen?" said one.

73   "Wasn't it this way?" said another, "the man you bought her of bought another of you for the same price, you both got the advertising, and not a dollar changed hands."

74   A third offered the man twenty cents a pound for her live weight. "It's easy to see she's an extra good hen," he admitted.

75   At first the man gloried in his shame. "Why, Mister," he replied to this, "that hen is worth more than your horse." But constant dropping wears away a stone, and bye and bye his neighbors' comment began to have its effect. He grew sensitive. The pullet was not his only folly. There was a cockerel also, which he had put off declaring, until now he was resolved not to declare it at all.

76   But if his neighbors would only have let him alone, he would have done very well. He was far from sick of his bargain. He remembered with satisfaction the reluctance of the birds' former owner to part with them. "Why, those birds," he said, "represent ten years of breeding—ten years of my life, brother. Don't ask me for them. To sell them at any price would be no more ruinous than to give them away. They're not for sale. Say I let them go—I should have to begin all over again at the beginning. What should I say for myself when I got home?"

77   And then he had always the score cards to peruse, even more reassuring to the novice than the sight of the birds themselves. One of them gave the pullet a score of 95 1/2, only one half point less than the limit for females, he understood. Neighbors might say what they pleased, but no amount of ungenerous detraction could take that from him. The birds might go off their feed and die, he still had the score cards to show for his money.

78   He had taken the precaution to ask their former owner if he considered them a well assorted pair for breeding, for it sometimes happens that the best birds in the world are obviously not mates.

79   "I should mate them," he had said, conservatively.

80   "Then I ought to get something good out of them next year?"

81   "You ought—you ought," with the same cautious reserve.

82   That was enough to build on. He felt almost certain of justification in the offspring of his purchases, in the show room of the next season. If others could sell pullets for ten dollars, and cockerels for—well, for considerably more, what was to prevent his doing so? Such prices were common, he believed. They were in the very air of the show room. Scrub birds at scrub prices for scrub buyers, was the cry there, and the imagination of the man had been kindled.

83   But his neighbors wouldn't let him alone. They came every day, ostensibly to form their judgment of fancy poultry on the high priced pullet, but in reality to take a good look at the man that bought her.

84   Gentlemen came every day, not so much "to see what my good hen did lay," as to quiz the man with the courage of his convictions, though they asked about the laying, too.

85   "I suppose she lays," said one reflectively, "just like any other hen, for all she cost,—say, heard you gave ten dollars for her, is that right?"

86   "Yes, she lays," said the man evasively.

87   "Two a day?" And then the visitor launched forth into tales of hens that had laid two eggs in a day, and how the fact was known. They came in doors on Sunday, and did their best to make the man unhappy. Their winks did not escape him. What the man did not realize was that they were in part inspired by jealousy.

88   They particularly resented his score cards—just as if, they said, the town had never had a scored fowl before. They plagued him with tales of 98 point hens here, there and everywhere. In vain he argued with them that a 98 point bird was impossible. He appealed to editors, but what could they help him in a community that recognized no authority but its own in its own affairs. He was taken to see 98 point hens with his own eyes. He hooted. He wanted to know who scored them. What judge had the courage to sign their cards! It was to no purpose.

89   The proud possessor of a 98 point hen came with a backing of scoffers, and made the man an offer. "I'll sell her to you," he said, "for five dollars, and you can call it you've *made* five."

90   "Why don't you let him have it for ten, just for the name of it, and give him a rebate ticket for five?" some one put in.

91   "How much would you let any one else have her for," another said.

92   "Well"—the wag paused for the effect they had all come for—"well, what I could get, I suppose, so much a pound, live weight."

93   The man felt his courage going. At this stage he was not quite sure whether he was sorriest for having paid ten dollars for a hen, or for having been found out. He might have regretted neither, had he been less alone in the community. But he lacked moral support altogether. At least so far as he knew he had not won so much as a boy to his way of thinking. He had accomplished nothing and had suffered much. He thought he was right, that is, he hoped he was right, that is,—well, perhaps it would have been better to leave it to others to find out. Martyrdom to an idea was more than as a man with a family he felt equal to.

94   Still, he was not ready to acknowledge himself beaten. He kept up the fight, but it was with half a heart. In some vague way he looked for vindication in the future. The pullet's every egg was saved for incubation. Chickens came and for awhile they looked their prize blood. Then for awhile they didn't, particularly those consigned to a brooder which left too much to the inexperienced man. Not that all these died as might easily have been the case; only their feathering was eccentric. One was completely feathered at four weeks like a little bird with full-grown trailing wings. Another had ridiculous pantalettes. Another ran mother naked like a little boat on legs. At this point the man's courage was at the lowest ebb.

95   But if he had given up he would have lived to regret it. For it was not two years after that the same neighbors who had come out of their way to make sport of the first up-to-date poultryman in their midst were turning up-to-date poultrymen themselves. Excitement over the new poultry culture struck the town with a rush. Everyone talked hens and built paper covered houses. There was talk of a local show. Perhaps all this must have come anyway. Perhaps the man's sacrifice made it come more easily. Perhaps his example had been worth something. He would have had that consolation, but the chances are he would not have thought of it. He would have been a man with a grievance—against himself. He could never have forgiven himself for not hanging on.

96   And yet he surely would not have hung on but for the merest accident. It happened one day in the fall when he had given up all thought, and almost all care of his fancy stock, that a business-looking man pulled up a spirited horse in the road before the house. His mouth had a muscular grip on an unlighted cigar, and he nodded unceremoniously, without speaking. What seemed to have caught his eye were the white chickens, now almost full grown, that ranged the young orchard.

97   "What you got there?" he said at last.

98   "Rocks—White Rocks," was the reply.

99   "Yes, I see, but—"

100   "Oh, they're good ones," said the owner, with assumed confidence.

101   The visitor looked at his horse irresolutely. "Just hold this mare," he said authoritatively, and got down. "Or no—can't I hitch her somewhere? I want you to call your chickens up where I can get a look at them."

102   The horse was hitched, the chickens were called. The visitor walked around them with a scowl.

103   "Some farm-raised cockerels are just what I'm after," he said. "You've got two or three very fair birds there. How much will you take for say three of them and let me choose?"

104   "I ought to get five dollars, hadn't I?" said the man in an agony of doubt.

105   "For the lot?"

106   "No, apiece," said the man, weakly.

107   The visitor said "Humph." There was silence for awhile. Then the visitor turned a quizzical look on the trembling man.

108   "How many birds have you ever sold for five dollars?" he said.

109   "Ask me how many I ever bought for five dollars," said the man.

110   Again there was silence. Then the visitor said, brushing his knees, "I guess you're new to the business. Just to encourage you I'm going to give you five apiece for five. You round them up and crate them now, and let me see you off to the station before I go."

111   The man nearly dropped down dead. He experienced a sudden return to the courage of his convictions. Before he had quite recovered from the shock, he found himself back from the station, poorer by the loss of five good cockerels, (which he now for the first time really appreciated) but richer by twenty-five dollars, and some new ideas. He was saved to the fancy.

112   The last thing the visitor had said as he handed him a card on leaving was, "Drop me a line if you care to part with any of those pullets. But keep the price within reason, I'm no millionaire."

113   If the neighbors only knew!

     R. L. F.

The Question of a Feather (July 15, 1903)

How an Editor Got out of the Frying Pan into the Fire

114   The editor sat at his desk. He had been writing about hens all day, and he hadn't heard a hen since he left home in the suburbs in the morning, and he was tired of it. Perhaps the nearest live hens were in the death coops of the

Faneuil Hall market. It was a hot day, and he had opened the window for air, but had let in only street noise and the smell of a livery stable. He was at his letters, and his brain reeled at the steady recurrence of the roup letter and the lice letter, and he was on the verge of things unimaginable when there came a fresh clear call from the fields.

115   It was just another letter, but the quaintness of it:—"You see many poultry places in a year," it ran, "but perhaps have not happened to see—we thought you might be interested to see—a place of which it could be truthfully said, as of ours, that it was the result of following your instructions to the letter. Sister Martha has read your paper ever since we began to keep hens, and gives you all the credit for what we have made of our Minorcas. You have been our only teacher, and we want you to be the judge whether it has been to our advantage. We learn that you pass near us every day on your way to and from the city. Would it be overmuch to ask that you turn aside sometime to visit us?"

116   Here was precisely what the editor had always feared—that someone would follow his instructions to the letter, and therefore it had been part of his instructions that they should do no such thing. Before everything he had advised the use of judgment in keeping hens. So that if sister Martha had fol-lowed his instructions to the letter, be it upon her own head. He was sorry about her Minorcas. He wondered what sister Martha had managed to make of them—Leghorns or only scrubs. Still, he did not feel that he was to blame, and if he was, what was sister Martha going to do about it?

117   He smiled at his fancies, and as he did so looked at the clock. "I doubt if 'tis as bad as that," he said, "but just to see how bad it is, or how amusing, why not knock off now, and look in on them this afternoon when I'm in need of the recreation? I never have seen a place of which it could be truthfully said that it was all my doing, and while I am not sure that I shall derive much plea-sure from seeing one, I had much rather see it myself than have anyone else see it."

118   As he found his coat and hat, he tried to picture to himself sister Martha, the poultry woman, his constant reader. He thought he knew the type—"Old maid," he said, "and the one that wrote the letter, too. Innocent, credulous kind, or under the circumstances I shouldn't trust myself to their tender mer-cies in a lonely suburb toward supper time. Now if it was a man that wanted to confront me with his failure to make money in hens—but why speculate when I shall soon know."

119   On the electric cars he referred to the letter again, once for the address, and once to refresh his memory of the contents. He considered himself as having one of the good times incident to his calling. He liked nothing

better than visiting a poultry farm, and visiting this one had a spice of real adventure.

120 "So here we are," he said at last, referring once more to the letter in front of a little vine clad cottage. The surroundings were almost rural. In the near distance lingered a dark clump of tall timber; there were fields and gardens and orchards. But here and there you saw a house going up, and you heard the sound of boards unloading, and of nails driven home. The city streets were there, too, though it was plain that the house he sought had been there before the streets, for it was set down without reference to their direction, like some mirage through which you might expect to see the more substantial objects behind it.

121 He satisfied himself from the safe side of the fence before it was too late to retreat had he cared to, that everything about the place was as it should be. The fruit trees were thrifty; the hen houses were right, and the yards were right, and, unless he was mistaken, the hens in them approximated Minorcas—Black Minorcas.

122 He thought as it was near feeding time he might catch someone out of doors, in which case he would make an informal yard call, and get home to an early supper and long evening. And sure enough, as he stood irresolute who should click the latch of the hen house door but sister Martha herself, (as her looks told him), in her hand, for a subject of conversation, a pailful of eggs.

123 "And so these are the Minorcas?" he said. "They lay well. How many do you keep?" He had been within a thought of saying, "So this is sister Martha," but had fortunately suppressed that as perhaps too much for a beginning. "I'm the editor of *Hendom*," he made haste to add at the sight of the lady's consternation.

124 "Oh, oh, Mr. Fulton. Won't—well, sister Martha—won't you come into the—" she appeared from her movements to break off in doubt as between house and hen house. She decided for the former. "Sister Martha will want to see you first. Won't you come into the house?"

125 So there was some mistake, and this was not sister Martha. Well, if it was not it ought to be, and he did not cease to assert her claims to the name until presently in the house he was confronted by the superior claims of the other.

126 His visit made the ladies sit up very straight. In their embarrassment they let slip precious moments without a word. As much to help them as to make himself at home, the editor conceived and executed a pleasantry.

127 "To which of you after myself, always after myself, am I to give most credit for the pailful of eggs I have just seen?" But while serving to compose nerves, it had rather a sobering effect than the reverse. It was the author of

the letter that spoke, "Sister Martha wouldn't be able to do much, you know, and so the work out of doors falls to me; but she is the one that is interested in showing and such things."

128   The editor, of course, had not known, but now he guessed. Sister Martha was an invalid, and the extent of her share in the hen business was looking at the hens through the window. It was only a sisterly fiction that made her chief poultryman.

129   The editor was properly subdued by the intelligence. Only after a prolonged pause did he attempt to give a more cheerful turn to the conversation by venturing to suggest that the subject of showing had been mentioned.

130   "Yes," said the author of the letter, "we have not shown yet, but if we are prospered in our stock this year, we intended to go to Boston in the winter, and perhaps New York, and that reminds me—Martha, that feather; you are just in time, Mr. Fulton, to help us with that feather on the leg of, I think, our best pullet."

131   "Pull it?"

132   "Yes, pullet."

133   "Help you pull it, I mean."

134   "Tell us whether it is right to pull it," she answered, flushed and serious.

135   His call to see the hens had degenerated into a call on sister Martha, which was more than he bargained for, and now he found himself confronted with a very nice question of ethics that up to this time in his life he had always managed to avoid. The question of pulling feathers was one to which he had always thrown his columns open for discussion—freely, but you could ask anyone if he had ever joined in the discussion. He was above suspecting that he had fallen into a trap set by his enemies, but he liked the situation none the better. Perhaps he was unreasonably shy of old maids disposed to follow his instructions to the letter.

136   He was thinking, thinking, and Martha, seeing his difficulty, came to his rescue. "Perhaps Mr. Fulton doesn't care to take it upon his conscience to decide for us in such a matter. It is too much to ask him."

137   The editor laughed uneasily at her penetration. "Oh, don't consider me," he said gallantly, "anything I can do to help you." But he was none the less inclined to temporize. "How comes a feather on the leg of a Minorca?" he asked.

138   "I know, and she from one of our best matings."

139   "Bring her in," said Martha.

140   The bird was brought, and sat cowering on the center table, unmistakably a picture pullet.
"Isn't it a shame?" sighed Helen.

141 "I am afraid it is the temptation that is the shame," said Martha. "We have had pullets before spoiled by a single defect, and have not felt as now. It is because the fault is so remediable. And people ought to face their own temptations, and not ask others to face them for them."

142 "But temptation implies wrong, and we only asked Mr. Fulton to tell us if it is wrong."

143 "We know it is wrong."

144 The editor was grateful to sister Martha for letting him out. "Really," he said, "I wish you wouldn't ask me to decide for you. But I shouldn't worry; 'tis a long time before the shows; the pullet may shed the feather."

145 "But if she doesn't?" said Helen, who was inconsolable.

146 "She may develop defects less remediable than a leg feather."

147 "Oh, but she won't," persisted Helen. "She is well along now, and you know how it is with the Mediterraneans."

148 He looked closer for the feather. He wondered if they would thank him for pulling it by stealth. What prevented him from pulling it, and so ending their perplexity, he did not know, unless it was the fear of lowering himself in the estimation of two very respectful ladies.

149 "Well," he said, "I don't see but that you will have to give up the idea of showing her."

150 The sisters were glum. His visit had done them no good. He was disappointed. He reached for the knob of the door.

151 "I must be going, and I haven't seen your place at all. Perhaps some other time."

152 But one thing and another prevented his repeating the visit. He often thought of the two, however, and once alluded to them indirectly in an article on "Women and Poultry." And at the Boston show he looked among the Minorcas for the outcome of their moral struggle. There was their pullet, disqualified. If those goody goodies hadn't compromised by frankly showing her with the offending feather intact. Who but two old maids would have thought of that way out of it?

R. L. F.

Old Welch Goes to the Show (August 15, 1903)

After Getting Ready—Good and Ready

153 Old Welch did not care about having his neighbors in when he was getting ready for the show, because, as he said, "The laity don't understand, and can't be expected to."

154   Still, he did not admit that there was anything to conceal. He used to say, "I guess 'tis fair enough to groom and tame the birds a little before showing." He scorned the defence that if he was bad others were worse. Others might be worse, he was not bad. He was an honest man.

155   His saying about grooming and taming the birds obtained wide currency. He was asked, when caught in the act, which he called going over the birds for black feathers,—grooming or taming. "Taming," he answered, with the suggestion of a wink.

156   Of course that made the uninitiated laugh. But as long as the gossip was confined to the neighborhood, Welch did not care, and he knew that as long as he showed that he did not care, it would go no further and do no harm.

157   There is something fascinating about the like of Welch that peculiarly fits them for corrupters of youth. Welch always had one or more boys around him; and the boys seemed never to tire of asking about the black feathers—whether they were a defect or not, and never to tire either of the old man's unvarying answer: "I calculate the judges would full rather not see any."

158   Welch loved to please the judges. One of their peculiarities was a passion for featherless legs, and Welch did what he could to see that they got them. There must have been a Brahma cross for blockiness somewhere back in his strain, for he often had legs as fringed as a cowboy's. But that was one of the easiest things remedied—according to the boys.

159   Old Welch's were White Wyandottes, and he was reported as saying that all he asked of nature was the Wyandotte, and he could supply the rest. "You just put a little of this here chloride of lime in the water on washing day, and—yes, it deadens the feathers, but a dead white is what you're after."

160   He revealed these trade secrets to the boys that sought him for their first taste of the fruit of the tree of the knowledge of good and evil. And the boys retailed them at the village store, where it was simply opined that Welch probably hated to win.

161   Welch usually had his chickens out early, and the showing season seldom found him unprepared. But one year his first hatches were so exceptionally fine that the gods fell in love with them, and they died young. His later ones were quite as good, but as they were too late to be of any use to him, he was allowed to keep them. Welch was eloquent in his racy way. His favorites among the boys sought his society every day, and he got all his dirty work done for nothing.

162   "What are you going to do about it?" one of them asked him.

163   "Do? I ain't got nothing to do with." For an artist like Mr. Welch this was a confession indeed.

164 "Can't you show yearlings?"

165 "This strain ain't bred for yearlings, sonny." By which he was understood to mean that his strain did not hold up well—were good for one year only.

166 "But can't you doctor yearlings?"

167 "Doctor, doctor. Don't use that word to me, son."

168 The boy was too old to be easily cowed, so he only said, "Well, groom and tame them, then."

169 This appealed to the sport in the old man, and he was mollified.

170 "Let's see how many we have got of that first lot," he said. "All I ask is maturity. They must have maturity. I can't furnish that. I suppose now a woman could—at least she could make them look younger than they are. But there's no use in my trying. I'm a man, and a plain one. I want 'em old enough, and surely that ain't asking much. I must get to the shows with something, or I shan't know 'tis winter, except by the cold."

171 "What's the matter with that fellow?" said the youngster, with something of the real air.

172 "Haven't I learned you no better than that? Why, there's pretty nearly everything the matter with him. His comb don't fit, his eyes ain't mates. He's yellow, and his legs ain't. He's too high posted. He's whale backed and hollow chested. But just to show you what I can do, I'm going to take that dog shaped specimen, and renovate him—renovate him."

173 "His eyes ain't mates, come to look at them. How will you fix that?"

174 "I've thought of a way. The hardest will be to make him throw a chest."

175 What follows rests on the authority of boys, and not particularly good boys. It received a partial confirmation from chance witnesses, and from the established fact that when the time came old Welch went to the show.

176 One day a visitor came upon Welch by the kitchen stove, with a cockerel between his knees, and a hot wire in his hand. "Taming that one?" was the ready question.

177 Welch was in a serious mood. "This is the way the pick of the comb is brought down to conformity with the head—by searing underneath." You would have thought it was the regular thing. The visitor's levity was rebuked.

178 Someone else was a witness to the finishing touches on the bird. Welch was polishing its legs, "just as you polish your shoes when you're out to be looked at," he explained. "That? Oh, that's butter color; brings out the yellow a little, maybe—but that's what the judges seem to like."

179 "Call it grooming or taming?" the other wanted to know.

180 Welch had heard this too often to resent it for anything but its age. "Speaking of taming," he answered patiently, "I never had a bird as tame as this one, especially on one side, where he's absolutely tame." He proved it by

making sudden passes at the left eye, which never blinked. "He's tame on the other side, too, but not *as* tame."

181   There was only the boys' word for it, but it was believed that Welch had employed the services of an oculist in renovating the bird. One of the bird's eyes had been yellow; after the encounter with the oculist it was red like the other, but he did not seem to notice anything with it.

182   The boys said "glass." The boys said almost anything. They told about what might be called a pneumatic front. Welch had got the idea from the Asiatics who, he had read, practiced inflating the skin of camels with air to make them salable. It was a delicate operation, almost requiring the services of a veterinary. His instruments were a sharp knife, a bicycle pump, and needle and thread. Of course this was left to the last moment for fear of mortification.

183   Now everything was accounted for but the bird's general shape. Let what follows be spoken with reserve. You are not asked to believe it. The poor, the much enduring bird's lines were corrected, it was said, with a pair of Wyandotte shaped corsets designed by Welch, and made to order. You may say that you never heard of such a thing. You never did hear of such a thing, because no such thing ever existed until Welch devised it (if he did devise it). Therein lay his originality as a breeder. He literally recast that cockerel. It took two weeks of the tightest lacing known to fashion to satisfy the old man. Once or twice the lifelike glass eye was actually squeezed out in the process, and had to be searched for and put back. But in the end science triumphed.

184   Old Welch was a proud man when he surveyed the finished product. "'Tis the best job I ever did," he said, "all things considered. What's the use of breeding in for a term of years, when you can make all the wonders you want practically out of mud, at trifling cost?"

185   "But," said one of the boys, doubtfully, "I should think a good deal would depend on the judge when you showed a bird like that."

186   "It does—it does. You have to be extra careful in choosing your judge. 'Tis with judges, as with other folks, there ain't only now and then one that's suited to your purpose. Now I only know one judge this year that that bird'll do to show to."

187   The old reprobate was so pleased with himself that he must take a boy to the show with him, and introduce him to the old timers as a natural born breeder.

188   The cockerel was Welch's only entry, and it had a red ribbon on its cage. The boy who told the story might as well have made it blue while he was

about it, but he said red, and red we must keep it. Red was satisfactory to Welch.

189   Welch might easily have sold the bird, but when it came to that his conscience smote him. He had a code of his own. If the right person had made him an offer he might not have been so virtuous, but he could not bring himself to palm his work off on a greenhorn, especially one that did not pretend to be anything else.

190   The greenhorn had picked up some of the technicalities, and he was particular to ask Welch, as a friend, if the bird was not a "chance bird."

191   "Chance bird," said Welch, with a twitch of the lips, "better say design. I designed him, made him out of whole cloth. I can talk this to you, because you won't understand. The fact is, he owes just the leastest leetle mite too much to the way he was groomed. I shouldn't want to recommend him to you, because I ain't quite sure that he'd breed true, and you may know that I wouldn't say so unless there was reason."

    R. L. F.

The Original and Only (September 1, 1903)

192   "You want to hear about our hen," said the practical poultryman, "the original and only—the hen that diverted us from the fancy, and laid the foundation for our present profitable egg business.

193   "Well, I bought her for her shape and color, and for nothing else, with no thought of the eggs in her—they might be solid gold for all I cared. She was a prize bird, but that wasn't what I bought her for. I bought her because she suited me. I had the mate to her, as cocky a cockerel as you ever saw, raised right on this place, and as I was going into the fancy for keeps, I paid twelve good dollars for that hen. It was a genuine plunge for a conservative farmer. I was five years younger than I am now, but I did just right. I'd do the same thing again today. She was a good beginning. She'd have been the making of us if we'd staid in the fancy, only she didn't let us stay.

194   "I remember well the day I got her home here. It was early in December, but cold as January. She was given the run of the barn for the time being, along with another bird I had picked up at the show, until I could make up the pen they were going into. The barn was no place for her in such weather, but she hadn't been there an hour when that boy of mine comes into the house and reports, 'That hen's laid another egg.'

195   "'Which one,' says I.

196   "'The one that laid in the box in the cars on the way—'tis the same egg.'

197   "I got to know that egg before long as well as my own name. It was a light glossy brown, flecked with pink. I can show you a specimen that we keep blown as a trophy.

198   "I said to myself, 'That's a pretty good hen not to let anything interfere with her plans like that. I wonder if it would stop her laying to pluck her.' I vow I don't believe it would, though come to think of it, I can't say that she ever laid in the molt, and that's about the same thing as being plucked by nature. But I never asked her to lay in the molt. She laid hard enough anyway to scare a man. I was always afraid she couldn't keep the pace, or something would go wrong, and finally it did. She got to making eggs faster than she could lay them. They came so fast that they crowded each other and broke, and she died of sort of an internal custard, so to speak. But I'm getting ahead.

199   "Along at first we didn't know which hen she was. I said to the boy, 'You make it a point to find out which hen is doing this.' He said he couldn't tell them apart. I told him to lift them off the nest and get the numbers on their leg bands. We didn't have any trap nests on the place then. The boy was our first trap nest. He deserves some of the credit for what followed.

200   "It turned out that No.5 was the layer—the prize bird, the one that cost twelve dollars. I paid for her show points and got her eggs thrown in, but her eggs alone were worth the money. Not that she laid enough to bring that much in the market, though there's no telling what she might have done if she'd lived long enough; but they were worth it for what they taught me. For one thing, they taught me the importance of the egg of the best bred hen, which is something I doubt if one in a thousand thinks of in buying, and it wouldn't do one much good if he did think of it. It was the contrast between her egg and that of the other hen, I suppose, that brought it home to me. The other hen laid about once a week, and when she did lay it was a dead white, gritty, thin shelled egg, just misshapen enough at the pick to be unhatchable. She was money thrown away, though she wasn't bad looking.

201   "Of course at first all I saw in No.5's eggs was fancy chickens. I was glad she laid good eggs, and laid often, because it meant chickens, and lots of them. But one day the boy said something that set me thinking. 'It seems to me,' he said, 'that that No.5 lays three days and rests one.'

202   "'Are you sure of that?' I said.

203   "'No, I'm not sure.'

204   "'Well, don't say anything you aren't sure of. Make sure. There's a calendar; you can keep score for her on that.'

205   "So a fire insurance calendar on the wall was our first egg record book.

206   "The boy was right; she did lay three days out of four; when the days got longer, four out of five. I said to myself: 'If there are other hens like that

there must be others still altogether *unlike* that to pull down the average, because we think we're doing well at this season if we get half as many eggs as we have hens. It looks as if there must be some hens that only lay one day a week to offset the work of those that lay every day but one. 'Tis plain that a poultryman is as much in need of a weeder as a market gardener, and what's the trap nest but a weeder?'

207   "Suddenly I saw the trap nest in a new light. Before that it had been associated in my mind with big egg stories and line breeding for eggs. But it has no necessary connection with either. One needn't abuse his trap nests to make his hens too prolific for the stamina of the stock, if such a thing is possible; neither need he lie about their findings, neither need he tell the truth about them if the truth was so remarkable as to look like a lie. He could keep his mouth shut in that case. There may be such a thing as a 300-egg hen, but I'm not going to be the fellow to say so—not at this stage of the game. If you watch you'll see how careful I am not to be too definite about No.5's laying. I am satisfied to claim for her about 200. It was more than that. But you don't catch me saying whether it was one more or a hundred more.

208   "I don't know whether I should have made a success of the fancy or not, and probably never shall know, because right at this point I was diverted from it for good and all. The trap nest as a weeder appealed to me as a sure thing. I felt that the fancy was considerably chancy. Fanciers are born, not made, and I wasn't sure that I felt particularly born, and as the ministers say that's the test, if you don't feel as if you are called you aren't called. There were already a lot of good men in the fancy who easily made the birds it would probably be cheaper for me to buy. And as far as I knew, the ranks of those who were tending strictly to the trap nests were mighty slim.

209   "You see what one hen can do. We knew that she laid 200 eggs—call it that. We didn't have to take anyone's word for it. It don't satisfy you, but it satisfied us. It gave us faith to go ahead. It gave us a sound basis to figure on, which is the hardest thing in this world to get. We have housed about 400 hens for years, and they laid for us upwards of 125 eggs a year; if they could be converted into 200-egg hens, by selection or otherwise, it would mean a clear gain of $1.50 per head with very little extra trouble. It would just double profits at what it costs us to feed, and what we get for eggs at wholesale.

210   "You may form some idea of what No.5 may have been for shape and size and constitution from the general appearance of our flock today, for they are all her offspring in the fifth and sixth generations. They were not bred exclusively to lay. They were bred for everything that No.5 was, and that was a good deal. But we are not afraid to say that we believe in eggs—we believe in the 200-egg hen. I am not prepared to say just how common she is, but prob-

ably not over-common. Two hundred eggs should be enough to entitle a hen to the name of the new hen, for of course we are not to have the new everything else without the new hen, and the new hen must distinguish herself from the old hen and the old pullet by marked superiority as a layer. She is not to crow or sport sickle feathers or talk politics. She must succeed without going out of her sphere.

211   "I'm going to observe the same caution about making claims for our 400 as I did for No.5. We haven't got them all up to the 200 mark yet, not by any manner of means, and we've got some above it. It would surprise you to see the average—if you could believe it. They do very well—very. Of course 400 hens are not many. Now neighbor Davis over here is a real poultry man. He has something like a thousand in a three story building with no dirt on the floors except what the hens supply. We can't compare with him. But I sometimes think neighbor Davis isn't as fat as he used to be, and he talks too much of Belgian hares and squabs and ginseng for a man that's satisfied with hens."

   R. L. F.

Three Phases of the Poultry Industry (December 15, 1903)

A Typical "Bred to Lay" Business

212   In Andover, Mass., may be seen what there is to see of a typical "bred to lay" business, that of Dr. C. Bricault—and heard what there is to be said for it.

213   Before going into what I saw at Dr. Bricault's place, I may state what I did not see. I saw 200-egg hens—or let us call them heavy layers—Dr. Bricault prefers that name—but no outward marks to distinguish them as such. We must take some things on trust in this world. Of course no one pretends to tell a 200-egg hen with the naked eye, or even with the help of the X-ray. A man may assert that he has exceptional layers, and we may believe that he has or not as we like. We may know whether he has or not, as we may know whether another man sells standard bred stock or not, by a small expenditure—the price of a sitting or two of eggs, say, or of a trio of birds. We generally have to pay to find out about the business that appeals to us from a distance through advertising.

214   What Dr. Bricault says about the part of his business that you must of necessity take his word for seems to me entitled to respect for its moderation. Perhaps as much as any breeder for eggs can claim is, (lst) that he has been at it long enough to have picked out a few good layers on which to build; (2d) that he has the apparatus to do with; (3d) that in so far as is practicable he is tending the trap nests. Dr. Bricault claims no more.

215 In the six years he has been breeding for eggs he has made a good beginning—that is all. He has come across some very heavy layers. This is not the place to discuss the existence of the 200-egg hen. Doubters may be referred to the recent bulletin of the Maine Experiment Station, which reports thirty-five 200-egg hens in a total of 1000 tested, or three in a hundred. Perhaps it will not be too much to ask the cautious to believe that Dr. Bricault has had and still has his 200-egg hens; that he has bred from them; that he has made something if not the most of them. It is early yet to speak of positive results in breeding for eggs; suffice it to say Dr. Bricault has achieved enough in that direction to encourage him to persevere.

216 It is interesting to know just how much Dr. Bricault pretends to devote himself to the trap nests. At this time of year all his nests are frankly and shamelessly fastened open. The record keeping ceased in July. He will base his opinion of the hens on their work for the nine months preceding. From November to July he was a slave to the trap nests—not absolutely, but more or less, and within reason. He made no bones of taking a day off occasionally. He is not a scientist, but a business man, and attempts only the practicable. His records then lay no claim to scientific accuracy, but are thought to serve the purpose if they discriminate roughly among the good, bad, and indifferent layers.

217 So much for Dr. Bricault's claims; now for what he thinks he can convince the most sceptical of by ocular demonstration. In entering upon his present work he has had to consider one important question: Can hens stand the strain of being bred to lay? He has answered this question in the affirmative, as he believes all must who having eyes will see. His growing stock are before you, some hundred and fifty pullets, practically all of them bred to lay. They have their family defects, as what breeders have not, but no outward signs of weakness. Dr. Bricault will back them to rough it with the hardiest. Some are destined as an experiment to winter in piano boxes with free range on the snow, and he has no fear of the result.

218 One can see for himself moreover, though he must take the 200-egg hens on trust, that Dr. Bricault has the apparatus by which the 200-egg hens are brought to light—the notorious trap nests. He has the houses too for effective work, well planned, with every convenience, and manifestly well kept. His farm is of five acres, large for a village place, and his stock have the run of it—at this season both old and young together.

219 Let me say here that for his purpose no more ideal place than Dr. Bricault's could be found. One of the pleasantest spots in an unusually attractive town, it is calculated to add materially to the effectiveness of its white feathered population. It is high and dry without being arid. In fact every square foot of

it would be available for almost any kind of farming. Not the least of its advantages is its convenience to the cars, leaving no one an excuse for condemning Dr. Bricault's stock or methods unseen.

220　Dr. Bricault has this to say about his position: "I do not insist too much on the 200-egg hens. Call them heavy layers. I took their measures when somewhat more enthusiastic than I have been this year or intend to be henceforth. Strictly speaking, I shall have no 200-egg hens this year. My best record is 160 eggs in a period of one year less three months. What the three months would have brought forth we shall not quarrel about. I am content to rest on what I am sure of. I do not wish and never did wish to be identified with the 200-egg interest. I wish to be known for what I am doing more than for what I possess. What if I have a few 200-egg hens? So have others. I am distinguished from most of these by what I am doing with my 200 egg hens. I am of those who believe that the 200-egg hens indicate an upward tendency that may be hastened by artificial selection; that they may be made to uplift all hendom in productiveness, and this without detriment to the stamina of the stock. I breed accordingly."

221　Whether we approve of Dr. Bricault's course or not, we must admit that he persists in it with his eyes wide open. He is familiar with the stock objections to his business. He divides them into two classes, the trivial and the general. The first make the trap nests their point of attack. The trap nests, it is said, worry the hens out of condition, make them feverish and so broody. The trap nests teach egg eating. The trap nests do not catch the eggs. Those who use the trap nests abuse them to pick out their poorest layers for sale. The general objections resolve themselves into two: that hens cannot be bred to lay more eggs, having already reached the limit; that they cannot safely be bred to lay more eggs. All these Dr. Bricault has heard and has answers for, or else he would not be doing business at the old stand.

The Nichols' Place

222　Before ever I saw the Nichols' place I had it from one of the best known butchers in Lawrence that the Nichols' fresh eggs always commanded a price of their own in the markets a cent or two above anything else.

223　Eleven years ago Mr. Nichols was a carpenter in the city; Mrs. Nichols a mill operative. They knew as much about the poultry business as they had heard, namely, that it was profitable. It seemed to offer the best means of escape from city life, for which they had no love. So they looked it up and went into it, like plenty of others who have since gone out.

224　They had five hundred dollars between them. Part of this went for a six acre place in a rather out of the way part of southern New Hampshire near the town of No. Salem, the rest they invested in hens. To sustain life until they should begin to realize on their investment, Mrs. Nichols continued at her work in the mills, which she drove to and from nine miles over the road.

225   Mr. Nichols turned his trade to account to build his own houses—and very neat houses they are. As the first one was, so is the last one, for Mr. Nichols found little to improve on in his original plan. They are rather high and pitch roofed, divided by wire netting into ten foot sections, with a passage in the rear. If they have a fault it is the draftiness, which I should think inevitable where there are no board partitions to break the air currents set in motion by the animal heat on a cold night; but if they serve the purpose, criticism is a waste of breath.

226   The Nichols adopted intensive methods, the only ones thought of by the enterprising beginner of eleven years ago. They have brought their plant to a capacity of from four to five hundred head, but I doubt if today it exceeds the limits of a large sized village lot. The hen house runs are many of them not over fifty feet in length, and, of course, verdureless; the chicken yards, probably no larger accordingly, are in no better condition. The stock are fed green stuff by hand. In fact, they do nothing for themselves—everything is done for them; but there can be no question about its being done well. There is not a better "kept up" place, cleaner looking or smelling within marketing distance of Lawrence. It is the Nichols' boast that they have not missed cleaning the roost platforms six times since they started in business.

227   They chose the broiler and egg business, and eschewed the fancy. They make no pretense at breeding. They take the American hen as they find her, get her eggs, and at the end of two years "turn" her. Showing and shows they have little use for.

228   In raising broilers and getting eggs they have been equally successful. They have been able to name their own prices for eggs, not because they had better eggs than others, but a more constant supply. The butcher and grocer could pay what they asked when eggs were plenty, or go without when no one but the Nichols had them for sale. In October the Nichols are sending eggs to Lawrence at the rate of sixty dozen a week, and October is a worse month than December or January, market quotations to the contrary notwithstanding. As for their broilers, the fact that these were always passed along to the retailer by the commission merchant in the original package, unopened and uninspected, is sufficient testimony as to their quality.

229   I speak of the broilers in the past tense. The fact is, the broiler business languishes, and an explanation is due. It seems that for some time, if not from the first, the poultry business has been regarded as a means to an end. The end is cows, and the end is in sight. Having amassed the capital necessary

to start with a good herd, they cast about for the time for their care. Something had to go, and it was the broilers, as the part of their work least to their liking.

230   So the Nichols have begun to enter into their reward; they have reached the point where they feel that they can afford to consult their tastes. The cows are the first thing; and they have begun to look around on their work and see how good it is. They take a natural pride in it. They have made a place literally bloom, that, judging from the original cost (inferred) could not have been much. They have increased it from six to over a hundred acres. They started with five hundred dollars; today their visible assets will foot up to four thousand, possibly more.

231   They have not done all this without setback. No one likes to be robbed of credit for his share of ill luck. Like others, the Nichols have had to learn by experience, but unlike some others they have hung on to tell the tale. Only this year they have known the greatest misfortune of all in an accident which befell Mr. Nichols, and threw all the work of caring for cows and hens on Mrs. Nichols. What can a woman do with hens, is a favorite theme with poultry writers; if they could meet Mrs. Nichols they would ask what can't a woman do with hens. She has run the place single handed, or practically so, having hired no more help than a man would hire in the same position.

232   But hard work has no terrors for the likes of Mr. and Mrs. Nichols. Whether from fear of being suspected of laziness or some other cause, they employ few labor saving devices in their establishment. There are no overhead tracks, no access for a wagon even to the pen windows. Sand is carried to and from the pens by the rear passage in coal hods. Everything is put through by main strength, but it is put through. And I surmise the fact is significant. The Nichols have succeeded, not because they started with ample capital, with previous knowledge of hens, with greater adaptation for it than for anything else they might have undertaken, or with special opportunities, but because they did not dislike hard up hill work.

A Typical Small Breeder

233   Mr. John A. Hall, of Atkinson, N.H., is a good type of the small breeder. He makes up in the care and real affection he lavishes on his stock for any lack of the business ability that distinguishes so many of our mere middlemen in the fancy. He is always heels over head in pets of one kind or another. In addition to White Wyandottes he indulges a taste for several varieties of ducks and geese, not to mention Runt pigeons and Angora cats on the side. All these creatures share the place of honor about the dooryard and everywhere under foot.

234   Mr. Hall has bred fancy fowl ever since he was "big enough to carry a dough dish." He has bred Rocks, Langshans, Cochins, Brahmas; and ribbons and trophies testify as to how he has bred them.

235   He has never faced the public as an advertiser. He might be regarded as a sort of breeders' breeder. That is to say, it is chiefly other breeders whose acquaintance he has made at the shows that find their way to him to buy. Still he says he has always been able to dispose of all the very good birds he could spare, and sometimes some that he could not spare.

236   But though he is a fancier first, he has never been so situated that he could afford to disregard the claims of the practical. He owns to having adopted the White Wyandotte for the most practical of reasons, to meet the requirements of his market for dressed poultry.

237   Mr. Hall has something like a hundred youngsters this year, all sired by one superannuated cock, and the family, though not over numerous, does the old bird credit. Not that they are all show birds, but there is a general freedom from disqualifications. There seems to be no feathered or willow legs. Eyes are good, plumage white to promising white. It is too early yet to judge of finer points of shape and style, but one thing is certain, the youngsters are all that they should be in weight, and that as White Wyandottes go in these parts is saying a great deal.

238   If houses are more to you than the inmates, you will go elsewhere than Mr. Hall's. The old timer will sometimes forget surroundings and accessories in the superior interest of the birds themselves. In the matter of housing Mr. Hall carries opposition to the sheltered life idea to an extreme. His houses have value to the observer only as illustrating what a hen will roost in and still live. They are airy to say the least. Mr. Hall apologizes for them, but I believe retains them on principle. He says the hens take no more harm from them than an occasional frozen wattle in winter, and on the whole are benefitted by them.

239   Two things in breeding he makes of first importance—size and vigor. It is his experience that weight tends constantly to decline. It is a simple matter to keep it up, only it cannot be left to take care of itself. As for vigor, it is easier to get this right than not. What the stock need is a little judicious neglect. Mr. Hall's geese roost in the trees even in winter. Such a toughening process would be too drastic for hens, but these have to take it according to their strength.

240   As might be expected, Mr. Hall gives everything free range the year round. He fences in instead of out, finding that two and a half feet will keep hens out where it takes five to keep them in.

241   Almost any year you may see specimens of Mr. Hall's land or water fowl

at some one of the shows, and as he lives rather out of the world, perhaps the easiest way to form an opinion of him as a breeder is there. It is worth a little trouble, however, to view his stock as a whole at home, especially his Wyandottes, because it is not everywhere in these days that you will see a lot as uniformly good.

R. L. Frost

The Cockerel Buying Habit (February 1, 1904)

242   The old gentleman took his corncob out of his mouth, and leaning toward me lowered his voice almost to a whisper: "What's your opinion of inbreeding, anyway?" he said.

243   "I'm a safe man to talk it over with," I laughed. "What's your opinion? There's no law against it, is there?"

244   "Law of nature," he suggested.

245   "I'd risk it."

246   "You're not afraid of it then?"

247   "Pshaw!"

248   He rolled his eyes on me with unfeigned admiration of my recklessness; but he shook his head.

249   "I snum I don't know," he reflected. "It's attended with awful consequences in the human family. You know how it's supposed to be when cousins marry. You can hear some awful stories against it."

250   "You can hear just as many the other way, and more authentic."

251   "Did ever I tell you how George Hill bred Cochins in till he got them that squat and fluffy and Cochiny they were a sight for sore eyes? But come to set their eggs one year there wasn't a single one fertile."

252   "I believe you have told me, but I don't think he proved anything. So many considerations enter into a case of the kind."

253   "Yes, of course it might have been something else. And maybe it's all prejudice on my part, but I snum I don't know. Don't seem as if anything'd ever make me feel about it as you do."

254   We had been on the point of considering his hens when the conversation took this serious turn. They were running at large, but as it was near feeding time a number had gathered around us as we talked. Our thoughts went back to them.

255   "Well, there they are, *such* as they are," said the old gentleman with a sweep of the hand. "It's as much as a year or two since you've seen them, I guess."

256   "What's the matter with those? They're a nice looking lot," I protested.

257   "If you don't see it, I'm not going to tell you."

258   All hens in a flock look pretty much alike at first glance, and it is hard to pick out individual characteristics. But I had to say something.

259   "Perhaps you mean they vary somewhat in size. You have some very white birds."

260   "I mean they're of all sorts and kinds. I've got some very white birds, and I've got some not so white. I've got some big ones, and I've got some all fired runts. The fact is they come every which way. I haven't anything like a strain."

261   As I looked I became convinced that there was something to what he said.

262   He sat down on his heels and pointed with his pipe stem. "There that one facing this way—tail to tail with that other one—she's eating now."

263   "Yes, I see her."

264   "Well, she's what I call a pretty middling fair bird—good full breast, and nice spread of tail. There may be a couple of others something like her in the flock—not exactly like—not on your life—but something like. I know where they come from. I know them as much as anything by a certain defect they all have—a hollow comb—worse in the males than in the females, of course— or more noticeable. They keep showing up since I bought a cockerel of So and so a few years back. Then take that one over there—alone—walking. She's likely to have a few stubs on her legs, though you can't see them from here. That's the tendency of the strain she comes from. But even if she hadn't feathered legs, and the other hadn't a bad comb, and both of them were all that they ought to be, they wouldn't be any more alike than the animals in a happy family at the circus."

265   I listened to this confession in silence.

266   As the old gentleman recovered his feet he shied a chip at another specimen. "And that one takes after what you may call 'im's strain. And there's another—I can tell you who breeds them like that—oh—now I know that as well as I know my own name—he lives out there in Milledge—never mind, it will come to me. You see I've got them all and some besides, especially the some besides, the combinations that are neither this, that, nor the other, all right here together where I can study and compare them. But of course I could do that at the shows, couldn't I?"

267   "Not so much at your leisure," I consoled him.

268   "No, no, you're right there. I've had a chance to improve myself a lot. And no one can accuse me of having bred in. I could leave it to a jury of summer boarders if it looked as if I had bred in, couldn't I? And now what? At the age of sixty the indications are that I'm about ready to begin over again—dress the lot and begin over again. And I call myself a breeder? So much for the

cockerel buying habit. And the question before the house is, another time shall I breed in?"

269 "Chance it—why don't you chance it?"

270 "That's what I asked you for—would you advise me to? I guess you don't think I could have come out any worse than I have, anyway."

271 "You don't think so yourself, do you? Come."

272 "Don't seem as if I could have, does it? But I snum I don't know."

R. L. F.

"The Same Thing Over and Over" (March 1, 1904)

273 One day an agent, who hated to take no for an answer, knocked at the door of Mr. Green with a poultry paper to sell. Mr. Green was at home.

274 Now Mr. Green is all right in his way. He has some nice hens, and he knows something about their care. Many in his place wouldn't shut them up so tightly, but then Mr. Green gets eggs, and eggs are what are wanted.

275 But Mr. Green confessed to the agent that he did not take a poultry paper—thought he didn't need one. He had taken one once, so that he knew what poultry papers were. He thought—and his wife agreed with him—that they were the same thing over and over.

276 "There's something to that," assented the agent with the best possible grace, "and I'm glad you spoke of it, because I know of nothing I'd rather talk about. There's necessarily a great deal of repetition in them."

277 "I was going to say it is all repetition," Mr. Green replied, "and between you and me, how much of it isn't? It was five or six years ago that I was taking a poultry paper, and I suppose they're still talking away just as they were then about cleanliness and warmth and a variety of feed. You see I have it all down pat."

278 "No, there has been a slight reaction from the high toned poultry keeping of those days, especially for those situated as you are, with many things to attend to besides your hens. It is allowable now for a farmer not to clean the droppings boards every day in the year. And as for warmth—warmth is not thought as much of as it was once. You may remember there was a time when people were putting steam pipes into their hen houses. I used to know a man that stacked his barn manure in compartments at either end of his hen house for heating purposes. The tendency would now seem to be all in the other direction—toward plenty of fresh air; it makes no difference how cold if only fresh. I spoke of your stoves just now when we looked over your houses. You say that you only use them on the very coldest days; but really they're the least bit out of date. And your double windows, too. The ten-

dency now is toward no windows at all. If you haven't seen a poultry paper for five years, it is probably news to you that some are building hen houses, even as far north as this, with not even a wall on the southern side. The open front scratching shed is made to do duty night and day. So you see there has been some progress—or at least change."

279   "I guess not enough to pay a man to keep track of the poultry papers for five years."

280   "Perhaps that's a matter of personal opinion; but if the progress has been anything at all, I think the live poultryman would want to keep pace with it. It's the little things that make the difference between success and failure you know. You understand that I do not claim that there has been as much progress as you seem to think there ought to have been; and I will tell you why."

281   "Because you can't."

282   "No, not that exactly. To be sure I can't, but I wouldn't wish to. For just consider, what would you have, the whole poultry industry revolutionized, made over by the editor with each issue of his paper? That would keep things rather stirred up, and many complain that they are unsettled enough as it is with one advocating one method, another another."

283   "You're right there, all right."

284   "That's the way it seems sometimes, doesn't it, when one looks at details? But we'll have to admit that there's a surprising unanimity of opinion among experts on essentials, and that what are regarded as essentials, while not the same yesterday, today, and forever, change so slowly that they make some restless folks tired waiting—which brings us back to your quarrel with the poultry papers."

285   Mr. Green laughed at the agent's pertinacity as much as to say, "You're a good one, but you mustn't forget you're up against another as good."

286   "You may laugh," said the agent, "but I want you to see that this repetition in the poultry papers is a thing I'm not afraid to admit—is a thing, in fact, I count in their favor. Of course if their object was sensationalism it would be different. When poultry journalism catches the yellows from the other kinds of journalism, I suppose their object will be to reconstruct the poultry business twelve or twenty-four times a year, as the case may be. Meanwhile they are content to be merely progressive and up to date. In the principles they lay down they are much the same from year to year. Of course we are not speaking of the details of illustration and example—there they are varied enough for anyone. But in general principles they preserve a certain sameness, and necessarily so, because it is their function to reflect the poultry business, which changes no faster than any other business.

287   "I suspect that in calling them 'the same thing over and over,' you mean

that they are not educational—at least for you—now that is that you have graduated from them. But even if you happen to be one of the few that know it all, they may still have their use in reminding you of things you know and are in danger of forgetting. And again, no matter how much they repeated themselves they would have a certain social value that must not be left out of account. Like intercourse with your fellow men, they are a luxury that amounts to a necessity.

288   "This is the way for you to look at it. Reading the poultry papers is precisely like talking hens with the most intelligent and enlightened, and where is the poultryman with soul so dead that he doesn't like to talk hens with almost anyone? It is not invariably educational, and one does not expect it to be, if he is an old hand; but it does stimulate and it does strengthen one in his convictions. It affords one a sort of moral support in his faith in hens—a support that he may not need, and then again he may, if he is not quite self-sufficient and lives isolated, as most of us live in communities that have little use for hens."

289   That's the way the agent talked to Mr. Green. I don't recollect that he told me whether he get his subscription or not. R. L. F.

The Universal Chicken Feed (April 1, 1904)

290   Mr. Call remained a seeker for truth to the end of his days in the hen business. (This is not an obituary. Mr. Call still lives, only not on the proceeds of his hens, or the expectation thereof.) In the fat months, when the hens laid, he staid at home and sawed wood, as the saying is; but in the lean months he went visiting. And because he was a pretty good sort of fellow, people always indulged his curiosity about their methods, and told him all they knew, especially with regard to feeding; but he never seemed to find out what he was after, for before long he was back again if possible more curious than ever.

291   "What are you feeding?" was his stock question, and though there was a discouraging sameness to the replies he got, he persevered with a devotion worthy of a loftier cause. He felt that there was something his hens lacked that once found would make them lay every day in the year. That something eluded him. Often he thought he had it. Once he grasped at sunflower seeds; he had heard of them before, but had clean forgotten them. Again, India wheat came to him as a revelation. He thought that an evening mash might be better than a morning. He tried everything, only to be disappointed in the result. But because he had been many times disappointed was no proof that he was always to be. Hope sprung eternal in his breast. Sometime, somewhere, unless the public wearied of his quest before he did, he would light upon the right thing, and then begin to get his money back.

292   "I guess Call thinks there's some dark secret in feeding, or something that we're all keeping back," one neighbor remarked to another as they stood in the barn door one winter day. "He was over here to talk hens yesterday, and here he comes again now."

293   "Having trouble with his hens?"

294   "This is the time of year when he has trouble with them. How do, Silas? Hens started up any since yesterday?"

295   Silas was an honest man, and he realized that the first condition of getting help was frankly confessing your need of help. Who was going to tell him how to get eggs if he was getting eggs? No egg stories as big as a fish story for him. He was a little sour about it, but he owned right up. "Nary one. Where did you say you got those beef scraps you showed me yesterday, neighbor?"

296   "Those? I got those of Carey. But I don't suppose it makes so much difference where they came from, or who cut them up. Beef scraps are pretty much the same everywhere, though it seems as if one lot I bought did have a little more twine and skewers in it than usual."

297   Mr. Call went to a feed bin and examined critically the "article of scraps" it contained.

298   "How much'll you sell me a little of that for—a pound or two—enough to try it?"

299   "Give you some. But say, Call, I could tell you a way to make your hens lay."

300   "Why in the dickens don't you, then?"

301   "Because it's too simple; you wouldn't take any stock in it. You want to feed them something you nor nobody else ever heard of."

302   "Let's hear your way."

303   "Feed them a mash (as much as they'll hold of it in the evening) of scraps, corn meal, shorts, and middlings. Feed them wheat, cracked corn, oats, and barley in a litter. Keep shells, grit, charcoal, and water before them always. Give them plenty of green stuff. I use big cattle beets pegged onto a headless nail; it's surprising how they demolish them. And give them a dust bath, and give them air."

304   "I guess I must have done most of that."

305   "Well, you want to do all of it."

306   "Well, I guess I've done all of it; but I didn't get the eggs."

307   "Maybe you did some extras that spoiled it. Maybe you didn't do it long enough. There must have been something wrong. Perhaps your hens weren't females. But I knew how you'd take it."

308   Mr. Call went back to the feed bin and re-examined the beef scraps. What was there about those beef scraps?

309   Then neighbor No.2 spoke up, and he was a wag.

310   "I'm not much of a poultryman, Mr. Call, but I manage to get eggs out of the few hens I keep."

311   "Table scraps?" beamed Mr. Call knowingly. "Yes, if we could only get enough table scraps to feed nothing else?"

312   "No; I have too many for that. You've never been over to my place. Better stop in some day when you're passing, and perhaps we can help each other."

313   "What are *you* feeding?"

314   "For one thing, protein."

315   This was a feeler. How much did Mr. Call know?

316   "Protein?" quoth Mr. Call. "Is that something new? Where did you get hold of it?"

317   "I take it you don't read the poultry papers, Mr. Call. Too busy, perhaps. Protein's something they recommend."

318   "It's a good thing, is it? Can you get it in town?" He turned to neighbor No.1. "Have you ever tried it?"

319   "Yes, I have, Mr. Call," he reluctantly admitted.

320   "Why didn't you tell me about it?"

321   "Well, I guess I didn't think of it," said neighbor No.1 rather lamely, and under restraint of a fearful wink from neighbor No.2.

322   Mr. Call's suspicions were aroused. Here was a strange omission on the part of a friend and adviser. He addressed himself to neighbor No.2.

323   "Where did you say you got it—or don't you want to say? Is it a feed?"

324   "Yes, you'd call it a feed—not a medicine. Carey keeps it."

325   Carey kept it? Then of course they all used it. And he had been kept in the dark all this time. He felt aggrieved. How better could he show his displeasure with neighbor No.1 than by ostentatiously thanking neighbor No.2 for his information? He laid it on pretty thick, and neighbor No.2 took it all with proper modesty, and saw him off for Carey's in quest of protein without a qualm of conscience.

326   But half way down the yard Mr. Call stopped. "Protein, protein," he had been saying. "Why drat my!" he exclaimed, "if it isn't in scraps. I've seen it in those analysises on bags—that's where. Seems to me it's in that last meat meal I tried." He half turned round, and then thought better of it.

327   "Smart, aren't they?" he said. "Well that's the last time, neighbor."
        R. L. F.

Dalkins' Little Indulgence—
A Christmas Story (December 15, 1905)

328   It is no matter how much Dalkins paid for the bird; the point is that the man who sold it to him somehow got the impression that he did not pay

enough—that he would have paid more. He could not have denied that Dalkins paid him all he asked. So that he had himself to blame if it was not enough. But he got to talking as if he had been cheated—and badly cheated. He enlarged upon the bird until he said he shouldn't wonder if Dalkins would get a cool fifty for it. He groomed it, so to speak, as he thought of it. He made it a little whiter than white, a little more symmetrical than symmetry.

329 As a matter of fact it was the kind of bird that is worth what one can get for it. It transcended scoring, as it was better than any score reputable judges are willing to sign. It was a bird framed by nature for comparison judging.

330 If the man who sold it to Dalkins made the mistake of parting with it for a cent less than fifty dollars, he deserved sympathy, but he was the only one who could see that Dalkins deserved blame. He showed himself a poor loser. He talked early and late to all comers about his misfortune that was another man's fault. But almost all comers had been in the same fix themselves, and knew how to make allowances. They did not believe too heartily in the pricelessness of his bird—a suspicion of which made him but talk the more.

331 The wonderful part of this story is that this fellow had picked the bird up away over back in Peacham, Vt., for one dollar and fifty cents. These figures I am willing to vouch for. In that case he did fairly well if he got a five for it. Mind you, I don't say what he got. At the time I heard various rumors. This part of the story must remain shrouded in mystery—men are such liars. I vouch for nothing that you cannot safely believe.

332 Though he was far enough away from this man and his troubles, the facts here stated somehow or other reached Dalkins. He had come by the bird through an agent of his who had spotted it by the merest accident from his carriage in passing. He had not been too curious about its history and antecedents at the outset; with him the bird in the hand was the thing. But a certain letter aroused his interest. It was anonymous, doubtless from someone in no way concerned, but bent on mischief making, and informed him that the remarkable bird had been raised by the writer's next door neighbor, and had been started on its career for one dollar and fifty cents. He questioned his agent about it. The agent had heard some such tale. Evidently gossip had been buzzing in the hill town of Peacham. He had heard also that the bird was of the Dalkins strain direct. That was calculated to please Dalkins. He wondered if they couldn't find out who raised it. He would have liked the poor benighted fellow who would part with such a jewel for one fifty to know by its fruits what a thing the Dalkins strain was.

333 "He didn't suspect what he was doing," he said.

334 "It isn't likely," said the agent.

335 "And the fellow who sold him to you?"

336   "He had some idea, because he's kicking himself for having sold it. I have seen him since. He is talking at a great rate."

337   "The bird has made some stir already, then; that's what they call the fatal gift of beauty, isn't it?"

338   The agent was duly embarrassed. Dalkins was thinking.

339   "Say," he said at last, "I want you to find that original owner and bring him to the New York show on me. And bring the other fellow, too—both of them. I guess I'm good for it. Tell them 'tis a Christmas notion of mine—the show is near enough to Christmas for that. It'll make it easier for you. We'll show them a thing or two, and we'll show the kicker that he only knows a little bit more than the other fellow. And I think I'll show you something. Not a word of this to anyone outside, and not too many words to them. Just say 'tis my treat—consolation treat. 'Tis an order."

340   Dalkins' agent found the original owner away over in Peacham one bitter cold morning a day or two after Christmas. Peacham is a New England street town, that is to say, it consists of but one street, which runs north and south along a sharp ridge that looks like the back of a razor backed world. The railroad, when it was built, missed it by about eight miles on the right, and that seemed to send it into a decline—such a close call, no doubt. Many of its fine old houses are going to ruin, and there is never a new one to take their place. The age and size of its shade trees suggested that it might do very well in summer; but on such a day in winter it made the agent fairly groan at the patience of the people who could abide there. He inquired at the postoffice store for his man, and was sent to the woods for him. He came upon him snaking out logs in a grove recently laid waste, as seriously at work as if he had entirely given up seeing Santa Claus that year. He laid before him his invitation, and while not persuading him on the spot to accept it, succeeded in making him regard it as worth considering. At any rate, he carried him away in triumph from his toil like a Cincinnatus, a Putnam, or a Parker. He left his ox team standing in a brush pile in the care of his fellow workmen.

341   Before he left he had dinner with him, and it was all arranged. The fellow was a little sheepish at first, as one accused of deliberately circulating counterfeit money—only in this case it would have been a counterfeit bird. He suspected that his punishment was going to take the form of a practical joke. But he decided he was equal to it if only it wasn't to cost him anything, and the return ticket the agent laid down for him set at rest his fears on that score.

342   The agent had less trouble with the other fellow—Durgin, if the name must out. He considered the invitation his due. "Aw yes," he yawped, "he knew how it all was. Nobody probably intended to do him. It was business, just business. Only he thought," etc. Of course he wasn't a fool. He knew a

good bird when he saw one. Only sometimes his mind didn't work quick enough, etc. Yes, he'd be glad to meet Mr. Dalkins. He bore no grudge. He wasn't that kind. Only he thought, etc. The main thing was that he accepted the ticket.

343   Scene, the New York show. Mr. Dalkins is doing the honors. When I say doing, I mean doing. He never let those two importations of his out of his sight for three days, and he never gave them a restful half hour. And it was not all inside the Garden. But let us draw a veil over anything that was irrelevant to the show proper. What have I to do with the Rialto and the Bowery? Suffice it to say that he gave two simple souls the time of their lives, and beat them out in his own enjoyment of it, in spite of the fact that it was on him and it came high.

345   The grand finale Mr. Dalkins had all prearranged, and he looked forward to it with the anticipation of a boy. No one had an inkling of what was coming, unless it was his agent to whom he once said in an aside: "The bird, *the* bird, was sold, I suppose you didn't know, before anything was placed, but he's not to change hands till the last day of the show. I want you to be there when he does."

346   And once he had said to the second in line of possession, "So it sticks in your crop that you should have had fifty for your trade. Well, we won't let that spectre intrude on our festivities. Time enough for discussion afterward. There's always a way to settle such matters between gentlemen."

347   But the victim, though disliking the tone of banter in this, smelt not a rat. He and the original owner came to the final catastrophe as unprepared as the babe new born. They were so absorbed in the pleasure of the hour that it never occurred to either that he might be destined in the mind of the master to point a moral or adorn a tale. When it suited Dalkins' sense of dramatic fitness, they were led like lambs to the slaughter.

348   He towed the brace of them round to a certain much beribboned coop in the last hours of the show. He had made it a point to take them there several times a day during their stay to punctuate their experiences and keep them from forgetting to whom they were indebted for their popularity. He had never said much in the feathery presence. He found it more impressive to look in silence. His charges divided their hushed regard between him and the bird, awed by the thought of what great things might be passing in the mind of such a man at such a moment.

349   Now he led them there for the last time. Tomorrow it was good bye. The tumult and the crowing would die away. He told them that they must have a last look at the prize they had let slip through their fingers. Might it be a lesson to them!

350   As it happened they found someone there before them. He showed himself more than usually interested, and they hung back until he should have
completed his scrutiny. Upon lifting his head from the note book he employed, he recognized Dalkins. He had been about to move off. He stood still.
There may have been a momentary gleam of fun in his eye. It passed unnoticed.

351   "Splendid," he said, with an indicative wave of the hand, "I want him."

352   "I thought of you, Wilson, when I put him in here. Isn't he what you were
looking for in the fall? I thought you would want him."

353   "I do. Your price?"

354   Dalkins made a movement with his fingers as if he despaired of having
enough to give the sign. He ended by holding up, side by side, and far forward, one finger on each hand.

355   The agent, Durgin, and the original owner, turned pale. The first thought
he was insane, the second that he was making a fake sale, the third that he
hadn't been so far wrong in his estimate of the bird. To these three the two
fingers meant two dollars.

356   "Shade it," said Mr. Wilson.

357   "Will you give me a dollar fifty?" laughed Dalkins.

358   "What are a few dollars here or there when it is a question of such a bird?"
said Wilson as he went down for his wad.

359   "This is the payee." Dalkins obtruded the original owner.

360   "His bird, is it?"

361   "In a way, yes. He raised it up back here a few hundred miles, and I don't
consider that he was ever honestly separated from it." This with a withering
eye to Durgin.

362   "It wasn't stolen?"

363   "It comes to that. He was induced to sell it for one dollar and fifty cents."

364   For a moment Wilson hesitated and drew back, but it was only a moment.
He looked at the bird again. "Well," he said, "I'm not supposed to know that.
A bargain's a bargain."

365   At the moment of being thrust into prominence by the collar, the original
owner, somewhat taken by surprise, had mechanically turned up a hand.
Now Dalkins seized upon this and held it as in a vice, while Wilson heaped
bills upon it till the count should have been lost, though it wasn't. The sum
total was two hundred dollars. All the time Durgin had been opening wider
and wider at the mouth.

366   "If I let go," said Dalkins to the original owner, "can I trust you to put that
money where it belongs, and not bother me with arguments? Remember it is
Christmas, or was a week or so since."

367   The original owner smiled weakly, but made no remonstrance.

368   "Where do I come in?" piped up poor Durgin.

369   "For a good time, and a valuable lesson," snapped Dalkins. "If there's any-thing else you want but can't seem to lay your hands on, just take it out in kicking."

370   Then Dalkins gently but forcibly closed the original's fingers over the pa-per in his hand, and headed him down the aisle. Durgin followed with a rat-tling in his throat that suggested roup, but merely indicated the impulse to speak without the ability.

371   Everybody followed, the little procession attracting considerable attention in the hall. It was thought someone had been arrested by a plain clothes man for stealing ribbons from the cages. The original had almost lost conscious-ness of what was going on around him. He heard as in a dream amid the up-roar of roosters, that sounded like a dying yell that wouldn't die, the voice of Dalkins saying, "Go tell that up in the hills, and make them stop breeding mongrel stock."

R. L. F.

Three Articles Associated with Pinkerton Academy

(1906–1910)

[Article for the Pinkerton Academy *Catalogue* (1906–07)]

1   Pinkerton Academy has been in successful operation since 1815, the year following its incorporation. It was named for Major John Pinkerton and Elder James Pinkerton, "old-time merchants of Londonderry," who gave an endowment sufficient to assure the permanence of the school during the first seventy years of its existence.

2   John M. Pinkerton, a son of one of the original founders, at his death in 1881, left a munificent bequest, which became available in 1886 and enabled the trustees to increase the facilities in respect to buildings, apparatus and number of instructors and to provide for an enlarged and advanced form of work.

3   Bronze tablets, recently placed in the outer vestibule of the main building, commemorate the special service of these three men, freshly linking the institution with the lives in which it had its foundation.

Aim and Character of Instruction.

4   The Academy has had a long and honorable record as a college preparatory school. At the same time it may be said that it has always been looked to by the youth of communities about it less as a means to education beyond it than as an aim and end in itself. Of these it sends yearly a large number directly to positions of usefulness in the world. It has been enough restricted in field to Derry and surrounding towns to take tone, to some extent, from the preponderance of day students over boarding students in its attendance.

5   While moving abreast of the times, the Academy has kept unspoiled by transient theory the educational ideals that are not transient. It would be rated as conservative in avoidance of pedagogic experimentation, though less so by comparison with other secondary schools than with many elementary schools. It undertakes to teach with sense and thoroughness the subjects proper to its curriculum. For the rest, its concern is to aim high enough. Work is methodical without subservience to methods. It is held that, for the

instructor, "no method nor discipline can supersede the necessity of being forever on the alert." Much must be left to the inspiration of the class-room and the exigency of the case. The constant appeal is to honor, reason and native energy. Government is less by rule than by suggestion. Pupils are taught to think for themselves, and to do things by having to do them for themselves. The whole plan of the school makes provision for diligent young people of character who have the definite purpose to be of use in the world.

6   As set forth in the act of incorporation, the Academy was established "for the purpose of promoting piety and virtue and for the education of Youth in the Liberal Arts and Sciences or Languages." While it is not sectarian it is truly Christian. It is not forgotten that character is more than scholarship, that "life is the highest of arts," that education means knowing how to live so as not to fail of life's great end. Chapel exercises, held daily, are so conducted as to furnish an incentive to scholarly ideals, true manliness and purity of character.

The Academy Town.

7   Derry is a healthful and attractive town forty-five miles from Boston on the Boston and Maine railroad, with six trains daily each way. It has a perfect water supply, well-paved streets and electric lighting. Easy of access and not behind in modern improvements, it preserves the wholesome social atmosphere of the villages that have made New England history. The Academy has exerted an important influence to make it what it is, giving it the right touch of culture and shaping it to the uses of education. The student mingles freely in the quiet life of such a town to his lasting benefit, never really out of the presence of the school. The danger, common to private preparatory schools, of too great detachment, at a critical time, from people and things, is here obviated. In few places are the conditions for study more unartificial. Town and school have thus grown together, with the happiest result, to form, in some sense, one institution.

[Drama at Pinkerton: A Series of Entertainments for the Benefit of the Academy Critic (1910)]

8   Beginning Thursday, May 26, and continuing at intervals of a week, the editorial board of the Pinkerton Critic will give in Academy Hall a series of noted plays illustrating four periods of English dramatic literature, Marlowe's Faustus of the sixteenth century, Milton's Comus of the seventeenth, Sheridan's Rivals of the eighteenth, and Yeats' Land of Heart's Desire and Cathleen ni Hoolihan of the latter nineteenth. The set, five in all (two of which will be

given the same evening as being by the same author), will constitute a good short course in literature, intended to cultivate in school a taste for the better written sort of plays. But while all are literary and the object in staging them is largely educational, it must not be inferred that they have not been selected without regard to the entertainment they are likely to afford. All belong to the class of good acting drama as distinguished from the kind that is only meant to be read. All were written for the stage and have won and held a place on the stage. Only last winter the oldest, Marlowe's Faustus, was presented in New York by the Ben Greet company. It is thought that the plays will lose nothing by being put on without any elaborate attempt at stage setting in the simple Elizabethan fashion that was good enough for Shakespeare. The audience will be asked to supply much of the costuming and most of the scenery from the imagination.

> "And let us
> On your imaginary forces work,
> For 'tis your thoughts that must now deck our kings."

9   The plays are sufficiently distinct in kind to warrant the belief that the series will not prove monotonous. Each exhibits some special phase of dramatic art, of which it is one of the best examples. In the weird and tragic Faustus we have one of the last written of the mediaeval morality plays. Itself based on the monkish tale of the man who sold his soul to the devil, it forms in turn the basis for Goethe's play and Gounod's opera of the same name. Milton's Comus gives us something in the high philosophical strain. Chiefly notable for its beautiful poetry it is not without its strong dramatic possibilities in character, situation and action. Sheridan's gay wit made his Rivals the best piece of comedy between Shakespeare's time and our own. We come to the two Yeats plays. Yeats is head and front of that most interesting of recent literary movements known as the Celtic Renaissance; most interesting of course to the Irish, but hardly less so to the rest of us who speak the same tongue. He is the exponent of the lyrical drama, in which kind The Land of Heart's Desire is the best thing he has done. This is a fairy story with a meaning for lovers. Cathleen ni Hoolihan, the other play, can hardly be called a fairy story, though the chief character in it is an old woman who is no less a person than old Ireland herself. It has the genuine stir of Irish patriotism. A recent Critic says, "It must be dangerous to represent in Ireland, for it is an Irish Marseillaise."

10   The plays will not be presented in chronological order, but the Yeats plays, The Land of Heart's Desire and Cathleen ni Hoolihan, will be given the eve-

ning of May 26 in the Academy hall at a quarter before eight. The following is the cast of characters:

> *Land of Heart's Desire*
> Maurteen Bruin, Roger Ladd
> Shawn Bruin, Robert Bartlett
> Bridget Bruin, Emily Healey
> Maire Bruin, Margaret Abbott
> Father Hart, George Seavey
> A Fairy, Lavinia Mack
> *Cathleen ni Hoolihan*
> Peter Gillane, Edmund Stearns
> Michael Gillane, John Bartlett
> Patrick Gillane, George Goldsmith
> Bridget Gillane, Annie Frazier
> Delia Cabel, Hazel Stevens
> A Poor Old Woman (typifying Ireland), Lillian Sawyer

11 Single admission will be twenty-five cents, tickets for the course, seventy-five cents. Cars will probably be running. Look for announcement next week.

[Description of English Curriculum, Pinkerton Academy *Catalogue* (1910–11)]

English.

12 The general aim of the course in English is twofold: to bring our students under the *influence* of the great books, and to teach them the *satisfaction* of superior speech.

English I.

13 Reading:—Treasure Island, Robinson Crusoe (not in class), Horatius at the Bridge, Sohrab and Rustum, selections from Odyssey, selections from Arabian Nights, ten short stories (in class). Expression in oral reading rather than intelligent comment is made the test of appreciation.

14 Composition:—Fifty themes, written and oral; given direction by assignment of subjects. Criticism addressed to subject matter equally with form.

15 Rhetoric:—Talks on the subject, what it is (with copious illustrations from the experience of the teacher) and where to be found.

16 Memorizing:—Twenty poems from the Golden Treasury; basis of subsequent study of the history of English literature.

English II.

17   Reading:—Pilgrim's Progress, Ivanhoe, thirty short stories (not in class), As You Like It, Ancient Mariner, Gareth and Lynette, Passing of Arthur, selections from Hanson's Composition (in class). Discussion proceeds more and more without the goad of the direct question.

18   Composition:—Fifty themes.

19   Rhetoric:—Talks chiefly on the technicalities of writing.

20   Memorizing:—Twenty poems learned from dictation. These form the basis for subsequent talks on literary art.

English III.

21   Reading:—Silas Marner, Tale of Two Cities, House of Seven Gables, Kenilworth (not in class), Julius Caesar, selections from Walden (in class); some voluntary work in Scott, Dickens and Hawthorne, or Shakespeare, Marlowe, and Sheridan, or the lyrics of Wordsworth, Browning, Tennyson and Kipling.

22   Composition:—Thirty themes. Woolley's Handbook is used in theme correcting.

English IV.

23   Reading:—College requirements. Especially in this year a point is made of re-reading a great many selections remembered with pleasure from previous years.

24   Composition:—Thirty themes.

25   Memorizing:—Lines from Milton.

26   Parts of such books as the following have been read from the desk to one class and another this year: Jonson's Silent Woman, Clemens' Yankee in King Arthur's Court, Gilbert's Bab Ballads, Goldsmith's She Stoops to Conquer, Maeterlinck's Blue Bird.

[Remarks on Form in Poetry (1919)]

1   A man who makes really good literature is like a fellow who goes into the fields to pull carrots. He keeps on pulling them patiently enough until he finds a carrot that suggests something else to him. It is not shaped like other carrots. He takes out his knife and notches it here and there, until the two pronged roots become legs and the carrot takes on something of the semblance of a man. The real genius takes hold of that bit of life which is suggestive to him and gives it form. But the man who is merely a realist, and not a genius, will leave the carrot just as he finds it. The man who is merely an idealist and not a genius, will try to carve a donkey where no donkey is suggested by the carrot he pulls.

[Address before the Amherst Alumni Council (1919)]

1   I ought to say at first perhaps that the Language and Literature Group is probably about as it was when you were in College. We do not change much. It is about as it was, I know, where I went to college—the language at one end—I take it that the two words are significant—the language at one end, and the literature at the other. Language for scholarship, we will say, and literature for art. At the one end we still have in our work here the men who are interested in books as scientists, as scholars; and at the other end men who are interested in books for what they were intended by the author; that is to say—I mean that (laughter) I myself have that feeling for all books that I would refuse to put them to any use that the author did not intend them for.

2   There is not very much for me to describe. I would just like to give you the spirit of the thing as I understand it. You know I have been a great deal worried lately, what with all this Bolshevism, and syndicalism, and anarchism, and socialism—I have been a great deal worried about an ancient institution, namely, poverty. (Laughter.) I have heard some people say they were going to abolish poverty, just as they might say, "Let us go up and abolish the Amherst House" because they don't like the looks of it; it is ugly. Now, poverty would be, perhaps, a good thing to lose. I don't know; I have my doubts about it, as a writer, as a person sympathetic with young aspirations. You see, poverty has always kept up in the world as a kind of institution of refuge, a kind of life which is suited to young genius, to young aspiration before it makes good its promise. The young scholar, the young poet, the young painter, the young inventor, the young musician has always found a Latin Quarter where he could decently live in a garret, or a Barbizon where he could decently live in a cottage; and go half hungry, and get along somehow, and wear old clothes until he got the thing done and could show it to the world. Let poverty be abolished and where will the young poet, the young scholar, the young painter go then? I only see one place left for him to go and that is to college. (Laughter.) The only place left for him where his inclinations will have a chance is here at College.

3   You remember when teachers began to talk against rote memory. The day of reason came in and they began to say, "Let us have a college where people

think for themselves." I say, yes, that is all right. Let us have a college where people think for themselves; but it is more important that we have a college where they make projects for themselves; where the believing and the desiring part of their nature has a chance. I like to think of a college as something like that—a place where something in it has a chance; I don't expect to make painters or musicians in my class; I don't make them; I hope I give them a chance; I hope I give the desiring part of their nature a chance. I value the college in this as it resembles the institution of poverty. It is calling an awful power to humble functions perhaps. It may seem so to you.

4   What is a department where inclination has its chance, where the will has its chance? Why, it is something like what Mr. Meiklejohn has described. It is where wills are pushing their way. At its best it is a confluence of wills, rather than a conflict of wills, young wills and older wills driving toward the same thing. It is as much made from below by the student as from above by the teacher.

5   It is hard for me not to have my own department particularly in mind in all this. Here we are a department of what I might call not philosophical ease but reminiscent ease, where everything that a man has ever done or read comes home to be a memory and a meaning and a phrase; where it comes home to be an expression; where it comes home to be either good talk or good writing. Such a department as that has to be conducted in its own special way. Like the rest of the College, it must, first of all, be for the man of inclination, who knows his likes and dislikes, and wants to cultivate his likes and dislikes. I should wish to conduct it always so that those who will, may, and those who won't, must. (Laughter.) I should want some sort of whip hand for those who won't, but I should like to be gentle enough and unassuming enough simply to stand aside to let the man who will have his chance. There was nothing I hated so much when I was young as to be told or commanded to do something I was about to do anyway. (Laughter.)

6   In my work with the boys in writing I like to stand aside entirely. The only whip I use on those with the will is the whip that the mother of George III used on him, "Be a king, George; be a king." I like to say to them "Oh, be a writer, be a writer; or oh, be a reader." If they come to me and say, "Help me to be a reader, tell me how to be a reader," I say, "That is too hard a thing to tell you. Read." I mean to be satisfied to have them readers; but I am always forgetting and telling them to be writers. Of course, the department must have two objects, must it not? One, to make the American writer who won't be very numerous; and the other, to make the American audience who ought to be very numerous; whoever he is. The other departments in my group have nearly as much to do with that, I take it, as mine—making the great American audience and making the great American writer.

[Address in Memory of J. Warner Fobes (December 1, 1920)]

1   My acquaintance with Mr. Fobes began in Franconia about five years ago. We found each other by accident first; then we sought each other for the support of friendship in bad times. There has seemed to be a good deal wrong with the world in the last five years. I know I have been a great deal troubled; I think Mr. Fobes was a little troubled. He shared some of my anxieties about the nations at war and the classes at odds, but not all of them. He was a man of far fewer misgivings than I, and so probably did me more good in the exchange of ideas than I did him. He was too quick, too generous, too forward-looking, too believing, for misgivings; a curious blend of the man of thought and action.

2   I asked a traveller from the Labrador once about the people down there—two thousand to a coast of one thousand miles—two people to the mile. What is their life? How do they live? "Oh they live as other people any-where," he said. "They live by two things, by bread and by pride." I knew about the living by bread, but needed help about the living by pride. "What pride?" "Oh, pride in doing more than is asked of them, more than the law demands, or the pay demands; pride in the extra touch, the grace touch, the flourish of strength and generosity." I thought I could have said something myself on the subject of good measure from the contemplation of such lives as Mr. Fobes'. But my traveller from the Labrador had said it for me.

3   The pride I am speaking of is not incompatible with humility. No one will misunderstand me. The pride in doing more than the world asks of you may very well go with a humility in doing less than the divine asks of you. The best natures must be conscious of falling somewhere between the standards of the market place and the standards of religion. My emphasis for the moment happens not to be on the humility.

4   I came on Mr. Fobes after his days as preacher and soldier were over. I knew him altogether outside the church and army. I may have heard that he had climbed mountains and hunted big game, and still kept a high-power rifle. But it was as farmers we met, and it was as farmer to farmer we exhibited our qualities. I suspect he was not a very different man farming from

what he was preaching. He leaned forward as he went with eagerness. He seemed to feel that freedom was out ahead before you were sent or dragged. That was the generosity I have spoken of. It made him a figure of vitality and zest, a man in the fifties still hoping and believing, on the defensive nowhere.

5   Of course the best of generosity is courage. Mr. Fobes showed it as preacher, soldier, citizen, and hunter. He showed it as a farmer too. He was a brave farmer. I didn't attempt always to conceal the misgivings I had for him personally there. I sat by smiling and tried to disturb him about farming on such a scale as he planned it on in Franconia. But he shed my lighter fears as he shed my more serious.

6   I wondered to myself if he never entertained a momentary fear of the thoughts that might close in on old age, should certain things in life fail us. I am sure he knew no such weakness. I might try more or less perversely to trouble him with a fear for the republic. I doubt if I persuaded him I was very sincerely troubled with any myself.

7   His ultimate generosity lay in owning that generosity was a privilege of too few. He dreamed of a world in which everyone would be free as he felt to give more than the law of Moses asked. He hated that there should be driven slaves, too pressed for time and strength to exceed in quality or quantity the assignment of the taskmaster. What he would not allow for was slave natures that would not be self-roused to action and were almost grateful to the whip. But these things were still unsettled between us when last we talked.

8   Between our houses on the side of Sugar Hill there was a tunnel road of white birches. I shall always see it alight away ahead at night with the head-lights of the car as we went back and forth on the errands of friendship in the long summers we both made of it up there.

[Some Definitions by Robert Frost (1923)]

1   "Sometimes I have my doubts of words altogether, and I ask myself what is the place of them. They are worse than nothing unless they do something; unless they amount to deeds, as in ultimatums or battle-cries. They must be flat and final like the show-down in poker, from which there is no appeal. My definition of poetry (if I were forced to give one) would be this: words that have become deeds."

2   "All poetry is a reproduction of the tones of actual speech."

3   "There are two types of realists: the one who offers a good deal of dirt with his potato to show that it is a real one, and the one who is satisfied with the potato brushed clean. I'm inclined to be the second kind. To me, the thing that art does for life is to clean it, to strip it to form."

4   "A poem begins with a lump in the throat; a home-sickness or a love-sickness. It is a reaching-out toward expression; an effort to find fulfilment. A complete poem is one where an emotion has found its thought and the thought has found the words."

[Preface to *Memoirs of the Notorious Stephen Burroughs* (1924)]

1   Pelham, Massachusetts, may never have produced anything else; it had a large part in producing the *Memoirs of the Notorious Stephen Burroughs*—this good book; or at least in starting the author on the criminal career of which it is a record. I like setting up the claim for Pelham, because I once lived there or thereabouts. But it is the kind of town I should have wanted to magnify anyway, whether I had lived in it or not, just one high old street along a ridge, not much to begin with and every year beautifully less. The railroads have worked modern magic against it from away off in the valleys and the woods have pressed in upon it till now there is nothing left but the church where Burroughs preached his unsanctified sermons, a few houses (among them, possibly, the one where he preached the funeral sermon that began his undoing), and here and there a good mowing field of about the size of a tea-tray in the sky.

2   I was back there the other day looking for Burroughs, and I saw three great ghosts instead of one, Burroughs, the rogue, Glazier Wheeler, the coiner, and Daniel Shays, the rebel, a shining company. Such places always have all their great men at once, as if they were neither born nor self-made, but created each other. I suppose I saw the three as they must have gotten together to talk subversion of an evening at the Leanders'. Poor old Shays! He was so scared by his own rebellion that once he started running away from it, he never stopped till he got to Sandgate, Vermont,—if you can imagine how far out of the world that is—at any rate it was then outside of the United States. Burroughs should have told us more about his Pelham friends, and especially about Glazier Wheeler, who on his serious side was concerned with the transmutation of metals and may have been a necromancer.

3   I was anxious to ask Burroughs if he wouldn't agree with me that his own chief distinction was hypocrisy. Many will be satisfied to see in him just another specimen of the knowing rascal. I choose to take it that he is here raised up again as an example to us of the naïve hypocrite.

4   We assume that by virtue of being bad we are at least safe from being hyp-
ocrites. But are we any such thing? We bad people I should say had appearances to keep up no less dangerously than the good. The good must at all
costs seem good; that is the weakness of their position. But the bad must
seem amiable and engaging. They must often have to pass for large-hearted
when it is nothing but a strain on the heart that makes the heart secretly sick.
That is one curse that is laid on them; and another is that in every out-and-
out clash with the righteous they must try to make themselves out more
right than the righteous. You can see what that would lead to. No, I am afraid
hypocrisy is as increasing to evil as it is diminishing to good.

5   I was not a church-goer at the time when Burroughs was preaching in Pelham, and there may have been circumstances in aggravation that he does not
set down, but, let him tell it, I see little in the story to count against him. If
the sermons were sound and the preacher able, it couldn't have mattered
much that they were stolen and he not ordained. Technically, he was an im-
postor, and I suppose I am too inclined to be lenient with irregularity in both
school and church. But I remember that Melchizedek was not a Levite and
men have taught in colleges with no degree beyond a bachelor's. And take
Burroughs' first serious lapse in attempting to pass counterfeit money in
Springfield. Crime couldn't be made more excusable. Just one little dollar at a
drugstore in the interests of scientific experiment and to save the tears of a
lovely lady. I suspect he was not frank with us about what brought him sneaking back to Pelham after he was driven out with pitchforks. The friendship of
the Leanders, was it? And equally that of Mr. and Mrs. Leander? And not at
all the poetic young dream of easy money? The sweet hypocrite, we must
never let him drop.

6   And couldn't he write, couldn't he state things? In his lifetime, he made the
only two revolts from Puritanism anyone has yet thought of, one backwards
into Paganism and the other, let us say, sideways into the Catholic Church. In
making the first, he put the case for Paganism almost as well as Milton puts it
in the mouth of the sorcerer Comus: "We that are of purer fire." How well
he argues against holding anyone locked up in a jail in a free country, and in
favor of free coining in a free country!

7   I should like to have heard his reasons for winding up in the Catholic
Church. I can conceive of their being honest. Probably he was tired of his un-
charted freedom out of jail and wanted to be moral and a Puritan again as
when a child, but this time under a cover where he couldn't be made fun of
by the intellectuals. The course might commend itself to the modern Puritan
(what there is left of the modern Puritan).

8   Let me tell the reader where he must put this book if he will please me and

why there. On the same shelf with Benjamin Franklin and Jonathan Edwards (grandfather of Aaron Burr). Franklin will be a reminder of what we have been as a young nation in some respects, Edwards in others. Burroughs comes in reassuringly when there is question of our not unprincipled wickedness, whether we have had enough of it for salt. The world knows we are criminal enough. We commit our share of blind and inarticulate murder, for instance. But sophisticated wickedness, the kind that knows its grounds and can twinkle, could we have been expected to have produced so fine a flower in a pioneer state? The answer is that we had it and had it early in Stephen Burroughs (not to mention Aaron Burr). It is not just a recent publisher's importation from Europe.

9   Could anything recent be more teasing to our proper prejudices than the way Burroughs mixed the ingredients when he ran off on his travels? He went not like a fool with no thought for the future and nothing to his name but the horse between his legs. He took with him a pocketful of sermons stolen from his father, in one fell act combining prudence, a respect for religion (as property) and a respect for his father (as a preacher). *He* knew how to put the reverse on a ball so that when it was going it was also coming. It argues a sophisticated taste in the society around him that he should have found friends such as the Leanders to enjoy his jokes with him.

10   A book that I for one should be sorry to have missed. I have to thank my friend W. R. Brown for bringing it to my attention.

South Shaftsbury, Vermont

1924

The Poetry of Amy Lowell (1925)

1   It is absurd to think that the only way to tell if a poem is lasting is to wait and see if it lasts. The right reader of a good poem can tell the moment it strikes him that he has taken an immortal wound—that he will never get over it. That is to say, permanence in poetry as in love is perceived instantly. It hasn't to await the test of time. The proof of a poem is not that we have never forgotten it, but that we knew at sight that we never could forget it. There was a barb to it and a toxin that we owned to at once. How often I have heard it in the voice and seen it in the eyes of this generation that Amy Lowell had lodged poetry with them to stay.

2   The most exciting movement in nature is not progress, advance, but expansion and contraction, the opening and shutting of the eye, the hand, the heart, the mind. We throw our arms wide with a gesture of religion to the universe; we close them around a person. We explore and adventure for a while and then we draw in to consolidate our gains. The breathless swing is between subject matter and form. Amy Lowell was distinguished in a period of dilation when poetry, in the effort to include a larger material, stretched itself almost to the breaking of the verse. Little ones with no more apparatus than a teacup looked on with alarm. She helped make it stirring times for a decade to those immediately concerned with art and to many not so immediately.

3   The water in our eyes from her poetry is not warm with any suspicion of tears; it is water flung cold, bright and many-colored from flowers gathered in her formal garden in the morning. Her Imagism lay chiefly in images to the eye. She flung flowers and everything there. Her poetry was forever a clear resonant calling off of things seen.

[Marion Leroy Burton and Education (1925)]

1   All you teachers and students know so well what you have lost by the death of Marion LeRoy Burton that I can hardly expect to tell you anything you don't know about it. I choose, therefore, not to try to instruct you. Let this be as if we sat down together to exchange recollections of a friend in words like, "Remember how tall he was in a crowd?" "Yes, and remember the determined smile with which he went at things?" "And remember what a great president of the University he was!" You probably remember the last time you met him. Well, I am going to tell you about the last time I met him and what we talked about,—my last impression of him.

2   But first, my first impression of him.

3   It was that at forty-five he was still accepting life like a boy, primarily by taking part in it and only secondarily on reflection. He was a natural participator. The type of the powerful administrator not to be stopped by trifles, minor considerations.

4   I doubt if the great State University, that scares so many people, especially east of us, ever gave him a moment's pause. Enough that there was such a thing. He accepted it as a task to go ahead with rather than as a question. Let detached superior people ask if it wasn't already a failure and ask, while they were about it, if democracy wasn't a failure. Well, wasn't democracy a failure? He would have laughed, "At least not yet, by the looks." Strength lay in never saying 'till we saw the outcome.

5   Just so with the elements that went to make up the University. Take buildings for example. There was such a thing as buildings in education, either buildings or groves or both. (For Michigan, happily, it is both.) Buildings may have been a question of the whole when Mark Hopkins drummed on a log like a partridge to bring his class to order. They had long since been reduced to a question of more or less. Some friends may have wanted him to be sorry and apologetic because he had to build lecture halls and laboratories. The time to be sorry would be when they turned out badly. Architecture, brick or stone and mortar have been no particular reproach to the

kings who have succeeded with them as well as he has on this campus of Michigan University.

6   Then there was the relation of the school to the government and the politics of the state. There *was* such a relation, as why should there not be in a democracy or even monarchy for that matter! Those might indulge in regretting it who had no official concern with maintaining it in harmony. We know people who look on any human give-and-take as degrading and who are proud of being bad at it. The friendship that President Burton maintained with the legislature of the state was an honor on both sides and will go down in the history of the University. No one was ever better at reminding the people of a state where their largest interest lay. No one, I should think, can ever have asked a legislature for more of value to education than he asked and obtained.

7   And so I might go on with my admiration for him as a man who drove ahead. There was the matter of vocational subjects in college—the dread practical that some people like to muddle their wits with. What is this fear?— that someone shall learn to cook who should have been taught Homer? That someone shall learn to do something humble too well? The cry is that at least we should keep one department of the University sacred to the non-utilitarian. So we must if we can. He agreed to that. Still it is very hard to make anything in this world that shall be either wise or beautiful for its own sake and not at the same time useful to God or man. Once a maker of vases swore his vases should sell for their form purely, and not for any use they might be put to. So to keep them from holding water and flowers he bored a hole in them at the bottom. But he soon found that brought them into use as flowerpots to hold earth and flowers which was as much worse than water and flowers as earth is baser than water. And you have to remember that for one of the arts after which the college is named, for writing, the college has been always vocational. It has always trained writers. And for teachers it has been more or less vocational. I can't help a sneaking wish to see it continue directly productive of literature—books. I am so far practical in my ambition for the college of arts that I would dedicate it outright to life insurance, that is to say, insurance for life against two formidable things, to wit, being made a fool of by failure, in the event of failure, and being made a fool of by success, in the event of success. A lot of nonsense has been uttered about the practical in education either from affectation or sheer parrotry.

8   A lot of nonsense about athletics too. You would think to hear our talk that serious play had nothing to do with the arts. Serious play nothing to do with the arts? Why we talk in the slack of the tongue. We don't mean

what we say. Men who have things to do are safe in disregarding our chatty misgivings.

9   Then there were undeniably electives. The gift of Charles Eliot.

10   And coeducation.

11   And finally, you students, your number, vast and always increasing in the nature of the case, boundless.

12   President Burton took his place in the middle of all these things, and seized them by what they were made to be seized by, as naturally as anyone with horse sense takes hold of a horse by the nose instead of by the heels or around the waist. He refused to be troubled by them. They were certainly not great questions any more, and if questions at all were long since reduced to questions of more or less.

13   In the end, administration and what it entailed was too much for his physical strength, powerful administrator though he was. But though it overtaxed him, it never consumed his spirit with doubts. He wanted it right, he wanted it beautiful, where he had set his signature. But administration was never enough to satisfy the idealism of his nature. He brushed it aside in his mind for something beyond, which as I came to see, was no less than the advancement of learning through magnanimous teaching. Buildings, discipline, entrance requirements, professional schools were but the spread and ramification of the tree. His heart was really in some slight branch away at the top by which alone the tree was gaining height. The height of teaching was what concerned him, how far up it could be carried into prouder scholarship in teacher and taught. We talked of nothing else the last time I saw him. My first impression of him was that he was an administrator. Now for my last impression—that he was a teacher and an idealist.

14   Some distance in education has been achieved by rigor and pressure to the tune of "'Those who won't, must a little." But you cannot require fineness of a student. Fineness has never been got out of anyone by force. Is the chance favorable for getting it out of him by some other appeal now in use? Always look for the makings of the future right here in the present. Beginning under feet, what had we?

15   There was the teaching chiefly designed to keep the student from cheating;

16   The teaching chiefly designed to keep the student from dodging work;

17   The teaching designed to keep the student from making mistakes or, in its degenerate form, to make him make mistakes. (I have delved in teachers' libraries where I found the books all penciled with corrections. All the teachers had seen in literature was something to correct.)

18   All these were well enough in their way, though destructive of the teacher, not to mention the student, if thought on too intently.

19   There is the teaching that would make every lesson one of thoroughness and the sharpening of wits, just as if there were no other qualities than thoroughness and sharpness to be cultivated in the human breast. Thoroughness is the last quality to be insisted on in reading a poem, for one thing. No one who cared for poetry could ever linger to have it out with ignorance over any one poem. Progress in poetry is circular. You read poem number one to help you understand poem number two to help you understand poem number three to help you understand poem number one again. Really any book suffers from too close scrutiny. All it needs for understanding it is that you should have read all the other books ever written in the world; which, when you stop to think of it, is thoroughness too of a kind.

20   We were away in the Berkshires in the back room of a little bookstore with vacation on our hands. So we went on to be exhaustive. We praised, I remember, the apples of discord man—the appleman—good at throwing one apple of discord a session into his class to start conflict and pass the hour in controversy:

21   And the baby-scarer, turned loose on freshmen, those babes in grace, to scare them out of their home-taught certainties and make them blink, shiver and laugh as their mothers made them when she said "boo" to them on her lap. But it is funniest when the scared babies come fresh from class to try to scare the poor old world with their new found "boo" at second hand:

22   And the radical thinker (he has his place) who holds that anything radical you got into your memory made you rank as a thinker whether you thought it up or not. Stock up with radicalism and you think; stock up with conservatism and you cannot be said to think. Such is the notion.

23   But we had the teaching he would build on still to seek. Students themselves easily transcend the teaching I have described. The best of them do. The question was how much of the way they mount above it can teachers be found to go with them. Not all the way of course. In every achievement there is a point beyond which they must go alone. But they have often had the company of teachers of the right kind a long, long time.

24   Remember now, I am reporting almost his very words. A change was coming over education. No one was ready yet to give that change a name. He preferred to describe it himself in terms of teachers. He built the future on teachers who knew how to get more out of a student by throwing an atmosphere of expectation round him than by putting the screws on him. They asked without asking. How? Not quizzingly, to test anyone. Indeed real teachers have always felt some embarrassment in asking for answers they

know too well themselves. The make-believe-they-didn't know question disgusted them as a classroom device. They knew it relaxed attention on both sides and enfeebled speech. What is the large demand they make? First, they demand that the student make his own trouble and not wait for teachers to make it for him. Second, they insist on turning the teachers' claim on the student into the student's claim on the teachers, absolutely the reverse of what it has been. In the name of sensitiveness they beg of him never to put a poem to any use it wasn't intended for by the person who wrote it.

25   In the name of polite conversation they beg him to give up trying to amuse any one even in a class by telling over in the order in which he read it the last history or fiction he read last night.

26   Should anybody ask what, besides thoroughness and sharpness, lessons may be in, here are two suggested lessons, one in sensitiveness and one in polite conversation.

27   And more and more we must remind the student that in both the arts and sciences a man shows the quality he is to be known by, strikes what is called his note, young, or, almost certainly not at all. He has no time to waste dawdling over good-enough marks. Between fifteen and twenty-five are the springing years. We keep men school boys too long in America for the good of our arts and sciences. We try to keep the spirit along on a diet of technique. It is a drag. The food of the spirit is properly matter—subject matter. It won't do to say, Get technique first and then if you ever have anything to say you will be sure to say it well. Getting something to say and getting technique are the same thing. The whole of art is getting something to say. Find out what ideas are and start at once to have them before the evil days come when you can't start anything.

28   We were talking, of course, of free, natural, life-like, magnanimous teaching.

29   Charles Eliot gave us freedom as among the courses. That has not been found to be enough. What we are after next is freedom within the course. We have the teachers ready and waiting to make this freedom out of. All that is needed is to reshape the institutions a little to fit them and make them comfortable. The unwilling student has long been provided for or against. He has had to do something however little. The question, the only question in education that is a question, is how to provide for the willing student so that he shall feel free to do simply everything.

30   Spoken like a teacher you will agree rather than a President set apart by the bigness of the State University to look after its business and politics. But Marion Burton refused to be a president altogether specialized in politics and business. It was his instinct to keep near teaching and the ideals of teaching

for his own happiness. And we did not want him to get far away from the ideals of teaching. And we do not want his successor to.

31   President Burton's plans were unfolding when he died. He had many things in his mind that he had not yet come to in action. We must feel for him cut off in the middle of his career. Others will go on with his work. But it will not be the same to friends who sympathized with him in ambition. Our loss may be great. How can it be so great as that of the man interrupted by death in the middle of his work?

THIRTEEN

[Introduction to *The Arts Anthology:*
Dartmouth Verse 1925]

1   No one given to looking under-ground in spring can have failed to notice how a bean starts its growth from the seed. Now the manner of a poet's germination is less like that of a bean in the ground than of a waterspout at sea. He has to begin as a cloud of all the other poets he ever read. That can't be helped. And first the cloud reaches down toward the water from above and then the water reaches up toward the cloud from below and finally cloud and water join together to roll as one pillar between heaven and earth. The base of water he picks up from below is of course all the life he ever lived outside of books.

2   These, then, are the three figures of the waterspout and the first is about as far as the poet doomed to die young in everyone of us usually gets. He brings something down from Dowson, Yeats, Morris, Masefield, or the Imagists (often a long way down), but lifts little or nothing up. If he were absolutely certain to do as doomed and die young, he would hardly be worth getting excited over in college or elsewhere. But you can't be too careful about whom you will ignore in this world. Cases have been known of his refusing at the last minute to abdicate the breast in favor of the practical and living on to write lyric like Landor till ninety.

3   Right in this book he will be found surviving into the second figure of the waterspout, and, by several poems and many scattered lines, even into the third figure. "The Heritage," "Sonnet," "I Have Built a Vessel," and "The Wanderer," good as they are of their kind—accomplished and all that—are of the first figure and frankly derivative. They are meant to do credit to anyone's reading. But "The Letter," "The Village Daily," "For a Salvationist," and best of all, "The Ski Jumper," at least get up the salt water. Their realism represents an advance. They show acceptance of the fact that the way to better is often through worse. In such a poem as "Underneath Sleep" the pillar revolves pretty much unbroken.

4   We are here getting a long way with poetry, considering all there is against

it in school and college. The poet, as everyone knows, must strike his individual note sometime between the ages of fifteen and twenty-five. He may hold
it a long time, or a short time, but it is then he must strike it or never. School
and college have been conducted with the almost express purpose of keeping
him busy with something else till the danger of his ever creating anything is
past. Their motto has been, the muses find some mischief still for idle hands
to do. No one is asking to see poetry regularized in courses and directed by
coaches like sociology and football. It must remain a theft to retain its savor.
But it does seem as if it could be a little more connived at than it is. I for one
should be in favor of the colleges setting the expectation of poetry forward a
few years (the way the clocks are set forward in May), so as to get the young
poets started earlier in the morning before the freshness dries off. Just setting
the expectation of poetry forward might be all that was needed to give us our
proportioned number of poets to Congressmen.

    R. F.

[Poet—One of the Truest (1928)]

1   Percy MacKaye has spent precious time trying to make the world an easier place to write poetry in. Everybody knows how he has spread himself over the country, as with two very large wings, to get his fellow poets all fellowships at the universities. That is but an incident in the general campaign he is forever on, to hasten the day when our national life, the raw material of poetry, having become less and less raw, shall at last cease to be raw at all, and poetry shall almost write itself without the intervention of the artist.

2   It is angelic of him to wish all poets a livelihood and a beauty of life that shall be poetry, without being worked up into poetry. That is why many think of him as an angel before they think of him as a poet. He is none the less a poet, one of the truest. He has come his way through three distinct periods of poetry, always Percy MacKaye, with no undue perturbations in his nature from what was going on around him.

3   I don't know how much he is read today, whether more or less than he has been in the past, but I am sure it is less than he will be in the future.—May he be read at least twice as much in the last fifty years of his life as he was in the first fifty!

FIFTEEN

[Introduction to *The Cow's in the Corn* (1929)]

1   This my sole contribution to the Celtic Drama (no one so unromantic as not to have made at least one) illustrates the latter-day tendency of all drama to become smaller and smaller and to be acted in smaller and smaller theatres to smaller and smaller audiences.

    R. F.

[Preface to *A Way Out* (1929)]

1   Everything written is as good as it is dramatic. It need not declare itself in form, but it is drama or nothing. A least lyric alone may have a hard time, but it can make a beginning, and lyric will be piled on lyric till all are easily heard as sung or spoken by a person in a scene—in character, in a setting. By whom, where and when is the question. By a dreamer of the better world out in a storm in autumn; by a lover under a window at night. It is the same with the essay. It may manage alone or it may take unto itself other essays for help, but it must make itself heard as by Stevenson on an island, or Lamb in London.

2   A dramatic necessity goes deep into the nature of the sentence. Sentences are not different enough to hold the attention unless they are dramatic. No ingenuity of varying structure will do. All that can save them is the speaking tone of voice somehow entangled in the words and fastened to the page for the ear of the imagination. That is all that can save poetry from sing-song, all that can save prose from itself.

3   I have always come as near the dramatic as I could this side of actually writing a play. Here for once I have written a play without (as I should like to believe) having gone very far from where I have spent my life.

[Address at the Dedication of the Davison Memorial Library (1930)]

1   I owe a debt to Wilfred Davison that I can't tell you about. It's between him and me. I didn't get a chance to tell him about it. He went away before we could talk it over. One way to pay that debt is to come here to-day to help prolong his memory by this ceremony. He speaks in his poem about the influence which passed through him to others. I don't care very much for the influence which merely passes through him. That's all right, too; but I want him to be personally remembered.

2   We don't know how dead a dead man is or live a live man is, but I like to see a person I care for remembered personally as long as possible. One way to get him remembered is with our talk to-day; a better way is with the Library. The time will come when people will ask us for whom it is named. The way I should like to see his memory prolonged would be by keeping the *bent* that he gave the School—keeping the bent as long as possible. I suppose that it cannot be kept up forever, but let us make it as long that way as we can.

3   I am honored to think I had something to do with this meeting here. Listening to him so many times, I got a good idea what he wanted the School to be, what bent he wanted it to have. The strange thing is that I didn't know about his poetry—very modest he was about that. (Most of my friends who write show it to me sooner or later). His writing explains something to me— explains the bent he gave the School—the poetic bent. I like to measure up poetry to everything. I don't think there is anything very important without poetry. I don't think mathematics, science, is important without poetry, or amounts to much.

4   A school of this kind, set amid the beauties of nature, I think would be a dismal thing—it would be a mere credit-hunting summer school up here— but for the bent of poetry he gave it. Now it isn't easy in just a few words to define rightly how or where he gave it that poetic bent. He just had always with him this poetic fineness: I think he never would willingly have any

teacher on the place who would give to literature a meaning that wasn't intended by the person who wrote it.

5   There are all sorts of perversions—in summer and winter schools—in the teaching of poetry. And he agreed with those of us who knew him best that we were to gather people here who were above the perversions of poetry. He made the whole thing unpedagogical and poetic. It was as if he had taken the view that he wasn't interested in credits but in life and beauty.

6   You can think of your courses almost anywhere you are in the light of the idea. That was the thing that made Bread Loaf what it was—that bent. I hope it will keep it a long time,—and he be kept alive in that way.

Education by Poetry: A Meditative Monologue (1931)

1   I am going to urge nothing in my talk. I am not an advocate. I am going to consider a matter, and commit a description. And I am going to describe other colleges than Amherst. Or, rather say all that is good can be taken as about Amherst; all that is bad will be about other colleges.

2   I know whole colleges where all American poetry is barred—whole colleges. I know whole colleges where all contemporary poetry is barred.

3   I once heard of a minister who turned his daughter—his poetry-writing daughter—out on the street to earn a living, because he said there should be no more books written; God wrote one book, and that was enough. (My friend George Russell, "Æ," has read no literature, he protests, since just before Chaucer.)

4   That all seems sufficiently safe, and you can say one thing for it. It takes the onus off the poetry of having to be used to teach children anything. It comes pretty hard on poetry, I sometimes think,—what it has to bear in the teaching process.

5   Then I know whole colleges where, though they let in older poetry, they manage to bar all that is poetical in it by treating it as something other than poetry. It is not so hard to do that. Their reason I have often hunted for. It may be that these people act from a kind of modesty. Who are professors that they should attempt to deal with a thing as high and as fine as poetry? Who are *they*? There is a certain manly modesty in that.

6   That is the best general way of settling the problem; treat all poetry as if it were something else than poetry, as if it were syntax, language, science. Then you can even come down into the American and into the contemporary without any special risk.

7   There is another reason they have, and that is that they are, first and foremost in life, markers. They have the marking problem to consider. Now, I stand here a teacher of many years' experience and I have never complained of having had to mark. I had rather mark anyone for anything—for his looks, carriage, his ideas, his correctness, his exactness, anything you please,—I would rather give him a mark in terms of letters, A, B, C, D, than have to use

adjectives on him. We are all being marked by each other all the time, classi-
fied, ranked, put in our place, and I see no escape from that. I am no sentimentalist. You have got to mark, and you have got to mark, first of all, for accuracy, for correctness. But if I am going to give a mark, that is the least part
of my marking. The hard part is the part beyond that, the part where the adventure begins.

8   One other way to rid the curriculum of the poetry nuisance has been considered. More merciful than the others it would neither abolish nor denature
the poetry, but only turn it out to disport itself, with the plays and games—in
no wise discredited, though given no credit for. Anyone who liked to teach
poetically could take his subject, whether English, Latin, Greek or French,
out into the nowhere along with the poetry. One side of a sharp line would
be left to the rigorous and righteous; the other side would be assigned to the
flowery where they would know what could be expected of them. Grade
marks where more easily given, of course, in the courses concentrating on
correctness and exactness as the only forms of honesty recognized by plain
people; a general indefinite mark of X in the courses that scatter brains over
taste and opinion. On inquiry I have found no teacher willing to take position
on either side of the line, either among the rigors or among the flowers. No
one is willing to admit that his discipline is not partly in exactness. No one is
willing to admit that his discipline is not partly in taste and enthusiasm.

9   How shall a man go through college without having been marked for taste
and judgment? What will become of him? What will his end be? He will have
to take continuation courses for college graduates. He will have to go to
night schools. They are having night schools now, you know, for college graduates. Why? Because they have not been educated enough to find their way
around in contemporary literature. They don't know what they may safely
like in the libraries and galleries. They don't know how to judge an editorial
when they see one. They don't know how to judge a political campaign.
They don't know when they are being fooled by a metaphor, an analogy, a
parable. And metaphor is, of course, what we are talking about. Education
by poetry is education by metaphor.

10   Suppose we stop short of imagination, initiative, enthusiasm, inspiration
and originality—dread words. Suppose we don't mark in such things at all.
There are still two minimal things, that we have got to take care of, taste and
judgment. Americans are supposed to have more judgment than taste, but
taste is there to be dealt with. That is what poetry, the only art in the colleges
of arts, is there for. I for my part would not be afraid to go in for enthusiasm.
There is the enthusiasm like a blinding light, or the enthusiasm of the deafening shout, the crude enthusiasm that you get uneducated by poetry, outside

of poetry. It is exemplified in what I might call "sunset raving." You look westward toward the sunset, or if you get up early enough, eastward toward the sunrise, and you rave. It is oh's and ah's with you and no more.

11   But the enthusiasm I mean is taken through the prism of the intellect and spread on the screen in a color, all the way from hyperbole at one end—or overstatement, at one end—to understatement at the other end. It is a long strip of dark lines and many colors. Such enthusiasm is one object of all teaching in poetry. I heard wonderful things said about Virgil yesterday, and many of them seemed to me crude enthusiasm, more like a deafening shout, many of them. But one speech had range, something of overstatement, something of statement, and something of understatement. It had all the colors of an enthusiasm passed through an idea.

12   I would be willing to throw away everything else but that: enthusiasm tamed by metaphor. Let me rest the case there. Enthusiasm tamed to metaphor, tamed to that much of it. I do not think anybody ever knows the discreet use of metaphor, his own and other people's, the discreet handling of metaphor, unless he has been properly educated in poetry.

13   Poetry begins in trivial metaphors, pretty metaphors, "grace" metaphors, and goes on to the profoundest thinking that we have. Poetry provides the one permissible way of saying one thing and meaning another. People say, "Why don't you say what you mean?" We never do that, do we, being all of us too much poets. We like to talk in parables and in hints and in indirections—whether from diffidence or some other instinct.

14   I have wanted in late years to go further and further in making metaphor the whole of thinking. I find someone now and then to agree with me that all thinking, except mathematical thinking, is metaphorical, or all thinking except scientific thinking. The mathematical might be difficult for me to bring in, but the scientific is easy enough.

15   Once on a time all the Greeks were busy telling each other what the All was—or was like unto. All was three elements, air, earth, and water (we once thought it was ninety elements; now we think it is only one). All was substance, said another. All was change, said a third. But best and most fruitful was Pythagoras' comparison of the universe with number. Number of what? Number of feet, pounds, and seconds was the answer, and we had science and all that has followed in science. The metaphor has held and held, breaking down only when it came to the spiritual and psychological or the out of the way places of the physical.

16   The other day we had a visitor here, a noted scientist, whose latest word to the world has been that the more accurately you know where a thing is, the less accurately you are able to state how fast it is moving. You can see why

that would be so, without going back to Zeno's problem of the arrow's flight. In carrying numbers into the realm of space and at the same time into the realm of time you are mixing metaphors, that is all, and you are in trouble. They won't mix. The two don't go together.

17   Let's take two or three more of the metaphors now in use to live by. I have just spoken of one of the new ones, a charming mixed metaphor right in the realm of higher mathematics and higher physics: that the more accurately you state where a thing is, the less accurately you will be able to tell how fast it is moving. And, of course, everything is moving. Everything is an event now. Another metaphor. A thing, they say, is an event. Do you believe it is? Not quite. I believe it is almost an event. But I like the comparison of a thing with an event.

18   I notice another from the same quarter. "In the neighborhood of matter space is something like curved." Isn't that a good one! It seems to me that that is simply and utterly charming—to say that space is something like curved in the neighborhood of matter. "Something like."

19   Another amusing one is from—what is the book?—I can't say it now; but here is the metaphor. Its aim is to restore you to your ideas of free will. It wants to give you back your freedom of will. All right, here it is on a platter. You know that you can't tell by name what persons in a certain class will be dead ten years after graduation, but you can tell actuarially how many will be dead. Now, just so this scientist says of the particles of matter flying at a screen, striking a screen; you can't tell what individual particles will come, but you can say in general that a certain number will strike in a given time. It shows, you see, that the individual particles can come freely. I asked Bohr about that particularly, and he said, "Yes, it is so. It can come when it wills and as it wills; and the action of the individual particle is unpredictable. But it is not so of the action of the mass. There you can predict." He says, "That gives the individual atom its freedom, but the mass its necessity."

20   Another metaphor that has interested us in our time and has done all our thinking for us is the metaphor of evolution. Never mind going into the Latin word. The metaphor is simply the metaphor of the growing plant or of the growing thing. And somebody very brilliantly, quite a while ago, said that the whole universe, the whole of everything, was like unto a growing thing. That is all. I know the metaphor will break down at some point, but it has not failed everywhere. It is a very brilliant metaphor, I acknowledge, though I myself get too tired of the kind of essay that talks about the evolution of candy, we will say, or the evolution of elevators—the evolution of this, that, and the other. Everything is evolution. I emancipate myself by simply saying that I didn't get up the metaphor and so am not much interested in it.

21   What I am pointing out is that unless you are at home in the metaphor, unless you have had your proper poetical education in the metaphor, you are not safe anywhere. Because you are not at ease with figurative values: you don't know the metaphor in its strength and its weakness. You don't know how far you may expect to ride it and when it may break down with you. You are not safe in science; you are not safe in history. In history, for instance—to show that is the same in history as elsewhere—I heard somebody say yesterday that Aeneas was to be likened unto (those words, "likened unto"!) George Washington. He was that type of national hero, the middle-class man, not thinking of being a hero at all, bent on building the future, bent on his children, his descendants. A good metaphor, as far as it goes, and you must know how far. And then he added that Odysseus should be likened unto Theodore Roosevelt. I don't think that is so good. Someone visiting Gibbon at the point of death said he was the same Gibbon as of old, still at his parallels.

22   Take the way we have been led into our present position morally, the world over. It is by a sort of metaphorical gradient. There is a kind of thinking—to speak metaphorically—there is a kind of thinking you might say was endemic in the brothel. It is always there. And every now and then in some mysterious way it becomes epidemic in the world. And how does it do so? By using all the good words that virtue has invented to maintain virtue. It uses honesty, first,—frankness, sincerity—those words; picks them up, uses them. "In the name of honesty, let us see what we are." You know. And then it picks up the word joy. "Let us in the name of joy, which is the enemy of our ancestors, the Puritans . . . Let us in the name of joy, which is the enemy of the kill-joy Puritan . . ." You see. "Let us," and so on. And then, "In the name of health . . ." Health is another good word. And that is the metaphor Freudianism trades on, mental health. And the first thing we know, it has us all in up to the top knot. I suppose we may blame the artists a good deal, because they are great people to spread by metaphor. The stage too—the stage is always a good intermediary between the two worlds, the under and the upper,—if I may say so without personal prejudice to the stage.

23   In all this I have only been saying that the devil can quote Scripture, which simply means that the good words you have lying around the devil can use for his purposes as well as anybody else. Never mind about my morality. I am not here to urge anything. I don't care whether the world is good or bad—not on any particular day.

24   Let me ask you to watch a metaphor breaking down here before you.

25   Somebody said to me a little while ago, "It is easy enough for me to think of the universe as a machine, as a mechanism."

26   I said, "You mean the universe is like a machine?"

26   He said, "No. I think it is one . . . Well, it is like. . ."

27   "I think you mean the universe is like a machine."

28   "All right. Let it go at that."

29   I asked him, "Did you ever see a machine without a pedal for the foot, or a lever for the hand, or a button for the finger?"

30   He said, "No—no."

31   I said, "All right. Is the universe like that?"

32   And he said, "No. I mean it is like a machine, only . . ."

33   ". . . it is different from a machine," I said.

34   He wanted to go just that far with that metaphor and no further. And so do we all. All metaphor breaks down somewhere. That is the beauty of it. It is touch and go with the metaphor, and until you have lived with it long enough you don't know when it is going. You don't know how much you can get out of it and when it will cease to yield. It is a very living thing. It is as life itself.

35   I have heard this ever since I can remember, and ever since I have taught: the teacher must teach the pupil to think. I saw a teacher once going around in a great school and snapping pupils' heads with thumb and finger and saying, "Think." That was when thinking was becoming the fashion. The fashion hasn't yet quite gone out.

36   We still ask boys in college to think, as in the nineties, but we seldom tell them what thinking means; we seldom tell them it is just putting this and that together; it is just saying one thing in terms of another. To tell them is to set their feet on the first rung of a ladder the top of which sticks through the sky.

37   Greatest of all attempts to say one thing in terms of another is the philosophical attempt to say matter in terms of spirit, or spirit in terms of matter, to make the final unity. That is the greatest attempt that ever failed. We stop just short there. But it is the height of poetry, the height of all thinking, the height of all poetic thinking, that attempt to say matter in terms of spirit and spirit in terms of matter. It is wrong to call anybody a materialist simply because he tries to say spirit in terms of matter, as if that were a sin. Materialism is not the attempt to say all in terms of matter. The only materialist—be he poet, teacher, scientist, politician, or statesman—is the man who gets lost in his material without a gathering metaphor to throw it into shape and order. He is the lost soul.

38   We ask people to think, and we don't show them what thinking is. Somebody says we don't need to show them how to think; bye and bye they will think. We will give them the forms of sentences and, if they have any ideas,

then they will know how to write them. But that is preposterous. All there is to writing is having ideas. To learn to write is to learn to have ideas.

39   The first little metaphor . . . Take some of the trivial ones. I would rather have trivial ones of my own to live by than the big ones of other people.

40   I remember a boy saying, "He is the kind of person that wounds with his shield." That may be a slender one, of course. It goes a good way in character description. It has poetic grace. "He is the kind that wounds with his shield."

41   The shield reminds me—just to linger a minute—the shield reminds me of the inverted shield spoken of in one of the books of the "Odyssey," the book that tells about the longest swim on record. I forget how long it lasted—several days, was it?—but at last as Odysseus came near the coast of Phaeacia, he saw it on the horizon "like an inverted shield."

42   There is a better metaphor in the same book. In the end Odysseus comes ashore and crawls up the beach to spend the night under a double olive tree, and it says, as in a lonely farmhouse where it is hard to get fire—I am not quoting exactly—where it is hard to start the fire again if it goes out, they cover the seeds of fire with ashes to preserve it for the night, so Odysseus covered himself with the leaves around him and went to sleep. There you have something that gives you character, something of Odysseus himself. "Seeds of fire." So Odysseus covered the seeds of fire in himself. You get the greatness of his nature.

43   But these are slighter metaphors than the ones we live by. They have their charm, their passing charm. They are as it were the first steps toward the great thoughts, grave thoughts, thoughts lasting to the end.

44   The metaphor whose manage we are best taught in poetry—that is all there is of thinking. It may not seem far for the mind to go but it is the mind's furthest. The richest accumulation of the ages is the noble metaphors we have rolled up.

45   I want to add one thing more that the experience of poetry is to anyone who comes close to poetry. There are two ways of coming close to poetry. One is by writing poetry. And some people think I want people to write poetry, but I don't; that is, I don't necessarily. I only want people to write poetry if they want to write poetry. I have never encouraged anybody to write poetry that did not want to write it, and I have not always encouraged those who did want to write it. That ought to be one's own funeral. It is a hard, hard life, as they say.

46   (I have just been to a city in the West, a city full of poets, a city they have made safe for poets. The whole city is so lovely that you do not have to write it up to make it poetry; it is ready-made for you. But, I don't know—the poetry written in that city might not seem like poetry if read outside of the city.

It would be like the jokes made when you were drunk; you have to get drunk again to appreciate them.)

47 But as I say, there is another way to come close to poetry, fortunately, and that is in the reading of it, not as linguistics, not as history, not as anything but poetry. It is one of the hard things for a teacher to know how close a man has come in reading poetry. How do I know whether a man has come close to Keats in reading Keats? It is hard for me to know. I have lived with some boys a whole year over some of the poets and I have not felt sure whether they have come near what it was all about. One remark sometimes told me. One remark was their mark for the year; had to be—it was all I got that told me what I wanted to know. And that is enough, if it was the right remark, if it came close enough. I think a man might make twenty fool remarks if he made one good one some time in the year. His mark would depend on that good remark.

48 The closeness—everything depends on the closeness with which you come, and you ought to be marked for the closeness, for nothing else. And that will have to be estimated by chance remarks, not by question and answer. It is only by accident that you know some day how near a person has come.

49 The person who gets close enough to poetry, he is going to know more about the word *belief* than anybody else knows, even in religion nowadays. There are two or three places where we know belief outside of religion. One of them is at the age of fifteen to twenty, in our self-belief. A young man knows more about himself than he is able to prove to anyone. He has no knowledge that anybody else will accept as knowledge. In his foreknowledge he has something that is going to believe itself into fulfilment, into acceptance.

50 There is another belief like that, the belief in someone else, a relationship of two that is going to be believed into fulfilment. That is what we are talking about in our novels, the belief of love. And the disillusionment that the novels are full of is simply the disillusionment from disappointment in that belief. That belief can fail, of course.

51 Then there is a literary belief. Every time a poem is written, every time a short story is written, it is written not by cunning, but by belief. The beauty, the something, the little charm of the thing to be, is more felt than known. There is a common jest, one that always annoys me, on the writers, that they write the last end first, and then work up to it; that they lay a train toward one sentence that they think is pretty nice and have all fixed up to set like a trap to close with. No, it should not be that way at all. No one who has ever come close to the arts has failed to see the difference between things written that way, with cunning and device, and the kind that are believed into exis-

tence, that begin in something more felt than known. This you can realize quite as well—not quite as well, perhaps, but nearly as well—in reading as you can in writing. I would undertake to separate short stories on that principle; stories that have been believed into existence and stories that have been cunningly devised. And I could separate the poems still more easily.

52   Now I think—I happen to think—that those three beliefs that I speak of, the self-belief, the love-belief, and the art-belief, are all closely related to the God-belief, that the belief in God is a relationship you enter into with Him to bring about the future.

53   There is national belief like that, too. One feels it. I have been where I came near getting up and walking out on the people who thought that they had to talk against nations, against nationalism, in order to curry favor with internationalism. Their metaphors are all mixed up. They think that because a Frenchman and an American and an Englishman can all sit down on the same platform and receive honors together, it must be that there is no such thing as nations. That kind of bad thinking springs from a source we all know. I should want to say to anyone like that: "Look! First I want to be a person. And I want you to be a person, and then we can be as interpersonal as you please. We can pull each other's noses—do all sorts of things. But, first of all, you have got to have the personality. First of all, you have got to have the nations and then they can be as international as they please with each other."

54   I should like to use another metaphor on them. I want my palette, if I am a painter, I want my palette on my thumb or on my chair, all clean, pure, separate colors. Then I will do the mixing on the canvas. The canvas is where the work of art is, where we make the conquest. But we want the nations all separate, pure, distinct, things as separate as we can make them; and then in our thoughts, in our arts, and so on, we can do what we please about it.

55   But I go back. There are four beliefs that I know more about from having lived with poetry. One is the personal belief, which is a knowledge that you don't want to tell other people about because you cannot prove that you know. You are saying nothing about it till you see. The love belief, just the same, has that same shyness. It knows it cannot tell; only the outcome can tell. And the national belief we enter into socially with each other, all together, party of the first part, party of the second part, we enter into that to bring the future of the country. We cannot tell some people what it is we believe, partly, because they are too stupid to understand and partly because we are too proudly vague to explain. And anyway it has got to be fulfilled, and we are not talking until we know more, until we have something to show. And then the literary one in every work of art, not of cunning and craft,

mind you, but of real art; that believing the thing into existence, saying as you go more than you even hoped you were going to be able to say, and coming with surprise to an end that you foreknew only with some sort of emotion. And then finally the relationship we enter into with God to believe the future in—to believe the hereafter in.

[Autobiographical Sketch (1933)]

1 Robert Frost was born in San Francisco, California, in 1875. His father, William Prescott Frost, was a New Englander of the ninth generation, and his mother, Belle Moodie, was a Scot, born in Edinburgh. He was brought up and educated in New England. He went to the city High School of Lawrance, Massachusetts, and to Dartmouth and Harvard colleges. In 1895 he married Elinor White, a New Englander of the tenth generation, and has four children, living, Lesley, Carroll, Irma and Marjorie.

2 His life has been spent in farming, teaching, and writing poetry.

3 Between 1900 and 1907 he kept a one man farm in Derry, New Hampshire. There he wrote a large share of his first two books. Since then, he has always had an interest in the land, and has owned a small farm in either New Hampshire or Vermont.

4 He has been a part time teacher in almost all kinds of schools, and in colleges. He has been in residence, in an honorary capacity, without duties, at the University of Michigan, in Ann Arbor, Michigan, for three years, and now going on for seven years, at Amherst College, in Amherst, Massachusetts. Many colleges have conferred honors on him. He was made a member of the American Academy in 1930.

5 He has published scattering poems in magazines since 1894. The first book he ever put together, *A Boy's Will*, was immediately accepted and published by David Nutt, in London, England, in 1913. His subsequent books have been *North of Boston*, 1914, *Mountain Interval*, 1917, *New Hampshire*, (awarded the Pulitzer Prize) in 1923, *West-Running Brook*, 1928, and *Collected Poems*, (awarded the Pulitzer Prize) in 1930.

6 The country and nature in New England have been his background, but the poems are almost without exception portraits of people. Of New England, they have proved of interest to more than New England: in fact, they first attracted considerable attention in Old England. The verse is regular iambic, rhymed and unrhymed.

TWENTY

[Comment on "Birches" (1933)]

1   (Old Knower): The tide of evil rises. Your Ark is sailing and you make me a last-minute allowance of a single plant on board for seed. (It would have to be two if animals, or there would be no seed.) Well, let it be a tree—Birches. Don't ask me why at a time of doom and confusion like this. My reasons might be forced and unreal. But if I must defend my choice, I will say I took it for its vocality and its ulteriority.

["Letter" to *The Amherst Student* (1935)]

1   It is very, very kind of the *Student* to be showing sympathy with me for my age. But sixty is only a pretty good age. It is not advanced enough. The great thing is to be advanced. Now ninety would be really well along and something to be given credit for.

2   But speaking of ages, you will often hear it said that the age of the world we live in is particularly bad. I am impatient of such talk. We have no way of knowing that this age is one of the worst in the world's history. Arnold claimed the honor for the age before this. Wordsworth claimed it for the last but one. And so on back through literature. I say they claimed the honor for their ages. They claimed it rather for themselves. It is immodest of a man to think of himself as going down before the worst forces ever mobilized by God.

3   All ages of the world are bad—a great deal worse anyway than Heaven. If they weren't the world might just as well be Heaven at once and have it over with. One can safely say after from six to thirty thousand years of experience that the evident design is a situation here in which it will always be about equally hard to save your soul. Whatever progress may be taken to mean, it can't mean making the world any easier a place in which to save your soul— or if you dislike hearing your soul mentioned in open meeting, say your decency, your integrity.

4   Ages may vary a little. One may be a little worse than another. But it is not possible to get outside the age you are in to judge it exactly. Indeed it is as dangerous to try to get outside of anything as large as an age as it would be to engorge a donkey. Witness the many who in the attempt have suffered a dilation from which the tissues and the muscles of the mind have never been able to recover natural shape. They can't pick up anything delicate or small any more. They can't use a pen. They have to use a typewriter. And they gape in agony. They can write huge shapeless novels, huge gobs of raw sincerity bellowing with pain and that's all that they can write.

5   Fortunately we don't need to know how bad the age is. There is something we can always be doing without reference to how good or how bad the age

is. There is at least so much good in the world that it admits of form and the making of form. And not only admits of it, but calls for it. We people are thrust forward out of the suggestions of form in the rolling clouds of nature. In us nature reaches its height of form and through us exceeds itself. When in doubt there is always form for us to go on with. Anyone who has achieved the least form to be sure of it, is lost to the larger excruciations. I think it must stroke faith the right way. The artist, the poet might be expected to be the most aware of such assurance. But it is really everybody's sanity to feel it and live by it. Fortunately, too, no forms are more engrossing, gratifying, comforting, staying than those lesser ones we throw off, like vortex rings of smoke, all our individual enterprise and needing nobody's cooperation; a basket, a letter, a garden, a room, an idea, a picture, a poem. For these we haven't to get a team together before we can play.

6   The background is hugeness and confusion shading away from where we stand into black and utter chaos; and against the background any small man-made figure of order and concentration. What pleasanter than that this should be so? Unless we are novelists or economists we don't worry about this confusion; we look out on it with an instrument or tackle it to reduce it. It is partly because we are afraid it might prove too much for us and our blend of democratic-republican-socialist-communist-anarchist party. But it is more because we like it, we were born to it, born used to it and have practical reasons for wanting it there. To me any little form I assert upon it is velvet, as the saying is, and to be considered for how much more it is than nothing. If I were a Platonist I should have to consider it, I suppose, for how much less it is than everything.

[Introduction to *King Jasper* (1935)]

1   It may come to the notice of posterity (and then again it may not) that this, our age, ran wild in the quest of new ways to be new. The one old way to be new no longer served. Science put it into our heads that there must be new ways to be new. Those tried were largely by subtraction—elimination. Poetry, for example, was tried without punctuation. It was tried without capital letters. It was tried without metric frame on which to measure the rhythm. It was tried without any images but those to the eye; and a loud general intoning had to be kept up to cover the total loss of specific images to the ear, those dramatic tones of voice which had hitherto constituted the better half of poetry. It was tried without content under the trade name of poesie pure. It was tried without phrase, epigram, coherence, logic and consistency. It was tried without ability. I took the confession of one who had had deliberately to unlearn what he knew. He made a back-pedalling movement of his hands to illustrate the process. It was tried premature like the delicacy of unborn calf in Asia. It was tried without feeling or sentiment like murder for small pay in the underworld. These many things was it tried without, and what had we left? Still something. The limits of poetry had been sorely strained, but the hope was that the idea had been somewhat brought out.

2   Robinson stayed content with the old-fashioned way to be new. I remember bringing the subject up with him. How does a man come on his difference, and how does he feel about it when he first finds it out? At first it may well frighten him, as his difference with the Church frightened Martin Luther. There is such a thing as being too willing to be different. And what shall we say to people who are not only willing but anxious? What assurance have they that their difference is not insane, eccentric, abortive, unintelligible? Two fears should follow us through life. There is the fear that we shan't prove worthy in the eyes of someone who knows us at least as well as we know ourselves. That is the fear of God. And there is the fear of Man—the fear that men won't understand us and we shall be cut off from them.

3   We began in infancy by establishing correspondence of eyes with eyes. We recognized that they were the same feature and we could do the same things

with them. We went on to the visible motion of the lips—smile answered smile; then cautiously, by trial and error, to compare the invisible muscles of the mouth and throat. They were the same and could make the same sounds. We were still together. So far, so good. From here on the wonder grows. It has been said that recognition in art is all. Better say correspondence is all. Mind must convince mind that it can uncurl and wave the same filaments of subtlety, soul convince soul that it can give off the same shimmers of eternity. At no point would anyone but a brute fool want to break off this correspondence. It is all there is to satisfaction; and it is salutary to live in the fear of its being broken off.

4   The latest proposed experiment of the experimentalists is to use poetry as a vehicle of grievances against the un-Utopian state. As I say, most of their experiments have been by subtraction. This would be by addition of an ingredient that latter-day poetry has lacked. A distinction must be made between griefs and grievances. Grievances are probably more useful than griefs. I read in a sort of Sunday School leaflet from Moscow that the grievances of Chekhov against the sordidness and dullness of his home-town society have done away with the sordidness and dullness of home-town society all over Russia. They were celebrating the event. The grievances of the great Russians of the last century have given Russia a revolution. The grievances of their great followers in America may well give us, if not a revolution, at least some palliative pensions. We must suffer them to put life at its ugliest and forbid them not as we value our reputation for liberality.

5   I had it from one of the youngest lately: "Whereas we once thought literature should be without content, we now know it should be charged full of propaganda." Wrong twice, I told him. Wrong twice and of theory prepense. But he returned to his position after a moment out for reassembly: "Surely art can be considered good only as it prompts to action." How soon, I asked him. But there is danger of undue levity in teasing the young. The experiment is evidently started. Grievances are certainly a power and are going to be turned on. We must be very tender of our dreamers. They may seem like picketers or members of the committee on rules for the moment. We shan't mind what they seem, if only they produce real poems.

6   But for me, I don't like grievances. I find I gently let them alone wherever published. What I like is griefs and I like them Robinsonianly profound. I suppose there is no use in asking, but I should think we might be indulged to the extent of having grievances restricted to prose if prose will accept the imposition, and leaving poetry free to go its way in tears.

7   Robinson was a prince of heartachers amid countless achers of another part. The sincerity he wrought in was all sad. He asserted the sacred right of

poetry to lean its breast to a thorn and sing its dolefullest. Let weasels suck eggs. I know better where to look for melancholy. A few superficial irritable grievances, perhaps, as was only human, but these are forgotten in the depth of griefs to which he plunged us.

8   Grievances are a form of impatience. Griefs are a form of patience. We may be required by law to throw away patience as we have been required to surrender gold; since by throwing away patience and joining the impatient in one last rush on the citadel of evil, the hope is we may end the need of patience. There will be nothing left to be patient about. The day of perfection waits on unanimous social action. Two or three more good national elections should do the business. It has been similarly urged on us to give up courage, make cowardice a virtue, and see if that won't end war, and the need of courage. Desert religion for science, clean out the holes and corners of the residual unknown, and there will be no more need of religion. (Religion is merely consolation for what we don't know.) But suppose there was some mistake; and the evil stood siege, the war didn't end, and something remained unknowable. Our having disarmed would make our case worse than it had ever been before. Nothing in the latest advices from Wall Street, the League of Nations, or the Vatican inclines me to give up my holdings in patient grief.

9   There were Robinson and I, it was years ago, and the place (near Boston Common) was the Place, as we liked afterward to call it, of Bitters, because it was with bitters, though without bitterness, we could sit there and look out on the welter of dissatisfaction and experiment in the world around us. It was too long ago to remember who said what, but the sense of the meeting was, we didn't care how arrant a reformer or experimentalist a man was if he gave us real poems. For ourselves, we would hate to be read for any theory upon which we might be supposed to write. We doubted any poem could persist for any theory upon which it might have been written. Take the theory that poetry in our language could be treated as quantitative, for example. Poems had been written in spite of it. And poems are all that matter. The utmost of ambition is to lodge a few poems where they will be hard to get rid of, to lodge a few irreducible bits where Robinson lodged more than his share.

10   For forty years it was phrase on phrase on phrase with Robinson and everyone the closest delineation of something that *is* something. Any poet, to resemble him in the least, would have to resemble him in that grazing closeness to the spiritual realities. If books of verse were to be indexed by lines first in importance instead of lines first in position, many of Robinson's poems would be represented several times over. This should be seen to. The only possible objection is that it could not be done by any mere hireling of the moment, but would have to be the work of someone who had taken his

impressions freely before he had any notion of their use. A particular poem's being represented several times would only increase the chance of its being located.

11   The first poet I ever sat down with to talk about poetry was Ezra Pound. It was in London in 1913. The first poet we talked about, to the best of my recollection, was Edwin Arlington Robinson. I was fresh from America and having read *The Town Down the River.* Beginning at that book I have slowly spread my reading of Robinson twenty years backward and forward, about equally in both directions.

12   I remember the pleasure with which Pound and I laughed over the fourth "thought" in

> Miniver thought and thought and thought
> And thought about it.

14   Three "thoughts" would have been "adequate" as the critical praise-word then was. There would have been nothing to complain of if it had been left at three. The fourth made the intolerable touch of poetry. With the fourth the fun began. I was taken out on the strength of our community of opinion here to be rewarded with an introduction to Miss May Sinclair, who had qualified as the patron authority on young and new poets by the sympathy she had shown them in *The Divine Fire.*

15   There is more to it than the number of the "thoughts." There is the way the last one turns up by surprise round the corner, the way the shape of the stanza is played with, the easy way the obstacle of verse is turned to advantage. The mischief is in it.

> One pauses half afraid
> To say for certain that he played—

a man as sorrowful as Robinson. His death was sad to those who knew him, but nowhere near as sad as the lifetime of poetry to which he attuned our ears. Nevertheless, I say his much-admired restraint lies wholly in his never having let grief go further than it could in play. So far shall grief go, so far shall philosophy go, so far shall confidences go, and no further. Taste may set the limit. Humor is a surer dependence.

> Once a man was there all night
> Expecting something every minute.

16   I know what the man wanted of Old King Cole. He wanted the heart out of his mystery. He was the friend who stands at the end of a poem ready in waiting to catch you by both hands with enthusiasm and drag you off your

balance over the last punctuation mark into more than you meant to say. "I understand the poem all right, but please tell me what is behind it." Such presumption needs to be twinkled at and baffled. The answer must be, "If I had wanted you to know, I should have told you in the poem."

17   We early have Robinson's word for it:

>   The games we play
>   To fill the frittered minutes of a day
>   Good glasses are to read the spirit through.

18   He speaks somewhere of Crabbe's stubborn skill. His own was a happy skill. His theme was unhappiness itself, but his skill was as happy as it was playful. There is that comforting thought for those who suffered to see him suffer. Let it be said at the risk of offending the humorless in poetry's train (for there are a few such): his art was more than playful; it was humorous.

19   The style is the man. Rather say the style is the way the man takes himself; and to be at all charming or even bearable, the way is almost rigidly prescribed. If it is with outer seriousness, it must be with inner humor. If it is with outer humor, it must be with inner seriousness. Neither one alone without the other under it will do. Robinson was thinking as much in his sonnet on Tom Hood. One ordeal of Mark Twain was the constant fear that his occluded seriousness would be overlooked. That betrayed him into his two or three books of out-and-out seriousness.

20   "Miniver Cheevy" was long ago. The glint I mean has kept coming to the surface of the fabric all down the years. Yesterday in conversation, I was using "The Mill." Robinson could make lyric talk like drama. What imagination for speech in "John Gorham"! He is at his height between quotation marks.

>   The miller's wife had waited long.
>   The tea was cold, the fire was dead.
>   And there might yet be nothing wrong
>   In how he went and what he said.
>   "There are no millers any more,"
>   Was all that she had heard him say.

21   "There are no millers any more." It might be an edict of the New Deal against processors (as we now dignify them). But no, it is of wider application. It is a sinister jest at the expense of all investors of life or capital. The market shifts and leaves them with a car-barn full of dead trolley cars. At twenty I commit myself to a life of religion. Now, if religion should go out of fashion in twenty-five years, there would I be, forty-five years old, unfitted

for anything else and too old to learn anything else. It seems immoral to have to bet on such high things as lives of art, business, or the church. But in effect, we have no alternative. None but an all-wise and all-powerful government could take the responsibility of keeping us out of gambling or of insuring us against loss once we were in.

22   The guarded pathos of "Mr. Flood's Party" is what makes it merciless. We are to bear in mind the number of moons listening. Two, as on the planet Mars. No less. No more ("No more, sir, that's enough"). One moon (albeit a moon, no sun) would have laid grief too bare. More than two would have dissipated grief entirely and would have amounted to dissipation. The emotion had to be held at a point.

> He set the jug down slowly at his feet
> With trembling care, knowing that most things break,
> And only when assured that on firm earth
> It stood, as the uncertain lives of men
> Assuredly did not—

23   There twice it gleams. Nor is it lost even where it is perhaps lost sight of in the dazzle of all those golden girls at the end of "The Sheaves." Granted a few fair days in a world where not all days are fair.

> "Well, Mr. Flood, we have the harvest moon
> Again, and we may not have many more.
> The bird is on the wing, the poet says
> And you and I have said it here before.
> Drink to the bird."

24   Poetry transcends itself in the playfulness of the toast.

25   Robinson has gone to his place in American literature and left his human place among us vacant. We mourn, but with the qualification that after all, his life was a revel in the felicities of language. And not just to no purpose. None could deplore,

> The inscrutable profusion of the Lord
> Who shaped as one of us a thing

so sad and at the same time so happy in achievement. Not for me to search his sadness to its source. He knew how to forbid encroachment. And there is solid satisfaction in a sadness that is not just a fishing for ministration and consolation. Give us immedicable woes—woes that nothing can be done for—woes flat and final. And then to play. The play's the thing. Play's the thing. All virtue in "as if."

> As if the last of days
> Were fading and all wars were done.

As if they were. As if, as if!

Robert Frost

[Contribution to *Books We Like* (1936)]

1 1 *The Odyssey* chooses itself, the first in time and rank of all romances. Palmer's translation is by all odds the best. As Lawrence in a preface to his own translation describes the author of the original, he is evidently a man much more like Palmer than like Lawrence. I can permit myself but one translation out of ten books.

2 2 *Robinson Crusoe* is never quite out of my mind. I never tire of being shown how the limited can make snug in the limitless.

3 3 *Walden* has something of the same fascination. Crusoe was cast away; Thoreau was self-cast away. Both found themselves sufficient. No prose writer has ever been more fortunate in subject than these two. I prefer my essay in narrative form. In *Walden* I get it and always near the height of poetry.

4 4 Poe's *Tales*. Here is every kind of entertainment the short story can afford, the supernatural, the horrific, pseudo-scientific, ingenious, and detective. (Every kind I should perhaps say but the character.)

5 5 *The Oxford Book of English Verse* and

6 6 Untermeyer's *Modern American and British Poetry* pretty well cover between them the poetry of our race. I am permitting myself two and one half numbers of actual verse in the ten—twenty-five per cent. That doesn't seem for the moment an undue proportion.

7 7 *The Last of the Mohicans* supplies us once for all with our way of thinking of the American Indian.

8 8 *The Prisoner of Zenda*—surely one of the very best of our modern best-sellers.

9 9 *The Jungle Book* (1st). I shall read it again as often as I can find a new child to listen to me.

10 10 Emerson's *Essays* and *Poems*—the rapture of idealism either way you have it, in prose or in verse and in brief.

Robert Frost
Key West
December 18 1934

[Introduction to Sarah Cleghorn's *Threescore* (1936)]

1   Security, security! We run in all directions for security in the game of Pussy-wants-a-corner. I find security chiefly in proper names—the thought of certain people, I mean people I can be certain of at their posts or postoffices. I am like Childe Roland on his way to the Dark Tower: I need someone pleasant to think of. They that are against us should be more than they that are for us by all present-day accounts.

> "May be true what I have heard:
> Earth's a howling wilderness
> Truculent with force and fraud."

It will not do to underestimate the relative strength of the enemy. But neither will it do to overestimate it. That, I take it, is one lesson of Grant's greatness as a general. It is necessary to keep in mind in a campaign just whom we can muster in an emergency. We in Vermont are taken care of on the north by three great ladies up the valley, three verities who can be depended on to hold Vermont true to its winter self against all summer comers. And one of these is wise and a novelist, one is mystic and an essayist, and the third is saintly and a poet. This book is about them all, but principally (and charmingly and naturally) about the poet. It is her own story of her life told with a beautiful unconsciousness of its beauty.

2   Saint, poet—*and* reformer. There is more high explosive for righteousness in the least little line of Sarah Cleghorn's poem about the children working in the mill where they could look out the window at their grown-up employers playing golf than in all the prose of our radical bound-boys pressed together under a weight of several atmospheres of revolution. The reformer has to be taken with the rest of it. And why not? Some of us have developed a habit of saying we can't stand a reformer. But we don't mean it except where the reformer is at the same time a raw convert to the latest scheme for saving the soul or the state. The last we heard of him may have been two or three fashions ago as one of the ultra-arty insisting that we join him in his minor vices at his wild parties. Now he turns up at our door to ask without ceremony—

You don't mean to say you don't love God or you don't mean to say you don't love humanity.—Don't you believe public confession is good for the soul?—Don't you believe so-and-so died a martyr to the cause of humanity?—Let me recall you to your better self.—Have you given anything any thought?

3   I don't know what makes this so nettling unless it is that it ignores so superciliously the strain we may have been under for years trying to decide between God and the Devil, between the rich and the poor (the greed of one and the greed of the other), between keeping still about our troubles and enlarging on them to the doctor and—oh, between endless other things in pairs ordained to everlasting opposition. No, it is not the reformer we object to. Nor is it yet the convert. The convert has his defense. It is the rawness, the egotism, the gross greed to take spiritual advantage of us. We have all had attempts on our self-respect of the kind, and we cringe at the memory. I have had four, one of them lately that would afford one scene in a comedy. But a reformer who has all her life long pursued the even tenor of her aspiration, is no one to resent. On the contrary she is one for me to claim friendship with and, if permitted, kindred spirit with. Pride enters into it, as may be seen.

4   Just after the great Democratic victory of 1932 I made occasion to bring the election into conversation with a Negress who had come to our door soliciting alms for a school for Negroes in the deep south.

5   "My people don't very much like the Democrats in power again," she said.

6   "Surely you aren't afraid of them anymore!"

7   "I wouldn't just say we weren't afraid of them. You wouldn't think there was much they could do. But there's small things an outsider wouldn't notice."

8   She was a poor creature, poorly clothed, but she touched her wrists with a pretty pathos for this:

9   "Here a shackle, there a shackle, and before we know it we're back in slavery."

10   "Not while Sarah Cleghorn lives in Manchester, Vermont," I answered. Then I went on to explain that Sarah Cleghorn was an abolitionist as of 1861. One of her best poems was about a Negress who personally conducted troop on troop of runaway slaves northward. Many lightly argue that since we have tolerated wage slavery and child labor, we might as well have tolerated Negro slavery. She reasons the other way round: that since we have abolished Negro slavery we are bound in logic to abolish all other slavery. She is the complete abolitionist. She has it in for race prejudice and many another ignobleness besides. Some time I intend to ask her if she isn't bent on having the world perfect at last.

11   Did I know her?

12   "Yes, very well," I said with effect.

13   I have just come indoors from boasting among the egrets of the Everglades of Florida that I was acquainted with the lady up north who by writing to the papers (see page 110) had done more than anyone else to get them free of the terrible yearly Minoan tax on the flower of their youth and beauty. I don't know what impression I made in this case. The egret standing nearest me in the water simply lifted stiffly and withdrew further into the Everglades, as unresponsive as a bank clerk with whom I should have attempted to establish credit. The fact remains that I do know one or two people who have done measurable good. And I think I have a right to speak of them when the chance offers.

14   You get some notion of Sarah Cleghorn's range of beneficence—all the way from pure black to snow white—which may sound dangerously like being an extremist—and typically a New Englander. But you have only to read to find out that she was not born a New Englander nor of wholly New England stock.

15   We can't all be judges. There must always be a thousand *ex parte* lawyers for one judge, sitting out impartial till sides have all but wiped each other out in encounter and judgment has all but pronounced itself. A philosopher may worry about a tendency that, if run out to its logical conclusion, might ruin all; but he worries only till he can make out in the confusion the particular counter tendency that is going to collide with it to the cancellation of both. Formidable equations often resolve into no more information than that nothing equals nothing. It is a common question: What has become of the alarming old tendency to come to grief from each one's minding his own business? Oh, if I remember rightly, that bumped head on into the tendency to come to grief from minding each other's business. The philosopher values himself on the inconsistencies he can contain by main force. They are two ends of a strut that keeps his mind from collapsing. He may take too much satisfaction in having once more remarked the two-endedness of things. To a saint and a reformer like Sarah Cleghorn the great importance is not to get hold of both ends, but of the right end. She has to be partisan and even a trifle grim. I heard a clergyman say she is the kind we need most of to get the world forward. Well, here we have her, her whole story from the first dawning on her in childhood of the need of goodness and mercy.

Robert Frost

[Contribution to *The Stag at Ease* (1938)]

1   I cook nothing and have never cooked anything except potatoes outdoors in wood ashes. They can be cooked without burning, but I like them with the skin burned black and hard as a shell.

    Robert Frost

[Letter to the Editor of *New Hampshire:*
A Guide to the Granite State (1938)]

1   Not a poem, I believe, in all my six books, from "A Boy's Will" to "A Further Range," but has something in it of New Hampshire. Nearly half my poems must actually have been written in New Hampshire. Every single person in my "North of Boston" was friend or acquaintance of mine in New Hampshire. I lived, somewhat brokenly to be sure, in Salem, Derry, Plymouth, and Franconia, New Hampshire, from my tenth to my forty-fifth year. Most of my time out of it I lived in Lawrance, Massachusetts, on the edge of New Hampshire, where my walks and vacations could be in New Hampshire. My first teaching was in a district school in the southern part of Salem, New Hampshire. Four of my children were born in Derry, New Hampshire. My father was born in Kingston, New Hampshire. My wife's mother was born in New Hampshire. So you see it has been New Hampshire, New Hampshire with me all the way. You will find my poems show it, I think.

The Doctrine of Excursions (1939)

1   You who are as much concerned as I for the future of Bread Loaf will agree
with me that once in so often it should be redefined if it is to be kept from de-
generating into a mere summer resort for routine education in English or
worse still for the encouragement of vain ambition in literature. We go there
not for correction or improvement. No writer has ever been corrected into
importance. Nor do we go to find a publisher or get help in finding a publisher. Bringing manuscript to Bread Loaf is in itself publication.

2   A writer can live by writing to himself alone for days and years. Sooner or
later to go on he must be read. It may well be that in appealing to the public
he has but added to his own responsibility; for now besides judging himself
he must judge his judges. For long the public received him not. Then the public received him. When were the public right? Why when the final authority
is his should he be bothered with any other? The answer is an article in the
doctrine of excursions. All we know is that the crowning mercy for an author
is publication in some form or other.

3   Undeniably the best form is a book with a reputable house at the expense
of the house. The next best is a book with a reputable house at the expense
of the author. Those two constitute publication in the first and second degrees. But there are several humbler degrees, among them the Bread Loaf
Conference. It must not be forgotten that much good poetry has never risen
above the second degree and some has undoubtedly come out in newspapers
that pay nothing for contributions. Publication in book form like this anthology of ours was not contemplated in the original scheme of Bread Loaf and
is not of the essence of the institution. It has simply been added unto us as a
reward for modesty.

4   Bread Loaf is to be regarded then as a place in Vermont where a writer can
try his effect on readers. There as out in the world he must brave the rigors
of specific criticism. He will get enough and perhaps more than enough of
good set praise and blame. He will help wear out the words "like" and "dislike." He will hear too many things compared to the disadvantage of all of
them. A handkerchief is worse than a knife because it can be cut by a knife; a

knife is worse than a stone because it can be blunted by a stone; a stone is worse than a handkerchief because it can be covered by a handkerchief; and we have been round the silly circle. All this is as it has to be where the end is a referee's decision. There is nothing so satisfactory in literature as the knock-out in prize-fighting.

5   But more than out in the world a writer has a chance at Bread Loaf of getting beyond this cavil and getting his proof of something better than approval in signs—looks, tones, manners. Many words are often but one small sign. There is the possibility of his winning through to the affections of the affectionate.

6   Beyond self-esteem and the critical opinion of others the scientist has a third proof I have envied for the artist. From the perturbation of a planet in its orbit he predicts exactly where in the sky and at what time of night another planet will be discovered. All telescopes point that way and there the new planet is. The scientist is justified of his figures. He knows he is good. He has fitted into the nature of the universe. A topical play of the eighties had in it a scene from the digging of the Hoosac Tunnel. The engineer had triangulated over the mountain and driven in shafts from opposite sides to meet each other under the middle of the mountain. It was the eleventh hour of the enterprise. There stood the engineer among the workmen in one shaft waiting to hear the workmen in the other. A gleam of pick ax broke through; a human face appeared in the face of the rock. The engineer was justified of his figures. He knew he was an engineer. He had fitted into the nature of the universe.

7   I should like to believe the poet gets an equivalent assurance in the affections of the affectionate. He has fitted into the nature of mankind. He is justified of his numbers. He has accrued friends who will even cheat for him a little and refuse to see his faults if they are not so glaring as to show through eyelids. And friends are everything. For what have we wings if not to seek friends at an elevation?

The Figure a Poem Makes (1939)

1   Abstraction is an old story with the philosophers, but it has been like a new toy in the hands of the artists of our day. Why can't we have any one quality of poetry we choose by itself? We can have in thought. Then it will go hard if we can't in practice. Our lives for it.

2   Granted no one but a humanist much cares how sound a poem is if it is only *a* sound. The sound is the gold in the ore. Then we will have the sound out alone and dispense with the inessential. We do till we make the discovery that the object in writing poetry is to make all poems sound as different as possible from each other, and the resources for that of vowels, consonants, punctuation, syntax, words, sentences, meter are not enough. We need the help of context—meaning—subject matter. That is the greatest help towards variety. All that can be done with words is soon told. So also with meters— particularly in our language where there are virtually but two, strict iambic and loose iambic. The ancients with many were still poor if they depended on meters for all tune. It is painful to watch our sprung-rhythmists straining at the point of omitting one short from a foot for relief from monotony. The possibilities for tune from the dramatic tones of meaning struck across the rigidity of a limited meter are endless. And we are back in poetry as merely one more art of having something to say, sound or unsound. Probably better if sound, because deeper and from wider experience.

3   Then there is this wildness whereof it is spoken. Granted again that it has an equal claim with sound to being a poem's better half. If it is a wild tune, it is a poem. Our problem then is, as modern abstractionists, to have the wildness pure; to be wild with nothing to be wild about. We bring up as aberrationists, giving way to undirected associations and kicking ourselves from one chance suggestion to another in all directions as of a hot afternoon in the life of a grasshopper. Theme alone can steady us down. Just as the first mystery was how a poem could have a tune in such a straightness as meter, so the second mystery is how a poem can have wildness and at the same time a subject that shall be fulfilled.

4   It should be of the pleasure of a poem itself to tell how it can. The figure a

poem makes. It begins in delight and ends in wisdom. The figure is the same as for love. No one can really hold that the ecstasy should be static and stand still in one place. It begins in delight, it inclines to the impulse, it assumes direction with the first line laid down, it runs a course of lucky events, and ends in a clarification of life—not necessarily a great clarification, such as sects and cults are founded on, but in a momentary stay against confusion. It has denouement. It has an outcome that though unforeseen was predestined from the first image of the original mood—and indeed from the very mood. It is but a trick poem and no poem at all if the best of it was thought of first and saved for the last. It finds its own name as it goes and discovers the best waiting for it in some final phrase at once wise and sad—the happy-sad blend of the drinking song.

5   No tears in the writer, no tears in the reader. No surprise for the writer, no surprise for the reader. For me the initial delight is in the surprise of remembering something I didn't know I knew. I am in a place, in a situation, as if I had materialized from cloud or risen out of the ground. There is a glad recognition of the long lost and the rest follows. Step by step the wonder of unexpected supply keeps growing. The impressions most useful to my purpose seem always those I was unaware of and so made no note of at the time when taken, and the conclusion is come to that like giants we are always hurling experience ahead of us to pave the future with against the day when we may want to strike a line of purpose across it for somewhere. The line will have the more charm for not being mechanically straight. We enjoy the straight crookedness of a good walking stick. Modern instruments of precision are being used to make things crooked as if by eye and hand in the old days.

6   I tell how there may be a better wildness of logic than of inconsequence. But the logic is backward, in retrospect, after the act. It must be more felt than seen ahead like prophecy. It must be a revelation, or a series of revelations, as much for the poet as for the reader. For it to be that there must have been the greatest freedom of the material to move about in it and to establish relations in it regardless of time and space, previous relation, and everything but affinity. We prate of freedom. We call our schools free because we are not free to stay away from them till we are sixteen years of age. I have given up my democratic prejudices and now willingly set the lower classes free to be completely taken care of by the upper classes. Political freedom is nothing to me. I bestow it right and left. All I would keep for myself is the freedom of my material—the condition of body and mind now and then to summons aptly from the vast chaos of all I have lived through.

7   Scholars and artists thrown together are often annoyed at the puzzle of

where they differ. Both work from knowledge; but I suspect they differ most importantly in the way their knowledge is come by. Scholars get theirs with conscientious thoroughness along projected lines of logic; poets theirs cavalierly and as it happens in and out of books. They stick to nothing deliberately, but let what will stick to them like burrs where they walk in the fields. No acquirement is on assignment, or even self-assignment. Knowledge of the second kind is much more available in the wild free ways of wit and art. A school boy may be defined as one who can tell you what he knows in the order in which he learned it. The artist must value himself as he snatches a thing from some previous order in time and space into a new order with not so much as a ligature clinging to it of the old place where it was organic.

8   More than once I should have lost my soul to radicalism if it had been the originality it was mistaken for by its young converts. Originality and initiative are what I ask for my country. For myself the originality need be no more than the freshness of a poem run in the way I have described: from delight to wisdom. The figure is the same as for love. Like a piece of ice on a hot stove the poem must ride on its own melting. A poem may be worked over once it is in being, but may not be worried into being. Its most precious quality will remain its having run itself and carried away the poet with it. Read it a hundred times: it will forever keep its freshness as a metal keeps its fragrance. It can never lose its sense of a meaning that once unfolded by surprise as it went.

R. F.

Boston, January 11, 1939.

[Remarks Accepting the Gold Medal of the National Institute of Arts and Letters (1939)]

1   "Have you ever thought about rewards," I was asked lately in a tone of fear for me that I might not have thought at my age. I don't know what I was supposed to think unless it was that the greatest reward of all was self-esteem. Saints like John Bunyan are all right in jail if they are sure of their truth and sincerity. But so also are many criminals. The great trouble is to be sure. A stuffed shirt is the opposite of a criminal. He cares not what he thinks of himself so long as the world continues to think well of him. The sensible and healthy live somewhere between self-approval and the approval of society. They make their adjustment without too much talk of compromise.

2   Still, an artist, however well he may fare within and without, must often feel he has to rely too heavily on self-appraisal for comfort. For twenty years the world neglected him; then for twenty years it entreated him kindly. He has to take the responsibility of deciding when the world was wrong. He can't help wishing there was some third more disinterested party such as God or Time to give absolute judgement.

> O Time whose verdicts mock our own
> The only righteous judge art thou.

3   The scientist seems to have the advantage of him in a court of larger appeal. A planet is perturbed in its orbit. The scientist stakes his reputation on the perturber's being found at a certain point in the sky at a certain time of night. All telescopes are turned that way, and sure enough, there the perturber is as bright as a button. The scientist knows he is good without being told. He has a mind and he has instruments, the extensions of mind that fit closely into the nature of the Universe. It is the same when an engineer has plotted two shafts to meet under the middle of a mountain and make a tunnel. The shafts approach each other; the workmen in one can hear the pick axes of the workmen in the other. A sudden gleam of pick ax breaks through. A human face shows in the face of the rock. The engineer is justi-

fied of his figures. He knows he has a mind. It has fitted into the nature of the Universe.

4   I should be sorry to concede the artist had no such recourse to tests of certainty at all. His hope must be that his work will prove to have fitted into the nature of people. Beyond my belief in myself, beyond another's critical opinion of me, lies this. I should like to have it that your medal is a token of my having fitted not into the nature of the Universe but in some small way at least into the nature of Americans—into their affections is perhaps what I mean. I trust you will be willing to indulge me here and let me have it so for the occasion. But whatever the medal may or may not symbolize I take it as a very great honor.

THIRTY

The Last Refinement of Subject Matter:
Vocal Imagination (1941?)

1   Ask me if I make the sound of poetry a matter of vowel and consonant sounds, a matter of alliteration and consonation, and my answer would have to be "No," but it might be any one of great many kinds of "No" all spelled exactly alike with the same vowel and consonant and yet all quite distinct. I might say:

> No, I should hardly be inclined to say that poetry was a matter of vowel and consonant sounds; or
> No, I tell you NO! Let's hear no more of that; or
> Oh no, you don't understand; or
> No, I can't hear it, no; or
> No, you wait a moment and I'll tell you.

These noes are not merely negative. In addition to being negative the first is lenient, the second is all but angry, the third is contemptuous, the fourth short and final, the fifth merely by the way and preliminary to the explanation I am about to give.

2   But don't think that because these noes are given as examples they are not to be taken seriously. I mean every one of them at once. You are to dismiss the idea that the sound of the letters in the word "No" or in any other word is the real stuff of poetry.

3   Still the point is not that so much as it is that neither is the simple negative sound of "No" the stuff of poetry. That would be too characterless, too unimaginative. It is the extra sound the "No" gets when in addition to being negative it becomes lenient, angry, contemptuous, or short and final.

4   The thing to notice is that orally in each case the "No" stands safely on its own legs alone. It can be made to convey its extra meaning without the help of any context. But in writing it is otherwise: in writing it begins to need the help of a setting of other words to determine its character. It has to take its place in a sentence, the other words of which shall act as a sort of notation to

indicate what particular "No" it is, the lenient, the angry, the scornful, or the short and final.

5   There are as many yes-tones as no-tones on our lips, I suppose, and probably more oh-tones than either. In speaking I can make the bare "Oh" express many things. In writing I have no way of making it express anything beyond exclamation except as it stands in a sentence.

6   Here we come on one of the principle uses of the sentence.

7   Poets have lamented the lack in poetry of any such notation as music has for suggesting sound. But it is there and always has been there. The sentence is the notation. The sentence is before all else just that: a notation for suggesting significant tones of voice. With the sentence that doesn't suggest significant tones of voice, poetry has no concern whatever.

7   There is place in the world to be sure for a kind of sentence like a mathematical formula that is content to convey no more meaning than belongs to a grammatical set of words. Such a sentence serves for much necessary workaday writing and also for certain over-intellectual writing that most of us find dull—for two extremes, hasty journalism and heavy philosophy. It goes toneless or in the lifeless tone of matter-of-fact statement. It has no part in poetry. No mechanical attempts to vary it by structural device can save it to poetry.

8   Once and for all the sentence that takes rank as poetry must do double duty. It will not neglect the meaning it can convey in words; but it will succeed chiefly by some meaning it conveys by tone of voice.

9   You hear the tone of lofty scorn in the first line of Yeats' "Rose of the World":

"Who dreamed that beauty passes like a dream?"

the weariness of it all in the first lines of Tennyson's "Ulysses":

"It little profits that an idle king
By this still hearth, among the barren crags,
Matched with an aged wife I mete and dole
Unequal laws unto a savage race";

the hate in Browning's "In a Cloister":

"Grrr! there go my heart's abhorrence,
Water your damned flower pots, do!"

the delight in Browning's

"The fancy I had today!"

the man's longing in Kipling's

"Put me down somewhere east of Suez where the best is like the worst."

10   Under everything in all these lines you have the metrical beat of the verse. I take that more or less as a matter of course although some of my friends don't nowadays. The writers of free verse dispense with it altogether. I'm not sure that it isn't possible to do without it. As it happens I don't do without it myself. I seem rather to want it where it is as something for the rhythm of the vocal tones to play across, to make a figure in, to make a posture in—say it as you like. It has its purpose.

11   But at the same time it is to be regarded as a danger. There is always the certainty that the voice will fall a prey to it if there is nothing worthier to engage the attention. The refuge from the deadly sing-song of the verse provided by real poetry is the tones of meaning clearly and sharply imagined and set down in black and white for the recognition of the reader. The sentence must never leave the reader in doubt for a moment as to how the voice is to be placed in it. So only will it save us from death by jingle.

12   I speak of imagination as having some part in the sound of poetry. It is everything in the sound of poetry; but not as inventor nor creator—simply as summoner. Make no mistake about the tones of speech I mean. They are the same yesterday, today, and forever. They were before words were—if anything was before anything else. They have merely entrenched themselves in words. No one invents new tones of voice. So many and no more belong to the human throat, just as so many runs and quavers belong to the throat of the cat-bird, so many to the chickadee. The imagination is no more than their summoner—the imagination of the ear.

13   It is the imagination of the eye we think oftenest of in connection with poetry. We remember the poet's injunction to poets to write with the eye on the object. We value poetry too much as it makes pictures. The imagination of the ear is more peculiarly poetical than the imaginative eye, since it deals with sound which is what poetry is before it is sight. Write with the ear to the speaking voice. Seek first in poetry concrete images of sound—concrete tone images. Poetry is a dwelling on the fact, a gloating over the fact, a luxuriating in the fact. Its first pleasure is in the fact of the voice.

14   So much for what the sounds of poetry are, where they come from and at what summons (the summons of the imaginative ear). It remains to show that not all tones of voice have the same poetical value. I am not so much afraid of vulgar tones or what might be dismissed off hand as vulgar. You never know what is vulgar till you try to see what you can carry off with thinking no evil. A scolding tone would seem to be hopeless for poetry. And yet—you never can tell. Bookish tones are surely to be avoided, such as belong to the balanced sentences, for example, and all tones that depend altogether on conjunctions and conjunctives. There are the tones of grandeur, of

sweetness, of invocation that poetry has had rather too much of. It could well get along with less for a while. There are the dull tones of plain statement which are almost no tones at all. They require no imagination in the summoning. Anybody can get them down on the page. And about half the poets are getting them down on the page by the bookfull.

15   What attests the imagination of the poet are significant tones of voice we all know and easily recognize, but can't say we have grown familiar with from having met with them in books.

16   I have gone to poets of the past for such examples of poetry as I have used for my theme. But there are poets of the present as we have all been made very much aware of late. I have decided to leave you these as material to try by my principles or try my principles by. You know their names. Which of them has no tones but those of plain statement? Which haven't tones enough for a refuge from the jingle of their verse? Which have none but the old familiar bookish tones? Which have none but the tones long established in poetry and have nothing to show that they have observing ears?

[Preface to a Selection of His Poems (1942)]

1   It would be hard to gather biography from poems of mine except as they were all written by the same person, out of the same general region north of Boston, and out of the same books, a few Greek and Latin, practically no others in any other tongue than our own. This was as it happened. To show that there was no rule about place laid down, I may point to two or three poems reminiscent of my ten years as a child in San Francisco and a few others actually written in California at the time of the Olympic games. More than a few were written in Beaconsfield and in Ryton, England, where I farmed, or rather gardened in a very small way from 1912 to 1915. My first two books were published in England by the Scotch and English, to whom I am under obligations for life for my start in life. This too was as it happened. I had on hand when I visited England the material of those two books and more than half of another. I had had poems in American magazines but not many, and my relative unsuccess with magazines had kept the idea of a book from ever entering my head. It was perhaps the boldness of my adventure among entire strangers that stirred me up to try appealing from the editors of magazines to the publishers of books.

2   I have made this selection much as I made the one from my first book, *A Boy's Will,* and my second book, *North of Boston,* looking backward over the accumulation of years to see how many poems I could find towards some one meaning it might seem absurd to have had in advance, but it would be all right to accept from fate after the fact. The interest, the pastime, was to learn if there had been any divinity shaping my ends and I had been building better than I knew. In other words could anything of larger design, even the roughest, any broken or dotted continuity, or any fragment of a figure be discerned among the apparently random lesser designs of the several poems. I had given up convictions when young from despair of learning how they were had. Nevertheless I might not have been without them. They might be turned up out of the heap by assortment. And if not convictions, then perhaps native prejudices and inclinations. I took thirty poems for *A Boy's Will* to plot a curved line of flight away from people and so back to people. For *North*

of Boston I took group enough to show the people and to show that I had for-given them for being people. The group here given brings out my inclination to country occupations. It began with a farm in the back yard in San Fran-cisco. This is no prejudice against the city. I am fond of several great cities. It is merely an inclination to country things. My favorite implements (after the pen) are the axe and the scythe, both of which besides being tools of peace have also been weapons of war. The Hungarian peasantry under Kossuth car-ried the scythe into battle in their attempt at independence from Austria, and the axle of an ancient war chariot was prolonged into a scythe at either end. In three of the poems I celebrate the axe, in one the scythe.

Robert Frost
Ripton, Vt.
July 26, 1942

[Essay on the Divine Right of Kings (1943?)]

1 We were talking about the Divine Right of a king or of anyone else who rules. A principle like that may vary in strength but even in a Democracy it never dies out. It is his right first of all to consult the highest in himself. His first answerability must be to the highest in himself, however close a second his answerability may be to his subjects and constituents. He needs the consent of the governed. But he is no sort of leader unless his pride is in providing them with something definite to consent to. Or dissent from! A ruler is distinguished by the proportions in which the two answerabilities are blended in his nature. Excess of one and he is a nobody marking time; excess of the other may bring him to the block. There can be no complaint that the rulers of our generation haven't been leaders. Roosevelt, Stalin, Hitler, Churchill, Mussolini have certainly known what they wanted the people to want.

[Contribution to 25th Anniversary Bread Loaf Booklet (1944)]

1   In my travels recently I have noticed beside the road now and then a diamond shaped sign with the picture of a run-away boy on it and the legend SLOW SCHOOL. I suppose the boy represents a truant and he is running away from school because it is too slow for him. He is an argument for "acceleration." The Bread Loaf School of English has had to accelerate somewhat to keep up with the others, but it is only temporarily, we trust. Education in English is properly a slow process of just staying around in the right company till you can speak of and handle a book in the author's presence without setting his teeth on edge. Many educated to the third degree still betray low culture by the way they bring up a book in polite conversation. The wholesale haste of eye reading may be to blame for this crudity. So also may too much reading of literature in translation. One good thing to be said in defense of poetry is that it holds the imagination down to the rate of the speaking voice. Another is that it will convince almost anyone in the long run that no translation of poetry will do: practically any book in any but your own language or languages is a closed book. The spirit moves with deliberate speed.

2   By the right company I mean such as I have visited with for 25 years at Bread Loaf: Wilfred Davison (Davy), former President Moody, Doctors Harrington, Wright and Collins, James Southall Wilson, Walter Prichard Eaton, Burges Johnson, Sidney Cox, the George Whichers, Donald Davidson, the Mirrielees sisters, John Crowe Ransom, Philip Wheelwright, Ted Greene, Hewette Joyce, Bob Gay, Theodore Morrison, Harry Owen, Henry Canby, the Colums, Marguerite Wilkinson, Elizabeth Drew, Hortense Moore and Raymond Bosworth, Fred Lewis Pattee, Perry Miller, not to mention my many friends of the Conference.

3   The wall of mountains around us and our distance from everywhere shuts us in on ourselves and makes the place cloistral enough to ensure an easy intellectual concentration. For those who have to go on serving for credits in English "under correction" (as Uriah would say) it is a most humane place to

contemplate. Indeed as I have said before, those who know enough to come here for credits ought to get a bonus credit or two extra for their taste and judgment. I know what I would do if I wanted a second language. I have never mastered a second. I would take Chaucerian as most nearly within my reach of all languages and improve a summer at Bread Loaf not learning to appreciate and admire Chaucer's greatness but merely learning to understand and pronounce his words. The quickest real bargain in education would be Chaucerian for a second language. It isn't far from English.

THIRTY-FOUR

The Four Beliefs (1944)

1   There are several beliefs that I know more about from having lived with poetry:

2   One is the self-belief, which is a knowledge that you don't want to tell other people about because you cannot prove that you know. You are saying nothing about it till you see.

3   The love belief has that shame shyness. It knows it cannot tell; only the outcome will tell.

4   And the national belief we enter into socially with each other to bring on the future of the country. We cannot tell some people what it is we believe, partly because they are too stupid to understand and partly because we are too proudly vague to explain. And anyway we are not talking until we know more, until we have something to show.

5   And then the one in every work of art. This is not of cunning and craft, mind you, but of art. You say as you go more than you even hoped you were going to be able to say, and come with surprise to an end that you foreknew only with some sort of emotion. You have believed the thing into existence.

6   And then finally there is the relationship we enter into with God to believe the future in. That by which we believe the future in is our belief in God.

ROBERT FROST

THIRTY-FIVE

[Preface to "The Death of the Hired Man" (1945)]

1 In asking me to preface my poem, Mr. Burnett's idea is no doubt to have me bring it up to date by connecting it with some such thing as National Labor Relations. I am always glad to give my poems every extraneous help possible. The employee here depicted is no longer numerous enough to be dealt with statistically by the Departments of Economics and Sociology. Nevertheless I should like to flatter myself that it is at least partly for his sake that the revolution is being brought on. In conclusion I beg to protest that it was with no such thoughts as these that the poem was written. By the way, it's in blank verse, not free verse.

The Constant Symbol (1946)

1   There seems to be some such folk saying as that easy to understand is contemptible, hard to understand irritating. The implication is that just easy enough, just hard enough, right in the middle, is what literary criticism ought to foster. A glance backward over the past convinces me otherwise. The *Iliad*, *Odyssey*, and *Aeneid* are easy. The *Purgatorio* is said to be hard. The Song of Songs *is* hard. There have been works lately to surpass all records for hardness. Some knotted riddles tell that may be worth our trouble. But hard or easy seems to me of slight use as a test either way.

2   Texture is surely something. A good piece of weaving takes rank with a picture as decoration for the wall of a studio, though it must be admitted to verge on the arty. There is a time of apprenticeship to texture when it shouldn't matter if the stuff is never made up into anything. There may be scraps of repeated form all over it. But form as a whole! Don't be shocking! The title of his first book was *Fragments*. The artist has to grow up and coarsen a little before he looks on texture as not an end in itself.

3   And there are many other things I have found myself saying about poetry, but the chiefest of these is that it is metaphor, saying one thing and meaning another, saying one thing in terms of another, the pleasure of ulteriority. Poetry is simply made of metaphor. So also is philosophy—and science, too, for that matter, if it will take the soft impeachment from a friend. Every poem is a new metaphor inside or it is nothing. And there is a sense in which all poems are the same old metaphor always.

4   Every single poem written regular is a symbol small or great of the way the will has to pitch into commitments deeper and deeper to a rounded conclusion and then be judged for whether any original intention it had has been strongly spent or weakly lost; be it in art, politics, school, church, business, love, or marriage—in a piece of work or in a career. Strongly spent is synonymous with kept.

5   We may speak after sentence, resenting judgment. How can the world know anything so intimate as what we were intending to do? The answer is the world presumes to know. The ruling passion in man is not as Viennese as

is claimed. It is rather a gregarious instinct to keep together by minding each other's business. Grex rather than sex. We *must* be preserved from becoming egregious. The beauty of socialism is that it will end the individuality that is always crying out mind your own business. Terence's answer would be all human business is my business. No more invisible means of support, no more invisible motives, no more invisible anything. The ultimate commitment is giving in to it that an outsider may see what we were up to sooner and better than we ourselves. The bard has said in effect, Unto these forms did I commend the spirit. It may take him a year after the act to confess he only betrayed the spirit with a rhymester's cleverness and to forgive his enemies the critics for not having listened to his oaths and protestations to the contrary. Had he anything to be true to? Was he true to it? Did he use good words? You couldn't tell unless you made out what idea they were supposed to be good for. Every poem is an epitome of the great predicament; a figure of the will braving alien entanglements.

6   Take the President in the White House. A study of the success of his intention might have to go clear back to when as a young politician, youthfully step-careless, he made choice between the two parties of our system. He may have stood for a moment wishing he knew of a third party nearer the ideal; but only for a moment, since he was practical. And in fact he may have been so little impressed with the importance of his choice that he left his first commitment to be made for him by his friends and relatives. It was only a small commitment anyway, like a kiss. He can scarcely remember how much credit he deserved personally for the decision it took. Calculation is usually no part in the first step in any walk. And behold him now a statesman so multifariously closed in on with obligations and answerabilities that sometimes he loses his august temper. He might as well have got himself into a sestina royal.

7   Or he may be a religious nature who lightly gets committed to a nameable church through an older friend in plays and games at the Y.M.C.A. The next he knows he is in a theological school and next in the pulpit of a Sunday wrestling with the angel for a blessing on his self-defensive interpretation of the Creed. What of his original intention now? At least he has had the advantage of having it more in his heart than in his head; so that he should have made shift to assert it without being chargeable with compromise. He could go a long way before he had to declare anything he could be held to. He began with freedom to squander. He has to acknowledge himself in a tighter and tighter place. But his courage asked for it. It would have been the same if he had gone to the North Pole or climbed Everest. All that concerns *us* is whether his story is one of conformance or performance.

8   There's an indulgent smile I get for the recklessness of the unnecessary commitment I made when I came to the first line in the second stanza of a poem in my book called "Stopping By Woods on a Snowy Evening." I was riding too high to care what trouble I incurred. And it was all right so long as I didn't suffer deflection.

9   The poet goes in like a rope skipper to make the most of his opportunities. If he trips himself he stops the rope. He is of our stock and has been brought up by ear to choice of two metres, strict iambic and loose iambic (not to count varieties of the latter). He may have any length of line up to six feet. He may use an assortment of line lengths for any shape of stanza, like Herrick in "To Daffodils." Not that he is running wild. His intention is of course a particular mood that won't be satisfied with anything less than its own fulfillment. But it is not yet a thought concerned with what becomes it. One thing to know it by: it shrinks shyly from anticipatory expression. Tell love beforehand and, as Blake says, it loses flow without filling the mould; the cast will be a reject. The freshness of a poem belongs absolutely to its not having been thought out and then set to verse as the verse in turn might be set to music. A poem is the emotion of having a thought while the reader waits a little anxiously for the success of dawn. The only discipline to begin with is the inner mood that at worst may give the poet a false start or two like the almost microscopic filament of cotton that goes before the blunt thread-end and must be picked up first by the eye of the needle. He must be entranced to the exact premonition. No mystery is meant. When familiar friends approach each other in the street both are apt to have this experience in feeling before knowing the pleasantry they will inflict on each other in passing.

10   Probably there is something between the mood and the vocal imagination (images of the voice speaking) that determines a man's first commitment to metre and length of line.

11   Suppose him to have written down "When in disgrace with Fortune and men's eyes." He has uttered about as much he has to live up to in the theme as in the form. Odd how the two advance into the open *pari passu*. He has given out that he will descend into Hades, but he has confided in no one how far before he will turn back, or whether he will turn back at all, and by what jutting points of rock he will pick his way. He may proceed as in blank verse. Two lines more, however, and he has let himself in for rhyme, three more and he has set himself a stanza. Up to this point his discipline has been the self-discipline whereof it is written in so great praise. The harsher discipline from without is now well begun. He who knows not both knows neither. His worldly commitments are now three or four deep. Between us, he was no doubt bent on the sonnet in the first place from habit, and what's the use in

pretending he was a freer agent than he had any ambition to be. He had made most of his commitments all in one plunge. The only suspense he asks us to share with him is in the theme. He goes down, for instance, to a depth that must surprise him as much as it does us. But he doesn't even have the say of how long his piece will be. Any worry is as to whether he will outlast or last out the fourteen lines—have to cramp or stretch to come out even—have enough bread for the butter or butter for the bread. As a matter of fact, he gets through in twelve lines and doesn't know quite what to do with the last two.

12   Things like that and worse are the reason the sonnet is so suspect a form and has driven so many to free verse and even to the novel. Many a quatrain is salvaged from a sonnet that went agley. Dobson confesses frankly to having changed from one form to another after starting: "I intended an Ode, And it turned to a Sonnet." But he reverses the usual order of being driven from the harder down to the easier. And he has a better excuse for weakness of will than most, namely, Rose.

13   Jeremiah, it seems, has had his sincerity questioned because the anguish of his lamentations was tamable to the form of twenty-two stanzas for the twenty-two letters of the alphabet. The Hebrew alphabet has been kept to the twenty-two letters it came out of Egypt with, so the number twenty-two means as much form as ever.

14   But there they go again with the old doubt about law and order. (The communist looks forward to a day of order without law, bless his merciful heart.) To the right person it must seem naïve to distrust form as such. The very words of the dictionary are a restriction to make the best of or stay out of and be silent. Coining new words isn't encouraged. We play the words as we find them. We make them do. Form in language is such a disjected lot of old broken pieces it seems almost as non-existent as the spirit till the two embrace in the sky. They are not to be thought of as encountering in rivalry but in creation. No judgment on either alone counts. We see what Whitman's extravagance may have meant when he said the body was the soul.

15   Here is where it all comes out. The mind is a baby giant who, more provident in the cradle than he knows, has hurled his paths in life all round ahead of him like playthings given—data so-called. They are vocabulary, grammar, prosody, and diary, and it will be too bad if he can't find stepping stones of them for his feet wherever he wants to go. The way will be zigzag, but it will be a straight crookedness like the walking stick he cuts himself in the bushes for an emblem. He will be judged as he does or doesn't let this zig or that zag project him off out of his general direction.

16   Teacher or student or investigator whose chance on these defenseless lines

may seize, your pardon if for once I point you out what ordinarily you would point me out. To some it will seem strange that I should have written my verse regular all this time without knowing till yesterday that it was from fascination with this constant symbol I celebrate. To the right person it will seem lucky; since in finding out too much too soon there is danger of arrest. Does anyone believe I would have committed myself to the treason-reason-season rhyme-set in my "Reluctance" if I had been blasé enough to know that these three words about exhausted the possibilities? No rhyming dictionary for me to make me face the facts of rhyme. I may say the strain of rhyming is less since I came to see words as phrase-ends to countless phrases just as the syllables *ly, ing,* and *ation* are word-ends to countless words. Leave something to learn still later. We'd have lost most of our innocence by forty anyway even if we never went to school a day.

TO THE RIGHT PERSON
Fourteen Lines
In the one state of ours that is a shire
There is a District Schoolhouse I admire—
As much as anything for situation.
There are few institutions standing higher
This side the Rockies in my estimation—
Two thousand feet above the ocean level.
It has two entries for co-education.
But there's a tight-shut look to either door
And to the windows of its fenestration
As if to say mere knowledge was the devil,
And this school wasn't keeping any more,
Unless for penitents who took their seat
Upon its doorsteps as at Mercy's feet
To make up for a lack of meditation.

Speaking of Loyalty (1948)

1   Charlie Cole and I, and George Whicher, are just back from having inaugurated the first president of a brand new college [Marlboro]. The extenuating
circumstance is that it is a seedling from Amherst College. The chief event of
the occasion for me was the history of the founding of Amherst College as
told by Charlie Cole, and the analogy he drew between the shoe-string start
of this new college on a mountain in Vermont and the shoe-string start of
Amherst College a hundred and so many years ago. My ear is always cocked
for anything democratic these days, and the most democratic thing I know
about America is shoe-string starts.

2   I don't know whether or not they have them in other countries to compare
with ours, but they move me—whether of an enterprise or of an individual,
of a person—these shoe-string starts. I read the obituaries in the *Times* and
the *Tribune* for the stories of them.

3   At the same place, Marlboro College, our national friend—our Vermont
lady of the manor—Dorothy Canfield Fisher made an attempt to define democracy in other terms. She would have it that Vermont, anyway, had always
had a classless society, whether Massachusetts had or not, or New Hampshire
had or not. And her proof of it was that the wife of the first governor of Vermont, Governor Chittenden, always cooked the meal before she sat down at
the table with the guests from New Haven and Boston to eat it. And Dorothy
Canfield insisted that was still the Vermont way of life. I'm only a bastard
Vermonter, and so I don't know. (I had that from Reed Powell [of Harvard
Law School] once. He told me I was only a bastard Vermonter. I'm really a
Californian.)

4   I'm here in a sort of grand bath of loyalties. And I'd like to say a little bit in
connection with this—the founding of this new college. There someone is
starting a new thing to be loyal to. And the one starting it, the president we
inaugurated, was of the class, I think, of 1917, Walter Hendricks. He was a
Bond Prize winner. I sat on the platform here in 1917 when his oration won
the Bond Prize, an oration on "Adventures in Education," and right there he
set out to establish something new to be loyal to.

5   You often wonder about that. There are talkers abroad who confuse the

word loyalty, make confusion with the word loyalty. They use Emerson and they use Josiah Royce to prove that you can be as loyal as Benedict Arnold or Aaron Burr, we'll say, and still be a loyal person. Loyal to something else, that's all they mean. The leading article in the *Harper's Magazine* a month or two ago was written to prove that. I heard a speech like that here many years ago confusing the loyalties. There is loyalty to chemistry, loyalty to physics, loyalty to geography, loyalty to history, and just incidentally, there might be loyalty to Amherst College and, more incidentally still, loyalty to the United States of America. The only hitch is that the United States is in a stronger position than chemistry, physics, or history to compel loyalty.

6   Most confusing of all there is loyalty to the next thing ahead of you.

> Heartily know
> When half-gods go,
> The gods arrive.

Emerson was the original heretic—the villain of the piece. But you have to ask yourself (without any help from semantics), "What is the meaning of loyalty to the common ordinary person, to me, for instance?"

7   I had a questionnaire the other day from an editor. He asked, "What in your opinion is the present state of middle-brow literature in America?" That was new slang to me. I'd got behind a little bit, being off in the country. I hadn't heard of "middle-brow" before. What he meant to say was, "You old skeezix, what's the present state of your own middle-brow stuff?" There was something invidious, I am sure, in that. But right away I thought of a way to use it, not here but in verse, in writing. You make it like this:

> High-brow, low brow,
> Middle-brow, and no brow.

There is a refrain for the next poem.

> High-brow, low brow,
> Middle-brow, and no brow.

8   Now what is the middle-brow attitude toward loyalty? There's the high-brow attitude—that is the one I speak of—Josiah Royce's and Ralph Waldo Emerson's. That is loyalty, not to your attachment, but to your attractions. The next one is your concern—let's see what comes next—who's the next lady?

> Heartily know
> When half-gods go,
> The quarter-gods arrive.

Emerson says the gods arrive, the whole gods, but you see we don't know that for sure. The loyalty as he defines it could be the loyalty of a quisling. That's loyalty too, to the next thing. But what's my own poor middle-brow, or low-brow notion of loyalty—not no brow, I won't grant that? . . . By the way, I've got a poem I'm going to write about that some day. It begins something like this. It's about the girl Hanno—I don't want to entertain you with too much scholarship, but about the girl Hanno and his sailors captured on the coast of Africa, down the Gold Coast, outside the Gates. It's one of those old Polybius stories. And the poem should begin like this:

> She had no brow but a mind of her own,
> She wanted the sailors to let her alone;
> She didn't like sailors, she didn't like men,
> So they had to shut her up in a pen.

And so on, offhand. They found her so incorrigible, or whatever you call it, that they got sick of it in the end. She scratched and bit, I suppose; so they skinned her alive and took her skin back to Carthage and hung it up to Astarte.

9   Well, to my loyalty question again. When someone asked a mother what service her son had been in, she answered proudly, "In the Intelligentsia." That's the high-brow of it. Nobody can escape it—it's everywhere. I was looking up "potatoes" in the *Columbia Encyclopedia*—I don't know whether you know the great book—but I was looking up "potato" and I stumbled onto "poetry." You know I write verse? I had never read about poetry before, and so I stopped and read about it. And this is what I read. (The same high-brow stuff. I wonder who wrote it. I should like to catch him before I cool off. He put it like this as if to embarrass me in particular.) He said: "Poetry is largely a matter of rhythm and diction; meaning is not essential, and by many is considered detrimental." I quote from memory.

10   Well, when Dorothy Canfield talked about a classless society in Vermont, you and I know how to shade it—into more or less classless. But there are these classes apparently, anyway: high-brow, low-brow, middle-brow, and no brow. And my view, whatever it is—I suppose it's somewhere between middle and low—about loyalty is just the plain one of her pride in Vermont. It pleases me, for instance, that Vermont after litigation for a hundred years has established it that New Hampshire has no right to tax the wharves of the seaports (or should we say riverports?) on the Merrimack River, on her side of the river. It took over a hundred years of litigation to establish that, and even now the line between the two states has to be re-perambulated every seven

years so as to keep the feeling open. That's the national feeling for you! That's the patriotism! That's the loyalty on both sides of the river.

11   A very high official in California, almost the highest, I guess the highest, said to me as a renegade native son—he said, "Why did you leave California?" I told him, "I went out very young. I was carried out screaming." That made it all right. I was on the spot, but I got out all right.

12   And right here and now I am looking at somebody who is watching me, too. He's from Dartmouth. And he's wondering how I straighten all this out with Dartmouth when I get back there. I remember once, one of the first times I appeared here, years ago, back in 1916 it was, that one of the faculty members, my fellows-to-be, said to me, "From Dartmouth!" he said. "I never saw a Dartmouth man yet who didn't deserve to be shot." We began like that. I was in that transition stage—it's one of the problems of life—that transition between one loyalty and another, between an attraction and an attachment.

13   How do you get from an attachment to follow an attraction? It ought to be painful to you, it ought to be, if you're any good. It ought not to be easy. You ought not to do it cheerfully, lightly, the way Emerson talked of doing it. He didn't do it in practice. I know people who do it in practice, however, on his advice. The loyalty I'm speaking of—I don't know whether I'm permitted here to deal with it in written words of my own—I've written a great deal about it; once away back when I was very young in a stanza I'll venture to say to you.

> Ah, when to the heart of man
> Was it ever less than a treason
> To go with the drift of things,
> To yield with a grace to reason,
> To bow and accept the end
> Of a love or a season?

14   Even a season—that pain of the end of summer—is in it for me, the person, the place, friendship, parting is such sweet sorrow, and so on. One of the poems I'll say has to do with the breaking off, with the cost of breaking off with one attachment to form another. And then I'll say a couple of short ones just to wind up and say goodbye.

15   [Mr. Frost then recited "The Gift Outright" (*Poems*, p. 399), which he called "a history of the United States in a dozen lines of blank verse."]

16   And that, I take it, is the whole thing. Lately I've been thinking more and more about it. All there is is belonging and belongings; belonging and having belongings. You belong and I belong. The sincerity of their belonging is all I

have to measure people by. I hate to take great names in vain, but I am tempted to call some men quislings that perhaps some of you would not like to hear me call quislings. Men in great places. I can't quite take them. My namesake anyway, Robert Lee, never came up to Washington to curry favor with those that had licked him. He sawed wood. That was the only thing for him to do when beaten.

17   You have to ask yourself in the end, how far will you go when it comes to changing your allegiance.

18   [In conclusion Mr. Frost recited "One Step Backward Taken" (*Steeple Bush*, p. 6), remarking: "So many of my poems have Amherst memories. This one remembers the time of the big flood, when I set out to come to see Mr. Pease inaugurated here and didn't get here." Next "Departmental" (*Poems*, p. 330): "I wrote this in entire detachment. . . . And you can't go looking into it with a Freudian eye for anything that's eating me. It's about an ant, A-N-T, that I met in Florida." And finally "A Considerable Speck" (*Poems*, p. 411): "This one has some of my animosities in it—buried, you know. Somebody said I didn't have to talk politics, they shone out of me."]

THIRTY-EIGHT

[Preface to *A Masque of Mercy* (1947)]

1   Robert Frost seems fated to keep on till he has pretty well covered New England, its stone walls, birches, belilaced cellar holes, its characters and weather. Now in this *Masque of Mercy* and his last year's *Masque of Reason* the Bible is taken care of. The two are intended to be brought into juxtaposition some time under the title TWO NEW ENGLAND BIBLICALS.

A Romantic Chasm (1948)

1   Having a book in London is not quite the same thing to-day as it was in 1913 when I had my first book there or anywhere—half a lifetime and two wars ago. To be sure by 1913 I had already had it from Kipling that I was hopelessly hedged from the elder earth with alien speech. But hearing then I heard not. I was young and heedless. My vitality shed discouragement as the well-oiled feathers of a healthy duck shed wetness. And to be merely hedged off was no great matter. What was a hedge to the poacher in my blood of a shiny night in the season of the year? It took an American, a friend, Henry L. Mencken, to rouse me to a sense of national differences. My pedantry would be poor and my desert small with the educated if I could pretend to look unscared into the gulf his great book has made to yawn between the American and English languages.

2   I wish Edward Thomas (that poet) were here to ponder gulfs in general with me as in the days when he and I tired the sun down with talking on the footpaths and stiles of Leddington and Ryton. I should like to ask him if it isn't true that the world is in parts and the separation of the parts as important as the connection of the parts. Isn't the great demand for good spacing? But now I do not know the number of his mansion to write him so much as a letter of inquiry. The mansions so many would probably be numberless. Then I must leave it to Jack Haines in Gloucester to tell me frankly if the gulf in word or idiom has been seriously widening since the night when to illustrate our talk about the internationality of ferns, he boosted me up a small cliff to see by matchlight a spleenwort he knew of there.

3   The Dea knows (as we still say in New England) I would go to any length short of idolatry to keep Great Britain within speaking, or at least shouting, distance of America in the trying times seen ahead. I might not care to go for a hero myself, but I could perhaps persuade some Mark Curtius of our race to leap into the gulf in the forum for me and close it as much as it was thought needful. Anyway I might be tempted to enlist with the forlorn hope who would sacrifice all the words in both languages except a very limited few

we could agree on as meaning the same in both; only with the proviso that I should be drawn on the committee for vocabulary where I could hold out for certain favorites for my own use, such as quackery for remedies too unorthodox, boustrophedon for a more scientific eye-reading (if science is really in earnest about advancing the humanities), ornery for the old-fashioned colonial pronunciation of ordinary with only one accent. And there are other good words I should have to consult Ivor Brown about before giving them up. Sursanure for instance for the way my wounds heal after cruel criticism.

4   It is beyond idealism of mine to think of closing the gulf so tight as to embarrass the beneficiaries of it on either verge. The Mother Country will hardly deny having profited in several ways by American independence in business and government. May she profit more. For me I should hate to miss the chance for exotic charm my distance overseas might lend me. Charm may be too strong a word. Suppose American had got as far away from English as present day English is from Chaucerian, or at least Elizabethan; obviously my verse by being in American would automatically, without mental expense on my part, be raised to the rank of having to be annotated. It might be advertised as with glossary. It might be studied.

5   I should surely hesitate to squeeze the Atlantic out from between the two continents lest it should raise the tide too high for ports in the Pacific to adjust their wharves to the change.

6   But I mustn't talk myself entirely out of respect for the gulf. I don't doubt its awesome reality. Still I begin to wonder if it is anything more than a "romantic chasm" of poetry and slang.

7   If that is a question, Phoebus replied (and touched my trembling ears), I can support you in your wild Coleridgian surmise. The estrangement in language is pretty much due to the very word-shift by metaphor you do your best to take part in daily so as to hold your closest friend off where you can "entertain her always as a stranger"—with the freshness of a stranger. It often looks dangerously like aberration into a new dialect. But it is mostly back and forth in the same place like the jumping of a grasshopper whose day's work gets him nowhere. And even when it is a word-drift, which is a chain of word-shifts all in one direction, it is nothing but that an average ingenuity with figures of speech can be counted on to keep up with, or in half a jiffy overtake. You are both free peoples so used to your freedom that you are not interested in talking too much about what you are free from. Your pride is in what you dare to take liberties with, be it word, friend, or institution. In the beginning was the word, to be sure, very sure, and a solid basic comfort it remains in situ, but the fun only begins with the spirited when you treat the word as a

point of many departures. There is risk in the play. But if some of the company get lost in the excitement, charge it up to proving the truth of chapter and verse in the Gospel according to Saint Mark, although the oracle speaking is Delphic. Remember the future of the world may depend on your keeping in practice with each other's quips and figures.

[Unpublished Contribution to *Understanding Poetry* (1950)]

1   The more trouble that can be shown to have been had with a poem the better the poem—anyhow for school purposes. I never had as much trouble with any poem I didn't reject as I have had in the last few years with that idea. I can't decide what there is to it. Yeats once told me he was nine hours over "The Song of the Wandering Aengus" sweating blood and chewing the pencil. I can well believe he tortured himself longer over some of his later poems. We learn from the Pseudodoxia that the bear is born shapeless and is licked (with the tongue) into shape by the mother. One of the giants is said to have been his mother's favorite because he cost her more keen pangs than her other children. I won't deny I have worried quite a number of my poems into existence. But my sneaking preference remains for the ones I have carried through like the stroke of a racquet, club, or headsman's axe. It is only under pressure from friends that I can consent to come out into the open and expose myself in a weakness so sacred and in the present trend of criticism so damaging. When I look into myself for the agony I am supposed to lay claim to as an artist it has to be over the poems that went wrong and came to grief without coming to an end; and they made me less miserable than I deserved when I discovered that though lost they were not entirely lost: I could and did quite freely quote lines and phrases of them from memory. I never wrote a poem for practice: I always extended for the best yet. But what I failed with I learned to charge up to practice after the fact. Now if I had only cherished my first drafts along with my baby shoes to bear me out in all this I should be more comfortable off in a world of suspicion. My word will be more or less taken for it that I played certain poems through without fumbling a sentence: such as for example "November Days," "The Mountain," "After Apple-Picking," "The Woodpile," "Desert Places," "The Gift Outright," "The Lovely Shall Be Choosers," "Directive." With what pleasure I remember their tractability. They have been the experience I couldn't help referring for more of—I trust I may say without seeming to put on inspired airs.

2   Then for a small chaser of the low-down under head, perhaps of curiosa I

might confess the trade secret that I wrote the third line of the last stanza in "Stopping By Woods" in such a way as to call for another stanza when I didn't want another stanza and didn't have another stanza in me but with great presence of mind and a sense of what a good boy I was I instantly struck the line out and made my exit with a repeat end. I left "The Ingenuities of Debt" lying around nameless for forty years because I couldn't find a fourth line to suit me. A friend, a famous poet, saw it in 1913 and wasn't so much disturbed by my bad fourth line as he was by the word "tesselation" further on. The same famous poet did persuade me to omit a line or two from "The Death of the Hired Man" and wanted me to omit the lines "Home is the place where when you have to go they have to take you in." The last three lines of "Nothing Gold Can Stay" were once entirely different. A lady in Rochester, New York has I think the earlier version. I haven't. "Birches" is two fragments soldered together so long ago I have forgotten where the joint is.

FORTY-ONE

[Letter to the American Booksellers' Association (1950)]

1   To the American Booksellers Association:

2   The first thing I do in any town I come to is ask if it has a bookstore. My first question at any college I visit is the same: Has it a bookstore to supplement with trade books (not just text books) the pleasures of the department of Literature? Furthermore I do all my thinking about economics and politics from the very satisfactory middle position bookstores and publishers occupy between me and the public. It may add to my prejudice in favor of bookstores that daughters of mine founded and once ran the Open Book in Pittsfield Mass.

    Sincerely yours

    Robert Frost

March 26 1950

in absentia

FORTY-TWO

[Contribution to *The World's Best* (1950)]

1   It would be a very false pose for me to pretend to know what I have done best. Any choice I made would mean little or nothing an hour after I had made it. Every new moon I could get up something entirely new. By the time my friend Whit Burnett had completed all the anthologies he could think of, I should have been in them with nearly everything I ever wrote. After all, what I have published represents a pretty strict essential selection as it is in my seven or eight books. But if I may be permitted to put forward a few that I have lately been looking fondly back over as deserving more attention than they get, let me seize the chance to name these.

     Robert Frost

[Poetry and School (1951)]

1   Why poetry is in school more than it seems to be outside in the world, the children haven't been told. They must wonder.

        . . .

2   The authorities that keep poetry in school may be divided into two kinds, those with a conscientious concern for it and those with a real weakness for it. They are easily told apart.

        . . .

3   School is founded on the invention of letters and numbers. The inscription over every school door should be the rhyme A B C and One Two Three. The rest of education is apprenticeship and for me doesn't belong in school

        . . .

4   The chief reason for going to school is to get the impression fixed for life that there is a book side to everything.

        . . .

5   We go to college to be given one more chance to learn to read in case we haven't learned in High School. Once we have learned to read the rest can be trusted to add itself unto us.

        . . .

6   The way to read a poem in prose or verse is in the light of all the other poems ever written. We may begin anywhere. We *duff* into our first. We read that imperfectly (thoroughness with it would be fatal), but the better to read the second. We read the second the better to read the third, the third the better to read the fourth, the fourth the better to read the fifth, the fifth the better to read the first again, or the second if it so happens. For poems are not meant to be read in course any more than they are to be made a study of. I once made a resolve never to put any book to any use it wasn't intended for by its author. Improvement will not be a progression but a widening circulation. Our instinct is to settle down like a revolving dog and make ourselves at home among the poems, completely at our ease as to how they should be taken. The same people will be apt to take poems right as know how to take

a hint when there is one and not to take a hint when none is intended. Theirs is the ultimate refinement.

. . .

7   We write in school chiefly because to try our hand at writing should make us better readers.

. . .

8   Almost everyone should almost have experienced the fact that a poem is an idea caught fresh in the act of dawning.

. . .

9   Also that felicity can't be fussed into existence.

. . .

10   Also that there is such a thing as having a moment. And that the great thing is to know a moment when you have one.

. . .

11   Also to know what Catullus means by *mens animi*.

. . .

12   Also to know that poetry and prose too regarded as poetry is the renewal of words.

. . .

13   Emotion emoves a word from its base for the moment by metaphor, but often in the long run even on to a new base. The institution, the form, the word, have regularly or irregularly to be renewed from the root of the spirit. That is the creed of the true radical.

. . .

14   Emotions must be dammed back and harnessed by discipline to the wit mill, not just turned loose in exclamations. No force will express far that isn't shut in by discipline at all the pores to jet at one outlet only. Emotion has been known to ooze off.

. . .

15   Better readers, yes, and better writers too, if possible. Certainly not worse writers as many are made by being kept forever at it with the language (not to say jargon) of criticism and appreciation. The evil days will come soon enough, and we shall have no pleasure in them, when we shall have dried up into nothing but abstractions. The best educated person is one who has been matured at just the proper rate. Seasoned but not kiln dried. The starch thickening has to be stirred in with slow care. The arteries will harden fast enough without being helped. Too many recent poems have been actually done in the language of evaluation. They are too critical in spirit to admit of further criticism.

. . .

16   And this constant saying what amounts to no more than variations on the theme of "I don't like this and I do like that" tends to aesthetic Puritanism. "For goodness' sake," said one teacher to a class, "write for a change about what you are neither for nor against." When one bold boy asked if there could be any such thing, he was told he had flunked the course.

· · ·

17   The escape is to action in words: to stories, plays, scenes, episodes, and incidents.

· · ·

18   Practice of an art is more salutary than talk about it. There is nothing more composing than composition.

· · ·

19   We were enjoined of old to learn to write now while young so that if we ever had anything to say later we would know how to say it. All there is to learning to write or talk is learning how to have something to say.

· · ·

20   Our object is to say something that *is* something. One teacher once said that it was something at once valid and sensational with the accent on both. Classmates punish us for failure better than the teachers by very dead silence or exchanging glances at our expense.

· · ·

21   One of the dangers of college to anyone who wants to stay a human reader (that is to say a humanist) is that he will become a specialist and lose his sensitive fear of landing on the lovely too hard. (With beak and talon.)

· · ·

22   Another danger nowadays to sensitiveness is getting inured to translations. The rarity of a poem well brought over from one language into another should be a warning. Some translation of course in course for utility. But never enough to get broken to it. For self assurance there should always be a lingering unhappiness in reading translations.

· · ·

23   The last place along the line where books are safely read as they are going to be out in the world in polite society is usually in so-called Freshman English. There pupils are still treated as if not all of them were going to turn out scholars.

· · ·

24   The best reader of all is one who will read, can read, no faster than he can hear the lines and sentences in his mind's ear as if aloud. Frequenting poetry has slowed him down by its metric or measured pace.

· · ·

25   The eye reader is a barbarian. So also is the writer for the eye reader, who needn't care how badly he writes since he doesn't care how badly he is read.

· · ·

26   It is one thing to think the text and be totally absorbed in it. There is however an ascendancy in the mood to spare that can also think ABOUT the text. From the induced parallel current in the mind over and above the text the notes are drawn that we so much resent other people's giving us because we want the fun of having them for ourselves.

· · ·

27   A B C is letters. One Two Three is numbers—mathematica. What marks verse off from prose is that it talks letters in numbers. Numbers is a nickname for poetry. Poetry plays the rhythms of dramatic speech on the grid of meter. A good map carries its own scale of miles.

· · ·

28   For my pleasure I had as soon write free verse as play tennis with the net down.

[Unfinished Preface to an Unpublished Collection of Poems by Hervey Allen (1951)]

1   The course of true poetry is from more ethereal than substantial to more substantial than ethereal. What begins lyric may be counted on if not broken off by death or business to end epic. By pure poetry some would seem to mean poetry purely not substantial at all. That's an extravagance of theory. But where has there ever been any such thing with success? It may have been tried for the purpose of sinning with originality. The result if any would be of scientific rather than esthetic interest. Such notion relegates to the realm where in the cyclotron nothing is perceptibly becoming something. That would be funny if it wasn't wicked. The surest thing we know is that the scale of soul is not quadruple, none, some, more, most, but eternally triple, merely some, more, most. Nothing can be done with nothing. Nothing but weight can put on weightiness. The most diaphanous wings carry a burden of pollen from flower to flower. No song without a burden.

2   What begins as lyric may be counted on if not broken off by death or business to end as epic. The principle was never better exemplified than in the fine poems of Hervey Allen and through the years to a book heard round the world it was translated from admiration into so many languages. The book was a novel in prose but only a poet could have written it and its very name rang with poetry. Unquestionably it is best regarded as just one more poem on top of all his others, longer than all the rest put together, an epic that had come in the disguise of prose to get past our modern prejudice against the epic. Hervey Allen would have wanted it taken as part and parcel of his life in poetry. He would live to regret it in the Elysian fields if it wasn't.

[Contribution to *The Tufts Weekly* (1952)]

1   Professor Charles Fay invited me to read the Phi Beta Kappa poem at Tufts thirty seven years ago and so began this career for me of reading poetry in public and looking to colleges for critical and financial support. I read him three poems at the time and have been reading poems at Tufts ever since. He was the one in those days as Professors John Holmes and Harold Blanchard are the special ones at Tufts today willing to risk the live bard on undergraduates. What the idea was or is nobody has yet told: possibly to test the judgement the young are supposed to have acquired from the long harsh study of the dead-sure reputations of the past; or simply to entertain them at an intellectual level, though for no credit toward a degree—to give them as it were a gay flyer in the insecurities of the moment. We should all owe Tufts much for pioneering thus somewhat out of bounds.

The Hear-Say Ballad (1953)

1   "An ordinary song or ballad that is the delight of the common people cannot fail to please all such readers as are not unqualified for the entertainment by their affectation or their ignorance."

2   Thus Addison with his challenge two hundred odd years ago and it might be Mrs. Flanders speaking today. We are defied not to love ballads on pain of being thought what Addison says. Balladry belongs to the none too literate and its spirit, and probably the spirit of all poetry, is safest in the keeping of the none too literate—people who know it by heart where it can weather and season properly. Ballads lead their life in the mouths and ears of men by hearsay like bluebirds and flickers in the nest holes of hollow trees. But that's no reason specimens shouldn't be brought in and brought to book now and then for sport and scholarship. We have a right to satisfy our curiosity as to what variants they may have been running wild into while our backs were turned. We can't touch their existence as a breed either to increase or destroy them. Nothing we do can. Trout have to be killed carefully so as not to exterminate them; have even to be fished out and multiplied artificially in captivity for re-stocking their own brooks. Ballads are different. Child hunted them, Mrs. Flanders hunts them; and they have the vitality to stay game at large, not to say gamey. You won't see the ballads of this book going back from here in print to alter the versions of the singers they were found on. No patronage of ours will smile them out of using "fee" for a rhyme word, "lily-white hands" for beauty, and lords and ladies for goodness knows what away off here three thousand miles across the ocean and after three hundred years of democracy. Their singers ought in consistency to be equally excited over the coronation and the inauguration that are in conjunction this graceful year of nineteen hundred and fifty-three.

3   One word more to speed the launching enterprise.

4   The voice and ear are left at a loss what to do with the ballad till supplied with the tune it was written to go with. That might be the definition of a true ballad to distinguish it from a true poem. A ballad does not or should not supply its own way of being uttered. For tune it depends on the music of

music—a good set score. Unsung it stays half lacking—as Mrs. Flanders knows full well. She has been at the same pains to recruit singers to sing the ballads for her on the stage as to collect the ballads. It is always interesting to watch how lowly the thing may lapse and still be poetry for the right people. It may flaw in metre, syntax, logic and sense. It may seem to be going to pieces, breaking up, but it is only as the voice breaks with emotion.

The Prerequisites (1954)

1   Some sixty years ago a young reader ran into serious trouble with the blind last stanza of a poem otherwise perfectly intelligible. The interest today might be in what he then did about it. He simply left it to shift for itself. He might see to it if he ever saw it again. He guessed he was no more anxious to understand the poem than the poem was to be understood.

2   He might have gone to college for help. But he had just left college to improve his mind if he had any. Or he might have gone to Asia. The whole poem smacked of Asia. He suspected a whole religion behind it different from the one he was brought up to. But as he was no traveler except on foot he must have gone by way of the Bering Strait when frozen over and that might have taken him an epoch from East to West as it had the Indians from West to East.

3   The poem was called "Brahma" and he was lilting along on such lines as the following in easy recognition:

> They reckon ill who leave me out
> When me they fly I am the wings.
> I am the doubter and the doubt
> And I the hymn the Brahmin sings.

which was all very pretty. For Brahma he naturally read God—not the God of the Old Testament nor of the New either, but near enough. Though no special liberal he valued himself on his tolerance of heresy in great thinkers. He could always lend himself to an unsound idea for the duration of the piece and had been even heard to wish people would cling to their heresies long enough for him to go and tell on them.

4   Success in taking figures of speech is as intoxicating as success in making figures of speech. It had to be just when he was flushed with having held his own with the poem so far and was thinking "good easy man" "What a good boy am I" that the disaster happened. The words were still Brahma's:

> The strong gods pine for my abode
> And pine in vain the sacred seven

> But thou meek lover of the good
> Find me and turn thy back on Heaven.

5   There he blacked out as if he had bumped his head and he only came to dazed. I remember his anger in asking if anybody had a right to talk like that. But he wasn't as put out as he let on to be. He didn't go back on poetry for more than the particular poem or on that for more than the time being. His subconscious intention was to return on it by stealth some day if only it would stay in print till he was ready for it. All was he didn't want the wrong kind of help. The heart sinks when robbed of the chance to see for itself what a poem is all about. Any immediate preface is like cramming the night before an examination. Too late, too late! Any footnote while the poem is going is too late. Any subsequent explanation is as dispiriting as the explanation of a joke. Being taught poems reduces them to the rank of mere information. He was sure the Muse would thank him for reserving a few of her best for being achieved on the spur of the moment.

6   Approach to the poem must be from afar off, even generations off. He should close in on it on converging lines from many directions like the divisions of an army upon a battlefield.

7   A poem is best read in the light of all the other poems ever written. We read A the better to read B (we have to start somewhere; we may get very little out of A). We read B the better to read C, C the better to read D, D the better to go back and get something more out of A. Progress is not the aim, but circulation. The thing is to get among the poems where they hold each other apart in their places as the stars do.

8   And if he stubbornly stayed away from college and Asia (he hated to be caught at his age grooming his brains in public) perhaps in time college and Asia, even the Taj Mahal, might come to him with the prerequisites to that poem and to much else not yet clear.

9   Well, it so happened. For the story has a happy ending. Not fifty years later when the poem turned up again he found himself in a position to deal with all but two lines of it. He was not quite satisfied that the reference to "strong gods," plural, was fair poetry practice. Were these Titans or Yidags or, perish the thought, Olympians?—Oh no! not Olympians. But he now saw through the "meek lover of the good" who sounded so deceptively Christian. His meekness must have meant the perfect detachment from ambition and desire that can alone rescue us from the round of existence. And the "me" worth turning "thy back on Heaven" for must of course be Nirvana—the only nothing that is something. He had grown very fastidious about not calling the round of existence a wheel. He was a confirmed symbolist.

[Message to the Poets of Japan (1954)]

1   This is looking towards you across 3000 miles of land and twice as many of water all in one flight unless I put down in San Francisco to make a fresh start from the city I was born in. Poetry is what makes you think of me and poetry is what makes me think of you. We aspire towards each other in the arts. But our aim is not soon to be lost in each other. We must always remember that a poet exists only by his difference from any other poet. He can be nobody's repetition. Our differences must be maintained even at the risk of their sometimes becoming acute and sanguinary. I do not change my little watch for every big clock it doesn't agree with. We must be brave but before all else brave about our differences to see them through to some real achievement. I have been slow to learn but it has not taken me all these eighty years to find out. An instinct told me long ago that I had to be national before I was international. I must be personal before I can hope to be interestingly interpersonal. There must first be definite nations for the world sentiment to flourish between. You may be more international than I am. I wish I were international enough to be speaking in Japanese the friendship some of you have made me feel by your writing. And I wish I could read in the original the Japanese poetry I have admired even as it was in translation.

[Caveat Poeta (1955?)]

1   Caveat poeta. I don't know where a poet could better mew his youth than in the academic world as long as he keeps one leg out of the grave. Caveat poeta. Let him look out for himself. Much goes on in college that is against the spirit. But so does it go on everywhere. The English departments may lean a little too far on the side of treating us all as if we were going to wind up as scholars like our teachers. The last place after high school where we were allowed to read books like men and women of the world was in the courses of Freshman English known at Harvard and some other places as English A. The authorities give themselves away in their attitude towards this. They are sure of the good their thoroughness is doing young scholars in prospect and sure they are not doing harm to the young business men in prospect. They can at least impose a respect for scholarship on the business men that will last them after graduation to keep contributing to the college fund for the rest of their lives. We have to admit that there aren't enough poets and other artists around to be worth much consideration. Such as there are, as I say, let them look out for themselves. Caveat poeta. He has less to fear perhaps if what he is out for is writing epics.

2   What I have been speaking of is partly the danger of too much analysis. I am glad to learn of the teachers' regret that their students come short in the initiative of discussion and question. My own personal regret is for their lack of initiative in getting up notions to surprise, shock, and amuse me. I mean rigmaroles and frame-ups that have some ingenuity of structure as in Meccano. They often show best in their own student publications provided they have no faculty adviser responsible for their deviations or effronteries.

3   One can't help a feeling, I suppose, of what is conventionally expected of him in school, on the stage, or in a book. The conventions have to be locked horns with somewhere. It may as well be in school as anywhere. We are the luckier given some choice where. It is hard to tell at this distance of time how much I was governed in writing by any demand there was or wasn't for my sort of thing. I don't know how much longer I might or might not have been able to do without readers.

4   I catch at the suggestion from someone that my encounter with the conventions may have always been with ironical detachment whether from school, from the stage, from the arts, from politics, or from life itself. One of the conventions of politics in America, for instance, is that we should belong with something almost like patriotism to one party or another. No one can accuse me of not having been ironical enough in my attachment to and my detachment from the Democratic party. It is the same with education for another example. I guess my open secret is that in the wrestling ring the hold with reality should be as much mine as my opponent's. I want, I am expecting everything and everybody in on me and my art, but as much as possible with a force tempered to my terms. There is always the chance it will be on their terms more than on mine and then I shall go down writing.

[Perfect Day—A Day of Prowess (1956)]

1   Americans would rather watch a game than play a game. Statement true or false? Why, as to these thousands here today to watch the game and not play it, probably not one man-jack but has himself played the game in his athletic years and got himself so full of bodily memories of the experience (what we farmers used to call kinesthetic images) that he can hardly sit still. We didn't burst into cheers immediately, but an exclamation swept the crowd as if we felt it all over in our muscles when Boyer at third made the two impossible catches, one a stab at a grounder and the other a leap at a line drive that may have saved the day for the National League. We all winced with fellow feeling when Berra got the foul tip on the ungloved fingers of his throwing hand.

2   As for the ladies present, they are here as next friends to the men, but even they have many of them pitching arms and batting eyes. Many of them would prefer a league ball to a pumpkin. You wouldn't want to catch them with bare hands. I mustn't count it against them that I envision one in the outfield at a picnic with her arms spread wide open for a fly ball as for a descending man-angel. Luckily it didn't hit her in the mouth which was open too, or it might have hurt her beauty. It missed her entirely.

3   How do I know all this and with what authority do I speak? Have I not been written up as a pitcher in *The New Yorker* by the poet, Raymond Holden?—though the last full game I pitched in was on the grounds of Rockingham Park in Salem, New Hampshire, before it was turned into a race track. If I have shone at all in the all-star games at Breadloaf in Vermont it has been as a relief pitcher with a soft ball I despise like a picture window. Moreover I once took an honorary degree at Williams College along with a very famous pitcher, Ed Lewis, who will be remembered and found in the record to have led the National League in pitching quite a long time ago. His degree was not for pitching. Neither was mine. His was for presiding with credit over the University of New Hampshire and the Massachusetts College of Agriculture. He let me into the secret of how he could make a ball behave when his arm was just right. It may sound superstitious to the uninitiated, but he could push a cushion of air up ahead of it for it to slide off from any way it pleased.

My great friendship for him probably accounts for my having made a trivial 10¢ bet on the National League today. He was a Welshman from Utica who, from having attended eisteddfods at Utica with his father, a bard, had like another Welsh friend of mine, Edward Thomas, in England, come to look on a poem as a performance one had to win. Chicago was my first favorite team because Chicago seemed the nearest city in the league to my original home town, San Francisco. I have conquered that prejudice. But I mean to see if the captain of it, Anson my boyhood hero, is in the Hall of Fame at Cooperstown where he belongs.

4   May I add to my self-citation that one of my unfulfilled promises on earth was to my fellow in art, Alfred Kreymborg, of an epic poem some day about a ball batted so hard by Babe Ruth that it never came back, but got to going round and round the world like a satellite. I got up the idea long before any artificial moon was thought of by the scientists. I meant to begin something like this:

> It was nothing to nothing at the end of the tenth
> And the prospects good it would last to the nth.

5   It needs a lot of work on it before it can take rank with *Casey at the Bat*.

6   In other words, some baseball is the fate of us all. For my part I am never more at home in America than at a baseball game like this in Clark Griffith's gem of a field, gem small, in beautiful weather in the capital of the country and my side winning. Here Walter Johnson flourished, who once threw a silver dollar across the Potomac (where not too wide) in emulation of George Washington, and here Gabby Street caught the bulletlike ball dropped from the top of George Washington's monument. It is the time and the place. And I have with me as consultant the well-known symbolist, Howard Schmitt of Buffalo, to mind my baseball slang and interpret the incidentals. The first player comes to the bat, Temple of the Redlegs, swinging two bats as he comes, the meaning of which or moral of which, I find on application to my consultant, is that we must always arrange to have just been doing something beforehand a good deal harder than what we are just going to do.

7   But when I asked him a moment later what it symbolized when a ball got batted into the stands and the people instead of dodging in terror fought each other fiercely to get and keep it and were allowed to keep it, Howard bade me hold on; there seemed to be a misunderstanding between us. When he accepted the job it was orally; he didn't mean to represent himself as a symbolist in the high-brow or middle-brow sense of the word, that is as a collegiate expounder of the double entendre for college classes; he was a common ordinary cymbalist in a local band somewhere out on the far end of the

Eeryie Canal. We were both honest men. He didn't want to be taken for a real professor any more than I wanted to be taken for a real sport. His utmost wish was to contribute to the general noise when home runs were made. He knew they would be the most popular hits of the day. And they were—four of them from exactly the four they were expected from, Musial, Williams, Mays and Mantle. The crowd went wild four times. Howard's story would have been more plausible if he had brought his cymbals with him. I saw I would have to take care of the significances myself. This comes of not having got it in writing. The moral is always get it in writing.

8   Time was when I saw nobody on the field but the players. If I saw the umpire at all it was as an enemy for not taking my side. I may never have wanted to see bottles thrown at him so that he had to be taken out by the police. Still I often regarded him with the angry disfavor that the Democratic Party showed the Supreme Court in the '30s and other parties have shown it in other crises in our history. But now grown psychological, shading 100, I saw him as a figure of justice, who stood forth alone to be judged as a judge by people and players with whom he wouldn't last a week if suspected of the least lack of fairness or the least lack of faith in the possibility of fairness. I was touched by his loneliness and glad it was relieved a little by his being five in number, five in one so to speak, *e pluribus unum.* I have it from high up in the judiciary that some justices see in him an example to pattern after. Right there in front of me for reassurance is the umpire brought up perhaps in the neighborhood of Boston who can yet be depended upon not to take sides today for or against the American League the Boston Red Sox belong to. Let me celebrate the umpire for any influence for the better he may have on the Supreme Court. The justices suffer the same predicaments with him. I saw one batter linger perceptibly to say something to the umpire for calling him out on a third strike. I didn't hear what the batter said. One of the hardest things to accept as just is a called third strike.

9   It has been a day of prowess in spite of its being a little on the picnic side and possibly not as desperately fought as it might be in a World Series. Prowess, prowess, in about equal strength for both sides. Each team made 11 hits, two home runs and not a single error. The day was perfect, the scene perfect, the play perfect. Prowess of course comes first, the ability to perform with success in games, in the arts and, come right down to it, in battle. The nearest of kin to the artists in college where we all become bachelors of arts are their fellow performers in baseball, football and tennis. That's why I am so particular college athletics should be kept from corruption. They are close to the soul of culture. At any rate the Greeks thought so. Justice is a close second to prowess. When displayed toward each other by antagonists in war and peace,

it is known as the nobility of noble natures. And I mustn't forget courage, for there is neither prowess nor justice without it. My fourth, if it is important enough in comparison to be worth bringing in, is knowledge, the mere information we can't get too much of and can't ever get enough of, we complain, before going into action.

10   As I say, I never feel more at home in America than at a ball game be it in park or in sandlot. Beyond this I know not. And dare not.

[Message to the Poets of Korea (1957)]

1   Korea is much on our mind nowadays with its national sorrows. It did me good to meet your poetess Youn-Sook Moh and hear from her in person in her own excellent English that in spite of everything you still have poets and poetry to support you and cheer you on. Poetry and the other arts are for me what a country chiefly lives by. They mark national characters better than anything else. And they bring peoples together in spirit the more apparently that they separate them in language. The language barrier has so much to do with individuality and originality that we wouldn't want to see it removed. We must content ourselves with seeing it more or less got over by interpretation and translation. We must remember that one may be national without being poetical, but one can't be poetical without being national. Youn-Sook Moh's visit made me wish I had as much Korean to read your poetry as she had English to read ours. Bless you in the name of whatever Muse of poetry may preside over your works in Korea.

Maturity No Object (1957)

1   Maturity is no object except perhaps in education where you might think from all the talk the aim and end of everything was to get sophisticated before educated. Shakespeare says it is the right virtue of the medlar to be rotten before it is ripe. Overdevelop the social conscience and make us all social meddlers. But I digress before I begin. My theme is not education, but poetry and how young one has to be or stay to make it. And it is not schools in general I reflect on, only bad schools which something should be done about before they get much larger. My excuse is that school and poetry come so near being one thing. Poetry has been a great concern of school all down the ages. A large part of reading in school always has been and still is poetry; and it is but an extension from the metaphors of poetry out into all thinking, scientific and philosophic. In fact the poet and scholar have so much in common and live together so naturally that it is easy to make too much of a mystery about where they part company. Their material seems the same—perhaps differs a little in being differently come by and differently held in play. Thoroughness is the danger of the scholar, dredging to the dregs. He works on assignment and self-assignment with some sense of the value of what he is getting when he is getting it. He is perhaps too avid of knowledge. The poet's instinct is to shun or shed more knowledge than he can swing or sing. His most available knowledge is acquired unconsciously. Something warns him dogged determination however profound can only result in doggerel. His danger is rhyming trivia. His depth is the lightsome blue depth of the air.

2   But I suppose the special distinction I was going to invest the poet with, that is making no object of maturity, was a mistake. It certainly belongs as much to the composer, the musician, the general, and I'm told the mathematician and the scientist. And it probably belongs to the scholar. Be that as it may, all poets I have ever heard of struck their note long before forty, the deadline for contributions to this book. The statistics are all in favor of their being as good and lyric as they will ever be. They may have ceased to be poets by the time appreciation catches up with them as Matthew Arnold complains somewhere. (I don't have to say exactly where because I'm not a scholar.) I

have personal reasons to trust that they may go phasing on into being as good poets in their later mental ages. For my country's sake I might wish one or two of them an old age of epic writing. A good epic would grace our history. Landor has set an example in prolonging the lyric out of all bounds.

3   Maturity will come. We mature. But the point is that it is at best irrelevant. Young poetry is the breath of parted lips. For the spirit to survive, the mouth must find how to firm and not harden. I saw it in two faces in the same drawing room—one youth in Greek sculpture, the other manhood in modern painting. They were both noble. The man was no better than the boy nor worse because he was older. The poets of this group, many of them my friends and already known to many of us, need live to write no better, need only wait to be better known for what they have written.

4   The reader is more on trial here than they are. He is given his chance to see if he can tell all by himself without critical instruction the difference between the poets who wrote because they thought it would be a good idea to write and those who couldn't help writing out of a strong weakness for the Muse, as for an elopement with her. There should be some way to tell that just as there is to tell the excitement of the morning from the autointoxication of midnight. Any distinction between maturity and immaturity is not worth making unless as a precaution. If school is going to proclaim a policy of maturing boys and girls ultimately it might become necessary for us to stay away from school or at least play hooky a good deal to season slowly out of doors rather than in an oven or in a tanning vat. And that seems too bad; for so many of us like school and want to go there.

5   As I often say a thousand, two thousand, colleges, town and gown together in the little town they make, give us the best audiences for poetry poetry ever had in all this world. I am in on the ambition that this book will get to them—heart and mind.

[Preface to *A Swinger of Birches*, by Sidney Cox (First Version)]

1   This is a book I am asked to introduce because it is about me and by a life-long faithful friend. Our intimacy was a curious blend of differences that if properly handled might prove an almost literary curiosity. That much might be gathered I should think from my letters to him as I remember them. Are they not on deposit in the Dartmouth College Library for anybody to read? If the book is a success in bringing out our protagonism, his character and mine, his as much as mine, I suppose I must as of obligation do what I can to give the book its chance. I have never really read it and have nothing but other people's word to rely on for what it is like. I drew back from one glimpse over the edge into the first part of it more or less out of inability to contemplate myself as others say in print they see me. I read enough to make out that his difficulty was the same as mine herein, that of striking the right tone about our relations. This may be getting too autobiographical, but I can't help relating that I was so abashed for him as well as for myself by what I found in the first chapter or two sent for approval years ago that I never approved of it and in fact never sent it back. My default I was willing to have taken as a nihil obstat. I find most attempts to describe me much too disturbing either for my pleasure or my discipline. I am assured and I assume from my knowledge of Sidney Cox that the book is one texture of honesty and as such I may concede it all the value you please, but be the responsibility of giving it to the world entirely on the head of others. An amusing situation I submit—me caught talking up anybody else's talk about me. We were a strange pair in our at-variances. We kept it up between us in a kind of magnanimity or high-minded tolerance of each other's taste. I remember how it began one evening in 1911 when we met as strangers looking on at a school dance at Plymouth, New Hampshire, where we were both teachers, he in one school and I in another. I didn't know who he was except that he looked very teasably young. He didn't know who I was except it seems I looked too old. By saying something flippant about the theme papers he had to hurry

away to correct I angered him to the point of his inquiring behind my back if it was because of alcohol I had got no further up in the world at my age. I was thirty seven. I was just teaching psychology in the Plymouth Normal School. He disdained to speak to me on the street for a while afterwards. But his seriousness piqued the mischief in me and I set myself to take him. He came round all right, but it wasn't the last time he had to make an effort to get over being bothered by me. He worked at it and I can well believe he may have got a real story out of it. He was a great, a triumphant teacher. He was all sincerity. He once wrote an article for *The New Republic* about my sincerity. I was very fond of him in my way. I really set my heart on his literary success.

[Preface to *A Swinger of Birches,* by Sidney Cox (1957)]

2   This ought to be a good book. Everybody who has seen it in manuscript says it is. The author probably knew me better than he knew himself and consequently contrariwise he very likely portrayed himself in it more than me. I trust it is in my favor. I know he would mean it to be. I don't read about myself well or easily. But I am always happier to hear that I am liked faults and all than that I am disliked. I had to tell Sidney once that I didn't believe it did me the least good to be told of the enemies he had had to defend me from. I have stolen look enough over the edge of the book to see that what went on between us is brought out much as in our correspondence. My letters to him I might mention are on deposit in the Dartmouth College library. I wish I had kept some of the great letters he wrote me but I am no curator of letters or anything else. He was at his best in his free letters. Yes, and of course in his teaching. A great teacher. He was all sincerity and frankness. He once wrote an article for *The New Republic* about *my* sincerity. I know that because it was in the title. We differed more in taste perhaps than in thinking. But we stood up to each other to support each other as two playing cards may be made to in building. I am a great equalitarian: I try to spend most of my time with my equals. He seemed worried at first lest it should appear I didn't seek him as much as he sought me. He respected me very highly. And he was more serious about such things than I. Not that he lacked a sense of humor. He liked a good story, and I am sure he would have enjoyed my version of our first encounter. It began one evening in 1911 when we met as strangers looking on at a school dance at Plymouth, New Hampshire, where we were both teachers, he in one school, I in another. I didn't know who he was except that he looked very teasably young. He didn't know who I was except, it seems, that I looked too old. By saying something flippant about the theme papers he had to hurry away to correct I angered him to the point of his inquiring behind

my back if it was because of alcohol I had got no further up in the world at my age. I was thirty-seven. I was just teaching psychology in the Plymouth Normal School. He disdained to speak to me on the street for a while afterwards. But his seriousness piqued the mischief in me and I set myself to take him. He came round all right, but it wasn't the last time he had to make allowances for me. He worked at it devotedly. He must have been about half my age then. He was all of two thirds my age when he died. He was catching up. He was cut off before he came all the way through with himself. But he had made up his mind to much. My heart was in his literary success and I have hopes this is it.

[Contribution to *Esquire's* Symposium on "What Worries You Most about America Today?" (1958)]

1   Worries is a hard word for me. I am interested in strengthening the high schools of America, bringing them up. A little thing I want is named chairs in the high schools. Once you got it, you would be in it for life. This would enrich the position of the high-school teacher. Their position is not dignified enough. The first chair, I'd have for mathematics. The other chair could be of the school's choosing. Instead of spraying money all over the colleges, I'd like to see something done for high-school teachers.

Merrill Moore (1958)

1   It was a life overflowing with poetic sympathy, whether in or out of form. His professional treatments seemed on the principle of poetry toward all. He may have written too many of what it amused him to call sonnets. And then again he may not. Louis Untermeyer was saying the other day he may prevail by sheer force of numbers; and numbers is after all the old-fashioned name for poetry. It can't be expected that the hundred thousand pieces he tossed off and never looked back at will be taken without discrimination. Louis Untermeyer made a beginning on the formidable task. Already he and such admirers as John Crowe Ransom, Dudley Fitts, William Carlos Williams, and Theodore Morrison have penetrated to seeing the trees in the woods. He was one of John Ransom's remarkable children at Vanderbilt University.

2   Serious physician and serious artist, he had no notion of being taken lightly; still there was something of the rogue there that was a part of his great charm. He seldom more than cracked a smile. The first time he ever called me in on a case, and in fact the first time I ever met him, was thirty years ago after a big party at the St. Botolph Club. He had hardly asked me if like a country swain he might see me home before he asked if he might use me for a visit at that hour of night at the house of a lady patient. It would do her a world of good to talk literary with me in particular at that hour of night. Anything once I said. He briefed me: she was a case of wanting to try one more doctor to see if she couldn't be cured of not knowing how to write. It sounded hopeless. Wouldn't he just have to tell that girl to be good? As a last resort he might. I think he would rather tell her to be brave than good. Besides poetry he dispensed courage. Like the boys that go aloft to crash the sound barrier he was a rebuke to the stupid give-it-ups who are willing to have it that heroism is out of date.

3   On a visit to Sanibel Island he had the bright idea of shovelling up from the beach with his own hands a ton or two of sea shells and shipping them North for his patients to sort out. I wish you could hear the disc recording of his speech about the therapeutic value of this exercise in beauty. Possibly he

thought it would do us the same kind of good to sort out the poems he left. Anyway I know he wouldn't mind my saying so.

4   No praise would mean anything to him that forgot he was a poet. Poetry was his rapture. He could hardly say it without singing it. I remember an evening out for a ride with him weaving through the traffic when he recited all of "L'Allegro" and "Il Penseroso" and to round them off with almost the same gentle sweetness and delight "The Ballad of the Revenge." On another evening he sang me somebody's setting of Omar. On another still in a cabaret he sang me and everybody present a long, long ballad of the World War (something he had picked up as Colonel in our army in China) to the ukelele accompaniment of a handsome Italian South Sea islander from South Boston. The South Sea islander might have sung it himself but for the laws of Petrillo. Merrill carried it off like a troubadour.

5   I looked for him once at Squantum. He was out swimming in the ocean somewhere between here and Europe. I might have to wait for him an hour or two. He was a great swimmer. He struck out boldly the same in the water as in poetry. As I have said he dispensed courage as well as poetry. He was a soldier poet, a true Tyrtaeus.

[Statement of Robert Frost in the Case of the United States of America versus Ezra Pound (1958)]

1   I am here to register my admiration for a government that can rouse in conscience to a case like this. Relief seems in sight for many of us besides the Ezra Pound in question and his faithful wife. He has countless admirers the world over who will rejoice in the news that he has hopes of freedom. I append a page or so of what they have been saying lately about him and his predicament. I myself speak as much in the general interest as in his. And I feel authorized to speak very specially for my friends, Archibald MacLeish, Ernest Hemingway and T. S. Eliot. None of us can bear the disgrace of our letting Ezra Pound come to his end where he is. It would leave too woeful a story in American literature. He went very wrongheaded in his egotism, but he insists it was from patriotism—love of America. He has never admitted that he went over to the enemy any more than the writers at home who have despaired of the Republic. I hate such nonsense and can only listen to it as an evidence of mental disorder. But mental disorder is what we are considering. I rest the case on Dr. Overholser's pronouncement that Ezra Pound is not too dangerous to go free in his wife's care, and too insane ever to be tried—a very nice discrimination.

2   Mr. Thurman Arnold admirably put this problem of a sick man being held too long in prison to see if he won't get well enough to be tried for a prison offense. There is probably legal precedent to help toward a solution of the problem. But I should think it would have to be reached more by magnanimity than by logic and it is chiefly on magnanimity I am counting. I can see how the Department of Justice would hesitate in the matter from fear of looking more just to a great poet than it would be to a mere nobody. The bigger the Department the longer it might have to take thinking things through.

/s/ Robert Frost

Robert Frost

[Remarks on Being Appointed Consultant to the Library of Congress (1958?)]

1   What would be said of me if I didn't hasten to acknowledge any notice taken of poetry by the government of the United States. One reason for my not hesitating is that poetry is my cause and so is the government of the United States. Another reason if needed would be more personal and selfish. I am far from insensible of the honor of being appointed as a poet to an office in the capital of the country among the rulers of the country. I have always thought and always said I should have liked nothing better than to be sent to Washington by my neighbors at home. I have envied with admiration the lives of fine senators like Flanders and Aiken from the state I vote in, but since there was no hope of my being elected like them by backers behind I can content myself with being selected from in front and a way may be found for my taking some small part in what I like to call politics. My father was seriously ambitious to represent California in Congress but he died young and never got nearer Washington than with a small book on the life of General Rosecrans in the Library to which I am becoming consultant. The inclination I myself own I had towards affairs of state will be amply and handsomely satisfied by the small token job I am to have down there. I promise.

2   I was not brought up to the distrust of politics that so many scholars and artists seem to suffer from. Neither was I to distrust of big business for that matter. Nor of small business either. Long before my luck changed I went on record as willing to accept the trial by market everything must come to.

3   I never believed in our being stand-offish with statesmen or letting them be stand-offish with us any more than we can help. Some of them are much more able than cultivated. A pathetic uneasiness often shows itself in their hurry to turn us over to their womenfolk to deal with. We are much more sympathetic with them however than they are with us. And we understand them better than they understand us. We know what's good for them better than they know what's good for us. And we're supposed to have language and should be willing to use it with them. I never shared the common artistic

prejudice against politics that tends to make artists too arty. I'm no Platonist to agree with Plato that the philosopher should be king. Neither do I agree with him that the poet should be suppressed. The poet would make a better king than the philosopher. Anyway poetry has had something to do with the magnificence of great government. But I musn't slur philosophy. I wasn't brought up to distrust philosophy or politics either. I look on enterprise as all one. In a great period there should be great statesmen, great soldiers, great artists, and great men of business. The whole nation seems full of one great undertaking. We have had two such times when we were flushed with spirit.

4   The Capital should be a place where all the ambitions should be thrown together in emulation and rivalry. I am only saying what should be, not what is. Give us an inch and we'll take an ell. There came a day when it occurred to someone that labor should be represented in Washington. My small toehold is in danger of rousing the proletariat to feeling the need of a Secretary of Poetry. My office will be merely that of consultant to everybody in general. I suppose even a statesman might consult me about what to do next.

The Way There (1958?)

1   It would be the footpath way. "Jog on, jog on, the footpath way and merrily hent the stile-a." The measured way, so many feet to the mile-a; so many feet to the line, seldom less than two or more than five in our language. Footbeats for the metre and heartbeats for the rhythm. The unevenness of the heartbeats will keep the footbeats from jogging dogged to the point of doggerel. You may not realize it, but it is the way you have all come thus far from the days of your Godmother Goose through books and nature, gathering bits and scraps of real magic that however flowery still clung to you like burrs thrown on your clothes in holiday foolery. You don't have to worry about clinging to such trophies. They will cling to you.

2   Sometimes it is a whole poem if short enough that takes possession of you. A little girl I heard of got so possessed of one of the poems in this book that she must hurry home and recite it to her mother. When her mother said, "Why, my dear, I knew that poem before you were born," the little girl came back with, "Then why didn't you tell me?" But perhaps it is parts of poems that season into most meaning for us. They will come lilting to mind unexpectedly in the most remote situations. We must remember that poetry is said to have been invented as an aid to memory. It might be described as the most unforgettable experience man can have of words. No painting can do the source of light. No poem even can describe itself. And here I am trying to define poetry in prose.

3   I could almost wish the stile of my quotation was spelled with a "y" so that I could use it for the airs and graces of poetry. The way there may be as airily as a bird's from tree to tree or as a squirrel's, or anyway a flying squirrel's, without touching the ground. It may be as airily airy as the course I have taken through this book with an inner logic I don't have to account for from the poem "Birches" to the poem "Wild Grapes." The first birches were trees I swung near the district school I went to in Salem, New Hampshire. The birch of "Wild Grapes" was one a girl swung in when she didn't weigh enough to bring it to earth. She told me about it eighty years later and asked me to write a poem about it for girls to match the other birch poem that she claimed was

written for boys. She clenched her hands in memory of the pain of having had to hang on in the tree too long. I had to write the poem for her because she was the first editor ever to publish me. Her name was Susan Hayes Ward. The poem was the first thing in prose or verse I ever wrote to order. She was my first publisher unless I count the Senior in the Lawrence High School who published three years earlier in our high school paper the first thing in prose or verse I ever wrote at all. And his name was Ernest Jewell.

4   The way there may be from tree to tree as in this book. Some day in another book, it may be from Nicasio to Ripton "if it comes in my mind just right."

Robert Frost

[Unpublished Preface to an Expanded *North of Boston* (1958?)]

1   North of Boston (I want it to say) was not written as a book nor towards a book. It was written as scattered poems in a form suggested by the eclogues of Virgil. Beginning with one about Julius Caesar in the year I was reading about Aeneas and Meliboeus, luckily (I consider it) in no vain attempt to Anglicize Virgil's versification, dactylic hexameter. It gathered itself together in retrospect and found a name for itself in the real estate advertising of *The Boston Globe*. It was written along with all sorts of briefer things in rhyme. It was what was left after these had gone through the sieve. Its public acceptance seemed to call for a sequel. At the time nothing seemed further from my mind. I even scouted the idea when it was proposed to me. But it turned out in the natural course of events that I was to write a second *North of Boston* and even a third as unintentionally as I had written the first. Only recently it has occurred to me that they may as well be added to the first under the same head in summing up. Some of them are a little nearer one act plays than eclogues but they seem to have something in common that I don't want to seek a better name for. I like its being locative.

[Letter to the Editor of *Poetry* (1958)]

Homer Noble Farm
Ripton
Vermont.
July 16, 1958.

1   Dear Henry Rago:

Your July number has what I mean. I shall keep it like one of my books. It illustrates the conflict set forth in the last paragraph of Simon Halkin's fine essay. It achieves a dominant idea without excogitation. All those young poets intent on themselves come out with an effect on me almost dramatically not to say tragically national. It is very striking. It is very very moving. I wish you more numbers like it. It is hard for us in a country two hundred years old to strike the same note at once individual and national that these young poets get in a young country. Being in on the ground floor of an enterprise heightens their double consciousness.

Sincerely yours

ROBERT FROST

Dorothy Canfield (1958)

1   Dorothy Canfield was the great lady of Vermont just as someone else we all admire might be called the great lady of the United States. But there was more to it than just that. It was as a great story teller with a book called *Hillsboro People* that I was introduced to her by her publisher, Alfred Harcourt, who was then my publisher too. There was nothing she was happier in than story telling in prose and speech unless it was doing good to everybody and anybody. She came from all directions from as far West as Kansas and from as far East as France. She was brought up by a nomadic mother who pursued the practice of art in Paris and New York. I believe she won her doctorate in old French at Columbia University. But everything that ever happened or occurred to her converged as into a napkin ring and came out wide on the other side of it Vermontly. I don't know whether she realized it or not, but even the Basques she lived with and wrote about read to me like Vermonters. The people of her witchcraft story among the Basques might well be Ethan Allen's Green Mountain boys.

2   Her benefactions weren't restricted to Vermont (I consider her work with the Book of the Month Club one of them). But of course they were most intimately felt there all up and down the state. She made it a welfare state. I remember her remarking that the Puritan word Commonwealth meant exactly the same thing. Her great good nature kept her from thinking too hard about doctrines, though she was plainly proud of a Vermont ancestry, Episcopalian, among the other sects non-conformist that came up from Connecticut and Rhode Island to settle the state.

3   Alfred Harcourt brought our families together from a notion he had that the White Mountains we lived in were neighborly to the Green Mountains she lived in. Many are our family obligations to her. She is often in our thoughts. Only the other day my granddaughter fresh from college asked me about her young resolution to devote her life to doing good. I used a parable to make it out better to do well. She was unconvinced. Hers was the last word: "Wouldn't it be enough of an ideal to do good well—like Dorothy Canfield?"

SIXTY-TWO

[List of Five Favorite Books (1958)]

1   The books that have meant the most to me in my lifetime:

2   1—The Old Testament.

3   2—"The Odyssey," by Homer.

4   3—"The Poems of Catullus."

5   4—"The Decline and Fall of the Roman Empire," by Edward Gibbon.

6   5—"Incidents of Travel in Yucatan," by John L. Stevens.

[On Emerson (1959)]

1   All that admiration for me I am glad of. I am here out of admiration for Emerson and Thoreau. Naturally on the proud occasion I should like to make myself as much of an Emersonian as I can. Let me see if I can't go a long way. You may be interested to know that I have right here in my pocket a little first edition of Emerson's poetry. His very first was published in England just as was mine. His book was given me on account of that connection by Fred Melcher, who takes so much pleasure in bringing books and things together like that.

2   I suppose I have always thought I'd like to name in verse some day my four greatest Americans: George Washington, the general and statesman; Thomas Jefferson, the political thinker; Abraham Lincoln, the martyr and savior; and fourth, Ralph Waldo Emerson, the poet. I take these names because they are going around the world. They are not just local. Emerson's name has gone as a poetic philosopher or as a philosophical poet, my favorite kind of both.

3   I have friends it bothers when I am accused of being Emersonian, that is, a cheerful Monist, for whom evil does not exist, or if it does exist, needn't last forever. Emerson quotes Burns as speaking to the Devil as if he could mend his ways. A melancholy dualism is the only soundness. The question is is soundness of the essence.

4   My own unsoundness has a strange history. My mother was a Presbyterian. We were here on my father's side for three hundred years but my mother was fresh a Presbyterian from Scotland. The smart thing when she was young was to be reading Emerson and Poe as it is today to be reading St. John Perse or T. S. Eliot. Reading Emerson turned her into a Unitarian. That was about the time I came into the world; so I suppose I started a sort of Presbyterian-Unitarian. I was transitional. Reading on into Emerson, that is into *Representative Men* until she got to Swedenborg, the Mystic, made her a Swedenborgian. I was brought up in all three of these religions, I suppose. I don't know whether I was baptized in them all. But as you see it was pretty much under the auspices of Emerson. It was all very Emersonian. Phrases of his began to come to me early. In that essay on the mystic he makes

Swedenborg say that in the highest heaven nothing is arrived at by dispute. Everybody votes in heaven but everybody votes the same way as in Russia to-day. It is only in the second-highest heaven that things get parliamentary; we get the two-party system or the hydra-headed as in France.

5   Some of my first thinking about my own language was certainly Emersonian. "Cut these sentences and they bleed," he says. I am not submissive enough to want to be a follower, but he had me there. I never got over that. He came pretty near making me an anti-vocabularian with the passage in "Monadnock" about our ancient speech. He blended praise and dispraise of the country people of New Hampshire. As an abolitionist he was against their politics. Forty per cent of them were states rights Democrats in sympathy with the South. They were really pretty bad, my own relatives included.

> "The God who made New Hampshire
> Taunted the lofty land
> With little men;—"

And if I may be further reminiscent parenthetically, my friend Amy Lowell hadn't much use for them either. "I have left New Hampshire," she told me. Why in the world? She couldn't stand the people. What's the matter with the people? "Read your own books and find out." They really differ from other New Englanders, or did in the days of Franklin Pierce.

6   But now to return to the speech that was his admiration and mine in a burst of poetry in "Monadnock":

> "Yet wouldst thou learn our ancient speech
> These the masters that can teach.
> Fourscore or a hundred words
> All their vocal muse affords.
> Yet they turn them in a fashion
> Past the statesman's art and passion.
> Rude poets of the tavern hearth
> Squandering your unquoted mirth,
> That keeps the ground and never soars,
> While Jake retorts and Reuben roars.
> Scoff of yeoman, strong and stark,
> Goes like bullet to the mark,
> And the solid curse and jeer
> Never balk the waiting ear."

7   Fourscore or a hundred is seven hundred less than my friend Ivor Richards' basic eight hundred. I used to climb on board a load of shooks (boxes that

haven't been set up) just for the pleasure I had in the driver's good use of his hundred word limit. This at the risk of liking it so much as to lose myself in mere picturesqueness. I was always in favor of the solid curse as one of the most beautiful of figures. We were warned against it in school for its sameness. It depends for variety on the tones of saying it and the situations.

8   I had a talk with John Erskine the first time I met him on this subject of sentences that may look tiresomely alike, short and with short words, yet turn out as calling for all sorts of ways of being said aloud or in the mind's ear, Horatio. I took Emerson's prose and verse as my illustration. Writing is unboring to the extent that it is dramatic.

9   In a recent preface to show my aversion to being interrupted with notes in reading a poem, I find myself resorting to Emerson again. I wanted to be too carried away for that. There was much of "Brahma" that I didn't get to begin with but I got enough to make me sure I would be back there reading it again some day when I had read more and lived more; and sure enough without help from dictionary or encyclopaedia I can now understand every line in it but one or two. It is a long story of many experiences that let me into the secret of:

> "But thou, meek lover of the good!
>   Find me, and turn thy back on heaven."

What baffled me was the Christianity in "Meek lover of the good." I don't like obscurity and obfuscation, but I do like dark sayings I must leave the clearing of to time. And I don't want to be robbed of the pleasure of fathoming depths for myself. It was a moment for me when I saw how Shakespeare set bounds to science when he brought in the North Star, "Whose worth's unknown although his height be taken." Of untold worth: it brings home some that should and some that shouldn't come. Let the psychologist take notice how unsuccessful he has to be.

10   I owe more to Emerson than anyone else for troubled thoughts about freedom. I had the hurt to get over when I first heard us made fun of by foreigners as the land of the free and the home of the brave. Haven't we won freedom? Is there no such thing as freedom? Well, Emerson says God

> "Would take the sun out of the skies
>   Ere freedom out of a man."

and there rings the freedom I choose.

11   Never mind how and where Emerson disabused me of my notion I may have been brought up to that the truth would make me free. My truth will bind you slave to me. He didn't want converts and followers. He was a Uni-

tarian. I am on record as saying that freedom is nothing but departure—setting forth—leaving things behind, brave origination of the courage to be new. We may not want freedom. But let us not deceive ourselves about what we don't want. Freedom is one jump ahead of formal laws as in planes and even automobiles right now. Let's see the law catch up with us very soon.

12   Emerson supplies the emancipating formula for giving an attachment up for an attraction, one nationality for another nationality, one love for another love. If you must break free

> "Heartily know,
> When half-gods go
> The gods arrive."

I have seen it invoked in *Harper's Magazine* to excuse disloyalty to our democracy in a time like this. But I am not sure of the reward promised. There is such a thing as getting too transcended. There are limits. Let's not talk socialism. I feel projected out from politics with lines like:

> "Musketaquit, a goblin strong,
> Of shards and flints makes jewels gay;
> They lose their grief who hear his song,
> And where he winds is the day of day.
>
> So forth and brighter fares my stream,—
> Who drink it shall not thirst again;
> No darkness stains its equal gleam,
> And ages drop in it like rain."

Left to myself I have gradually come to see what Emerson was meaning in "Give all to Love" was Give all to Meaning. The freedom of all freedoms is ours to insist on meaning.

13   The kind of story Steinbeck likes to tell is about an old labor hero punch drunk from fighting the police in many strikes, beloved by everybody at headquarters as the greatest living hater of tyranny. I take it that the production line was his grievance. The only way he could make it mean anything was to try to ruin it. He took arms and fists against it. No one could have given him that kind of freedom. He saw it as his to seize. He was no freedman; he was a free man. The one inalienable right is to go to destruction in your own way. What's worth living for is worth dying for. What's worth succeeding in is worth failing in.

14   If you have piled up a great rubbish heap of oily rags in the basement for your doctor's thesis and it won't seem to burst into flame spontaneously,

come away quickly and without declaring rebellion. It will cost you only your Ph.D. Union Card and the respect of the Union. But it will hardly be noticed even to your credit in the world. All you have to do is to amount to something anyway. The only reprehensible materiality is the materialism of getting lost in your material so you can't find out yourself what it is all about.

15   A young fellow came to me to complain of the department of philosophy in his university. "There wasn't a philosopher in it. I can't stand it." He was really complaining of his situation. He wasn't where he could feel real. But I didn't tell him so I didn't go into that. I agreed with him that there wasn't a philosopher in his university—there was hardly ever more than one at a time in the world—and I advised him to quit. Light out for somewhere. He hated to be a quitter. I told him the Bible says, "Quit ye, like men." "Does it?," he said. "Where would I go?" Why anywhere almost. Kamchatka, Madagascar, Brazil. I found him doing well in the educational department of Rio when I was sent on an errand down there by our government several years later. I had taken too much responsibility for him when I sent him glimmering like that. I wrote to him with troubled conscience and got no answer for two whole years. But the story has a happy ending. His departure was not suicidal. I had a post card from him this Christmas to tell me he was on Robinson Crusoe's island Juan Fernandez on his way to Easter Island that it had always been a necessity for him someday to see. I would next hear from him in Chile where he was to be employed in helping restore two colleges. Two! And the colleges were universities!

16   No subversive myself I think it very Emersonian of me that I am so sympathetic with subversives, rebels, runners out, runners out ahead, eccentrics, and radicals. I don't care how extreme their enthusiasm so long as it doesn't land them in the Russian camp. I always wanted one of them teaching in the next room to me so my work would be cut out for me warning the children taking my courses not to take his courses.

17   I am disposed to cheat myself and others in favor of any poet I am in love with. I hear people say the more they love anyone the more they see his faults. Nonsense. Love is blind and should be left so. But it hasn't been hidden in what I have said that I am not quite satisfied with the easy way Emerson takes disloyalty. He didn't know or ignored his Blackstone. It is one thing for the deserter and another for the deserted. Loyalty is that for the lack of which your gang will shoot you without benefit of trial by jury. And serves you right. Be as treacherous as you must be for your ideals, but don't expect to be kissed good-bye by the idol you go back on. We don't want to look too foolish, do we? And probably Emerson was too Platonic about evil. It was a

mere Τὸ Μὴ ὄν that could be disposed of like the butt of a cigarette. In a poem I have called the best Western poem yet he says:

"Unit and universe are round."

18   Another poem could be made from that to the effect that ideally in thought only is a circle round. In practice, in nature, the circle becomes an oval. As a circle it has one center—Good. As an oval it has two centers—Good and Evil. Thence Monism versus Dualism.

19   Emerson was a Unitarian because he was too rational to be superstitious and too little a story teller and lover of stories to like gossip and pretty scandal. Nothing very religious can be done for people lacking in superstition. They usually end up abominable agnostics. It takes superstition and the prettiest scandal story of all to make a good Trinitarian. It is the first step in the descent of the spirit into the material-human at the risk of the spirit.

20   But if Emerson had left us nothing else he would be remembered longer than the Washington Monument for the monument at Concord that he glorified with lines surpassing any other ever written about soldiers:

"By the rude bridge that arched the flood
Their flag to April breeze unfurled
Here once the embattled farmers stood
And fired the shot heard round the world."

Not even Thermopylae has been celebrated better. I am not a shriner but two things I never happen on unmoved: one, this poem on stone, and the other, the tall shaft seen from Lafayette Park across the White House in Washington.

The Future of Man (1959)

1   It's the word "challenge" that interests me, of course—the challenge of the future to the prophet—and I am the prophet. I am going to tell you about the future—I'm not going to advocate the future; I'm going to tell you what it will be.

2   The standing challenge—the great challenge—is of man's originality to his law and order, to his government. And that will always be the challenge— that of man's energy and daring and originality to his law and order. That means that looking ahead into the future with my eyes shut—I see govern- ment paired with government for the championship of its era—to see after whom the period will be named, in this era for instance, us or the Russ. Un- fortunately, we haven't a very good name for ourselves. All my South Ameri- can friends object to our calling ourselves America—we shall have to call our- selves "us," to rhyme with "Russ."

3   Add to that, that there will always be an issue for the two powers to pair off on, and the Lord is the Great Provider; He'll provide the issue. There's al- ways been an issue, a great issue, a grave issue, like the one between Persia and Greece, Rome and Carthage, Christendom and Islam—for every period. We see a great issue today. I never can bear to blackguard an enemy; I like him to be an intelligible enemy, a worthy antagonist.

4   Next, are we going on to be another kind of people? Young people of our day, in studying anthropology and listening to the anthropologists, think it's such an amusing distance between the monkeys and us that it will only be an- other amusing distance from us to the superman. It's a field day for all comic strip teasers, you see, every man can make his own comic strip. Let me tell you about that—I know just what's going to happen or not happen. Our self- consciousness is terminal—there's nothing beyond us. Life in us has reached a self-consciousness that terminates the growth.

5   I saw a little while ago a list of all the thoughts man has had—published in Chicago, I think. There weren't over a hundred or two. I looked for the word evolution, and there it was. I looked for the word growth, the plain word growth, and there it wasn't. Apparently in Chicago growth is not an idea but

I take it that evolution comes under the head of growth. Only it has a strange illusory way of making you think it goes on forever. But all growth is limited—the tree of life is limited like a maple tree or an oak tree—they all have a certain height, and they all have a certain life-length. And our tree, the tree Yggdrasill, has reached its growth. It doesn't have to fall down because it's stopped growing. It will go on blossoming and having its seasons—I'd give it another hundred or two hundred million years. Make that anything you please. It'll go on leaving out and blooming into successions of the doubleness, I foresee, just like the doubleness of the sexes. There'll be two parties always to it, some way. I hope that this tree is self-fertilizing—I guess I hadn't thought of that—and it doesn't need another tree besides it, and in itself has all the doubleness I ask, good and evil, two sexes, one of *them* good and the other evil.

6   I wish the young people would relieve themselves of the responsibility of attending to the future of our height. There's nothing coming beyond us. The tree Yggdrasill has reached its growth.

7   Then I want to say another thing about the god who provides the great issues. He's a god of waste, magnificent waste. And waste is another name for generosity of not always being intent on our own advantage, nor too importunate even for a better world. We pour out a libation to him as a symbol of the waste we share in—participate in. Pour it on the ground and you've wasted it; pour it into yourself and you've doubly wasted it. But all in the cause of generosity and relaxation of self interest.

8   But I think I've said enough about it. There are many details that I had in mind, but I don't want to be too long about it. The point is that the challenge will always be there between man's originality and his law and order, his government. I sometimes think the scientists have got themselves scared; they're afraid they'll run away with themselves they are so original. They needn't worry; the executives will take care of them.

The Future of Man

(Unpublished Version [1959])

1   Challenge seems to be the word. I have never before used it in prose or verse. I should hope the meaning of it hadn't escaped me. There is the challenge of the future to the prophet: guess me. The great challenge, the eternal challenge, is that of man's bursting energy and originality to his own governance. His speed and his traffic police. We become an organized society only as we tell off some of our number to be law-givers and law-enforcers, a blend of general and lawyer, to hold fast the line and turn the rest of us loose for scientists, philosophers, and poets to make the break-through, the revolution, if we can for refreshment. Science is the most formidable in challenge but philosophy has been formidable too. Philosophers have had to be given hemlock and burned at the stake. The party of the holding part, the defender of the state and status, is of course the chief executive. Let us call him king for short and for the purposes of this conclave.

2   The challenge of science to government takes the form of asking What will you do with our latest? Will you use it as a weapon or a tool or both? If you ignore it, we shall go elsewhere with it and try it on your rivals. If you suppress it, we will do the same.

3   The challenge of science to the run of us, the small fry intelligensia, takes the form of asking What are you going to say to our latest? How are you going to take our having hit the moon for Russia? With chagrin rightly. You should hate not to win. Nothing can be done with people who don't mind losing. You are not that bad. It must have been more painful for you to be beaten in the race for the moon than it would have been to lose the races at Melbourne. You seem thrown into consternation and confusion by the truck load of new words for fuel we poured rattling down the chute into your old coal bin in the cellar. Find something to say to our posers. You must learn to sass the Sphinx. It seems a shame to come on you with our new novelties when you are hardly up around after what Darwin, Spencer, and Huxley did to you last century. But I suppose you will be taken care of as you were the

last time by the king's editorial writers, column writers, and commentators. Remember how you were helped by being reminded all you were asked to do was change from your old idea that God made man out of mud to the new idea that God made man out of prepared mud.

4   Now science seems about to ask us what we are going to do about taking in hand our own further evolution. This is some left-over business from the great Darwinian days. Every school boy knows how amusingly short the distance was from monkeys to us. Well it ought not to be much longer from us to supermen. We have the laboratorians ready and willing to tend to this. We can commission them any day to go ahead messing around with rays on genes for mutations or with sperm on ovules for eugenics till they get us somewhere, make something of us for a board or foundation to approve of. But I am asked to be prophetic. As far into the future as I can see with my eyes shut people are still pairing for love and money, perhaps just superstitious enough to leave their direction to what the mystic Karl Marx called historical necessity but what I like to call passionate preference, to the taste there's no disputing about. I foresee no society where artificial insemination won't be in bad taste.

5   But while I am in the mood to comply, why don't I go on prophesying to the limit? I am in danger of making all this sound as if science were all. It is not all. But it is much. It comes into our lives as domestic science for our hold on the planet, into our deaths with its deadly weapons, bombs and airplanes, for war, and into our souls as pure science for nothing but glory; in which last respect it may be likened unto pure poetry and mysticism. It is man's greatest enterprise. It is the charge of the ethereal into the material. It is our substantiation of our meaning. It can't go too far or deep for me. Still it is not a law unto itself. It comes under the king. There never was a scientist king and there never will be any more than there will be a philosopher king. (The nearest a poet king was Henry VIII who acquired the art in Freshman English under the poet Skelton.) Science is a property. It belongs to us under the king. And the best description of us is the humanities from of old, the book of the worthies and unworthies. The passing science of the moment may contribute its psychological bit to the book like one of the fleeting elements recently added to the chemical list. As one of the humanities itself, it is jealous for their dignity and importance. I see it is getting, it has already got, in such technological schools as M.I.T., Cal Tech, and Case, so the students can divide their time between cyclotrons, and listening to generalizations about Socrates and his boys, Alcibiades and Critias; about Talleyrand and his peace of Vienna; and about the symbolism of *Moby Dick*.

6   The view from the top of Ararat is into the vale of prevalure, where igno-

rant armies clash by night, more or less ignorant. Only the general or king can be thought great who can go into action or before Congress and Parliament on less information than he wishes he had. By night and by day too for the next ten thousand years I see nation pairing with nation for the championship of the age to see whose king the age will be named for. It was Greece against Persia, Republican Rome against Carthage, Caesar's Rome against the world. And so on down to England against the Continent to outdo it in colonization. The one the mystic Karl Marx calls historical necessity can be trusted in to supply the great issues for us to quarrel about forever. God send that the issues be genuine as they are between us and Russia today. And that they be not too ignoble.

7   And how would this be for an idea to wind up with: if we are thought to have matured to a point where we can take control of our own evolution to go on with, why can't it be to stop ourselves in or tracks if there isn't too much the matter with us as we are. The free-for-all has been very exciting since man began to drag down man and nation nation. I am tempted to think that we may be that in the tree Yggdrasill that determines its length of growth. No tree we are acquainted with but has to stop or be stopped or self-stopped somewhere. The tree hasn't to fall down just because it can't get any taller. I see it blossom into one dominant civilization era after era. Its eras are like its seasons, each with a glory of its own. We are warned not to be too ambitious in our ideas what it should be. We must take Sunday off. We must let down in tribute to the generosity of waste with now and then a libation on to the ground or down our own gullets where the waste is double. The burnt offering must be burnt to cinders and ashes not servable on the dinner table.

[Talk and Reading, 25th Anniversary Dinner of the Academy of American Poets (1959)]

1   Poetry has always been a beggar. Homer was a beggar. He begged through seven cities. He ate at the table of the patrons—I suppose in those days he sat at the foot of the table instead of up where I have been sitting tonight. He sat, probably, under the table. *(Laughter)* Scholarship has always been a beggar too. But scholarship delegates its begging to the presidents of its colleges. And it is pleasant to have the beggars brought to meet their patrons as at a meeting like this. A great occasion, profoundly moving. I suppose half of us here are poets; I assume the other half are our patrons, and we are happy in their praise. We know we are getting somewhere. *(Laughter)* The president of my college, Amherst, spends most of his time begging for me. He goes soon to join a Foundation and I think I will get more out of them, maybe. *(Laughter)*

2   It is a strange situation in the world to hear poetry described as what might give us a new age at any moment by some one phrase, I suppose, some one phrase—I always wonder about it. Some little phrase by somebody like Emerson. A poet has said:

> "We in the ages lying
>   In the buried past of the earth
>   Built Nineveh with our sighing
>   And Babel itself with our mirth."

They ruined Nineveh with sighing and Babel with mirth. They destroyed one city by sighing and the other city by laughing. *(Laughter)* There is a lot of hope for poetry, and its power in that, isn't there? *(Laughter)*

3   My own idea of poetry isn't of its climbing on top of the earth. Nor is it of its sitting on top of the earth nor of its standing on top of the earth but of its reclining on top of the earth and giving way to its moods. *(Applause)* Like a spoiled actress, you know, the day after she has been on stage, reclining on top of the world and giving way to her moods.

4   I am supposed not to talk but to read. It is hard, however, for me to turn to poetry after all this prose. *(Applause)* I know where poetry gets off, where it always gets off, second to prose. Though there is this satisfaction that always in school and whatever language you study more than half your reading will be in verse. It gets rubbed into you in school, anyway; go out and forget it afterwards, if you can and will.

5   Am I supposed to read a poem? Before I begin do you want to hear a definition of poetry? I once heard a pretty one. I don't know where I heard it. It was some years ago. It is in prose, but one of these things following me around like a stray dog. It sounds as if it came from another century. "Poetry is the honey of all flowers." That would be all the way from clover to buckwheat, the common-man stuff, you see. Some of my friends write that kind of honey. "Poetry is the honey of all flowers; the quintessence of all the sciences" (plural, all the sciences). "It is the marrow of wit. And the very phrase of angels." It doesn't say "phrases of angels," "the very phrase of angels,"— phrase in the singular number, the most poetic expression in it all. I could make a talk out of every one of those four things. But the most beautiful one of all, "the very phrase of angels." And that is such an unearthly thing, that you wonder it could change anything or give any nation a turn for the better or worse. Still you see, the poets did give Babel and Babylon a turn for the worse, they turned them both too frivolous with laughing and crying. I guess that's why they went.

6   Well now, one poem from me. There have been four poets here tonight, four of us up against the patrons. *(Laughter)* An unequal stand off. There's been lots about politics; lots about affairs; lots about nations and the breaking of nations. Suppose I let it go at that. Almost as if I broke into delirium, though not rated a very delirious poet. *(Laughter)*

ONE MORE BREVITY
I opened the door so my last look
Should be taken outside a house and book.
Before I gave up seeing and slept
I said I would see how Sirius kept
His watch dog eye on what remained
To be gone into if not explained.
But scarcely was my door ajar
When past the leg I thrust for bar
Slipped in to be my problem guest
Not a heavenly dog made manifest,
But an earthly dog of the carriage breed,

Who having failed of the modern speed,
Now asked asylum—and I was stirred
To be the one so dog-preferred.
He dumped himself like a bag of bones,
He sighed himself a couple of groans,
And head to tail then firmly curled
Like swearing off on the traffic world.
I set him water, I set him food.
He rolled an eye with gratitude
(Or merely manners it may have been),
But never so much as lifted chin.
His hard tail loudly smacked the floor
As if beseeching me, "Please, no more
I can't explain—tonight at least."
His brow was perceptibly trouble-creased.
So I spoke in tones of adoption thus:
"Gustie, old boy, Dalmatian Gus
You're right, there's nothing to discuss.
Don't try to tell me what's on your mind,
The sorrow of having been left behind,
Or the sorrow of having run away.
All that can wait for the light of day.
Meanwhile feel obligation-free.
Nobody has to confide in me."
'Twas too one sided a dialogue,
And I wasn't sure I was talking dog.
I broke off puzzled. But all the same
In fancy I ratified his name,
Gustie, Dalmatian Gus, that is,
And started shaping my life to his,
Finding him his right supplies
And sharing his miles of exercise.
Next morning the minute I was about
He went to the door to be let out
As much as to say, "I have paid my call.
You mustn't be hurt if now I'm all
For getting back somewhere or further on."
I opened the door and he was gone.
I was to taste in little the grief
That comes of dogs' lives being so brief,

Only a fraction of ours at most.

He might have been the dream of a ghost

In spite of the way his tail had smacked

My floor so hard and matter-of-fact.

And things have been going so strangely since

I wouldn't be too hard to convince,

I might even claim, he was Sirius

(Think of presuming to call him Gus),

The star itself, Heaven's greatest star,

Not a meteorite, but an avatar,

Who had made an overnight descent

To show by deeds he didn't resent

My profiting by his virtue so long,

Yet doing so little about it in song.

A symbol was all he could hope to convey,

An intimation, a shot of ray,

A meaning I was supposed to seek,

And finding, was indisposed to speak.

(Applause)

7   Now back to one of my very early ones that I came on the scene with. It's called "A Tuft of Flowers." It has another definition of poetry in it. It is in rhymed couplets, as that last one was, paired rhymes as it were. This is about mowing, and turning the grass behind the mower. I was the one that turned the grass behind the mower.

I went to turn the grass once after one
Who mowed it in the dew before the sun.

The dew was gone that made his blade so keen
Before I came to view the leveled scene.

I looked for him behind an isle of trees;
I listened for his whetstone on the breeze.

But he had gone his way, the grass all mown,
And I must be, as he had been,—alone,

'As all must be,' I said within my heart,
'Whether they work together or apart.'

But as I said it, swift there passed me by
On noiseless wing a bewildered butterfly,

Seeking with memories grown dim o'er night
Some resting flower of yesterday's delight.

And once I marked his flight go round and round,
As where some flower lay withering on the ground.

And then he flew as far as eye could see,
And then on tremulous wing came back to me.

I thought of questions that have no reply,
And would have turned to toss the grass to dry;

But he turned first, and led my eye to look
At a tall tuft of flowers beside a brook,

A leaping tongue of bloom the scythe had spared
Beside a reedy brook the scythe had bared.

The mower in the dew had loved them thus,
By leaving them to flourish, not for us,

Nor yet to draw one thought of ours to him,
But from sheer morning gladness at the brim.

The butterfly and I had lit upon,
Nevertheless, a message from the dawn,

That made me hear the wakening birds around,
And hear his long scythe whispering to the ground,

And feel a spirit kindred to my own;
So that henceforth I worked no more alone;

But glad with him, I worked as with his aid,
And weary, sought at noon with him the shade;

And dreaming, as it were, held brotherly speech
With one whose thought I had not hoped to reach.

'Men work together,' I told him from the heart,
'Whether they work together or apart.'

(Applause)

8   And then this last one. It is called "Away."

Now I out walking
The world desert,

And my shoe and my stocking
Do me no hurt.

I leave behind
Good friends in town.
Let them get well-wined
And go lie down.

Don't think I leave
For the outer dark
Like Adam and Eve
Put out of the Park.

Forget the myth.
There is no one I
Am put out with
Or put out by.

Unless I'm wrong
I but obey
The urge of a song:
I'm—bound—away!

And I may return
If dissatisfied
With what I learn
From having died.

(Applause)

9   A goodbye one. I thought I'd say it over again to you.

Now I out walking
The world desert,
And my shoe and my stocking
Do me no hurt.

I leave behind
Good friends in town.
Let them get well-wined
And go lie down.

Don't think I leave
For the outer dark
Like Adam and Eve

Put out of the Park.

Forget the myth.
There is no one I
Am put out with
Or put out by.

Unless I'm wrong
I but obey
The urge of a song:
I'm—bound—away!

And I may return
If dissatisfied
With what I learn
From having died.

(Applause)

10   Then an old one, "Birches," a child's play one. Just about bending birches
down to the ground. That's all there is to it.

> When I see birches bend to left and right
> Across the lines of straighter darker trees,
> I like to think some boy's been swinging them.
> But swinging doesn't bend them down to stay
> As ice-storms do. Often you must have seen them
> Loaded with ice a sunny winter morning
> After a rain. They click upon themselves
> As the breeze rises, and turn many-colored
> As the stir cracks and crazes their enamel.
> Soon the sun's warmth makes them shed crystal shells
> Shattering and avalanching on the snow-crust—
> Such heaps of broken glass to sweep away
> You'd think the inner dome of heaven had fallen.
> They are dragged to the withered bracken by the load,
> And they seem not to break; though once they are bowed
> So low for long, they never right themselves:
> You may see their trunks arching in the woods
> Years afterwards, trailing their leaves on the ground
> Like girls on hands and knees that throw their hair
> Before them over their heads to dry in the sun.
> But I was going to say when Truth broke in

With all her matter-of-fact about the ice-storm
I should prefer to have some boy bend them
As he went out and in to fetch the cows—
Some boy too far from town to learn baseball,
Whose only play was what he found himself,
Summer or winter, and could play alone.
One by one he subdued his father's trees
By riding them down over and over again
Until he took the stiffness out of them,
And not one but hung limp, not one was left
For him to conquer. He learned all there was
To learn about not launching out too soon
And so not carrying the tree away
Clear to the ground. He always kept his poise
To the top branches, climbing carefully
With the same pains you use to fill a cup
Up to the brim, and even above the brim.
Then he flung outward, feet first, with a swish,
Kicking his way down through the air to the ground.
So was I once myself a swinger of birches.
And so I dream of going back to be.
It's when I'm weary of considerations,
And life is too much like a pathless wood
Where your face burns and tickles with the cobwebs
Broken across it, and one eye is weeping
From a twig's having lashed across it open.
I'd like to get away from earth awhile
And then come back to it and begin over.
May no fate willfully misunderstand me
And half grant what I wish and snatch me away
Not to return. Earth's the right place for love:
I don't know where it's likely to go better.
I'd like to go by climbing a birch tree,
And climb black branches up a snow-white trunk
Toward heaven, till the tree could bear no more,
But dipped its top and set me down again.
That would be good both going and coming back.
One could do worse than be a swinger of birches.

(Applause)

11   Then, I ought to end with a prayer. Do you want to hear me pray? *(Applause)*

> Forgive, O Lord, my little jokes on Thee,
> And I'll forgive Thy great big one on me.

(Applause)

[A Poet's Boyhood (1960)]

1   One of my earliest San Francisco memories is political, of crossing the bay to Oakland to see my father off on a train as delegate to the Democratic National Convention at Cincinnati in 1879 to help nominate Hancock. We were Democrats and very intense ones. I remember my father's disappointment in Hancock's defeat and his even greater disappointment when Hancock as an old friend and fellow soldier of Garfield's went to Garfield's inauguration and shook hands with him in public right on the platform.

2   Four years later at the age of nine I was marching all over San Francisco in uniform in the great torchlight processions that I thought elected Grover Cleveland. At first I rode on a fire engine pulled by many men on the same loop of rope till it was decided a girl would look better up there and I was taken down to carry my torch on foot in the middle of the loop. The cause was too serious for any vanity on my part either way. As I have said we were Democrats in those days.

3   My father was chairman of the Democratic City Committee and my health not being very good I was kept out of school and taken down town with him to his office many, many days. I rode around with him in a buggy electioneering and tacking his card to the ceilings of saloons with a silver dollar for tack hammer. I often acted as his errand boy to the City Hall and to the office of the Democratic boss, Buckley, who was my kind friend. I had my lunches free off the saloon counters. I wasn't drinking myself.

4   Of course I remember a few preliminary earthquakes. I got away before the big one. And there was Woodward's Gardens with its animals, and the Cliff House where the seals yelped. Have I not written poems about both these places? I wish I could get you to read "Once by the Pacific" to yourself before I have to read it to you. It took me a long, long time to get over the idea that the Pacific Ocean was going to be more important in our history than the Atlantic. If I ever got over it. I left the Coast in '85 at the death of my father. (My father, William Prescott Frost, was a newspaper man with papers long discontinued, "The Post" and "The Bulletin.") As late as six or seven years afterwards, I was writing lines like these:

"Europe might sink and the wave of its sinking sweep
And spend itself on our shore and we would not weep.
Our cities would not even turn in their sleep.
Our faces are not that way or should not be.
Our future is in the West on the other sea."

The rest is lost. I wish I could recapture it. It was never published. Many things have happened since to confute me. But I don't know—

5   Nothing but idyllic politics. Corruption may have been in it. Lincoln Steffens says so. Looking back I can see where it might have come in.

Cambridge Mass

Oct 6 1960

Robert Frost

[A New England Tribute (1961)]

1   Hard of course to judge of the importance of an event at the time of it, but an election like that, an inauguration like this, may well be looked back on as a turning point in the history of our country, even perhaps in the history of Christendom. It was such a great jump forward toward settling it once for all that the church's reformation both from within and from without had been accomplished; the old agonies and antagonisms were over; it was tacitly conceded that our founders were not far wrong; safety lay in a plurality of denominations and doctrines unenforced by secular law. I come fresh to say this from communion with portraits by Stuart of four of them who are on record to this effect, Washington, Jefferson, Adams, and Madison, enshrined in a temple on the North Shore of Massachusetts.

> "How still a moment may precede
> One that may thrill the world forever.
> To that still moment none would heed
> Man's doom was linked no more to sever."

So someone said of the first Christmas of all seven hundred and sixty three years after the founding of Rome. Such was our gift for Christmas confirmed by vote one hundred and eighty years after the first election.

2   For New Year's the inauguration might be another gift, a more than New Year's resolution, to make sure of the more than social security of us all in a greater strength, a greater formidability. A little more decisiveness at the points of decision, we don't exactly see where or how. We look forward with confidence to young leadership to show us where and how. We can afford a little stimulation of our will to win all the way from the sports to the sciences and arts.

> We have the Olympic games as yet.
> Where is the Olympic spirit gone?
> Of two such lessons why forget
> The nobler and the manlier one?

3   We have given ourselves before: we may have to give ourselves again. I have heard the despairers of the Republic say we may need the discipline of being invaded. Our Revolution was:

> OUR GIFT OUTRIGHT
> The land was ours before we were the land's.
> She was our land more than a hundred years
> Before we were her people. She was ours
> In Massachusetts, in Virginia,
> But we were England's, still colonials,
> Possessing what we still were unpossessed by,
> Possessed by what we now no more possessed.
> Something we were withholding made us weak
> Until we found it was ourselves
> We were withholding from the land of living,
> And forthwith found salvation in surrender.
> Such as we were we gave ourselves outright
> (The deed of gift was many deeds of war)
> To the land vaguely realizing westward,
> But still unstoried, artless, unenhanced,
> Such as she was, such as she will become.

SIXTY-NINE

[Shakespeare Festival of Washington (1961)]

1   It seems to all of us that Shakespeare is one of the greatest things that ever happened in the world's history. Four hundred years of art and science have given us nothing more important. It is as necessary for libraries and theatres to keep him going—read and acted—as it is for armies and navies to keep the language he wrote in alive, so he won't have to be translated into Esperanto and Volapük.

2   There is nothing to compare with his position with us, but the King James' version—with us and with the whole world apparently. He should be staged often and well. We need him more than his reputation needs us. I am especially urging support for this enterprise in the Capital of the country.

   Robert Frost

[Tribute to Ernest Hemingway (1961)]

1   Ernest Hemingway was rough and unsparing with life. He was rough and unsparing with himself. It is like his brave free ways that he should die by accident with a weapon. Fortunately for us, if it is a time to speak of fortune, he gave himself time to make his greatness. His style dominated our story telling long and short. I remember the fascination that made me want to read aloud *The Killers* to everybody that came along. He was a friend I shall miss. The country is in mourning.

SEVENTY-ONE

[Comments on "Choose Something Like a Star" (1962)]

1   I am not partial with my poems, any more than a mother with her children. But your choice, "Choose Something Like a Star," is one I like to say.

2   I seem to fancy it as rather Horatian in its ending. Then I like the two ways of spelling 'staid'; that's playing the words. And I like to mingle science and spirit here—as I do so deliberately in my new book.

3   But there are things beyond all this which I care more about, and hope we all do.

    Robert Frost

[Tribute to William Faulkner (1962)]

1   I had to admire him for the position he won for us in the world as an American. I read him for the deep dark magnificence of his "Tale Told by an Idiot" in the same way I admire the passage in Shakespeare that he takes the title from. His humor has the same macabre quality as in the story of the Choctaw Indians with their negro slaves and even in the story "That Evening Sun." Our personal acquaintance was but slight. My chief recollection would be of my daughter and me seeing him off from Rio de Janeiro, Brazil, to attend his daughter's wedding in Mississippi. I should like to have known him better. Sixty five is too young for a man to retire from the world or from his occupation.

SEVENTY-THREE

[Comments on "The Cold War Is Being Won" (1962)]

1   Dear Mr. Heineman:

The very name of your magazine gives me conscientious qualms for my not having given the attention I should have to who's running the county. I should be writing you an article about that but articles seem nothing I can undertake. I hate a cold war of sustained hate that finds no relief in blood letting but probably it should be regarded as a way of stalling till we find out whether there is really an issue big enough for a big show-down. We are given pause from the dread of the terribleness we feel capable of. I was sometimes like that as a boy with another boy I lived in antipathy with. It clouded my days. But here I am almost writing the article I was going to tell you I couldn't write. My limit seems to be verse and talk. I am dictating this.

    With regrets
    Sincerely yours,
    Robert Frost

[Statement Concerning the Beginning of His Career (1963)]

1   This letter is right out of events that capped the climax of four of the most lucky years of my life.

2   Edward Garnett's article was an unexpected extra gratuity after all the British had been doing for me before I came home. Ellery Sedgwick had been teasing me about publishing the poems he had already accepted: "Birches," "The Road Not Taken," "The Sound of Trees." He had been teasing me about publishing them and had gone on to tease me about the article. He said that he wasn't sure he would publish them, but he probably meant to publish both, and he now did at the best time of the year for all concerned. And the splash made waves that still keep coming to me after forty-five years.

3   The warmth of the letter is as much out of gratitude to the British in general as to Edward Garnett for giving me my start as a poet of our common language. (It still glows in me from my friends at Oxford, Cambridge, Durham—and Dublin.) And this always without prejudice to my own country. As I say elsewhere at the end of a poem, "I would not be taken as ever having rebelled"—except possibly for a moment now and then, as when an editor (in fact the editor of *The Atlantic*), in his natural misgivings about new things, rejected several of the *North of Boston* eclogues in a curt letter with *regrets that his magazine had no place for my vigorous verse.* (I quote him verbatim.) It is a happy continuation of the story of my discovery, to be still further discovered as a stranger by Edward Garnett's generosity. He apparently hadn't heard of what had happened to me over there before I came home.

4   It is all a very pleasant adventure to look back on.
    Robert Frost

SEVENTY-FIVE

[Press Release on Being Awarded the Bollingen Prize (1963)]

1   A sweet coincidence to have the great doctors of this great hospital,—Dr. Hartwell Harrison, Dr. George Thorn, Dr. Roger Hickler,—hand me a virtual new lease to live and on the same day and hour, the Bollingen Prize Committee of Yale University Library gives one new reason to live. I am in a critical position to appreciate the Committee's unanimity. It is magnificent. I was not always too sure of where all of them stood and that is as it should be, John Hall Wheelock, Allen Tate, Louise Bogan, Richard Eberhart, Robert Lowell, poets one and all of first esteem. And I musn't forget to thank the Librarian of Yale University, James T. Babb, for rounding them up. You should have seen the excitement in the hospital when his news came. This year or so has been a year for me taken to the President's side for his inauguration, and allowed to stand around listening where Premier Kruschev declared Russia a Western nation to be trusted as such in heroic rivalry.

Robert Frost

SEVENTY-SIX

[Statement Written for the 53rd Annual Dinner of the Poetry Society of America (January 17, 1963)]

1   Here we are again the Poetry Power of America and me sorry to be missing. May we never grow less and may our prizes be more felt over the whole country. For the moment I am in no strength to give you anything more than my blessing. May the country never doubt that poetry is it and it is the country.

2   I may wobble when I'm sitting up but I never waver.
     R. F.

Editorial Principles

Notes

Line-End Hyphenation

Acknowledgments

General Index

Index of Items by Title

Editorial Principles

This edition of Frost's prose writings includes works for which the author's finished or nearly finished manuscripts and typescripts survive, and works for which the published form provides the only surviving text. In the case of works from the latter group, Frost's finished manuscripts or typescripts have been lost, or, what is rarer, the manuscripts that do survive represent such early versions of the text that they cannot form the basis for an edition of the finished essay. Here I have relied on the published text as providing the best record—in fact, the sole record—of Frost's intentions. When the only surviving text of an essay is the published form, my editorial interventions are usually limited to the correction of misprints. However, in a few instances, early, incomplete versions of an essay have provided the basis for emendations to the published form, which serves as the copy-text.

Fortunately, much documentation is available for a great many more of Frost's essays and articles, among them his best known and most important. My aim in these cases, as throughout the edition, is to produce the text of each essay as Frost intended it to read in published form. The question of punctuation is the most difficult one an editor of Frost's prose must confront. Frost often dictated drafts of his essays, and had assistants prepare typescript drafts of them. Similarly, in revising several lectures for publication, he worked on transcripts prepared from stenographers' reports or from audio recordings. Consequently, the punctuation of his published essays often does not issue completely (or even at all) from his pen. In various degrees difficult to measure precisely, his punctuation is at times supplied by other people, whether a stenographer, his secretary Kathleen Morrison, or someone else; in fact, the revision, and at times even the composition, of his essays meshes with the labors of others. In considering Frost's punctuation, I have, then, worked from a definition of his intentions that accommodates the circumstances under which he typically chose to compose and publish his essays. This means that I accept the effects on his texts of these three related factors: the distinction he drew in practice between the punctuation of private and public texts, the occasional determination of his punctuation by transcribers of the talks he revised for publication, and his association with Kathleen Morrison and other assistants like her. If one decides, as I have, to respect the consequences of these circumstances in editing Frost's prose, it follows that, barring unusual circumstances, the final version of a text prepared under their regime is to be preferred. Whether or not this text is the published one varies case by case.

A brief description of Kathleen Morrison's relationship to Frost is in order here. She began working for him, as secretary and manager, in 1938, several months after Elinor White Frost, the poet's wife, died, and she remained with him until his death in 1963. She describes her work with the poet in a memoir, *Robert Frost: A Pictorial Chronicle* (New York: Holt, 1974): "In my new secretarial and managerial capacity the understanding was that I should go from Cambridge to Boston [where Frost had taken an apartment] around half past nine in the morning and supposedly leave at four in the afternoon. But from the time I first began to work with him until the end, time was of no consequence. I could be summoned after hours, on Saturdays and Sundays, on holidays, sometimes finding real problems but more often emotional upsets" (20).

During the summers after 1939, Morrison and her family lived together with Frost on his Homer Noble Farm in Ripton, Vermont. Frost lived in a cabin set off from the main house, which the Morrisons occupied. Morrison remembers working with him on the farm where "the days involved a rigidly divided pattern. From ten in the morning until three in the afternoon Robert's life was his own, a time he might write, read, or merely think. During these hours I was the only presence allowed in the cabin with him" (27). She took dictation, handled correspondence with his publisher, and managed his lecture engagements. In preparing essays for publication, Frost often dictated a working draft to Morrison. The two of them then went over the draft together as Frost dictated further revisions. At other times, Frost wrote his draft out in manuscript before bringing it to Morrison. Of course, whether the original was his manuscript, or hers as dictated by him, she next prepared from it a neat typescript, which might be corrected and revised yet again. On these typescripts, corrections usually appear in both her hand and in Frost's, but occasionally only in hers, which is to be expected given Frost's practice of dictation.

It seems clear that an edition of Frost's published prose presenting his essays in the unconventional punctuation that characterizes his private manuscripts would do some violence to his wish, expressed often enough in his writings, to be original (and even subversive) in covert, rather than in overt, ways. In the published writings, he almost always works within accepted institutions and conventions, though with a keen sense of his ironic relationship to them. He understood well Emerson's admonition in "New England Reformers": "It is handsomer to remain in the establishment better than the establishment" (*EL* 596). Frost begins his introduction to E. A. Robinson's *King Jasper* by looking out upon the welter of technical and cosmetic reforms in modernist poetry with a specifically Emersonian impatience: "It may come to the notice of posterity (and then again it may not) that this, our age, ran wild in the quest of new ways to be new. The one old way no longer served. Science put it into our heads that there must be new ways to be new. Those tried were largely by subtraction—elimination. Poetry, for example, was tried without punctuation. It was tried without capital letters," and so on (22.1). For his part—and he enlists Robinson for support—he remained content with "the old way to be new," as against the "new" ways of e. e. cummings and others (22.2). Frost would not have sanctioned any edition that presented his essays in a form radically different from the more or less conventional one he grew comfortable working inside over the course of his fifty-year career as a published writer.

The present edition attempts to collect all of the prose that Frost prepared for print. Collected also are several unpublished essays and prefaces that are of significant interest; here, I have included only essays that seem to have been finished and that stand alone as separate works. Robert Faggen has edited *The Notebooks of Robert Frost* (Cambridge, Mass.: Harvard University Press, 2006), many of which contain essay-like entries of much interest. Selections from these notebooks had previously been published in *Prose Jottings: Selections from His Notebooks,* edited by Edward Connery Lathem and Hyde Cox (Lunenburg, Vt.: Northeast-Kingdom, 1982). See also the appendix to *IMO,* "Robert Frost's English Notebooks." Margot Feldman edited for publication a notebook kept by Frost between 1918 and 1921; for this, see Frost, "Notebook: After England" *Antaeus* 61 (Autumn 1988): 147–64. But Faggen's edition of the notebooks supersedes all previous efforts to bring these fascinating documents into print, alike in its comprehensiveness and in its rigor. I have included letters written to editors of several periodicals and books because Frost seems to have intended these for publication. Finally, I have chosen to include as well a series of short stories Frost wrote for his children while living on his farm in Derry, N.H., from 1900–1909. These have been published before as *Stories for Lesley,* edited by Roger Sell (Charlottesville: University Press of Virginia, 1984), now out of print. Additionally, three of the stories were reprinted from Sell's edition in *CPPP* (657–61). I include them here, somewhat in violation of my general standards of inclusion, because of their intrinsic interest, because they seem to me rather to belong alongside the published "poultry-farming" stories that succeed them in the present edition, and because they are not likely soon to find preservation in print in any other edition.

Omitted materials include talks and lectures never revised for publication by Frost; interviews; interviews edited by other hands to read like an address or speech; and articles consisting entirely of extracts from interviews or speeches.

A word more about Frost's public lectures and readings: Many of these survive on audiotapes and in transcripts in major collections of his works at Dartmouth College, Amherst College, and the University of Virginia. But the great resources of even these libraries are not adequate to prepare a reliably comprehensive edition of his talks. Lisa Seale has catalogued more than 700 public readings in the period 1940–1962. The earliest transcripts I know of date from 1916, the latest from 1962. These were delivered in scores of cities across America and abroad. It was not uncommon for Frost's talks to be mechanically recorded in some form beginning in the early 1930s. The 1940s and 1950s saw an increase both in his lecturing and in his fame. Dozens of audio recordings of his talks survive from this period, though these lie scattered across the country in various libraries. It is beyond the scope of this edition to undertake a census and presentation of Frost's unpublished talks, which, in any case, involve very different kinds of textual problems from those presented by the prose. No selection can be confidently made until as many talks as can be gathered have been examined. However, as I indicate in the Introduction, I have reprinted in the notes many (often extensive) extracts from the unpublished transcripts of talks that I have examined, when they illuminate the published prose.

Some further explanation of my criteria for inclusion seems called for, and I will give several examples. The first involves a so-called "Introduction" by Frost for Frederic Fox, *14 Africans vs. One American* (New York: Macmillan, 1962, xi–xii). This is not, properly speaking, an article prepared by Frost for this purpose. It is a brief excerpt, in which Frost describes his friend Fox, from a talk given at Ford Hall Forum, Boston, on December 3, 1961. Frost is named neither on the title page nor in the table of contents for the book; the excerpt was lifted from the speech and prepared for separate publication by other hands. Frost himself played no part beyond granting permission for the transaction. Since this "Introduction" is but a quotation borrowed from another context without his editorial intervention, I do not reprint it in the present edition.

Another item of this sort is a pamphlet titled *The Mona Bronfman Sheckman Lectures* (Bronxville, N.Y.: Sarah Lawrence College, 1962). This pamphlet reprints extracts from the Sheckman lecture series, in which Frost spoke on April 17, 1962; he played no editorial role in preparing these extracts for press. A third example is a Frost item published as "Playful Talk" in *American Academy of Arts and Letters, Proceedings* 12 (1962): 180–89. To the reader of the *Proceedings* "Playful Talk" appears to be the text of a speech delivered by Frost on April 11, 1961, before the Institute of Arts and Letters. However, examination of the original transcript of the talk (prepared by The Master Reporting Company) indicates that Glenway Wescott, President of the Institute, took what was an informal question-and-answer performance by Frost and edited it to read like a continuous speech. He accomplished this by removing the remarks of Frost's various interlocutors, and by making certain further revisions which that removal necessitated. Because neither of the latter two items represents the text of remarks prepared by Frost for publication, or the text of an integrated "talk," I omit them from the present edition.

Similar problems rule out the inclusion of three other talks familiar to Frost's readers: "Poverty and Poetry," "The Poet's Next of Kin in College," and "What Became of New England?" The first two of these appeared together in *Biblia* 9 (February 1938). "Poverty and Poetry" was delivered at Haverford College on October 25, 1927, "The Poet's Next of Kin in College" at Princeton University on October 26. Lawrance Thompson explains how they came to be published:

> One thing which furthered that friendship [i.e., Thompson's friendship with Frost] even more was my telling him, after he had completed his talk, that I had been so bold as to put a stenographer in the audience at Haverford, another in the audience at Princeton; that if he wanted the transcripts torn up, he could say the word. No, he was glad I had done that. After he had gone, I had another idea: why not have those two speeches printed in the Princeton University Library periodical, *Biblia*. It would make a nice collector's item. So I wrote him, asking if he would give his permission, and he wrote back on November 22 [1937] from Amherst: "Yes, if you will undertake to make them read like something. Cutting might help." Well I undertook it all right. I edited them heavily, and even took the liberty of compressing sentences where he had spoken with a certain amount of clumsiness . . . [O]n January 15 [1937], he wrote me the following letter: "Dear Lawrance: I'm not anxious to hear that you printed my speech on the Poets Next of Kin but I am to hear that if you printed it or tried to print it it didn't get you in trouble with the athletic authorities. I assume you got my telegram of permission. You know my feeling about these speeches. I am getting less and less reluctant to have them published. Thats because my scattered thoughts of a lifetime are beginning to group up into natural shapes." (*TLY* 359–60)

The original stenographic records of the two talks have apparently been lost. My efforts to locate them at Princeton University Library and at the University of Virginia's Alderman Library (where most of Thompson's papers are deposited) proved fruitless. As Thompson's remarks suggest, the talks as published do not provide an accurate record of Frost's actual words. The Thompson papers held at the Firestone Library, Princeton University, contain a folder pertaining to his service as editor of *Biblia* (subsequently called *The Princeton University Library Chronicle*). In that folder is a copy of the February 1938 number of *Biblia* reprinting Frost's two lectures. Opposite the first of these, Thompson has written in ink: "Here is a Frost item that's a Thompson item. I put stenographers in the audience at Princeton and Haverford, got the lectures, then with Frost's permission—and at the suggestion of Frost—compressed them to their present form. The sentences are *mostly* his. I wanted the lectures printed separately in pamphlet form, but Princeton said no." The innuendo of the phrase "the sentences are *mostly* his" raises questions about how extensive Thompson's editorial work on the talks might have been.

"What Became of New England?" presents a related problem. The history of that talk begins with Frost's spoken performance at the Oberlin College commencement ceremonies, on June 8, 1937. A stenographic record of that performance formed the basis for a typescript of the address—held now in the Oberlin College Archives—prepared by Robert S. Newdick of the Department of English at Ohio State University. This typescript next went through a further battery of revisions, performed by Newdick, before appearing in the *Oberlin Alumni Magazine* 34.7 (May 1938): 5–6. The text of the address likely went through this last set of revisions before Newdick submitted it to Lesley Frost for approval in the spring of 1938. (Frost's wife had recently died; Newdick did not wish to bother him with the matter.) Lesley Frost did approve the text, according to a note, presumably written by Newdick himself, on the last page of the *Oberlin Alumni Magazine* in which the address appears: "Mr. Robert S. Newdick of the Department of English of Ohio State University is an enthusiastic admirer of Mr. Frost and thoroughly familiar with his thought and style. He has, through paragraphing and punctuation, brought out the nature and quality of the talk. Mr. Frost's daughter, Lesley, also graciously consented to check-read the copy." However, that final typescript, which would have been the copy-text for the first appearance (if it was distinct from the one now held at Oberlin), has been lost, and it is impossible to determine whether the last set of revisions was entirely Newdick's, or whether some were suggested by Lesley Frost after she saw a draft of the speech as reflected in the Oberlin typescript. Only one thing is clear: as a *precise* record of Frost's words, "What became of New England?" is unreliable. The tightly focused text of the Oberlin typescript certainly represents a significant revision of Frost's actual remarks, since he spoke extemporaneously. In the auction catalog of his collection of Frostiana, William Stitt quotes an August 23, 1937, letter to him from Virginia Van Fossman, Resident Alumni Secretary of Oberlin: "It was the general consensus of opinion that the rambling remarks which Mr. Frost made [at the commencement] were not worthy of him." Newdick thought otherwise and prepared the published, apparently much-edited version of the address. The only record of his emendations to the address exists in the differences in wording between the Oberlin typescript and the published text. The extent of Newdick's revisions of the stenographic record itself remains a mystery.

My view is that "What Became of New England?"—together with "Poverty and Poetry" and its companion piece—may best be handled in a volume of Frost's informal talks, or in a heterogeneous edition of his writings in all genres, rather than in a critical edition dedicated to his written prose. In any case, the three talks just discussed are readily available in *CPPP* (where a textual caveat is given in the notes). Additionally, a number of the talks Frost delivered at the Bread Loaf Writers' Conference and School of English in the later years of his life have been edited from tape recordings for publication by Reginald L. Cook in *Robert Frost: A Living Voice* (Amherst: University of Massachusetts Press, 1974). Two of Frost's earliest talks are reprinted in Elaine Barry, *Robert Frost on Writing* (New Brunswick, N.J.: Rutgers University Press, 1973), and again in *CPPP*. The latter volume includes as well Frost's late lecture "On Extravagance," in a transcription prepared anew from the original tape recording. In the second and third volumes of his biography of Frost, Lawrance Thompson quotes extensively from a number of otherwise unpublished talks and lectures. Other published talks are listed in my article "Robert Frost's Prose Writings: A Comprehensive Annotated Checklist" (a full citation is given in note 5 to the Introduction). Readers interested in Frost's career as a lecturer and public speaker should consult these sources.

This edition does not aim to reproduce non-textual features of the copy texts. Titles that appear within brackets, are editorially supplied, either by me or by a previous editor. Titles without brackets are Frost's. Dates following titles have been editorially supplied. Throughout the edition I use italics to indicate emphasis, though in the original typescripts and manuscripts such emphasis is indicated by underlining. As for the styling of titles of books, magazines, and so on: in manuscripts and typescripts, Frost's own usage is inconsistent. I have usually adopted the conventionalized styling that appears in his published texts. The contents of the edition are presented chronologically by date of first publication, or, in the case of previously unpublished materials, by date of composition.

Notes

The notes for each item give its textual history, together with any other significant information bearing on it. Collations, which follow the textual notes for each item, describe all emendations in wording and punctuation made to the copy-texts for this edition, as well as significant variants in wording from other authoritative texts of the essays and articles. Following each collation are explanatory notes, except where no such notes are needed; these gloss quotations and references, and provide other information of interest. As a rule, I have not annotated names and terms readily available in common reference works.

All entries in the collations and explanatory notes are keyed to the present edition by item and paragraph number (in some cases, I have grouped a number of texts into a single "item," as with the high-school journalism, the items associated with Pinkerton Academy, the children's stories, and the poultry-farming stories). An asterisk before an entry in the collation indicates an emendation; entries with no asterisk record variant wordings where no emendation is involved. The reading of the present edition always precedes the bracket in each entry. When an emendation comes from a documentary source, published or unpublished, that source is given immediately after the bracket. When no source is indicated, the emendation is first made here by the present editor. The rejected copy-text reading follows the bracket, or, when a source for the emendation is indicated, the semicolon. Comments inside braces {} are mine. When text is repeated verbatim from one side of the entry—that is, of the bracket—to the other, a ~ sign is used to indicate the repetition. Two braces with a space in between {   } placed to the right of a bracket indicate that the copy-text has a blank space at this point, dropping a word or punctuation mark. For example, the following:

> *27.1 has ever been] 1st; was ever

indicates that this entry describes an emendation (hence the asterisk), that the phrase is to be found in paragraph 1 of item 27 of the present edition; that the copy-text has been emended from "was ever" to "has ever been" (copy-texts are always identified in the notes preceding the collations); that the emendation follows the reading as it stands in the first appearance, as identified in the textual notes.

The same list and system of abbreviation are used to record variant wordings in other significant forms of the texts. Variant readings in punctuation are generally not given, except when the variant punctuation changes a statement to a question, or vice versa; when the meaning is clearly affected; or when the variant punctuation incidentally occurs within the citation of a variant wording. As with emendations, the reading of the present edition always precedes the bracket in each entry; variant readings succeed the bracket, followed by abbreviations identifying their source. When variant texts of a given article differ so widely from the copy-text as to constitute a distinct version, I have generally not recorded the variations, in order to avoid over-complicating the collations. For example, the following:

36.3 And there are many other things I have found myself saying about poetry,
but the chiefest of these is that it is metaphor] There are ~ ML; The supreme
thing is metaphor MS

indicates: that the entry—lacking an asterisk—does not describe an emendation; that the
phrase is to be found in paragraph 3 of item 36; that the reading in this edition is "And
there are many other things I have found myself saying about poetry, but the chiefest of
these is that it is metaphor"; that the reading in the Modern Library text ("ML": abbreviation identified in the relevant notes) is "'There are many other things'", etc.; that the reading at this point in the manuscript identified in the notes (and abbreviated "MS") is "The
supreme thing is metaphor."

1. Articles and Editorials from the Lawrence, Massachusetts, *High School Bulletin* (1891–92)

Frost's classmates elected him editor of the Lawrence, Mass., *High School Bulletin* in the
spring of 1891. (He had previously published two poems in the *Bulletin,* but no prose.)
Frost assumed his duties in the fall, writing five editorials for the paper's September 1891
editorial page and serving as editor through the October, November, and December numbers of the *Bulletin.* After resigning early in 1892, Frost filled in as editor of the May 1892
number, supplying four editorials. Later, the *Bulletin* for June 1892 reprinted his valedictory
address, "A Monument to After-Thought Unveiled." Following is a checklist of articles and
editorials published in the *Bulletin* known or thought to be written by Frost:

> [Five unsigned editorials.] Lawrence, Mass. *High School Bulletin* 13.1
> (September 1891): 4.
> [Two unsigned editorials.] 13.2 (October 1891): 4.
> [Three unsigned editorials.] 13.3 (November 1891): 4.
> "Petra and Its Surroundings." 13.4 (December 1891): 1–2.
> "Physical Culture." 13.4 (December 1891): 2.
> "The Charter Oak at Hartford." 13.4 (December 1891): 2.
> "M. Bonner, Deceased." 13.4 (December 1891): 3.
> [Three unsigned editorials.] 13.4 (December 1891): 4.
> "L.H.S.D.U. Unofficial Report" [Column of the debating union.] 13.4 (December
> 1891): 6–7.
> [Four editorials.] 13.9 (May 1892): 4.
> "A Monument to After-Thought Unveiled." 13.10 (June 1892): 10.

The editorials are typically unsigned, the exception being the fourth in the May 1892 number. Frost's contributions to the December number, exclusive of those appearing on the
editorial page, are signed pseudonymously. I retain the pseudonyms here. "A Monument
to After-Thought Unveiled" is signed "Robert Frost."

The copy-texts for the present edition are the first appearances. I have corrected a number of misprints, as recorded in the collation. I have also supplied the dates given parenthetically after the title of each item. Three asterisks centered in the text as a divider indicate a typographical device in the original. A detailed account of Frost's high-school
literary career, together with complete facsimiles of the numbers of the *Bulletin* edited by

him, is given in Edward Connery Lathem and Lawrance Thompson, *Robert Frost and the Lawrence, Massachusetts, "High School Bulletin"* (New York: The Grolier Club, 1966), now out of print.

Collation

*1.6   there are eighteen] their ~
*1.9   sub-master,] sub-master
*1.9   years'] year's
*1.14   years'] year's
*1.15   known that] known th t
*1.31   wake.] wake
*1.41   proportions] proportions,
*1.59   For hundreds] For hnndreds
*1.59   really conquered.] really conquered,
*1.60   C.B.] C B.
*1.64   develops] developes
*1.80   naught.] naught."
*1.83   arc-light] arc light
*1.84   The wrapping] he wrapping
*1.89   Mitchel's] Mitchell's {See explanatory note 1.89.}
*1.113   noiselessly] noisely
*1.117   poverty,] poverty.
*1.126   after-thought] afterthought {The hyphenated spelling is otherwise consistent throughout the speech in the copy-text.}
*1.128   may seem] may see
*1.128   influence on] influence{not present}
*1.128   as scientists] as scientist

Explanatory Notes

1.3   Raleigh's words] Raleigh, it is said, inscribed the line "Fain would I climb but that I fear to fall" on a palace window, to which Elizabeth replied with her own inscription: "If thy heart fail thee, climb not at all."

1.18   L.H.S.] Lawrence, Mass., High School.

1.41   Holmes] Oliver Wendell Holmes (1809–94), American essayist, poet, novelist.

1.41   *spruch-sprecher*] German: author of sententious remarks.

1.46   Mt. Hor] A mountain on the border of ancient Edom.

1.48   Petra] Ancient city situated in a valley west of ancient Edom. The site of the city is reached by passage through a gorge called the Siq, which Frost refers to later in this essay.

1.60   C.B.] Frost's pseudonym; perhaps a nod to his friend and former classmate Carl Burrell.

1.67   Sinon] Frost's pseudonym; name of the Greek warrior who, having pretended to desert the Greek army besieging Troy, accompanied the Trojan horse inside the city gates. He is a proverbially treacherous figure, placed by Dante in the eighth circle of Hell. Why Frost should have signed his article on "physical culture" with this name is not clear; perhaps he had no more fondness for "physical culture" than many modern high-school kids have for what we now call "PE."

1.68   Andros] Sir Edmund Andros (1637–1714), colonial governor of the province of New York and, later, of all New England. As James II's deputy, Andros revoked the charters of the colonies, precipitating the events Frost alludes to here. At Hartford in 1687, colonists led by Captain Joseph Wadsworth (1650–1729) hid the charter in an oak when Andros tried to secure it. Frost likely cribbed his account of the "charter oak" from J. Hammond Trumbull, *Memorial History of Hartford County, Connecticut, 1633–1884* (Boston: Edward L. Osgood, 1886).

1.70   Mr. Stuart] Isaac W. Stuart (1809–61), historian, came into possession of the property on which the "charter oak" stood in 1840.

1.73   A.C.C., '94] Frost's pseudonym; explanation unknown.

1.76   Rapheal] I assume this is the spelling Frost intended, not "Raphael." Perhaps he indicates a comic, bumpkinish pronunciation of the name given his plagiarizing artist: "Raph*eel*."

1.85   Kthon] Frost's pseudonym; from the Greek work for earth. For speculation as to why he might have chosen this name, see the Introduction.

1.89   Mitchel's "Stellar World"] Ormsby MacKnight Mitchel (1809–1862), American army officer, astronomer, engineer; author of *The Planetary and Stellar Worlds* (1848).

1.93   H.L.M.] Frost's pseudonym; explanation unknown.

1.94   L.H.S.D.U.] Lawrence High School Debating Union.

1.98   Cushing's Manual] Frost refers to Luther Stearns Cushing (1803–56), author of *Manual of Parliamentary Practice; Rules of Proceeding and Debate in Deliberative Assemblies* (Boston, 1867).

1.111–112   A Monument to After-Thought Unveiled] Frost's valedictory speech, delivered at the commencement exercises. He shared valedictory honors with Elinor White, his future wife.

2. [The American About and Abroad (1895)]

Relatively little is known about Frost's brief career at two Lawrence, Mass., newspapers in the winter of 1895. In a January 30, 1895, letter he reported the following to Susan Hayes Ward, literary editor of the New York City-based *Independent*, the first professional magazine that had published his poetry: "You are not to pardon my remissness: but it is the truth that you have wished me well to such good purpose that I have been busy night and day for two weeks. I am a reporter on a local newspaper! . . . My newspaper work requires a brave effort. They assure me I have much to learn particularly in the way of writing; but what care I: I have done the best I can with what I know: and if I know everything I have reached my limit. Let them teach me" (*SL* 26). Frost refers to the Lawrence *Daily American*, in which the February 2 column here reprinted first appeared, among a collage of testimonials for Dr. Greene's Nervura, Japanese Liver Pellets, and Lydia E. Pinkham's Vegetable Compound.

Frost had occasion to remember his work as a reporter in November 1924 and in March 1925 when he gave interviews to, respectively, the *Boston Sunday Globe* and the Lawrence *Telegram*. Gardner Jackson quotes him in the *Sunday Globe:* "It's amusing that I once had a column on a newspaper before columnists were ever known. Of course it wasn't like the present columns. I wrote about things I'd seen. Sort of prose poems. I remember one thing was about women I'd watched from my window picking up coal along the railroad tracks. Another was about an eagle that flew over Lawrence and alighted on the brass ball at the top of the flag pole on the Postoffice Building. An ardent hunter got out his gun and shot the eagle on the flagpole perch. That was worth writing about." The interviewer for the *Telegram* writes: "Like many authors living today Robert Frost was also something of a newspaper reporter, but unlike many of them his reportorial work did not influence his poetic career. In the interval between his two times at college, Dartmouth and Harvard, Mr. Frost was a reporter on the old *Sun* and *American* [the *Sun* was the Sunday issue of the *American*]. His greatest interest in his newspaper work was a column which he wrote. When he was a student at Harvard he edited the *Sentinel* which was a weekly publication. But he never pulled a scoop, and commenting on his ability as a newspaper man he said, with a sly banter: 'I was as bad a newspaper reporter as I was a farmer.'" The "column" alluded to is no doubt the "American About and Abroad" in the *Daily American*. That Frost "edited" the *Sentinel* is a suggestion made in the 1925 interview for the first time. It is apparently corroborated by Frost in a letter written to Louis Untermeyer twenty-five years later, though the letter dates his editorial work in the spring of 1895, not in 1897–99 when he was a student at Harvard.

Early in 1950, Untermeyer was preparing a biographical essay on Frost to be published as an introduction to *The Road Not Taken,* a selection of the poet's work. At his request, Frost supplied information about his early days in Lawrence in two letters of February 15 and 21. In the first he writes: "One year I was editing all by myself the old *Lawrence Sentinel* newspaper. Another I was writing paragraphs as a sort of columnist on *The Lawrence American*" (RFLU 353). And in the second: "In '94 I began as a reporter on the Lawrence *American* but gravitated to the editorial page where I wrote 'paragraphs' some of which though in prose were really eclogues. I remember the subject of two or three. Out of them came 'Mending Wall,' 'The Woodpile,' and 'Two Look at Two'" (RFLU 355). Untermeyer asked Frost to clarify certain particulars of the two letters, among them his work at the newspapers. Frost responded: "The *Sentinel* was a dying old weekly we had sent us from Lawrence when I was a child in San Francisco. I was asked to try putting life back into it when I was teaching private school with my mother. I failed. A young Irishman who succeeded me put so much life in to it that he got put in jail" (RFLU 357). In an interview with Neil Hertz published in *The Amherst Student* for May 10, 1951, Frost "recalled an incident that occurred when he was a newspaper reporter. It seems he was to accompany a lady who planned to expose a spiritualist. At the appropriate time during the séance Frost, who was concealing an oil lantern beneath his coat, was to focus a beam on the medium, while the 'exposer' would pull aside a curtain and reveal the hoax. All went well until Frost's lantern pervaded his surroundings with a suspicious smell and 'two big men came and chucked me out.' That was the last of the poet's anti-medium operations" (4). And in a short interview with Ruth Selzer published in *The Philadelphia Bulletin* on November 18, 1954, Frost remarked: "I was young and shy. My editor said I should get around to saloons more. I wasn't a very good reporter." These few references, together with evidence from the papers themselves, provide the basis for the following account of Frost's newspaper career.

Frost began as a reporter for the *American* in early to mid-January 1895. (He remembers it as 1894 in the letter to Untermeyer, but Frost's January 30, 1895, letter confirms mid-January as the earliest date.) He did routine reporting and contributed to a column called "The American About and Abroad." That column, always unsigned, appeared almost daily on the editorial page of the *American*. It ran long before and long after the period in which Frost could have written for the paper, and so was by no means exclusively his column. The column usually dealt with local political matters, and at times with what we now call "human interest" stories. During the time Frost definitely worked for the *American,* the character of the column changed somewhat, depending more consistently on the sort of "paragraphs" Frost wrote in the article here reprinted. It is possible that he wrote quite a few of the columns for January and February, though I can definitely assign him only the one for February 2 on the basis of his allusion to its subject in the 1924 interview. (No story about the eagle on the flagpole appears in the column during this period; neither does any dealing with the subjects of the poems Frost names in the letter to Untermeyer.) Why Frost left the paper sometime in February is not clear. Lawrance Thompson reports that he quit the paper in disgust after its managing editor, then involved in "litigation concerning graft and embezzlement," sent him to cover a private wedding: "He was ordered to threaten the father of the bride by saying that if Frost was not permitted to attend the wedding he would write and publish a story about it anyway. It took a little time for him to realize that he had been asked to perform a kind of blackmail. After he had thought it over, he stayed away from the wedding, and quit his job" (*TEY* 195). I find in the *American* and in the rival *Evening-Tribune* no mention of an embezzlement suit at this time. Beginning in early March, however, there is coverage of a libel suit which named the editor and the manager of the *American,* John F. Gilden and William S. Jewett, respectively. Yet it seems likely that Frost had by this time already left the paper to join the *Sentinel,* a newly regenerated weekly.

Frost's remarks in the letters to Untermeyer are supported circumstantially, at least in some details, by advertisements and articles in the *American* and in the *Evening-Tribune*. A talk-of-the-town column called "Lend Me Your Ears" ran regularly in the *Evening-Tribune*. In it, there appeared this story on January 28, 1895: "So the old 'Sentinel,' which for 45 years expounded Andrew Jackson's blessings on government 'like dew from heaven,' has given up the ghost. It is understood that the goodwill of the paper has been purchased by License Commissioner Donoghue." Apparently, then, the *Sentinel* failed and was bought out in January 1895. By mid-February advertisements began running in the *American* and in the *Evening-Tribune* for the "new" *Sentinel*. It was to be a Sunday weekly of literary tendencies. Advertisements promised new columns on cultural, political, and community affairs. It was probably at this time that Frost was hired by the fledgling-phoenix newspaper "to try to put some life into it," as he says to Untermeyer. Frost further reports to Untermeyer that he wrote for the paper while teaching in a private school run by his mother. And, indeed, this he did do during the spring of 1895, precisely when the new *Sentinel* was getting underway. All of this suggests that Frost worked for the paper in late winter and early spring of 1895, after he left the *American*. Unfortunately, the *Sentinel* for 1895 has been lost, as has been the Sunday *Sun-American* for winter and spring of 1895. The present editor inquired at public libraries in Essex County and at the Massachusetts Newspaper Program, a project based in the Boston Public Library that has compiled a record of library holdings of newspapers published in Massachusetts. No institution reports either the *Sentinel* or the *Sun* among its collections for the winter and spring of 1895. (A great many back issues of the two newspapers were destroyed in paper drives during World War I.) Unless copies of the newspapers turn up in private hands, it seems that Frost's first professional writings are lost, or unassignable to him, with the exception of the February 2 column from the *American* reprinted here in full.

Collation

*2.1   sone one else.] some one else,

*2.2   Sultan,] Sultan

*2.3   superior,] superior

*2.4   compelling] compeling

*2.6   defunct? I] defunct I?

*2.6   neighborhood,] neighborhood

*2.6   windows,] windows

*2.6   inscription] insciption

*2.6   Nommore!"] Nommore!

*2.6—Nommore!"] Nommore!"

Explanatory Notes

2.1   The Armenian] Melkon Garabedian, a member of Lawrence's large and politically active Armenian community, whose letter to the *Daily American* appeared on January 19, 1895:

> I am an Armenian born in Gormey, Harpoot, Turkey in Asia. In religion I am a Congregationalist. I will become a citizen next March. My family is in Turkey and this is my experience. My only hope is in the people of America. Your friend would like to tell you of the treatment of his people by the Turkish government and by the Hammedey soldiers. The Armenians are persecuted more today than ever before, because the Turkish sultan would like to destroy all the Christian nations in the world[.] He believes in his own prophet, Moh[a]mmed[,] and thinks that all others should. When I was in Asia Minor I saw some churches that had been closed to the Armenian Christians for two or three years. When I went home to my country last summer I was put into jail without reason. While there I met a young Armenian who told me this story. He said that the servant of the Turkish Pasha had stolen from him his wife and that he himself had been cast into prison by the Turks who declared that his wife had become Mohammedan and had embraced the true religion. But he told them that she was his wife and he could not let her become the Pasha's servant. So they found false witnesses against him and sentenced him to prison as an enemy of the church and state, and there they would have killed him if he had not accepted the faith. Oh, how they have treated our women and girls, and pillaged us since we fell 500 years ago—and we are all perishing under their hands! How our families cry in despair! The prophet Isaiah said[,] announcing the Christ: "He anointed me to preach good tidings to the poor and to set at liberty them that are bruised; to proclaim the acceptable year of the Lord." Our Saviour left that example to every one of his followers.

2.2   The author of Ben Hur] Lewis Wallace (1827–1905), American lawyer, soldier, author, and diplomat. His *Ben Hur: A Tale of the Christ* was published in 1880. In 1881, Wallace was appointed Minister to Turkey by President Garfield. He served until 1885, enjoying an especially close relationship with Sultan Abdul-Hamid II (reigned 1876–1909), whose administration oversaw the massacre of thousands of Armenians beginning in 1894.

2.2   Walker] John Brisben Walker (1847–1931), editor and publisher of *Cosmopolitan Magazine,* had earlier served in China under Ambassador John Ross Browne as a military advisor. Against his expectations the Sino-Japanese War (1894–95) ended in a Japanese victory.

2.6   A.P.A.] The American Protective Association was an anti-Catholic political lobby which sought strict limits on immigration. The A.P.A. claimed a membership of over two million in 1896. It soon went into decline, ceasing activities in 1911. As regards Frost's own attitude toward nativism, see his remarks in a 1923 interview with Rose Feld: "I had an aunt in New England who used to talk long and hard about the foreigners who were taking over this country. Across the way from her house stood a French Catholic church which the new people of the village had put up. Every Sunday my aunt would stand at her window, behind the curtain, and watch the steady stream of men and women pouring into church. Her mouth would twist in the way that seems peculiar to dried up New Englanders and she would say, 'My soul!' Just that. 'My soul!' All the disapproval and indignation and disgust were concentrated into these two words. She never could see why I laughed at her, but it did strike me as funny for her to be calling upon her soul for help when this mass of industrious people were going to church to save theirs. New England is constantly going through periods of change. In my own State, in Vermont, I mean, there have been three distinct changes of population. First came the Irish, then the French and now the Poles. There are those among us who raise their hands in horror at this, but what does it matter? All these people are becoming, have become, Americans. If soil is sacred, then I would say that they are more godly in their attitude to it. The Pole in New England today gets much more out of his plot of ground than does his Yankee neighbor. He knows how to cultivate it so that each inch produces, so that each grain is alive. Today the Pole may not be aware of the beauty of the Colonial houses he buys and may in some cases desecrate, but three generations from now, two generations, his children will be proud of it and may even boast of Yankee heritage. It has been done before; it will be done in the future. And if there be poets among these children, as surely there will be, theirs will be the poetry of America. They will be part of the soil of America as their cousins may be part of the city life of America. I am [im]patient with this jealousy of the old for the young. It is change, this constant flow of new blood which will make America eternally young, which will make her poets sing the songs of a young country, virile songs, strong songs, individual songs. The old cannot keep them back. I was amused years ago by the form this jealousy of tradition will take. One of the most brilliant pupils in the class was the son of a Polish farmer. Everybody admitted his mental superiority. But the old New Englanders would not swallow the pill as given. They sugar-coated, by backstairs gossip, which insisted that the real father of the boy must have been a Yankee. We are supposed to be a broad-minded country, yet in this respect we are so very narrow. Nobody worries about foreign strains in English or French literature and politics. Nobody thinks that England has been tainted by Disraeli, or Zangwill, or Lord Reading. They are taken as Englishmen, their works are important as English works. The same is true of French writers of foreign strain. We seem to lack the courage to be ourselves. I guess that's it. We're still a bit afraid" (*New York Times Book Review,* October 21, 1923).

3. [Children's Stories]

These stories exist in a notebook Frost kept while living on the farm in Derry, N.H., from 1900 to 1909. They have appeared once before as *Stories for Lesley,* edited by Roger Sell, in a slim volume now out of print. Three stories were reprinted from that source in *CPPP* (657–661). I have transcribed them afresh from the notebook, held now at the University of Virginia, and generally known as "The Derry Notebook." For reasons chiefly practical I have silently regularized the punctuation of the stories, as Frost is, in these notebooks, "standard" enough in his own habits to justify the presumption that he'd not wish them handled in any other way. And yet to record here every missing quotation mark I have added in transcribing the copy-text would clutter the collations with some four or five score entries which, in my judgment, are quite unnecessary. I do record the two emendations I made to the words themselves.

Collation

*3.8   you're full] your full MS
*3.162   tassel] tassle MS

Explanatory Notes

3.48   The cow's yours] See RF's poem "The Cow in Apple Time" (*CPPP* 120–21).

3.75   Two birds sat in a bare ruined tree] Doubtless an allusion to the phrase "bare ruined choirs, where late the sweet bird sang" in Shakespeare's sonnet 53, though whether RF had also been reading the sonnet to his children I do not know.

4. [Stories for *The Eastern Poultryman* and *Farm-Poultry* (1903–1905)]

The first three of Frost's stories for poultry journals, written while he was himself raising poultry on his Derry, N.H., farm, appeared in *The Eastern Poultryman,* a monthly published at Freeport, Me., between February and July of 1903. Eight more stories later appeared in the rival journal *Farm-Poultry,* a semi-monthly published in Boston, which also reprinted one of the stories that had originally appeared in *The Eastern Poultryman.* A checklist of Frost's contributions to the periodicals follows:
In *The Eastern Poultryman:*

> "Trap Nests." February 1903: 71.
> "A Just Judge." March 1903: 89–90.
> "A Start in the Fancy." July 1903: 147–48.

In *Farm-Poultry:*

> "A Just Judge." May 1, 1903: 221–222. (Reprinted from *The Eastern Poultryman.*)
> "The Question of a Feather." July 15, 1903: 301–302.
> "Old Welch Goes to the Show." August 15, 1903: 334–335.
> "The Original and Only." September 1, 1903: 352–353.
> "Three Phases of the Poultry Industry." December 15, 1903: 481–482.
> "The Cockerel Buying Habit." February 1, 1904: 54.

"'The Same Thing Over and Over.'" March 1, 1904: 110.
"The Universal Chicken Feed." April 1, 1904: 169.
"Dalkins' Little Indulgence—A Christmas Story." December 15, 1905: 513–514.

The copy-texts for the present edition of Frost's stories are the original appearances, complete runs of which are held at the National Agricultural Library in Beltsville, Md. I have corrected misprints. The collation lists variant wordings between the two appearances of "A Just Judge," the only one of Frost's contributions to the poultry journals to have been reprinted during his lifetime. All eleven of Frost's stories and articles were reprinted in Edward Connery Lathem and Lawrance Thompson's *Robert Frost: Farm Poultry-Man* (Hanover: Dartmouth Publications, 1963), now out of print.

On page 2 of the February 1903 number of *The Eastern Poultryman,* the editors print a note regarding Frost's first contribution:

> We publish in this issue a story entitled 'Trap Nests,' which we trust will interest and amuse our readers. The experiences of Mr. and Mrs. Aiken are similar to those met by many others who look upon the poultry business as one in which no skill or knowledge is required, and so venture in without any preparation, and later find to their sorrow that 'things are not what they seem.'
>
> The subject of trap nests has probably been more misunderstood than any other in which poultry keepers are interested. This misunderstanding may be due to the prejudice which opposes every new [i]nvention. Skepticism retards progress, and until quite recently there has not been a determination to learn the truth regarding the individual system. Many of those who have wished to use the system have invested in the impractical styles of nests, or have constructed nests from some free plan, and have found that the hens would not enter 'without bait' or would find that a single visit to the nest was as much as the hen would care to make.
>
> We trust our readers will understand the story in the spirit in which its author intended, and that like Mr. Aiken they may look for 'results' as being of as much importance as following a method of feeding or management that may seem popular whether it is based upon science, common sense or the caprice or greed of its originators.

A similar note appears in *Farm-Poultry* on July 15, 1903. This note also offers, incidentally, an expert poultry editor's reading of Frost's story "The Question of a Feather"—the first published commentary on the writings of Robert Lee Frost:

> By way of giving readers a little light reading for warm weather we present in this issue a bit of fiction, which we imagine many will find as entertaining as we have. A little while ago we reprinted an entertaining little story by the same author which first appeared in the *Eastern Poultryman.*
>
> Thereby hangs a tale of some interest to those who have MSS. to offer poultry editors. Some time before Mr. Frost wrote us offering articles a little out of the usual line, but with instructive ideas in them. We are always ready to investigate anything offering possibilities of good copy, so we wrote him to send us an article for examination. He did so, and we didn't like it a bit; sent it back. Then picking up a copy of the *Eastern Poultryman,* we came across what to us was a

very interesting story in a style somewhat familiar. We couldn't place it at first, but later recalled that the initials were those of the correspondent whose story weighted with information had been returned. So we wrote him if the story in the *Eastern Poultryman* was his to send us what plain stories he had, and we would make him an offer for any we could use. From the stories sent we selected three, the one appearing in this issue ["The Question of a Feather"], and two others which will come at intervals during the summer.

    Moral: It is sometimes better to let an editor see all your articles than to send him only those you think ought to suit his paper.

    Going back to Mr. Frost's story, whoever tries can of course find lessons in it. What strikes us most forcefully is its fine illustration of the way people have of endeavoring to shift responsibility for decision on all sorts of questions to editorial shoulders. That particular editor, however, seems to have been one of the kind that is different. The ordinary editor would have told them in a minute to pull the feather, if they wanted to show the bird, and would probably have told them how to leave no evidences of the feather having been pulled. Then having done his duty as an editor by giving full information, he would have gently shifted the responsibility to where it belonged by saying that the decision as to whether to show or not when showing involved such a question of ethics was one for the individual to decide for himself; finally impressing upon his hearers that 'if you don't pull the feather, don't show,' was the last word in the case. Others will find other lessons—and some fair but[t]s at 'the editor' will entertain them. We need not point these out.

    In addition to stories and articles, Frost published two letters to the editor in *Farm-Poultry,* one under his own name, one under the name of his friend John Hall. The occasion was Frost's error in "Three Phases of the Poultry Industry." In the third section of that article, "A Typical Small Breeder," Frost describes Hall's poultry farm in Atkinson, N.H., mentioning in passing Hall's flock of geese: "Mr. Hall's geese roost in the trees even in winter. Such a toughening process would be too drastic for hens, but these have to take it according to their strength." *Farm-Poultry* printed a letter from an H. R. White on January 15, 1904: "Will you kindly inform me through your next issue what kind of geese Mr. Hall has that Mr. R. L. Frost speaks of in your issue of Dec. 15th? According to Mr. Frost these geese roost in trees even in the winter time. Now I am 45 years old and have been among geese all my life time, and I can never remember seeing a goose in a tree. I thought if I could get a breed of that kind I could dispense with the coops. Doylestown, Mass. H. R. White." The editor added a note: "Letting Mr. Frost's statement pass is one 'on' us. The writer's attention was called to the evident error before the paper was mailed, but too late to make correction. Then we thought we'd wait and see how many would notice it. Mr. Frost will have to explain." Mr. Frost's temporizing explanation appeared in the February 15 number:

    In reply to Mr. White's (and yours) of recent date in regard to the error in the article on Mr. Hall's place, there is this to say:—

      Geese would sleep out, or float out, let us say, where hens would roost in the trees. To be sure. But what more natural, in speaking of geese in close connection with hens, than to speak of them as if they *were* hens? 'Roost in the trees,' has here simply suffered what the grammarians would call attraction from the subject with which it should be in agreement to the one uppermost in the mind. That is all. But the idea will have to stand, viz., that Mr. Hall's geese winter out,—and that is the essential thing. Mr. White is not after geese that roost in the trees, but geese that don't need coops. Well, Mr. Hall has them that prefer not to use coops, whether they need them or not. My impression is that he has them in several varieties, and I'll risk my impression. But Mr. Hall is a good fellow and will be glad to tell Mr. White about his geese himself—doubtless, also, to do business with him. R.L.F.

To which the editor added: "Mr. Frost seems not to be aware of the fact that geese generally remain out of doors by choice practically all the time. The same thing may be said of ducks. My Indian runner ducks (now deceased) would stay out in a snow storm from daylight to dark rather than go into a comfortable shed where they were sheltered and amply provided with bedding." The matter did not rest here. Lathem and Thompson explain in *Robert Frost: Farm-Poultryman:* "Before his own letter (with this unexpected editorial comment and correction) appeared, Frost had decided it might be well to protect himself further by having John Hall write a letter in his defense. But . . . John Hall had had little schooling, and his talents did not include epistolary abilities. The best he could do was to enter into collusion with his friend by giving approval to a letter actually composed by Frost" (19–20). The letter appeared on March 1:

I noticed Mr. H. R. White's letter in your paper asking about the kind of geese I kept that sleep out in the winter. They are Toulouse, Embden, and Buff. They don't roost in trees. I don't know how Mr. Frost made that mistake, for of course he knows better.

We have often talked about the way they take to the water at night, a favorite place for them to hang up being on a stone just under water. A good many nights in winter, as well as in summer, I have no idea where they are; and I think they are better every way out doors as long as there is any water not frozen over. But speaking of geese in trees, I don't suppose Mr. White has ever seen a duck in a tree. I have. And I once had a duck that laid her eggs in a tree high enough to be out of reach from the ground, and brought off twenty-two ducklings. These were Brazilians, and I don't know what they won't do.

It has always seemed strange to me how people succeed in keeping geese shut up. If I shut mine up they begin to be restless right away, and go off in looks, especially plumage. Mr. White needn't think because I let my geese run wild I think any less of them than other folks. They are good ones,—as they ought to be with the advantages I give them. They win, too, where they are shown.

The records in your paper ought to show what they did in Lawrence this year; but I notice they don't. So Mr. Frost was pretty near right about my geese; and if Mr. White wants some good ones that a little rather than not sleep out, I've got them.
John A. Hall

Frost confessed his authorship of the letter much later, in a 1913 letter to John Bartlett: "I wrote up one or two poultrymen . . . filling in the gaps in my knowledge with dream material. I think I managed fairly well except for the time I spoke of John Hall's geese roosting in the trees. I should have let geese severely alone. It took an artistic letter from John Hall himself (I wrote it for the douce man) to save me from the scandal that started" (*SL* 67).

Collation

2nd = Second appearance of "A Just Judge."

*4.8   beasts).] beasts.)

*4.38   trampled] tramp ed

*4.38   drove the others] drove the other

*4.44   someone asked him] some one ~ {The single word is otherwise consistently used in the copy-text.}

*4.49   It was doubted] If ~

*4.49   One said,] ~ said

*4.50   committee] committe

4.56   be all] be called 2nd

4.56   superadded] superadds 2nd

*4.63   getting so old] getting old

4.69   they were hard to find—they were hard to find."] they were hard to find." 2nd

*4.75   Mister,"] Mister,

*4.76   sick of his bargain.] ~ bargain

*4.90   some one put in.] ~ in?

*4.94   The pullet's] ~ pullets'

*4.103 "Some] Some

*4.110 knees, "I] knees, ¶ "I

*4.112 was, "Drop] was, ¶ "Drop

*4.120 before the streets] ~ street

*4.128 that made her] tha ~

*4.152 R.L.F.] R.S.F.

*4.206 weeder?'] weeder?

*4.210 generations.] generations."

*4.211 hens."] hens.

*4.224 Salem,] Salem.

4.311   {The phrasing of Mr. Call's "beaming" reply is obscure, and some may consider it corrupt; but I think it is correct. The sense of his remark seems to be: "Table scraps?— that is, so long as we have enough to feed the chickens table scraps and nothing else?"}

*4.316 "Is] Is

*4.321 of a] of {not present}

*4.332 what a thing the] ~ th

*4.333 He didn't] H ~

*4.333 suspect what] ~ wha

*4.340 winter it] winter { }

*4.341 all arranged] al ~

*4.341 counterfeit money] counterfe t ~

*4.345 The bird,] The bird

*4.347 But the victim,] But the victim

*4.347 like lambs] ~ ambs

*4.348   had made it] had made { }
*4.351–52   him." ¶ "I] him. I {It seems evident that Dalkins begins speaking at "I . . .",
and that the omission of the new quotation and paragraph is a misprint.}
*4.359   Dalkins] Dalkan
*4.363   sell] ell

Explanatory Notes

4.212   Dr. C. Bricault] Dr. Charlemagne Bricault, French-Canadian veterinarian and poultry farmer, helped Frost get started in the poultry-farming business in Methuen, Mass., in 1899.

4.233   John A. Hall] Hall, a successful poultry-farmer and good friend of Frost's, is also the inspiration for two of Frost's poems: "A Blue Ribbon at Amesbury" and "The House-keeper."

5. Three Articles Associated with Pinkerton Academy (1906–1910)

Frost began teaching part-time at Pinkerton Academy, in Derry, N.H., in the spring of 1906. The next fall he became a full-time member of the faculty, a post he held through June 1911, when he resigned to take a position at the New Hampshire State Normal School in Plymouth. He once remarked of his time at Pinkerton: "I began to teach part time at Pinkerton Academy. That got too absorbing. They took me on gingerly because I had no degree. Gradually they took me in more and more. It really became so consuming I had to run out on it. The school knew they had me, and they piled the work on. Knew I didn't have a degree so I might not get another job. I had four children. They didn't know I was the kind who would run out whether I had anywhere to go or not" (interview with Mary Handy, *Christian Science Monitor,* December 21, 1955).

While at Pinkerton Academy Frost wrote and published the three items presented here. The first, a general article on Pinkerton Academy, appeared in the *Catalogue of Pinkerton Academy* (West Derry, N.H.: E. P. Trowbridge 1906). Frost's authorship was confirmed in 1938 when Robert Newdick, then writing a biography of the poet, prepared a typescript copy of the article and submitted it to him for review. That typescript is now at Amherst College. Frost returned it to Newdick with several annotations. In the margin on page 1 he writes: "This seems to be largely mine. As I remember it, my original was both added to and cut down a little." He brackets the paragraph beginning "While moving abreast of the times," attaching a note: "This has all my marks hasn't it?" Finally, beside the paragraph beginning "As set forth in the act of incorporation," he writes: "I suspect this is none of mine." Comparison of the article to the corresponding articles from the previous two editions of the *Catalogue* suggests that Frost is responsible for the text reprinted in this edition, with the following exceptions. Two passages remain unchanged from the 1904–05 *Catalogue* and consequently could not have been written by Frost: "John M. Pinkerton . . . form of work" at 5.2 above, and "[the Academy] was established . . . purity of character" at 5.6. Frost incorporated these sentences into the text of his article from earlier editions of the *Catalogue.* I include them here since they are integral to the article. The copy-text for the present edition is the first appearance of the article in the *Catalogue.* Incidentally, Frost once told Lawrance Thompson that the Pinkerton Board of Trustees paid him $50 to write this article (NOTES March 1, 1940).

The second item associated with Pinkerton Academy is an unsigned notice of a series of dramatic productions given by Academy students under Frost's direction. The notice appeared in the *Derry News* (May 27, 1910): 2. Lawrance Thompson first identified Frost as its author, and he gives a useful account of the ambitious dramatic series (*TEY* 360ff). I reprint the text from the *Derry News,* correcting several misprints.

The third item is a description of the Pinkerton Academy English curriculum, which Frost wrote for the 1910–11 *Catalogue.* I reprint the text of the first appearance, correcting three misprints. As Thompson points out, Frost's revision of the curriculum was highly innovative: "By contrast [to Frost's program], the *Catalogue* for 1905–06 . . . listed as required reading in English a total of four books on rhetoric, a book entitled *Principles of Argumentation,* representative orations by various Americans, Burke's *Conciliation with the American Colonies,* and other discouraging titles, along with old stand-bys from Irving, Whittier, Dickens, George Eliot, Longfellow, Cooper, Scott, Shakespeare, Tennyson" (*TEY* 567). Frost's teaching methods came to the attention of Henry C. Morrison, Head of the State Education Office in New Hampshire during Frost's tenure at Pinkerton. Morrison visited Frost's classroom while on a routine inspection of the Academy and later gave this account of the visit to Robert Newdick. It sheds much light on Frost's appeal as a teacher:

> On the occasion of this particular visit of inspection I dropped into a classroom in English literature and was at once struck by a rare phenomenon: a class of boys and girls of high school age were listening open-mouthed to the teacher who was talking to them about an English classic. As I looked at the teacher I saw slumped down behind the desk a young man who was commenting on the work he had in his hand and perhaps other work by the same author on the desk. He was neither raising his voice nor cutting up any pedagogical monkey shines but rather talking to them as he might talk to a group of friends around his own fireside. But he 'had them' as few teachers ever do 'get them' . . . I did not know Mr. Frost at that time but I invited and urged him to come over to Exeter soon where I was holding a teachers' institute and just talk to high school teachers about how he taught literature. As I recall it he rather demurred at the proposal, professing that he knew nothing about the subject of teaching. Anyhow I finally prevailed and he did, on the day appointed, appear. I recall, with some amusement, that I have seldom seen anybody so thoroughly overcome by stage fright as he was, but he did what I wanted and made his point and afterward I came to rely upon him a good deal in his general field to simplify the whole problem of the high school teacher of English literature. (*Newdick's Season of Frost: An Interrupted Biography of Robert Frost,* edited by William A. Sutton [Albany: State University of New York Press, 1976], 287–88)

We can get an idea of Frost's theme in the Exeter lecture from an account he gave of it to Lawrance Thompson on February 22, 1940: "In the Exeter talk, when he had gotten the stone in his shoe [a painful distraction meant to counteract stage fright], he had two little ideas to expound . . . His two ideas were on teaching the students to absorb ideas and to impress ideas. So use the books in school that they would be lonely forever afterwards without them. In other words, get the students so interested that they could not leave books alone. This was a way of catching them. That meant teaching them to make little libraries of their own. In expression, teach them a satisfaction and pride in saying or writing an idea so well that you remembered it once it had been expressed. This is all he has been trying to convey to his Harvard students this year—by passing out cards and asking them to put down one single sentence they could remember that they had said or written—that they liked so much that they were willing to be boastful about it. At Exeter he had said also that the student should be encouraged to search for the right words and to seek shades of meaning so that when they spoke thoughtfully they could get the satisfaction of feeling themselves drawn on for words" (NOTES).

Frost had a sympathetic, if unusual, way with students at Pinkerton. In the following, also from Thompson's "Notes," the reference is to one of Frost's favorite students at the Academy: "Another was the boy who eventually became editor of the [literary paper] after [John] Bartlett. He gave RF the idea for the White Tailed Hornet by describing hornets in a hornet nest. One sentence was good. Frost spoke to the boy and said he liked the sentence; keep it up. Self-consciously the boy didn't know from RF's laconic phrasing of praise whether he had done well or poorly. Authorities thought [the] boy should be kicked out, but at the end of the first year he managed to hold on. RF encouraged him slowly. His little descriptions were done with an eye for detail. But his themes were always sloppy—on poor paper, badly written, with dreadful misspellings. RF never used blue-pencil to point out misspelled words but he one day said to the boy that his themes were so much improved that he should begin to work on his spelling. But the boy didn't know which ones of the words he misspelled. Then start looking up a, an, the, Frost said, and so on until he had looked up every word in the theme. The boy learned to spell. Became editor of the school paper and one of the outstanding students."

Collation

*5.8   the same author),] ~ author)
*5.8   will be asked to] ~ o
*5.9   literary movements] ~ movement
*5.9   Land of Desire is] ~ i
*5.9   Hoolihan, the other play,] Hoolihan the other play
*5.9   Irish Marseillaise."] ~ Marseillaise.
*5.10   Yeats plays,] ~ play
*5.10   Hoolihan,] Hoolihan
*5.17   selections from] from;
*5.21   from Walden] ~ Walden,
*5.26   Clemens'] Clemen's]

Explanatory Notes

5.5   Much must be left . . . for themselves.] Frost later carried this idea much further. He remarks in a 1926 lecture at Wesleyan College: "I would . . . run a course [in school] by self-withdrawal. I would begin a course by being very present, and then slowly disappear. A sort of vanishing act. I'd rather melt away just as I stood there, and leave a fellow more and more alone, and let him feel deserted, like a baby in a room alone. Give him that terribly abandoned feeling, left to the horrors of his own thoughts and conscience. That's what I've worked at more than anything else. I've probably ruined many people. They've probably gone right into mischief when I've left them. But then there have been some who have not. I've had boys that I remember as meditative people . . . You may say there's plenty of provision for that in school. But is there? Freedom to do more than you're asked to do? No . . . Every minute's provided for. I would say to my class, 'I am entitled to nine hours of your time—three in class and two outside for each of those. All right, I present it to you. This is the time you can lose yourselves. You've got to do some losing of yourself to find yourself. I touch it and remit it, as Kipling says. I'll keep the institution off your back to that extent.' Nothing may happen nine weeks out of ten. All those hours may be wasted. I think in the years, though, something may happen. Let it stand for a kind of a gravestone for what you didn't do. I contributed that much to your dead mind." The talk was recorded stenographically and published without Frost's permission or editorial intervention as "The Manumitted Student" in *The New Student* (January 12, 1927): 5–7, 2.

    5.7–8   Drama at Pinkerton] The students performed versions of the plays that Frost himself had condensed and revised. See *TEY*, 360ff.

    5.8   the Ben Greet company] Ben Greet (1857–1936) was an English actor, director, and producer. He spent twelve years in America (1902–14) touring with his company.

    5.8   And let us . . . kings] Frost combines several phrases from the prologue to *Henry the Fifth*. Lines 17–18 of the prologue read: "And let us, ciphers to this great accompt, / On your imaginary forces work." Line 28 reads: "For 'tis your things that now must deck our kings."

    5.13   Horatius . . . Sohrab and Rustum] The poem "Horatius" appears in the volume *Lays of Ancient Rome* by Thomas Babington Macaulay. "Sohrab and Rustum" is a poem by Matthew Arnold.

    5.13   Expression in oral reading . . . test of appreciation.] Frost held to this throughout his teaching career. Consider his remarks a generation later in a talk at Allegheny College in May 1938: "I can only read as fast as I can hear because I have read poetry all my life. I do not get the final meaning of a thing unless I hear *how* it was said. Everything depends on the *how*, the final meaning is in the *how*, no question of that to me. Poetry is absolutely so. No reading of poetry except at the speed at which you can hear it. The teachers have been told that they were to get over reading by ear, [that] they must become eye readers and [. . .] sort of pillagers of books, skippers and rippers. Some lady got up and said she had tried very hard and she couldn't seem to read anything without hearing it. What should she do? It was a kind of experience meeting. The psychologist, or whatever he was, psychiatrist, said, 'You must use your will.' We used to hear that about being good when we were young. All that frightens me about reading[;] I wonder if reading is going by" (unpublished typescript, Amherst College Library).

    5.16   Golden Treasury] Francis Turner Palgrave's *Golden Treasury of the Best Songs and Lyrical Poems in the English Language* (1861), a popular anthology. Frost was fond of the book, to which he alludes in the poem "Waiting: Afield at Dusk" (*CPPP* 24).

    5.17   Gareth . . . Hanson's Composition] Frost refers to "Gareth and Lynette" and "The Passing of Arthur," poems from Tennyson's Arthurian cycle *The Idylls of the King* (1859–72), and to Charles Lane Hanson's *English Composition* (Boston: Ginn & Company, 1908).

    5.22   Woolley's Handbook] Almost certainly a reference to Edwin Campbell Woolley's (1878–1916) *The mechanics of writing, a compendium of rules regarding manuscript-arrangement, spelling, the compounding of words, abbreviations, the representation of numbers, syllabication, the use of capitals, the use of italics, punctuation, and paragraphing* (Boston: D.C. Heath & Co., 1909).

5.26   Jonson's Silent Woman . . . Blue Bird] The full title of Jonson's play is *Epicoene; or, The Silent Woman* (1609). *Bab Ballads* (1869) is a volume of comic poetry by Sir William Schwenck Gilbert (1836–1911), English barrister and librettist of comic operas (with composer Sir Arthur Sullivan). *The Blue Bird* (trans. 1908) is a play by the Belgian poet, dramatist, and essayist Maurice Maeterlinck (1862–1949).

6. [Remarks on Form in Poetry (1919)]

These remarks appeared first in Marguerite Wilkinson's study of recent poetry, *New Voices* (New York: Macmillan, 1919), 207. She later reprinted them exactly in *The Way of the Makers* (New York: Macmillan, 1925). Frost and Wilkinson knew one another. Doubtless she got the remarks directly from their author and appears to have confirmed them with Frost before going to print. An April 21, 1919, letter from Frost to Wilkinson reads: "I didn't telegraph because I saw nothing to object to in what you said about my processes. As nearly as I can tell that's the way I work" (*SL* 237). I reprint Frost's remarks exactly as they appear in *New Voices*.

7. [Address before the Amherst Alumni Council (1919)]

Frost's speech appeared in *Proceedings of the Alumni Council of Amherst College at the Meeting Held in Amherst November 7–9, 1919* (Amherst: The Alumni Council, 1920). He joined the faculty in January 1917, replacing Professor George B. Churchill, who had taken a seat in the Massachusetts State Senate. A January 1 article in *The Springfield Republican* announced the appointment in a little article that suggests enough about Frost's habits as to indicate he may have supplied information for it. "Although nominally a farmer," the article reports, "Mr. Frost has already acquired a varied experience of academic life. After studying at Dartmouth and at Harvard he became a teacher of English in the Pinkerton Academy at Derry, N.H., and later taught psychology in the New Hampshire State normal school. His first volume of poems, 'A Boy's Will,' was published while he was living in England. Two subsequent books, 'North of Boston' and the recently-issued 'Mountain Interval' established his reputation as a poet of original rhythms and a keen student of New England character. Mr. Frost will take over two courses already begun by Prof. Churchill, a special senior seminar on the theory of poetry and an elective course for juniors on the rise and development of English drama. He will also work with a freshman section in composition." Frost's letters on the "sound of sense" and "sentence sounds" (sent to Sidney Cox and John Bartlett, among others, during 1914 and 1915) perhaps suggest something of what he contributed to the seminar on the theory of poetry.

Each department of the college was represented in the 1919 meetings. Frost spoke for the Language and Literature Group on November 7. I have found no other texts of this speech, nor any correspondence regarding it. The present edition reprints the text exactly as it appears in the *Proceedings,* with one correction. As this document marks the first appearance of Amherst College in the story of Frost's life as an educator and writer of prose, I include here, for the nonce, the texts of the four Amherst College New Year's greetings cards for which Frost supplied the copy, the last of which is a line from his poem "Choose Something Like a Star," together with the dates for each:

1931: "Amherst would be remembered for her wisest and loveliest lessons no less than for her sternest."

1950: "Greetings from Amherst and she would like to think your enterprises in or out of books are still in some sense one with hers."

1953: "Amherst's wish of the year is that she should have disposed you forever to look for a book side to everything."

1957: "It asks of us a certain height."

Collation

*7.6   I take it,] ~ it

Explanatory Notes

7.2   You see, poverty has always . . . refuge] A November 27, 1921, article by one Stirling Bowen, published in the book section of the *Detroit News,* and for which Frost was obviously interviewed, reads as follows (the occasion for the article was Frost's appointment to hold a fellowship in poetry at the University of Michigan): "Perhaps [Frost] will not mind in this most friendly article, if it is noted that the Frost larder in one bad period contained only oat meal. A full meal for the family was gained by the addition of milk from their one cow and salt of the kind farmers buy for their stock, scraped, in this instance, from the coarse grains in the barrel in the barn. There were small children in the family then, too. But oat meal, milk, and rock salt will prevent serious result and permit a man to write. His first volume of poetry, published in England when he was 38 years old, contained 30 comparatively short poems chosen from 20 successive years of work. He sold his first poem for $18 when he was 18 years old. He thought his reputation was made. But in the next 20 years he was paid an average of $10 a year by the magnates. 'Suffering we undergo, and even the bitterness we feel at times, plays its part in our development, for better or for worse,' Mr. Frost said once. 'It makes us think, probably, as we not have thought otherwise.' But it does more than that. It either tempers and strengthens, giving endurance and poise of understanding, among other things, or it breaks the mind and spirit of a man utterly. It did not break Mr. Frost. And so for just one reason it is possible to be glad Mr. Frost has lived as he lived, and has faced the discouragements, the insults, and the blows of a world that is too often blind to beauty. For as long as millions of men, women, and children who are not artists are required to withstand such hardships it is desirable that occasionally a poet should withstand them also, in full measure, to the end that poetry shall not consist purely of pretty graces, to the end that the brave though sometimes stupid yearnings of poor people shall be on record unforgettably—for the sake of such people as for the sake of art—and to the end that poetry and art shall become more and more the possessions of the millions who work."

7.4   Mr. Meiklejohn] Alexander Meiklejohn, who at the time had been President of Amherst College since 1912.

7.5   those who will, may] RF remarks to similar effect in an interview printed in *The New Student* 5.13 (January 6): 1,3: "I am for a wide open educational system for the freeborn. The slaves are another question. I will not refuse to treat them as slaves wherever found. Those who will, may, would be my first motto, but my close second[,] Those who won't, must. That is to say I shouldn't disdain to provide for the slaves if slaves they insisted on being. I shouldn't anyway unless I were too busy with the free-born. One mark of the free-born, however, is that he doesn't take much of your time. All he asks of his teacher is the happiness of being left to his own initiative; which is more of a tax on the teacher's egotism than on the teacher's time. Give me the high-spirited kind that hate an order to do what they were about to do of their own accord" (3).

7.5   There was nothing . . . anyway.] Frost remarks in an October 1962 appearance at Kenyon College: "One might list the things that you have to have it out with yourself about, and the distresses involved. I think that one of the things that ought to distress you is: What about your own age in college? What mental age, as they say in psychology, you're of, and the mental age you're in, ought to be between liking to be told and liking to do the telling. It's the business of the teacher to play it at that delicate point. I've thought sometimes I would sit in front of a class until it spoke, but I've always got embarrassed into speaking, and angrily embarrassed. That's the great thing, that's been my life, that place betwixt and between: needing to be told or liking to be told, and wanting to do the telling—not contradicting, not conflicting, necessarily, except with yourself; having it out with yourself." The talk was published in the *Kenyon College Alumni Bulletin* 21.1 (March 1963): 6–9, from a transcription prepared for publication without Frost's assistance.

8. [Address in Memory of J. Warner Fobes (December 1, 1920)]

Frost's address appeared in a booklet titled *Service in Remembrance of Reverend J. Warner Fobes at the Congregational Church, Peace Dale, Rhode Island, on Wednesday Evening, December the First, Nineteen Twenty* (Peace Dale, R.I., 1920), copy-text for the present edition. It was never reprinted and no other forms of the text survive. I am grateful to John Lancaster for bringing this item to my attention. Frost's speech is given a title in the booklet: "'A Friend's Memory'—Robert Frost." The Frosts first met Fobes and his wife, Edith Hazard Fobes, in June 1915 when they bought a farm in Franconia, N.H. The Fobes's estate, used by them as a summer residence, lay adjacent to the Frosts' new farm. In later years the Frosts often retreated to Mrs. Fobes's guest-cottage to escape the worst hay-fever weeks in lower New England.

9. [Some Definitions by Robert Frost (1923)]

These "definitions" appeared first in *Robert Frost: The Man and His Work* (New York: Henry Holt, 1923), a brochure printed by Frost's publishers for marketing purposes. The booklet was reprinted at least as late as the 1930s and these particular "definitions" were sometimes printed on the dust jackets of Frost's books. I have found no indication in his correspondence with Henry Holt and Company as to what Frost's role was in preparing the remarks for publication. The copy-text for the present edition is the 1923 brochure.

Explanatory Notes

9.3   the one who offers a good deal of dirt] In this same year, 1923, Frost was quoted in an interview with Rose Feld for the *New York Times Book Review:* "When and where has it been written that a poet must be a club-swinging warrior, a teller of barroom tales, a participant of unspeakable experiences. That, today, apparently is the stamp of poetic integrity . . . I can't see that a man must needs have his feet plowing through unhealthy mud in order to appreciate more fully the glowing splendor of the clouds. I can't see that a man must fill his soul with sick and miserable experiences, self-imposed and self-inflicted, and greatly enjoyed, before he can sit down and write a lyric of strange and compelling beauty. Inspiration doesn't lie in the mud; it lies in the clean and wholesome life of the ordinary man. Maybe I am wrong. Maybe there is something wrong with me. Maybe I haven't the power to feel, to appreciate and live the extremes of dank living and beautiful inspiration." The remark comes in the context of Frost's defense of Longfellow as "one of the real American poets of yesterday," an unfashionable opinion in this year after the publication of Eliot's *The Waste Land*. See the *Book Review* for Sunday, October 21, 1923.

10. [Preface to *Memoirs of the Notorious Stephen Burroughs* (1924)]

Frost's preface first appeared in an edition of Stephen Burroughs's *Memoirs* published by The Dial Press (New York, 1924). Lincoln MacVeagh, an editor at Dial, had met Frost a few years earlier while working at Henry Holt and Company, Frost's American publisher. The two men became so close that Frost considered leaving Holt when MacVeagh resigned in 1923. Frost's preface appeared only one other time during his life, in *The Cupid and the Lion* (1924), a pamphlet issued by The Dial Press as a supplement to lists of their publications. I have been unable to locate any manuscripts or typescripts of the preface. The *Cupid and the Lion* text differs from that published in the *Memoirs* in several respects, all of which reflect the circumstances of the pamphlet's separate publication. My conclusion is that Frost prepared the text printed in the book edition since the reading of the first sentence as it stands there seems authorial: "Pelham, Massachusetts, may never have produced anything else; it had a large part in producing the *Memoirs of the Notorious Stephen Burroughs*—this good book; or at least in starting the author on the criminal career of which it is a record." The phrase "this good book," not present in the pamphlet, is superfluous to the sense of the sentence and would not have been added by MacVeagh or a copy-editor. On the other hand, one can readily see why it would have been cut from the pamphlet text. The copy-text for the present edition is the book edition of the preface.

Collation

CL = The text of the preface as reprinted in *The Cupid and the Lion* (1924).
10.1—this good book] {not present} CL
10.8   put this book] put *Memoirs of the Notorious Stephen Burroughs* CL
10.10   South Shaftsbury, Vermont ¶ 1924] {not present} CL

Explanatory Notes

10   *MEMOIRS OF THE NOTORIOUS STEPHEN BURROUGHS*] Published first in 1811. Stephen Burroughs (1765–1840) spent time in the army, from which he deserted, and at Dartmouth College, which he left without a diploma. He became "notorious" for impersonating an ordained minister with plagiarized sermons, and for counterfeiting. He ended up in Canada, a convert to Roman Catholicism.

10.2   Glazier Wheeler . . . Daniel Shays] Glazier Wheeler, Burroughs's co-counterfeiter and a reputed alchemist, was born ca. 1724 in Lancaster, Mass. He is introduced in Burroughs's *Memoirs* on page 60 of the 1924 edition: "Glazier Wheeler, a money-maker, known throughout all New England, had the art of transmuting metals, so as to make copper into good silver, which would stand the test of every essay made upon it." Wheeler was jailed in 1755, 1763, and again in 1785. Daniel Shays (1747–1825), who served for a time in the Continental Army, became the leader in 1786 and early 1787 of a rebellion in western Massachusetts.

10.2   the Leanders'] This seems to be a mistake. In the *Memoirs*, Burroughs's friends in Pelham, Mass., are called the "Lysanders." I assume that the mistake is owing to a lapse in Frost's memory that slipped by unnoticed, not to a misprint. Of course, characters named Lysander and Leander appear in *A Midsummer Night's Dream*. Perhaps Frost unconsciously made a substitution.

10.5   Melchizedek] See Genesis 14:18–20 and Hebrews 7.

10.6   "We that are of purer fire."] Line 111 of John Milton's *Comus*.

10.10   W. R. Brown] Warren R. Brown, Amherst real-estate agent and friend of Frost's.

11. The Poetry of Amy Lowell (1925)

"The Poetry of Amy Lowell" appeared first in *The Christian Science Monitor* (May 16, 1925): 8. It was reprinted a year later in the anthology *Prose Preferences* (New York: Harper and Brothers, 1926), edited by Sidney Cox and Edmund Freeman.

Lowell died on May 12, 1925. A few days later a reporter from the *Monitor* called at Frost's Amherst house asking for a tribute to her. According to Lawrance Thompson, Frost wrote the essay while the reporter waited outside (*TYT* 277). Some weeks later Frost said to Louis Untermeyer: "I didn't rise to verse, but I did write a little compunctious prose to her ashes" (*RFLU* 174). An incomplete holograph manuscript of the essay is held at the Jones Library, Amherst. It lacks some five sentences, about a third of the total, and differs with the published version in a number of other cases, chiefly in punctuation. The Jones Library also holds two two-page typescripts of the essay, whose texts are identical. It seems unlikely that the typescripts were copied from the *Monitor*. They disagree with it in one important respect: the typescripts (as does Frost's early manuscript) read "toxin" where the *Monitor* reads "tocsin." The typescripts were likely prepared either by Frost or by his wife. The co-editor of *Prose Preferences*, Sidney Cox, was a friend and frequent correspondent of Frost. After the book was published Frost wrote to Cox, referring to his eulogistic headnote to "The Poetry of Amy Lowell": "You *would* exaggerate me into the most conspicuous prose writer in your collection, you doting friend and so disqualify me for doing anything to boost the book . . . You have more to lose by your act than I have. I am stopped from using or recommending for use any anthology in which I am made to shine" (*Robert Frost and Sidney Cox: Forty Years of Friendship*, edited by William R. Evans [Hanover, N.H.: University Press of New England, 1981], 177). Had Cox printed a corrupt text, Frost presumably would have mentioned it. The Jones Library typescripts match the text of *Prose Preferences*, and as the text of the latter seems accurately to represent Frost's intentions, it is the copy-text for the present edition.

Collation

1st = First appearance in the *Christian Science Monitor*. MS = Manuscript, Jones Library, Amherst.

11.1   toxin] MS; tocsin 1st {Perhaps the *Monitor* hoped to ward off suspicion that RF was getting mischievous with Lowell.}

11.7   that we owned to] 1st; {not present} we owned to MS

11.7   How often {. . .} to stay.] 1st; {not present} MS
11.2   breathless] 1st; {not present} MS
11.2   in the effort] 1st; ~ resolve MS
11.2   a larger] 1st; larger MS
11.2   helped] 1st; She {not present} MS
11.3   The water {. . .} things seen.] 1st; {not present} MS

Explanatory Notes

11.2   We throw our arms wide with a gesture of religion to the universe] George Foxhall reports in the October 21, 1937, number of *The Worcester Gazette* a talk Frost gave at Clark University, during which the poet said: "'Poetry, when I read it or write it, induces in me a mood of forgiveness. Forgiveness of what? Of the outrage of the universe.' But you must not misunderstand him here. He is not a radical screaming at outrages of the rich against the poor. He means something far more pitiful and more implacable. That sense of helplessness that confronts us when we are brought face to face with those personal tragedies of event and of situation which prove that the laws of the universe are as impersonal as they are personal." See also Frost's remarks before a Boston audience, as quoted in the *Christian Science Monitor* for May 6, 1940: "Literature is a kind of forgiveness. Something happens to you and it hurts too much at first to do anything about it, but after a while you write a poem about it—when there is only just enough sting left to make you eloquent, and then you find it doesn't bother you any more."

12. [Marion Leroy Burton and Education (1925)]

Frost taught at the University of Michigan twice—in 1921–23 and in 1925–26—during the first of which terms he worked under the administration of President Marion LeRoy Burton (1874–1925). On April 10, 1925, Acting President Alfred Lloyd invited Frost to deliver an address at a memorial service for Burton in Ann Arbor. At first Frost demurred, fearing (or so he said) that he could not make himself heard in Hill Auditorium, the venue for the event, and explaining that he had never before undertaken such a thing; he suggested that someone else would be better suited for the task. However, Lloyd persuaded him to accept the invitation, and Frost prepared the text of his address in typescript beforehand (in later years he tended to extemporize much more freely). The address was widely quoted in the Ann Arbor and Detroit press, in *The Michigan Alumnus* 31.32 (June 6, 1925), and also in *The Christian Science Monitor* for May 29, 1915. From the latter source Lawrance Thompson quoted several paragraphs in Volume 2 of his biography of the poet.

The copy-text for the present edition is a typescript bearing the heading "Address by Robert Frost / To be delivered May 28th / On M. L. Burton," which is held at the Bentley Historical Library at the University of Michigan. Comparison of the typescript to several reports of the event in Michigan newspapers and in the *Monitor* indicate that Frost, in delivering his address, hewed fairly closely to the typescript he had prepared.

Collation

*12.6   I should think,] ~ think
*12.7   that someone shall] ~ some one ~
*12.21   But it is] (But ~

*12.24   name. He] name, He
*12.27   It won't] ~ wont
*12.29   comfortable] confortable

Explanatory Notes

12.5   Mark Hopkins] Presumably a reference to Mark Hopkins, president of Williams College from 1836 to 1872. Hopkins favored a student-centered approach to education, highly unusual in his day, and for it he was immortalized by his one-time student President James A. Garfield, who once observed: "The ideal college is Mark Hopkins on one end of a log and a student on the other." Garfield's remark was often quoted.

12.7   productive of literature] The *Christian Science Monitor* for October 18, 1920, quotes a letter Frost wrote to students at Bryn Mawr College to similar effect: "We shall have to get a little more American literature directly out of the colleges or know the reason why . . . I see no better way to do it than by laying on our younger students the obligation to produce something besides exercises to be blue-penciled for details by teachers . . . The colleges haven't dared to expect absolute literature of mere students. Yet when you stop to consider, you find that before they were past the age of being students, nearly all the real writers that ever wrote had done something definite of the kind they were to be known for all the rest of their lives. Probably the colleges haven't expected enough of young writers. But perhaps it is the country's fault. A young country is too easily satisfied with a mechanical proficiency in the arts that can at best never be better than amateurish. The country may not expect enough. And then again I am not sure the country is to blame. I don't know that either the country or the colleges could expect enough of young artists. The young artists must expect it of themselves, by some miracle, if it is to be enough" (3).

12.9   Charles Eliot] Charles William Eliot (1834–1926), named President of Harvard University in 1869. Among his many innovations was the introduction of an "elective system," which broadened the range of courses offered and allowed students to choose from among them.

12.20   apples of discord man] The allusion is to the Greek goddess Eris, whose name means "Strife." In one of the old tales, Eris is said to have begun the Trojan war. At the wedding of Peleus and Thetis, to which she had not been invited, she tossed a golden apple into the party bearing the inscription: "For the most beautiful one." This set the attending goddesses at odds as to who ought to receive it. Paris, Prince of Troy, was told to settle the dispute by naming the prettiest goddess, each of whom attempted to bribe him. Aphrodite won by promising him Helen, who, of course, was already married to Menelaus of Sparta.

12.22   the radical thinker] See RF's remarks as reported in *The New Student* 6 (January 12, 1927): 5–7, 2: "There are a lot of radical teachers talking to [students] and giving them their freedom. Very few, for all that's said, getting up and taking their freedom, or acting like freemen. Of course, the whole object of education is to get freedom and give freedom, to enjoy freedom . . . When I say freedom I say I may want to give you freedom of something—freedom of the city, or the freedom of your subject. I might mean 'expertness.' I saw a man who was particularly free with hats. He was a juggler with straw hats, and he must have worked for years and years to get his freedom with straw hats. That's one sort of freedom—a juggler's freedom. There's a lot of that in education—freedom *of.*

Also there is freedom *from*. One's relatives, for instance—freedom *from*. Most young people think it's a question of this—freedom from America; young people want to take themselves somewhere" (5). As for the latter observation, bear in mind that RF was speaking during the expatriate period about which Malcolm Cowley was later to write so elegaically in his memoir *Exile's Return*. Incidentally, *The Student* printed RF's remarks under the title "The Manumitted Student, a Speech by Robert Frost," but in fact they were stenographically recorded without his knowledge during an appearance he had lately made at Wesleyan College.

12.24   the student's claim on the teachers] RF often touched on this theme, as in this interview, quoted in *The New Student* 5.13 (January 26): 1.3: "Half the time I don't know whether students are in my classes or not; on the other hand, I can stay with a student all night if I can get where he lives, among his realities. Courses should be a means of introduction, to give students a claim on me, so that they may come to me at any time, outside of class periods. If the student does not want to press his claim, well, for him I must give an examination. But he has already lowered his estimation. The student who does not press his claim has to that extent been found wanting. I favor the student who will convert my claim on him into his claim on me" (3). RF's generosity to his students was, indeed, extraordinary in this regard. Held at the University of Michigan is a letter dated June 10, 1938. Its author, a student of Frost's, is unknown, as is also its recipient, their names having been deliberately opaqued out of the document at some point. I quote it here in part: "Last night six of us had dinner with Robert Frost. We had ushered at the services here for his wife [in April] and had been in the very informal class which he had this year . . . After dinner, Frost shooed off the other profs. And we went out on the back porch of the Inn and sat in the moonlight talking about Capitalism, which he calls 'the struggle for existence with the dollar sign just a little ahead,' and Communism, Walter Lippmann, new poetry, selling on the market, and any number of interrelated and unrelated things. As they come into our minds we talk about them. Those evenings with Frost have been the apotheosis of conversation. When we were about to leave he gave us each a copy of his Collected Poems inscribed by himself. In mine is 'To [———], in memory of a day in April, 1938, from his friend, Robert Frost.' I wouldn't part with that book for love or money. Then he shook hands with each of us and we left; he didn't say a word outside of telling us that he was giving us the books in thanks for what we had done. Kindness, wit, wisdom, charity— all the old virtues in a new way—that's Robert Frost. It's hard to say how we feel about Mr. Frost. I remember that after the first evening with him, we were all so mentally exhausted and so amazed at the man that none of the eleven of us at that time said a word as we walked all the way back through town to the campus. I'm sure there's no deification, no idolizing on our part; he accepts us as human beings and we accept him as one. It's the easiest thing in the world to talk to him. I suppose that if each us were tied down and made to 'fess up, we would each say, 'I love him.' Only that can express it. One fellow broke down and wept after we had left him; I had to take him home and talk to him to keep his spirits up." The students had been planning to publish a magazine in tribute to Frost as a teacher. But they decided against it: "What we have learned and absorbed from Mr. Frost," the unnamed author of the letter concludes, "couldn't be put between the covers of a magazine anyway, perhaps not even in words" (typescript, University of Michigan Library). These young men were unusual neither in their verdict as to Frost's talent as an educator (unorthodox though his methods always were), nor in their depth of gratitude. Frost quite sincerely delighted in having students "make their claim on him." His generosity towards others, as Donald Sheehy points out, was quite unfairly impeached by Lawrance Thompson in his biography. See *"Your Success Is My Success": Robert Frost to Hugh Saglio,* with introduction and notes by Donald Sheehy (Amherst: Friends of the Amherst College Library, 2004). Saglio studied with Frost at Amherst in the late 1920s.

13. [Introduction to *The Arts Anthology: Dartmouth Verse 1925*]

This essay appeared first as the introduction to *The Arts Anthology: Dartmouth Verse 1925* (Portland, Me.: Mosher Press, 1925). The contributors to the anthology were Dartmouth undergraduates, many of whom Frost knew. I have found no manuscripts of the introduction. But a copy of the book signed by Frost in June 1925 (the month the book appeared) is held at the Dartmouth College Library. He offers no corrections and I have reprinted the text exactly as published. Frost does, however, make one marginal note in the Dartmouth copy. Alongside the somewhat harsh paragraph beginning "Right in this book" he adds: "Written in haste, some of this now repented." It is worth mentioning that the author of "The Village Daily," cited in Frost's introduction, is the poet Richard Eberhart.

Explanatory Notes

13.2   Imagists] Poets associated with Ezra Pound in England in the mid-1910s; the group included T. E. Hulme, F. S. Flint, and H. D. in England, and Amy Lowell in America. Lawrance Thompson reports a 1951 conversation in which Frost singles out Flint's contribution to the movement: "F. S. Flint. Frost says he would like to do an article on Flint, to show that he was the one who should have gotten the credit that Pound tried to appropriate. F. S. Flint translated from the French a book by Sorel which T. E. Hulme paid him 25 cents a page to translate; but Hulme published it without acknowledging that Flint had done the hack work. F. S. Flint got Pound interested (says Frost) in the French and in 'Imagisme'"(NOTES).

13.2   Landor] Walter Savage Landor (1775–1864) was an especially long-lived English poet.

14. [Poet—One of the Truest (1928)]

Frost's tribute to the poet and dramatist Percy MacKaye appeared in *Percy MacKaye: A Symposium on His Fiftieth Birthday, 1925* (Hanover, N.H.: Dartmouth Press, 1928), 21. According to a note in a copy held at Dartmouth College Library, three hundred copies of the book were printed for private distribution only, not for sale. The published text is apparently the only extant version of Frost's tribute. I reprint it here exactly.

Explanatory Notes

14.1   fellowships at universities] MacKaye helped Frost secure an appointment as Poet in Residence at the University of Michigan for the 1921–22 academic year. Frost was reappointed as Fellow in Creative Arts for 1922–23, and again as Fellow in Letters for 1925–26. MacKaye had himself been awarded a fellowship by Miami University (Oxford, Ohio) in 1920. As Frost implies, he then began a "campaign" on behalf of artists, starting with an article published in *The Forum* magazine in June 1921: "University Fellowships in the Creative Arts."

15. [Introduction to *The Cow's in the Corn* (1929)]

Frost's introduction appeared in the book publication of this comic playlet: *The Cow's in the Corn A One-Act Irish Play in Rhyme by Robert Frost* (Gaylordsville, Vt.: Slide Mountain Press, 1929). The "play" itself had previously appeared in the *Dearborn Independent* on June 18, 1927. A variant holograph manuscript of the introduction, which seems to represent an earlier draft, is held at Amherst College Library. The variants in wording registered in the published text of the introduction are, however, certainly authorial. The copy-text for the present edition is Frost's manuscript. I have incorporated into it all variant wordings in the first appearance.

Collation

1st = First appearance in *The Cow's in the Corn.*

*15.1   sole] 1st; one

*15.1   no one] 1st; Who

*15.1   at least one] 1st; ~ one?

*15.1   illustrates the] 1st; illustrates, among a number of other things, the

Explanatory Notes

15.1   smaller and smaller audiences] Frost touched on this subject in an interview printed in *The Christian Science Monitor* (July 14, 1925). He is speaking about the modern possibilities for drama: "If you took Shakespeare to build on, you would have to face the question of whether to base upon the speaking passages or the rhetorical passages or on both. There has been a danger that modern poetic drama might base itself entirely upon the rhetorical passages, the long speeches, but to my mind that way sacrifices opportunity for effect, leads to small audiences or to none, which is certainly not what the author would desire."

16. [Preface to *A Way Out* (1929)]

Frost's preface first appeared in the book edition of his one-act play *A Way Out* (New York: Harbor Press, 1929). The play had previously appeared without a preface in *The Seven Arts* 1.4 (February 1917) and in Helen Louise Cohen, editor, *More One Act Plays by Modern Authors* (New York: Harcourt Brace, 1927). Roland Wood (of Harbor Press) first suggested to Frost that he prepare a book edition of the play in April 1928. On June 29 of that year Wood sent Frost proof of the play and asked him to write an introduction. Frost agreed, but did not send the preface to Wood until the following March. Amherst College Library holds a set of proofs of this preface corrected and revised in Frost's hand. That text perfectly matches the text published by Harbor Press and I reprint it here exactly. Frost dedicated the Harbor Press edition: "To / Roland A. Wood / Who created the part of Asie / Academy of Music / Northampton, Mass. / February 24, 1919." The reference is to the premier performance of the play, in which Wood (a student of Frost's at the time) had acted.

Explanatory Notes

16.1   Stevenson . . . Lamb] Robert Louis Stevenson traveled to Samoa and the South
Pacific in 1888. Charles Lamb's *Essays of Elia* appeared first in *The London Magazine* in 1823.

17. [Address at the Dedication of the Davison Memorial Library (1930)]

Frost delivered these remarks at the dedication of the Wilfred Davison Memorial Library
on July 21, 1930, at the Bread Loaf School of English. Davison, Dean of the Bread Loaf
School of English since 1921, died in September 1929. Joan St. C. Crane gives the date of
the address as January 21 in her *Robert Frost: A Descriptive Catalogue of Books and Manuscripts
in the Clifton Waller Barrett Library, University of Virginia* (Charlottesville: University Press of
Virginia, 1974). But this is apparently incorrect. Frost writes to Louis Untermeyer in a July
14, 1930, letter: "I have been come after by President Moody [of Middlebury College] to be
present and help them dedicate the Memorial Library to Wilfred Davison on Monday July
21st" (*RFLU* 201). I have found no pre-publication forms of Frost's address, which was published twice: in a booklet titled *Wilfred Davison Memorial Library* (Middlebury, Vt.: Bread
Loaf School of English, 1930), and in *Give Me No Marble Slab Nor Sculptured Bronze* (Bread
Loaf Folder No. 8 [Middlebury, Vt.: Bread Loaf School of English, 1930]). (The title of the
latter is taken from one of Davison's poems.) The texts of the two printings are identical.
Alderman Library at the University of Virginia holds a copy of the first inscribed by Frost
and Dartmouth College Library holds a copy of the second signed by him in 1950. In neither case does he offer corrections or remarks. The copy-text for the present edition is the
first appearance. I have omitted the tag at the beginning of the address, which reads: "Mr
Frost spoke as follows." I have also omitted the quotation marks around the body of the
address that this tag made necessary.

Explanatory Notes

17.1   I owe a debt to Wilfred Davison] Lawrance Thompson reports a June 1946 conversation in which Frost told how his association with Bread Loaf began: "It seems that
Davidson [sic] came down to Amherst to get Frost interested in the Bread Loaf idea. And
on his way up to Franconia that first year, with Mrs. Frost and the children [apparently in
1921], he had stopped at Bread Loaf to read and talk. But the adulation and the failure to
include the family in the cordiality of the welcome dampened their spirit, and Frost probably would not have come back if Davidson hadn't pleaded. So it began, and they soon laid
claim to him, although he had congenital doubts as to the value of such a conference for
writers" (NOTES).

17.1   He speaks in his poem] Wilfred Davison was the first Dean of the Bread Loaf
School of English, where Frost taught during the 1920s and after. Davison's poem was reprinted in the folder with Frost's address. The lines alluded to read: "My monument be
what of living truth / Has flowed through me to other men. / So shall survive what is of
lasting worth. / Thus though I die, then shall I live again."

18. Education by Poetry: A Meditative Monologue (1931)

Frost delivered this address before the Amherst College Alumni Council on November 15,
1930. It was published first in the *Amherst Graduates' Quarterly* in February 1931 and was re-

printed with a few excisions in the *Boston Evening Transcript Magazine* on February 21. It was then reprinted in full (from the plates of the first appearance) as a supplement to *Amherst Alumni Council News* 4.4 (March 1931). I have examined five different texts of "Education by Poetry": (1) a typed transcript of Frost's spoken performance, with question and answer period, based on a stenographic record; (2) a typescript based on that transcript, with heavy manuscript revisions in Frost's hand, and some in his friend George Whicher's (reprinted in facsimile in *The Parkman Dexter Howe Library Part VII,* complied by John Lancaster [Gainesville: University of Florida, 1990]); (3) a typescript which incorporates those manuscript revisions, but which introduces a few variant readings and misprints of its own; (4) the first published appearance; (5) a facsimile of a copy of the published lecture, heavily revised by Frost some years later, probably between 1939 and 1942. In the following notes I refer to these documents by the numbers given here. Typescript 3 may be dispensed with quickly, as internal evidence suggests that neither Frost nor George Whicher prepared it: the text introduces a handful of nonsensical variants in wording for which neither man could have been responsible.

Typescript 2 is now held in the Parkman Dexter Howe Library at the University of Florida. John S. Van E. Kohn, who gave the typescript to Howe, supplied with it a letter identifying the typist as "one of [Frost's] very closest Amherst friends." That friend, according to John Lancaster, who prepared the catalogue of the Parkman Dexter Howe collection of Frostiana, is the aforementioned George Whicher, Frost's colleague at Amherst, and, in 1931, editor of the *Amherst Graduates' Quarterly.* Whicher, then, almost certainly prepared typescript 2. But he did so under Frost's direct oversight. In typescript 2, all of the false starts and incidental remarks present in the raw transcript of the talk have been cut, as have the transcriber's bracketed notes ("[Laughter]," "[Renewed laughter]," and so on). Whicher might have done this much on his own. But there are a number of places—and here I refer only to the typed portions of typescript 2, not to the manuscript revisions made on it at a later date—where typescript 2 revises the wording, or omits entire paragraphs. These latter revisions are almost certainly authorial. The version as published, then, derives from a typescript prepared by Whicher with Frost's assistance; which typescript in turn derives from a transcript of a stenographic record of Frost's spoken performance. Because I have sought to respect the character of Frost's working relationships, it follows, for me, that the result of those collaborations has a special authority. In the case before us now, Frost's editor, "publisher," and assistant are the same man: George Whicher. Accordingly I reproduce here the text of the first appearance of "Education by Poetry," correcting several misprints. I have also corrected an error that apparently crept in when the talk was transcribed from Frost's spoken performance and which remained in the text as originally published. At 18.41 the copy-text reads "the coast of Phoenicia." I have corrected this to "Phaeacia," as did Hyde Cox and Edward Connery Lathem in *SP.* The collation lists all variants in wording between the Frost-Whicher typescript and the first appearance of "Education by Poetry."

There remains to be discussed text number 5. The lecture was reprinted a month after its first appearance as a supplement to the *Amherst Alumni Council News.* After Frost's death Edward Connery Lathem and Hyde Cox found among his papers a copy of this supplement to the *Alumni Council News* with heavy manuscript revisions in Frost's hand. Lathem makes no guess as to the date of these revisions in his introduction to a publication of the document in facsimile in 1966. But circumstantial evidence suggests Frost may have undertaken them between 1939 and 1942. In 1938, he tried to leave the firm of Henry Holt and

Company only to discover that he was bound to it by contract and by long association. He could not be assured of their cooperation, for example, in the event that he should try to publish a collected edition with another firm. The best he could do was to renegotiate his contract. The terms of the new arrangements required that Frost prepare a volume of prose. He wrote in an October 17, 1940, letter to William Sloane at Holt: "I hereby promise in the presence of Kathleen, my secretary, that I will give you both the books you want, prose and verse, at approximately the times you name. Tell me right back in your next letter what's the latest you can wait for the prose book . . . You know me well enough to know that I wouldn't make these undertakings if I hadn't the books practically written already" (unpublished letter, Princeton University Library). Sloane wanted the prose volume for publication in the spring of 1941 and in April of that year made arrangements for J. J. Lankes, a woodcut artist, to design a cover for the book. That is as far as the project went. Frost never delivered a manuscript. Indeed, this is as close as he ever came to producing a volume of prose. For this reason I conjecture that he made further revisions to "Education by Poetry" in or around 1940.

As for the revisions themselves: they are comprehensive in character and affect hundreds of words, a few entire paragraphs, and a number of entire sentences throughout the ten-page lecture. By "comprehensive" I mean that Frost seems to have had some general aims in mind, in addition to simply fine-tuning the prose. Each particular revision has more than a merely local purpose. For example, Frost apparently wanted to remove from the lecture all traces of the occasion of its delivery. He cut references to Amherst College and to some other lecturers who had recently spoken at Amherst. He cleaned up some of the talkish aspects of the prose, with the effect that it reads much less like a lecture than it did before. Since many of the particular revisions are part of this larger, integrated revision, it would be hard to justify accepting only some of them. One must either accept them all, or accept none of them, as the two texts represent distinct versions of "Education by Poetry." But there are practical obstacles to accepting them all. Some of the revisions are unrecoverable owing to two torn sheets. In the cases of a number of others Frost left ambiguous indications as to how they are to be executed, and some are illegible. For textual as well as practical reasons this revised text ought not to be conflated with the original published text.

After Frost delivered "Education by Poetry" in 1931, he entertained questions, as he often did in public appearances. His responses are preserved in the transcript of the performance held at Amherst College, and I reproduce the more interesting ones among them here:

President PEASE. Mr. Frost would be very glad to have questions asked.
Professor FROST. I would hate to think I had been so dogmatic. Who was it telling me—I guess it was—some one was telling me about Sinclair Lewis. He says a thing so positively that you can't—that it is like being knocked on the head—you can't think of any answer until a long time afterwards. But take the matter of thinking and metaphor. That seems to me the important thing of all. When you are very young, you know, you shall start putting this and that together. It was Mr. Finley that said the good one about Washington and the not so good one about Theodore Roosevelt; and it is all we remember. It is all we live by. It is all that gives us any claim to being anybody, that we now and then

put something together that is something, that makes for validity—a real something.

Question: Mr. Frost, would you explain your belief as to why it is a metaphor never is satisfying to poetry if it is something too immediate? I mean that you can compare something in poetry to an inverted shield, but if you apply it to a monkey-wrench or a carburetor, it doesn't have the same effect.

Professor FROST . . . I don't think it has to be something remote. I think it is the sort of an unexpected that always has something to do with it [sic]. There is always this element of dipping here and here, you know. Time and space. I suppose it is a feeling of great freedom, mental freedom. I suppose it is the only freedom. I could go on talking about this. I think the great freedom of your material is to be able in connection with the thing in front of you to dip anywhere in time and space for its strange analogue, its surprising analogue, that gives you a sense of freedom. A schoolboy is, by definition, the boy who knows everything he knows in the order in which he learned it. It is to break up that order, to break up the order of experience and all reading or all experience, break it up and dip in anywhere for the analogue, that gives you the sense, gives you the freedom. That is where the making is, where the creation is. I don't care for the word creation in connection with the arts, because it has got attached to it courses in writing, and I always feel ashamed or abashed, if you know what I mean, when I hear the words creative writing. But creation is a good word in its place.

It doesn't matter where it comes from. It may be homely. It may be an aristocrat. It may be lofty. It may be courtly. You know you get poetry both ways. I don't [know] why they don't mix, but a person like William Butler Yeats, very aristocratic and fastidious in his nature, thinks everything started in courts and that all this folk-poetry is just degenerated court poetry, decadent court poetry, leavings from the court table—the swill. But it comes—like the hen and the egg; which came first, the court and the court poetry, or the folk poetry? I guess they always existed together. It is like this evolution. The Yeats people naturally believe in devolution, and the folk people would call it evolution; it came up from the gutter. But the whole is mixed and side by side; there are no beginnings in either place. They have all been going always.

Take the various forms of marriage, you know; they try to make you put in some order of devolution or evolution. They all always existed side by side, and still do.

Did I answer you? Is that what you mean?

Question: I think in part. My feeling was that a certain antiquity had to be associated with the things with which you compare.

Professor FROST. Then I answered that, because I don't think so.

Professor FROST . . . I am often amazed. Suppose somebody said, "Existence is all gland." It is all right. I say it could be worse, and so on. It is good, you know, a certain distance—something there. I just ran my eye over a book that my wife said I didn't do justice, that seemed to be a novel on the gland theory, and it was a pretty tight little novel. You can see where that gland thing breaks down—the metaphor. It goes a little way, and then it breaks down. But he trusts it entirely.

He hasn't had proper poetical education, that is all. He isn't used to letting the metaphor drop at the right point. That you have got to learn. I dislike more than anybody to go too far with a metaphor, the way I went too far with that fellow's metaphor about the machine. Don't think it is anything that carries you to the end of everything. I think I have attempted to bring him to the end because he thought it did carry him to the end. I don't see any objection to any of it. I don't hate the machine age. I don't hate machinery. I don't hate machinery metaphors, and I am not afraid of mass production. I don't know—I didn't get that up, so, as I say, it doesn't interest me particularly . . . Take leadership in politics. I think leadership in politics is a gift of making little metaphors. The man goes farthest who says the little thing that leads us.

There is an old [bit] of poetry

We are the music-makers

We are the dreamers of dreams,

and so on. It is not just about prophecy. It is everything that makes metaphors. We do it with metaphors. We build Babel and we overthrow Babel with metaphors. A new way of thinking . . .

They had a discussion in the Parisian papers a year or two ago, as to whether they should keep a light burning in the tomb of the unknown soldier. Some people said, "Well, there ought to be a light burning there. He ought always to be where we could see him, ought never to be out of our sight." That was their way of thinking of it. And then others answered, "Well, the poor man ought to have some rest. It ought to be dark part of the time. He ought to sleep." You see they bring in what they connect it with that makes their thinking. I don't know who won. I don't know which prevailed. But they were seeking, seeking conviction in analogy. Always seeking conviction in analogy.

The strangest thing is that it should be so in science. One of the expressions that that is so is that people in our time have deliberately thrown away the distinction between axioms and postulates. They have deliberately chucked the distinction so that they could have more fun thinking anything that metaphors let them in for.

Collation

TS = Frost's corrected typescript, held in the Parkman Dexter Howe Collection of the University of Florida Library. TS2 = Frost-Whicher typescript. 1st = First appearance in *Amherst Graduates' Quarterly.*

*18.8   Anyone who liked] Any one ~ 1st {Elsewhere in the copy-text the form is one word, not two.}

*18.14   I find someone] ~ some one 1st {Elsewhere in the copy-text the form is one word, not two.}

*18.19   that the individual particles] TS; ~ particle {The typescript has "particles" here, as is consistent with the same phrase in the previous sentence.}

*18.21   the point of death] TS2; ~ death, {The use of a comma in this situation is most uncharacteristic of Frost.}

18.35   That was when thinking] ~ teaching to think TS2

18.37   Greatest of all] The greatest ~ TS2

*18.41   Phaeacia] Phoenicia 1st {See textual notes to the essay, above.}

18.54   can make them;] can; TS2

Explanatory Notes

18.3   George Russell] George Russell ("AE"), Irish poet (1867–1935).

18.14   making metaphor the whole of thinking] See Emerson, "Poetry and Imagination": "All thinking is analogizing, and 'tis the use of life to learn metonymy" (*Ralph Waldo Emerson,* ed. Richard Poirier [New York: Oxford University Press, 1990], 445).

18.41   one of the books of the "Odyssey"] Frost refers to Book 5. However, consulting George Herbert Palmer's translation—Frost's favorite—I find in the account of Odysseus's landing at Phaeacia (after what Frost calls "the world's longest swim") no image of an "inverted shield."

18.42   a better metaphor in the same book] See the concluding lines to Book 5 of *The Odyssey.*

18.49   There are two or three places where we know belief outside of religion.] Frost often recurred to the topic, as in a 1931 lecture at the New School for Social Research in New York: "I saw a list of nine beliefs that a fellow considered to see if any one was like the belief that we call poetry. They were all just commonplaces of belief. 'I believe it is going to rain tomorrow,' 'I believe you are a liar' . . . all too dull for anything. All belief is really interesting to us in our day because so many people say they don't have any, and don't know what it is about. I saw a picture on a telephone book of a man with a telephone and he says he uses it, he believes in it, and he owns it. There is something there . . . why do we take the telephone up and put it down so carefully and not let the receiver off, except for some belief? I think belief is as I see it in a boy 16–20 yrs of age, adolescent as they say . . . who knows something about himself that he can't prove, that he would not dare to tell you or me or anybody because he just doesn't know what it is so that he can tell it. It is something he is going to . . . believe himself into. That may be a purely physical thing . . . it may be spiritual. Again, this man talking about marriage. Passion is a believing thing. It has been made a joke of because it often fails. But so often it succeeds. It is a making thing, an unfolding thing. It knows its end without being able to tell its end. We Americans are hard put to it to tell what it is about America . . . We are easily shaken in our belief by foreigners. I am too proud to go into it even with you Americans, to say what I think about it. I run away if I think I am going to be asked about it. I don't want to talk about my belief." But then Frost proceeds to do so: "We may say that there are certain countries that are in the dead wood, certain countries that are in the live wood, and we are in the cambium layer" (unpublished typescript, Dartmouth College Library). Lawrance Thompson reports a 1951 conversation in which Frost had this to say about belief: "Frost said that at Dartmouth in 1950–51, he had been invited to come up to talk in the Great Issues session, just after a Canadian philosopher. So he chose to talk on 'Three Gifts of God': Two beliefs and one unbelief. I heard him give this talk, I think, at Bread Loaf last summer. 1. Belief that the world could be made liveable. This was the belief fostered by science, which would arrange the world to be liveable. 2. Belief that the world could never be made liveable; but that Heaven would correct the shortcomings of earth: This was the belief fostered by religion. 3. The Unbelief which denied the two beliefs. This was the skeptical philosophical position. The poet's position was that of 'unbelief' in that the poet was never trying to sell either one of the other beliefs but was fond of pointing out the shortcomings of the other beliefs, not for the sake of setting up the denials but merely for the pleasure of setting up the discrepancy between the way of beliefs and the way things were. The poet, says Frost, is never systematic. He is more like the man in the streets, who sees things unsystematically. He views life in fragments" (NOTES).

19. [Autobiographical Sketch (1933)]

This brief autobiographical sketch is explained by a letter from Mrs. William Vanamee, Assistant to the President of the American Academy of Arts and Letters, to Frost, dated April 24, 1933: "In March Mr. Huntington wrote to President Butler [of the Academy] that the editor (Jean Boyere) of *Le Manuscrit autographe,* a quarterly printed in Paris, had asked him whether a number of that publication devoted to the Academy would be welcome . . . The plan is to have each member send me within two weeks a hand written article or poem, either prepared especially for this number or taken from his/her previous writings . . . In addition to the autographed manuscript the editor wishes to include approximately 350 words devoted to the biography and bibliography of each member, preferably prepared by the member (although the fact that he/she prepared it would not appear)." Frost supplied a signed manuscript of "An Old Man's Winter Night," which had originally appeared in *Mountain Interval* (1916), together with a brief sketch of his life. The letter just quoted is held, with a manuscript of the sketch in Elinor Frost's hand, in the library of the American Academy of Arts and Letters and the Institute of Arts and Letters in New York City. Frost dictated the sketch to his wife. Elinor Frost writes to Richard Thornton, of Henry Holt and Company, on May 31, 1933: "About two weeks ago, Robert composed a short biography of about 330 words for the American Academy. Some French enterprise wants one of all the members" (395). The Academy's library also holds a variant typescript of the sketch, origin unknown. Had Elinor Frost or Frost himself prepared it there would, of course, have been no need to send the manuscript in her hand to the Academy. In any event, the sketch as excerpted in French translation for *Le Manuscrit autographe* appears to have been based on Elinor Frost's manuscript, which I reprint here. I have conventionalized the styling of book titles.

   As this is the only item reprinted herein personally associated with Elinor White Frost, I include at this point some remarks about her marriage to Frost from Lawrance Thompson's "Notes on Conversations with Robert Frost." The entry is dated 1940, two years after Elinor died: "He talked much about his wife . . . and he found her always the most intelligent critic. Kay's [i.e., Kathleen Morrison's] society manners and academic approach to poetry bother him now, in contrast to Eleanor's [sic]. He never got much from her; her silences were as eloquent as any spoken criticism. And the early reviews filled her with delight. But when more came, she began to be jealous of the public acclaim that took him from her" (NOTES).

Collation

*19.5   *A Boy's Will*] A Boy's Will
*19.5   *North of Boston*] North of Boston
*19.5   *Mountain Interval*] Mountain Interval
*19.5   *New Hampshire*] New Hampshire
*19.5   *West-Running Brook*] West-Running Brook
*19.5   *Collected Poems*] Collected Poems

Explanatory Notes

19.1   1875] Lawrance Thompson was the first to determine that Frost was actually born in 1874, not 1875.

19.1   New Englander of the ninth generation] In a 1923 interview with Rose Feld, Frost remarked: "People do me the honor to say that I am truly a poet of America. They point to my New England background, to the fact that my paternal ancestors came here sometime in the sixteen hundreds. So much is true, but what they either do not know or do not say is that my mother was an immigrant. She came to these shores from Edinburgh in an old vessel that docked at Philadelphia. But she felt the spirit of America and became a part of it before she even set a foot off the boat. She used to tell about it when I was a child. She was sitting on the deck of the boat waiting for orders to come ashore. Near her some workmen were loading Delaware peaches on to the ship. One of them picked out one of them and dropped it into her lap. 'Here, take that,' he said. The way he said it and the spirit in which he gave it left an indelible impression on her mind. 'It was a bonny peach,' she used to say, ' and I didn't eat it. I kept it to show my friends.' Looking back would I say that she was less the American than my father? No. America meant something live and real and virile to her. He took it for granted. He was a Fourth of July American, by which I mean that he rarely failed to celebrate in the way considered proper and appropriate. She, however, was a year-around American" (*New York Times Book Review*, October 21, 1923).

19.6   they have proved of interest to more than New England] In a talk at Boston University in May 1940, Frost said: "I hear too much these days abut regionalism in art. People are always asking me what to do about New England. Let's don't do anything about it. Let's don't get self-conscious because we think we have to do something about it. Let's just read and write." And he continued: "The trouble with most of you young writers today is that you are too bookish. You write unconscious memories from what you have read. You are afraid to tell on your families or on yourselves. I always feel when I see a disclaimer in the front of a book, you know, 'all the characters in this book are fictitious and so on,' that what it really should say is, 'all the characters in this book are real.' I've written seven books and I haven't had to use one disclaimer line. All my poems are from life. Of course they all go through changes—'sea changes,' but they're all real people. Once a lady read, in my presence, a poem which I intended as a portrait of herself. At first I was worried that she would recognize herself and then I was annoyed when I found she hadn't. All of my poems come from a little circle about 14 miles in diameter—that's where they come from but not where they go to" (quoted in the *Christian Science Monitor*, May 6, 1940). Frost's having said so much about his own commitments to "region," it is perhaps worth reprinting here a previously unpublished (and likely unfinished) "essay," of sorts, on the topic of New England. It survives in manuscript, as dictated to Kathleen Morrison by Frost:

> Very few left would want to put on any airs about New England that would keep people from coming to live or play here summer or winter. Have I not said in verse to the immigrants:
>   "No ship of all that under sail or steam
>   Have gathered people to us more and more
>   But Pilgrim-manned the Mayflower in a dream
>   Has been her anxious convoy in to shore."
> We want the other parts of the country and the world to like us even if they

have to take us down a peg to common in their estimation by twitting us now and then for the Salem witchcraft. It has to be said however that hanging and burning witches was the most sophisticated religious thing to go in for at the time. Good Christians were finding and executing nearly a hundred thousand in Europe to our twenty individuals. It was a mark of intellectuality and Massachusetts, then the most college-educated community in the world, was the only colony not too busy for intellectuality while getting a foothold in the wilderness. I recently had occasion to tell a friend I still believed in witches though I don't take any stock in what they tell me about what stocks to invest in. Just so we still believe in God though we no longer believe in what the Jews claim he told us to do to witches and perverts. We and the Jews have put all that behind us. But we do owe something to Salem for a figure of speech that ought to keep us from being too hard on ex-pro Russians. I mean the word witch-hunting.

But to be really serious. The Puritans when the Mayflower's boats grounded at Plymouth gave the continent a "shog," as the Scottish poet would say, that we trust the country will never be demoralized out of. They gave us the ideal of government that before all else the ruler as giver and bestower would want to give his people character. Comfort, schooling, and security—yes, of course. But never more of these than makes for character. The Puritanism of the Puritans was at worst too distilled an isolation of a chief element in all religions, ancient and modern, Greek and Roman, old Roman and recent Roman, Anglican and Protestant, namely the fear in a man of his own delight and pleasure. Even before we eased off from the sternness that came to our stern and rock-bound coast, the life in these parts must not be thought of as entirely graceless. The church came first in Boston but I have it on the authority of my friend, Sam Morison, that there were ten silversmiths in Boston before there was a single lawyer. There was a beautiful architecture that had no rival except in Virginia. The only first folio of Shakespeare in the New World was in the library of one of the Mathers. Milton though he never came here was of our party and is always ours as Wordsworth quoted him in bad times, as times often will be:

"Milton, thou shouldst be living at this hour:
England hath need of thee: she is a fen
Of stagnant waters: alter, sword and pen,
Fireside, the heroic wealth of hall and bower,
Have forfeited their ancient English dower
Of inward happiness. We are selfish men:
Oh, raise us up, return to us again;
And give us manners, virtue, freedom, power.
Thy soul was like a Star, and dwelt apart."
He shared in the great decision we took in 1648 which was the last news dateline Thoreau had any interest in, so he said. We have had a brave history of decisiveness. Then and again in 1775 when
"By the rude bridge that arched the flood
Their flag to April's breeze unfurled
Here once the embattled farmers stood
And fired the shot heard round the world."
There you have the best piece of occasional poetry ever written—for

Thermopylae or any other fight. New England poets, Emerson, Longfellow, and Whittier, took their part towards the mighty decision of '61 to end slavery. Edgar Allen [*sic*] Poe's first book was published in Boston. One could say poetry has really flourished in the region. We have kept on having poets clear down to now, such as Emily Dickinson, Robinson to mention only the dead and gone. This may well be because the region has such a shrewdly beautiful climate and a scenery of beauty subdued to poetry and not grand or grandiose enough for rhetoric." (unpublished manuscript, University of Michigan)

The phrase "gave the continent a 'shog'" is apparently an allusion to Robert Burns's "Address to the Deil": "Then you, ye auld, snick-drawing dog! / Ye cam to Paradise incog, / An' play'd on man a cursed brogue, / (Black be your fa'!) / An' gied the infant warld a shog . . ." "Sam Morison" is the historian Samuel Eliot Morison (1887–1976).

20. [Comment on "Birches" (1933)]

Frost's remarks appeared with his poem "Birches" in *Fifty Poets: An American Auto-Anthology*, edited by William Rose Benet (New York: Duffield and Green, 1933). Benet wrote to Frost in December 1932 asking him to contribute to the anthology. Having received no response, Benet wrote again in February 1933. He refers to these letters in a headnote to Frost's contribution: "The editor wrote him at Amherst where he now resides a good part of the time as a literary consultant. Absorbed in his musing he promptly mislaid the letter. We kept after him, however, and were rewarded by his choice of *Birches,* and the following characteristic reply, with its bearing on present-day affairs." I have found no manuscript or typescript of Frost's remarks, which were not reprinted during his lifetime. Amherst College holds a copy of *Fifty Poets* signed by Frost in 1937 on the page where "Birches" appears. He offers no corrections or remarks. I reprint the text exactly as published in 1933, except that the copy-text is set in italic type.

Explanatory Notes

20.1   Your Ark] Apparently, *Fifty Poets* was to be the sole record of American poetry after the Flood. The "time of confusion and doom" in question is, of course, the Great Depression.

20.1   ulteriority] See "The Constant Symbol": Poetry "is metaphor, saying one thing and meaning another, saying one thing in terms of another, the pleasure of ulteriority" (36.3). See also Lawrance Thompson's report of a 1953 talk Frost gave at Bread Loaf: "He said that in writing a poem, he was aware of saying two things at once; but of wanting to say the first thing so well that any reader who liked that part of the poem might feel free to settle for that part of the poem as sufficient in itself. But, he added, it was of the nature of poetry to say two things at once, and it was of the nature of literary appreciation to perceive that an ulterior meaning had been included in the particular meaning" (NOTES).

21. ["Letter" to *The Amherst Student* (1935)]

The copy-text for the present edition of Frost's "Letter" is its first appearance in *The Amherst Student* (March 25, 1935) 1–2. *The Student* is an undergraduate newspaper published at Amherst College. Frost's manuscript, as supplied to *The Student*, has apparently been lost. All that survives is an incomplete, early holograph manuscript held now at Dartmouth College Library. The collation records differences in wording between this early text and the text as published. I have made a number of changes in the copy-text, in three cases incorporating readings from the manuscript. The Dartmouth manuscript, though provisional, clearly reads "stroke" for "strike," and the context favors this reading (at 21.5). Again following the manuscript, I have corrected "award" to "aware" (at 21.5). At 21.6 Frost's manuscript unmistakably reads "The background is," not "The background in"—though the latter reading has consistently been given in reprintings of the essay. Finally, the sentence to which I have added "it" (at 21.17) is not present in the manuscript, though the context requires the pronoun. Lawrence Thompson, in *SL*, and Hyde Cox and Edward Connery Lathem, in their *SP*, make the same correction. Because Frost's finished manuscript for the "Letter" does not survive, it is not possible definitely to determine which among the departures from convention in punctuation in *The Student* text derive from Frost's own final manuscript. I have therefore relied on my general knowledge of Frost's habits in writing for publication. I have supplied the additional comma in the series at 21.5 according to the usage the newspaper elsewhere implies, and according to Frost's habits of punctuation in published texts. The punctuation of the phrase "the artist the poet" 21.5 is a little more problematic. The sense of the phrase, in context, seems to be: "the artist and the poet might . . ." The second term does not evidently narrow the sense of the first term. I treat the two terms simply as in a series rather than in apposition, supplying one comma between them. I have omitted the inter-titles to the essay supplied by the editors of *The Amherst Student,* as they are not Frost's. These occur before paragraphs at 21.5 ("Man Is Form Born of Chaos") and 21.6 ("Economists Worship Form"). Portions of the "Letter" were reprinted by Grant Dahlstrom as a Christmas card for private distribution in 1936. Dahlstrom cribbed his text from a partial, and apparently unauthoritative, reprinting of the letter in the *New York Times*. Moreover, he did so without the knowledge of its author. See Crane, *Descriptive Catalogue,* 111–12, for an account of Dahlstrom's variant edition.

Collation

MS = Frost's manuscript fragment, Dartmouth College Library.

21.1–2   It is {. . .} such talk.] {not present} MS

21.2   claimed the] ~ that MS

21.2   it rather for themselves.] the honor for themselves rather. MS

21.2   immodest of] immodest for MS

21.2   think of himself as] he is MS

21.2   God.] ~ What it took to stop him is to be the measure of his importance on his tombstone. MS

21.3   great deal] good ~ MS

21.3   Heaven.] ~ They had to be for the world to justify its separate existence from Heaven. MS

21.3   hearing your] the MS

21.3   say your] call it MS

21.3   your integrity] or integrity MS

21.4   worse] better or worse MS

21.4   a donkey] a whole donkey MS

21.4   Witness] And the proof is in MS

21.4   tissues and the muscles] muscles MS

21.4   huge shapeless novels, huge gobs of raw sincerity] huge gobs of raw sincerity, shapeless novels MS

21.4   write] do MS

21.5   how bad] bad MS

21.5   age is.] ~ We can maintain and go on with form in our modest ways. MS

21.5   so much] the MS

21.5   admits of form] permits ~ MS

21.5   And not only {. . .} go on with.] {not present} MS

21.5   achieved the least] ever achieved MS

*21.5   stroke] MS; strike 1st

21.5   faith] ~ in MS

21.5   right way.] ~ Nothing is so composing as composition. MS

*21.5   artist,] artist 1st

*21.5   aware] MS; award 1st

21.5   really] really in MS

*21.5   engrossing,] engrossing 1st

21.5   staying] and staying MS

21.5   For these] {not present} MS

*21.6   The background is] MS; ~ in 1st

*21.6   out on it] out on{ } 1st

21.6   background any small {. . .} than everything.] 1st {with the exception noted at 21.6}; {not present} MS

Explanatory Notes

21.1   my age] The letter is in reply to birthday greetings extended by the students of Amherst College. The "Letter" appeared in the *Student* for March 25, 1935, the day before what Frost then believed to be his sixtieth birthday. He later learned that he had been born in 1874, not in 1875.

21.4   huge shapeless novels] Frost remarked in a July 20, 1936, talk at Bread Loaf: "If I were teaching, I would simply say, 'Now you are to report to me as hard as you can!' That is the way I would outline a year's work. Bring in words that belong to your family and locality—words, then incidents, characters, family stories and, best of all, ideas of your own—insights of your own into people and affairs—it doesn't matter what. Then I should say, 'What's to prevent that from being very tiresome? Why shouldn't that be just like Thomas Wolfe's novels? What's to prevent that from being just wholesale?' FORM—FORM—You can't bring anything in here that you can't bring in in form. It has got to make up—to shape up and only that can get in which can shape up. Form is a very exclusive thing" (unpublished typescript, as prepared by Elsie Waterman and Charles DuBois, Amherst College Library).

21.5   Anyone who has achieved the least form] See Emerson, "The Method of Nature": "The history of the genesis or the old mythology repeats itself in the experience of every child. He too is a demon or god thrown into a particular chaos, where he strives ever to lead things from disorder into order. Each individual soul is such, in virtue of its being a power to translate the world into some particular language of its own; if not into a picture, a statue, or a dance,—why, then, into a trade, an art, a science, a mode of living, a conversation, a character, an influence" (*EL* 122–23). See also Frost's remarks in the July 1936 talk at Bread Loaf cited above: "I am just going to make short work of that and tell you where poetry—where ideals—may exist. I suppose they exist in the making of form— wherever that is. You take a poem, a picture, a garden, a family, a state—all forms achieved in different media. I like myself best to work in words and rhymes and meters because I have it to do myself. I should hate the job of having to shape up a state and hold it in shape. I could stand it if that were cut out for me—I am enough of a ruffian to take that roughly with all its approximations. And I would not call it 'compromises'—I hate the word—never use it. But if I were working in marble, carrying out ideals in marble, should I find I had to compromise my ideals with the marble? No! My whole aim includes both the ideal and the marble. It would not be the same—different grains would make it differ- ent. But I cannot bring myself to expect to compromise my ideals. My ideal and my me- dium are one."

21.6   If I were a Platonist] See the February 20, 1940, entry in Lawrance Thompson's "Notes on Conversations with Robert Frost": "RF said he likes to think of people in two categories: the Platonists who thought of life at its best as perfection, and of people work- ing toward that perfection; the nihilists who thought of life as being whatever they found it to be ('This is hell, nor am I out of it'.) and were willing to give some shape or form to whatever they found at hand. The latter, instead of saying, 'This building would be best if built with a certain permanent material found in Zanzibar; too bad I can't get it,' said rather, 'Here's clay to use for a building; its not the best, but its the best available.['] The former thought of trying to overcome all drawbacks that hindered them from attaining perfection and eventually grew disappointed with what they called a *compromise*. The latter never used the word compromise because there couldn't be any such condition in doing the best with whatever there was—unless one didn't care to do the best. And then he might be compromised but he couldn't care enough to call it such. Connected with this was the whole story of how one stood up under sorrow. 'My November Guest' is built around this idea of sorrow. It was written during the sadness after his loss of the child— and I think it locks up closely with the point of view in 'Home Burial.' Which sorrow shall we dwell on—and how openly. Can we find pleasure in sorrow—or can pleasure and sor- row go hand in hand—joy and sadness with arms intertwined? His poetry is always a com- bination of these" (NOTES). And see the following remarks, again from Frost's July 20, 1936, talk: "The only way we see ideals in the state, in the family, in teaching and politics, is when you put them in yourself by mastery and skill—in the place for form. Now that does not mean a Platonic thing at all—I am talking Anti-Platonism. That does not come from looking at perfection. It means just the desire to take whatever comes to hand—whatever is in front of you—and shape it. Shape is something to do with the consistency of parts, and there is this more to it—that the form you work in has got almost to have some rela- tion to the larger forms around you or it is not 'national' enough."

22. [Introduction to *King Jasper* (1935)]

This essay appeared first as the introduction to Edwin Arlington Robinson's *King Jasper* (New York: Macmillan, 1935). James Putnam, assistant to the president of Macmillan, asked Frost to write the introduction in April 1935. In mid-August 1935, Frost mailed typescripts of it to Macmillan and to his friend Louis Untermeyer, who later reprinted this first version of the preface (*RFLU* 261–64), which ends with the sentence: "The utmost of ambition is to lodge a few poems where they will be hard to get rid of, to lodge a few irreducible bits where Robinson lodged more than his share" (22.9). This draft of the introduction does not mention *King Jasper*, nor does it refer specifically to any other poems by Robinson. Almost immediately, Macmillan returned the essay to Frost. George P. Brett, President of Macmillan in New York, explained the situation in a September 5 letter to Harold Latham, who had been Robinson's editor for twenty years: "As you know we have asked Robert Frost to write an appreciative introduction to *King Jasper*. It has come in and is impossible, terrific. It simply can't be used" (unpublished letter, Macmillan papers, New York Public Library). Brett then proposed to Latham that *he* write the introduction. Nevertheless, the sales department at Macmillan wanted a Frost introduction. James Putnam had already written Frost on August 22: "What we really want is an introduction to the poem that will be, at the same time, an appreciation of Robinson and a general estimate of his place in literature." Putnam went on to suggest that Frost submit the first draft of the introduction to *The Saturday Review of Literature* (unpublished letter, Dartmouth College Library). Upon receiving Putnam's letter, Frost took up the essay where he had left off, adding four pages and doubling its length. He explained to Untermeyer on September 21: "I've been bothered a little by the preface to King Jasper. They wanted more and, if I could manage it, a quotation or two from Robinson" (*RFLU* 264). Frost returned a new, complete typescript of the introduction (now held at Amherst College) to Macmillan in early September. This expanded version of the introduction was in galley proofs by September 27, when Brett wrote to Louis Ledoux, the friend and patron of Robinson who, upon the poet's death some months earlier, in April, had been appointed his literary executor: "I think the last time we talked about Robert Frost's introduction I told you I thought it was perfectly terrible and we simply couldn't use it. I seem to recall that you were rather of the opinion that it didn't make any difference; that you even rather preferred that the book be published without any introduction at all. Since that time Frost has done a new introduction and our editorial and sales folk feel that it is most important that it be included in *King Jasper*. Feeling that you would perhaps like to see it I send along a set of the galley proofs" (unpublished letter, Macmillan Papers, New York Public Library). Ledoux replied on September 30: "I must say that Frost's introduction to *King Jasper* seems to me about as bad as it could be . . . I am convinced that it would add nothing to the dignity or importance of the volume . . . Nearly ninety percent of what Frost has written seems to me an expression of his own personal 'grievances' against the present economic, social and financial regime of the Government, and his irritability with modernistic trends in contemporary verse. The little that is said about Robinson might have been said at least as well by any hack writer or undergraduate" (unpublished letter, Macmillan Papers, New York Public Library). Brett answered on October 4: "Yesterday we all went into a huddle over your letter of September 30. I think we all agree that the Frost introduction is not appropriate for *King Jasper*, but, on the other hand, Frost is surely one, two or three among the living American poets, and it is for that reason that our folk here feel that it must be included with *King Jasper*. There is a very definite sense or feeling here that more reviewers will give more space to *King Jasper* because of a Frost introduction" (unpublished letter, Macmillan Papers, New York Public Library). And so the preface, for which Frost received $200, was published.

Frost read and corrected proofs of the completed preface. In several cases the wording of the published version differs from his complete typescript, and the evidence suggests that Frost was directly responsible for two of these changes, since both are also made in his hand on a surviving manuscript of the complete preface. The first of these revisions (see note *22.5) was suggested to Frost by Untermeyer, as is indicated by a letter Frost wrote him in January 1936: "Anybody who follows me with the close attention you displayed in noticing the loss of effect from the introduction of a good figure in my Wrong Twice story, can do anything he pleases with my works up to ten corrections and suggestions in the rest of my life!" (*RFLU* 268). Frost made the correction in ink on the complete manuscript and I accept it as authoritative. There is no indication of Frost's motive for making the second revision in view here (see note *22.15). But there is no doubt that he made it, as it also appears in his hand, written over the original wording in the complete manuscript.

One other difference in wording between the typescript and the published version needs to be addressed (see 22.21 in the collation). This revision, unlike the two just noted, does not appear on Frost's complete manuscript. Possibly it was made, or suggested, by George Brett, who was dissatisfied with the tone of the introduction. Indeed, his confidant Louis Ledoux had raised vehement objections to its politics—especially to its hostility to the New Deal. I have let the passage stand as it reads in Frost's manuscript and complete typescript, as perhaps more faithful to his intentions. In any event, the fact that he registered the two revisions in the passages discussed above on the manuscript, but left this third one as it stood, suggests that, even if he agreed to make the third one, he did not place the three of them on a par.

The copy-text for this edition of the introduction to *King Jasper* is Frost's complete typescript. It is the one Frost prepared for publication and therefore best represents the punctuation he intended the essay to have in publication. Furthermore, in almost all cases where the complete typescript and published text disagree in punctuation or in wording, Frost's complete manuscript supports the typescript against the published text. Two exceptions are the revisions discussed above (at *22.5 and *22.15), which I have incorporated into the copy-text. I have also corrected several misprints in the typescript. Frost's complete typescript is inconsistent on one point. Sometimes he encloses indented quotations of poetry in quotation marks, sometimes he does not. I have omitted all quotation marks in these cases, except when they indicate the quoted speech of a character in a poem. The collation also records variants in wording in Frost's quotations from Robinson's poems, which were apparently quoted from memory. I have conventionalized the styling of titles.

Collation

TS = Frost's finished typescript (copy-text for this edition). 1st = First appearance of the essay in *King Jasper.* MS = Frost's complete manuscript, held at Dartmouth College; unless otherwise indicated, this manuscript agrees in wording with the finished typescript. STS = Short typescript, representing the first finished draft of the essay; held now at Dartmouth College Library. EAR = *Collected Poems of Edwin Arlington Robinson.* New York: Macmillan, 1937.

*22.1 logic and consistency] 1st; ~ consistancy TS

22.2 unintelligible] 1st; inadmissable MS {STS: the typing reads "inadmissable"; Frost's manuscript correction reads "unintelligible"}

*22.4 Chekhov] 1st; Chekov TS

22.4   great followers] 1st; great imitators MS {STS: the typing reads "imitators"; Frost's manuscript correction reads "followers"}

*22.5   full of propaganda."] 1st, MS; as full of propaganda as a child's stocking is with coal when he boasts of having lost his faith in Santa Claus." TS

*22.8   there will be no] 1st; ~ not TS

22.8   in the least inclines] ~ incline 1st

22.9   we would] ~ should 1st

22.11   and having] and from having 1st

*22.11   *The Town Down the River*] 1st; The Town Down the River TS

*22.14   "adequate"] 1st; "adeguate" TS

*22.14   praise-word then] 1st; ~ they TS

*22.14   to complain of if it] MS, 1st; ~ it if TS

*22.14   sympathy] MS, 1st; sumpathy TS

*22.14   *The Divine Fire*] 1st; The Devine Fire TS

22.15   number of the "thoughts."] number of "thoughts." 1st

*22.15   His death was] 1st, MS; ~ is TS

22.15   Once] And once 1st, EAR

22.16   behind it."] ~ it?" 1st

*22.20   "Miniver Cheevy"] 1st; Miniver Cheevy TS

*22.20   "The Mill"] 1st; The Mill TS

*22.20   "John Gorham"] 1st; John Gorham TS

22.21   the New Deal against processors (as we now dignify them).] some power against industrialism. 1st

22.21   gambling] the gamble 1st

*22.22   "Mr. Flood's Party"] 1st; Mr. Flood's Party TS

*22.22   ("No more, sir, that's enough").] ~ enough.") TS; ~ sir; that will do"). 1st; sir; that will do." EAR

*22.23   "The Sheaves"] 1st; the Sheaves TS

Explanatory Notes

22.3   We began in infancy . . . broken off.] Frost often touched on the theme in his lectures, as in these remarks in a 1931 talk at the New School for Social Research: "I have a kind of picture of correspondence all through life. I noticed it with babies. I was in a babies' ward in a big hospital with one of the doctors, looking at all sorts of things, and watching them catch at us in passing with smiles or gestures or a reaching of the hand. I noticed it in children very much younger than that. No child could be much younger than one I saw . . . 7 months old with frozen hands and frozen feet. It had been found out in the street . . . too early to be out on the street. I did not see much of it. From the first with a child it doesn't look toward anywhere but the eye. It seems to me that they always seem to get to the eye very quickly. It may be a little random at first, but the eyes seem to find the eyes. That's one of the very first . . . I don't want to get too physical. It is one of the very first correspondences established between human beings . . . eyes for eyes. And then the motion of the face, of the feet, the hands . . . for years, as if all the child wanted to do was correspond with your motions. It seems almost miraculous when the first invisible motions are corresponded with, when a motion a way down in your throat is corresponded with by a child. I noticed a year or so ago a young child wanted to whistle to a dog and could not get it, and in the end made a very good reproduction of a squeal in his throat. He made the dog pay attention to him. Correspondence goes on and on until you see people corresponding with you merely in idea, moving some part of the brain that you move. Take me sitting here tonight. I am trying to wag some lobe of my brain and satisfy myself that you can wag back with the same one. I don't know unless I examine you. But I can tell something about it, that there is some correspondence, by the fact that you stay here and don't go out. I take it that there is the idea of all of it. That's as far as we ever get. The best thing I can do to a poem is sort of say . . . nod with my whole nature to it" (unpublished typescript, Dartmouth College Library).

22.6   I don't like grievances . . . poetry free to go its way in tears.] Lawrance Thompson reports a February 1940 conversation he had with Frost on a similar theme: "He said some nice things about the relationship between argument and statement in poetry. The reason why poetry fails when it becomes propaganda is because it has to do with denials of social values that are debatable. But poetry is at its best when it makes observations in the realm of spiritual values which are perceived in realms where there is no room for argument. The crowding of points of view occur in social relationships, but in the higher realm of spiritual perceptions the atmosphere is not crowded. We can all find room for agreement on the point of a pin! And thus the wisest poet works toward the realm of spiritual perceptions. 'We don't join together in singing an argument.' Songs are built around everlastingly perceived spiritual values which are true for us all—love and longing and sorrow and loneliness" (NOTES).

22.9   There were Robinson and I] At a bar in Boston in 1915 (*TYT,* 44).

22.9   we could . . . poems are all that matter.] With this passage, and with the passage that begins the essay, read the following remarks from a lecture Frost gave at the New School for Social Research in 1931: "I have met a lot of people in what they call the new movements in poetry, and most of them are not poets at all. They are what they used to call the Chicago Cubs, what they call technical kids. They are very interested in what you call the ground rules and tinkering with ground rules. I am one of these people who doesn't care whether you change the size of the tennis court or the hopscotch court. You can have the court any shape that you please. It is for me to play . . . change the rules if you want to, but don't bother me with it. No, these fellows in poetry don't know that they are not poets at all, they are changers of the rules. I can sympathize with them a tiny bit in their preoccupation [with] changing the rules of the game. They have not changed them materially. I wish they had changed them more than they had, for their own sakes. The beginning of it as I saw it was in what was called the new kind of free verse. And the new kind of free verse was derived not from the minor Latin poets[. That is,] the form wasn't[;] the *idea* was, the *spirit* was[. B]ut the rules of the game were derived from [Bohn's] translations . . . those horribly dull translations of the minor Latin poets . . . those fellows that were working so hard on starting a new form always had [Bohn's] translation in front of them. That's facts. I saw them doing it" (unpublished typescript, Dartmouth College Library).

22.11   *The Town Down the River*] This book, Robinson's fourth volume of poetry, appeared first in 1910.

22.12   Miniver thought] From Robinson's poem, "Miniver Cheevy."

22.14   May Sinclair . . . *The Divine Fire*] May Sinclair (1865–1946), English novelist. Her novel, *The Divine Fire,* was published in 1904.

22.15   One pauses] From Robinson's poem "Flammonde," collected in *The Man against the Sky* (1916).

22.15   His death was sad] Robinson died on April 6, 1935.

22.15   Once a man] Slightly misquoted from Robinson's poem "Old King Cole," collected in *The Man against the Sky* (1916).

22.17   The games we play] From Robinson's sonnet "Dear Friends," collected in *The Children of Night* (1897), his second book.

22.18   Crabbe] English poet (1754–1832) and subject of Robinson's poem "George Crabbe": "Of his plain excellence and stubborn skill / There yet remains what fashion cannot kill, / Though years have thinned the laurel from his brows . . ."

22.19   Tom Hood] Thomas Hood (1799–1845), English poet. See these lines in Robinson's sonnet, "Thomas Hood":

> The man who cloaked his bitterness within
> This winding-sheet of puns and pleasantries,
> God never gave to look with common eyes
> Upon a world of anguish and of sin . . .
> And there are woven with his jollities
> The nameless and eternal tragedies
> That render hope and hopelessness akin.
> We laugh, and crown him; but anon we feel
> A still chord sorrow-swept . . .

22.19   One ordeal of Mark Twain] An allusion to Van Wyck Brooks's controversial book, *The Ordeal of Mark Twain* (1920).

22.20   "The Mill" . . . "John Gorham" . . . The miller's wife] "The Mill" was collected in Robinson's book *The Three Taverns* (1920), "John Gorham" in his *The Man against the Sky* (1916). Frost quotes from "The Mill," not "John Gorham."

22.22   "Mr. Flood's Party"] "Mr. Flood's Party" was collected first in *Avon's Harvest* (1921).

22.23   "The Sheaves"] "The Sheaves" was collected first in *Dionysus in Doubt* (1925). Frost alludes to the closing lines of the poem: "A thousand golden sheaves were lying there, / Shining and still, but not for long to stay—/ As if a thousand girls with golden hair / Might rise from where they slept and go away."

22.25   inscrutable profusion of the Lord] Frost adapts a passage from Robinson's poem "The Rat," collected first in *The Three Taverns* (1920): "As often as he let himself be seen / We pitied him, or scorned him, or deplored / The inscrutable profusion of the Lord / Who shaped as one of us a thing so mean," etc.

22.25   immedicable woes] Frost borrows the phrase from the once popular American poem "The Man with a Hoe," by Edwin Markham (1852–1940). The populist-sympathizing Markham wrote not in praise of immedicable woes, but for their alleviation; his is a poem of grievance, not grief. Frost quotes him mischievously.

22.25   play's the thing . . . All virtue in 'as if.'] See Hamlet's famous lines: "The Play's the thing / Wherein I'll catch the conscience of a king," and also Touchstone's in *As You Like It*: "I knew when seven justices could not take up a quarrel, but when the parties were met themselves, one of them thought of an If—as, 'If you said so, then I said so,' and then shook hands and swore brothers. Your If is the only peacemaker. Much virtue in If" (5.4).

22.25   As if the last of days] From Robinson's poem "The Dark Hills," collected first in *The Three Taverns* (1920).

23. [Contribution to *Books We Like* (1936)]

Frost's description of ten favorite books first appeared in *Books We Like; Sixty-Two Answers to the Question: 'Please choose, and give reasons for your choice, ten books, exclusive of the Bible and Shakespeare, dictionaries, encyclopedias, and other ordinary reference books, that you believe should be in every public library,' edited, and with a preface, by Edward Weeks* (Boston: Massachusetts Library Association, 1936). A manuscript of Frost's contribution (signed "Robert Frost, Key West, December 18, 1934") is held at the Jones Library, Amherst, together with a typescript of uncertain origin which matches its text exactly. The typescript and manuscript differ from the published version as noted below in the collation. Frost's manuscript is the copy-text for this edition, as the variant punctuation in the first appearance does not seem authorial. I have, however, incorporated into the copy-text two variants in wording from the first appearance that seem authoritative. These variations represent a wry specificity in expression that I associate with Frost and which must have been made on a final typescript which he submitted to Weeks. I have also conventionalized the styling of book titles.

Collation

1st = First appearance in *Books We Like*. MS = Manuscript.
*23.1   *Odyssey*] 1st; Odyssey MS
*23.2   *Robinson Crusoe*] 1st; Robinson Crusoe MS
*23.3   *Walden*] 1st; Walden MS
*23.3   In *Walden*] 1st; ~ Walden MS
*23.4   *Tales*] 1st; Tales MS
23.4   the horrific] {not present} horrific 1st
*23.5   *The Oxford Book of English Verse*] 1st; The Oxford Book of English Verse MS
*23.6   *Modern American and British Poetry*] 1st; Modern American and British Poetry MS
*23.6   and one half numbers] 1st; books MS
*23.6   twenty-five] 1st; twenty MS
*23.7   *The Last of the Mohicans*] 1st; The Last of the Mohicans MS
*23.8   *The Prisoner of Zenda*] 1st; The Prisoner of Zenda MS
*23.9   *The Jungle Book*] 1st; The Jungle Book MS
*23.9   (1st).] (1st) MS {In entry number four—Poe's *Tales*, where the title also does not begin the sentence that follows—Frost puts a period after the title in the manuscript. I assume his omission of the period is a misprint in the later case.}
*23.10   Emerson's] 1st; Emersons MS
*23.10   *Essays* and *Poems*] 1st; Essays and Poems MS

Explanatory Notes

23.1   Palmer] George Herbert Palmer (1842–1933), American classicist, translator of Homer. His *The Odyssey of Homer* appeared first in 1884.

23.5   *Oxford Book*] Edited by Sir Arthur Quiller-Couch. Frost often read from the anthology at lectures.

23.6   Untermeyer] Frost's friendship with Louis Untermeyer, American poet, anthologist, and translator, began in 1915 and continued until Frost's death in 1963. Among Untermeyer's numerous anthologies is *Modern American and British Poetry.*

23.8   *The Prisoner of Zenda*] By Sir Anthony Hope Hawkins (1863–1933), English novelist. Hawkins wrote under the pseudonym "Anthony Hope." *The Prisoner of Zenda* appeared in 1894.

24. [Introduction to Sarah Cleghorn's *Threescore* (1936)]

Frost's introduction appeared in Sarah Cleghorn's autobiography, *Threescore* (New York: Smith and Haas, 1936). Apparently Dorothy Canfield Fisher asked Frost to write the introduction in the autumn of 1935. Dartmouth College Library holds a November 2 letter from her to Frost thanking him for agreeing to do it. Also at Dartmouth is a January 16, 1936, letter from Robert Haas (of Smith and Haas) acknowledging receipt of the finished introduction, which Frost completed while wintering in Miami. The Jones Library in Amherst holds a manuscript that represents an early draft of the introduction. I have been unable to find any other typescripts or manuscripts of the essay. The text reprinted here is exactly as published in *Threescore.* The collation records all differences in wording between the Jones Library manuscript and the published text. Frost met Sarah Cleghorn in 1919 when he was invited by the newly formed Poetry Society of Southern Vermont—of which she was a member—to give a reading in Arlington, Vt. In June 1922 Frost was elected Poet Laureate of Vermont by the Vermont State League of Women's Clubs. When an editorialist in the *New York Times* treated the announcement with derision, Sarah Cleghorn (among others) wrote letters in Frost's defense (*TYT* 202–203).

Collation

MS = Early holograph manuscript, held now at Jones Library, Amherst. PRWE = *Poems of Ralph Waldo Emerson* (New York: Oxford University Press, 1914).

24.1   for security] ~ like a thousand children off their bases at once MS

24.1   certain of] ~ of, dead or alive,

24.1   have heard] had heard PRWE

24.1   force and fraud] fraud and force PRWE

24.1   necessary to keep in mind in a campaign] well in our campaign to keep in mind MS

24.1   depended on to hold Vermont true to its winter self against all summer] counted on to hold Vermont true to itself against all summer and winter MS

24.1   one of these] ~ them MS

24.1   one is mystic] ~ esthetic MS

24.1   but principally] but it is ~ MS

24.2   righteousness in the] righteousness in one MS

24.2   in the mill] in the mills MS

24.2   out the window] ~ windows MS

24.2   in all the prose] in all the piled up prose MS

24.2   pressed together under a weight of several atmospheres of revolution.] put together MS

24.2   can't stand] don't like MS

24.2   or the state] or state MS

24.2   may have been] was MS

24.2   one of the ultra-arty insisting that we join him in his minor vices at his wild parties.] an ultra-arty rotter insisting that we join him at his parties in his minor vices. MS

24.2   at our door] at our door and knocks MS

24.2   died a martyr] was a martyr MS

24.3   so nettling] so irritating MS

24.2   trying to decide] trying to decide for ourselves MS

24.3   Nor is it yet] Nor is it even MS

24.3   would afford] would make at least MS

24.3   aspiration] ~ for the race MS

24.3   she is one for me] she is{not present} MS

24.3   as may be seen] {not present} MS

24.4   the election] politics MS

24.5   like the] like to see MS

24.7   You wouldn't think there was much] There isn't much you'd think MS

24.8   creature, poorly clothed] poor creature in poor clothes MS

24.8   with a pretty] with MS

24.10   explain that] tell how MS

24.10   was about] was a ballad about MS

24.10   bound in logic] in logic bound MS

24.13   up north] {not present} MS

24.13   free of] off MS

24.13   The fact remains] The fact remains, however, MS

24.13   done measurable] done some measurable MS

24.13   when the chance] when occasion MS

24.14   which may sound] which sounds MS

24.14   was not born a New Englander nor of wholly] wasn't New England born or altogether MS

24.15   for one judge] to one judge MS

24.15   in encounter] in conflict MS

24.15   A] The MS

24.15   in the confusion] {not present} MS

24.15   the particular counter tendency] the counter tendency MS

24.15   Formidable] ~ looking MS

24.15   resolve into no more information than that nothing equals nothing. It is a common question:] give no more information in the end than that nothing equals nothing. We commonly hear it asked MS

24.15   from each one's minding] through each one's minding too much MS

24.15   business?] ~. MS

24.15   from minding] through minding MS

24.15   contain] hold together MS

24.15   may take too much satisfaction in] is apt to gloat over MS

24.15   and a reformer] {not present} MS

24.15   grim] ~ (if it were only to be preserved from being self-conscious and goody-goody) MS

24.15   need most] need mostly MS

Explanatory Notes

24.1   May be true] From Emerson's poem "Berrying."

24.1   And one of these] The novelist is Dorothy Canfield Fisher (1879–1958); the essay-ist is Zephine Humphrey Fahenstock (1875–1956), who was well known also for her fiction; the saint is Cleghorn.

24.2   poem about the children] "The Golf Links," published in the New York *Tribune* in 1915:

> The golf links lie so near the mill
> That almost every day
> The laboring children can look out
> And see the men at play.

24.2   saving the soul] See Frost's "'Letter' to *The Amherst Student*" (21.3)

24.13   I have just come indoors] Frost wrote the introduction to *Threescore* while in southern Florida in 1935 (*TYT* 664).

24.13   page 110] In the first edition of *Threescore*.

24.15   not to get hold of both ends, but of the right end] Frost may be thinking of a passage in Emerson's "The American Scholar": "But the old oracle said, 'All things have two handles: beware of the wrong one'" (*EL* 54). Emerson is himself quoting from Epictetus's *Enchiridion*, 43: "Everything has two handles, by one of which it ought to be carried and by the other not" (Loeb Classical Library edition, Cambridge, 1928).

25. [Contribution to *The Stag at Ease* (1938)]

Frost's recipe for ash-baked potatoes appeared in *A Cookbook; The Stag at Ease; Being the Cu-linary Preferences of a Number of Distinguished Male Citizens of the World* (Caldwell, Idaho: The Caxton Printers, 1938), 64. Dartmouth College Library holds a galley sheet on which Frost's contribution appears, signed by him in ink. The text is identical to the published form, which I reprint here. The recipe is hardly interesting from a culinary point of view. But the fact that Frost was asked to supply it for a volume of this kind suggests something interesting about his public profile in 1938, the year his wife Elinor died.

26. [Letter to the Editor of *New Hampshire: A Guide to the Granite State* (1938)]

Frost's letter appeared in *New Hampshire: A Guide to the Granite State* (Boston: Houghton Mifflin, 1938), 103. The volume was prepared under the auspices of the Federal Writers' Project of the Works Progress Administration of the State of New Hampshire. Frost's re-marks were solicited by the unnamed author of the article on "Literature" in the *Guide*. I cannot locate the original manuscript of the letter or any other text of it. The text re-printed here is from the *Guide*.

Explanatory Notes

26.1   Not a poem] Lawrance Thompson offers a commentary on the biographical data Frost gives in this letter (*SL* 454).

27. The Doctrine of Excursions (1939)

"The Doctrine of Excursions" appeared first as the preface to *Bread Loaf Anthology* (Middlebury, Vt.: Middlebury College Press, 1939). Dartmouth College Library holds a manuscript of the essay. At the foot of the last of its six leaves is a note in Frost's hand: "This letter with a deletion or two and a slight alteration of the first sentence can be used as a preface my dear." The note is addressed to Kathleen Morrison ("my dear"). The finished draft that Frost produced with her assistance has apparently been lost. The published version differs from the manuscript in a number of details, most of them minor. Since I cannot establish that Frost is responsible for all of the changes introduced in the published version, I have chosen the manuscript as copy-text, incorporating into it five readings from the first appearance which seem authorial. I have also corrected several misprints in the manuscript, following the first appearance in each case. All of these are listed in the collation, together with five variant wordings in the first appearance that I have rejected as non-authorial. Of the six variants in wording between the manuscript and the first appearance I have adopted two. In his note to Morrison on the manuscript, Frost mentions the "slight alteration of the first sentence" he intends to make for publication. He probably refers to the ameliorating change from "integrity" to "future" in the phrase "the integrity of Breadloaf." The second variant in wording ("was ever"/"has ever been") is more difficult to account for. But I do not see why someone at Middlebury College Press would have undertaken the change. As for the rest of the variants in wording in the published text: "Typical" is a misprint in the first appearance. "Topical" makes more sense: plays of the eighties were not "typically" about tunnels. The plural "mountains" in the first appearance is a misprint. "Hear *from* the workmen," as by mail, seems to make less sense in its context than "hear the workmen"; I cannot suppose Frost made this change. In his manuscript, Frost wrote "accrued," not "acquired." Finally, the sense of the last sentence prefers "what" (as in Frost's manuscript) to "why." The sentence seems to me an alternate form of: "*What* have we wings *for* if not," etc. I have also adopted from the published version three variants in punctuation that I am persuaded Frost must himself have adopted in the lost typescript. The question mark at 27.2 has for precedent the one in the sentence immediately before it. I have adopted the comma after "humbler degrees" at 27.3 since "among them" is attached grammatically to what follows, not to what comes before; in such cases Frost and Morrison typically follow the demands of grammar. Finally, though Frost seldom puts commas in series of nouns or adjectives in his manuscripts, in typescripts prepared for publication he invariably does. I have therefore adopted the two commas in "looks, tones, manners" at 27.5.

Collation

MS = Frost's holograph manuscript. 1st = First appearance of the essay, in *Bread Loaf Anthology*.

*27.1   future of Breadloaf] 1st; integrity of Breadloaf MS
*27.1   has ever been] 1st; was ever MS
*27.2   any other?] 1st; any other. MS
*27.3   humbler degrees,] 1st; humbler degrees MS
*27.4   referee's decision] 1st; referees' decision MS
*27.5   looks, tones, manners.] 1st; looks tones manners. MS

27.6   topical] typical 1st
*27.6   Hoosac] 1st; Hoosic MS {See explanatory note 185.17.}
*27.6   Tunnel.] 1st; Tunnel MS
27.6   over the mountain] over the mountains 1st
27.6   the workmen] from the workmen 1st
27.7   accrued] acquired 1st
27.7   For what] For why 1st

Explanatory Notes

27.4   he must brave the rigors of specific criticism] In an interview with Mary Handy published in *The Christian Science Monitor* on December 21, 1955, Frost remarked: "If people are looking for something to be brave about, there's their chance in poetry. It's one of the ways of being brave. Some like hostile criticism. Some like bullets flying around. You can get neglect flying around, too, and you can feel it like invisible television waves. There is nothing to it except valor and courage. A special kind of courage for a special kind of punishment. The fun is more than the punishment, if you'll only see it that way. There aren't enough poets. My advice to young people is to write poetry. There are 1,500 colleges in this country, and each year every one graduates, say, ten who have had A's in English. Some in poetry. Some in prose. Where are they all? Why don't some of them go through with it? They're either afraid of it, or someone's afraid of it for them. They don't presume to be one of 'those people.' They think it couldn't happen in their family. Or teachers think it couldn't happen in their classes. I remember one professor when he heard I'd had a few things published looked down his nose and said to me, 'So we're an author, are we?' I just got up and left. It's an old story. Courage and adventure. Courage for that kind of adventure. To write is not the horrible thing. The horrible thing is not having anybody want it for a long time. You get a job for a while. I knew one poet who was a silversmith. So many land in teaching English where they have too many papers to read. That's exhausting."

27.6   Hoosac Tunnel] The Hoosac Tunnel, completed in 1876, extends 4.73 miles under the Hoosac Mountains in Massachusetts.

28. The Figure a Poem Makes (1939)

"The Figure a Poem Makes" appeared first as the preface to *Collected Poems of Robert Frost 1939* (New York: Henry Holt and Company, 1939). Thereafter it prefaced *Complete Poems of Robert Frost, 1949*, as well as the Limited Edition Club's two-volume edition of the same book, published in 1951. Frost completed the essay late in 1938. Kathleen Morrison probably prepared the final typescript of the essay. A manuscript of the essay held at Dartmouth College includes some instructions, apparently to Morrison, in Frost's hand. Moreover, the manuscript differs in a number of respects from the published text, which indicates that a final typescript of the essay did exist, though I have not been able to find it. (Correspondence between Frost and the collector Earle J. Bernheimer suggests that he may have sold the final manuscript to Bernheimer, though the published catalogue of the auction of Bernheimer's collection makes no mention of such a document. Reference to the transaction is made in the letters of Frost and Bernheimer held now at the University of Virginia among the Thompson-Frost Papers.) Morrison mailed the finished text of "The Figure a

Poem Makes" to Frost's editor at Henry Holt and Company, William Sloane, on January 11, 1939, as is indicated by a letter of that date from her to Sloane held now at Princeton University Library. I have examined Frost's complete manuscript, as well as the 1939, 1949 (both early and late printings), and 1951 published texts of the essay. I have also examined a set of page proofs of the essay for *Complete Poems of Robert Frost, 1949* held at Dartmouth College Library. Collations of the three published texts show them to be identical, with one exception: 1939 has "school boy," as does Frost's manuscript, where all other published texts have "schoolboy" (28.7 in the present edition). This correction is indicated, though not in Frost's hand, on the page proofs for *Complete Poems of Robert Frost, 1949.* No other marks or corrections appear on the proofs. The present edition reprints the text of the first appearance. Since the 1939 edition's use of "school boy" matches Frost's usage in the manuscript, I have left it as it stands. The collation records all differences in wording between the manuscript and the first appearance.

Collation

MS = Frost's manuscript, held now at Dartmouth College Library.

28.1   for it.] ~ (They have given their whole lives and not just part of their lives for a partiality MS

28.2   sentences, meter] sentences, metrics MS

28.3   have a tune] have tune MS

28.4   runs a course] runs its course MS

28.4   discovers the] discovers its MS

28.5   it for somewhere.] it. MS

28.6   to establish] establish MS

{In the margin of page 7 of the manuscript (beside the paragraph beginning "Scholars and artists thrown together" at 28.7) Frost has written these words, which appear nowhere in the published text: "soon learns that they don't know when they are learning: No time can be regarded as waste time." It is unclear how this should be incorporated into the text of the essay.}

28.8   delight to wisdom.] delight to delight in the wisdom. MS

Explanatory Notes

28.0   The Figure a Poem Makes] Lawrance Thompson reports a conversation he had with Frost in September 1941: "He said he had often tried to say that his chief interest was in 'the figure a poem makes,' which is the title of his prose introduction to the expensive 'Collected Poems.' His first interest in it was to see if it had a kind of character and shape or form of its own. He liked to think that each poem was as distinct as each stroke of a good golfer, so that the hands and arms were in it, the twist of the body and the shift of the weight. He had never thought of it before, but what he meant was that a poem had to show that the poet was 'getting his body into it.' Or like tennis, there were the different strokes for the different demands made on the player. And there must be the follow through there—always remembering that the form, the stroke was nothing unless the shot was made successfully; unless the ball went where it was intended to go. And that going, in turn, was after all the most important part of it to him, although it was the sending it with grace that made the difference between poetry and prose. And yet there must be as much cunning about the thought as about the performance. The epithet, the aphorism must be two-edged, with a deeper meaning than that immediately apparent. It must have a subtlety and force at the same time. And the combination of the thing said and the manner of the saying makes the poem" (NOTES).

28.2   no one but a humanist] Frost remarks in a talk at Bread Loaf in the mid-1940s: "I once ventured to put in prose this sentence, that nobody but a humanist cares how sound a poem is if it's only *a* sound. I defended it. I went into a class one time and the humanist teacher had written this sentence on the board. He told me to defend it. When I got through one hour of trying to puzzle him, he said to me, 'You're a humanist.' Does wisdom matter? Does it matter whether you're right or wrong? Does that make any difference in poetry? The important poem is one that performs on a high plane of wisdom-unwisdom. It's up there where the big things are. It only matters that it's wisdom-unwisdom. Your wisdom is my unwisdom" (unpublished typescript, Dartmouth College Library).

28.2   sprung-rhythmists] The reference is to the followers of Gerard Manley Hopkins. In an unpublished manuscript, apparently a preliminary draft for a talk delivered in about 1940, Frost says: "I shall talk in bureaucratic (sp) on Present-day Party Lines in Poetry. There is the division between the serious radical propagandists and the old fashioned love-and-understandists. There is the other division between the Gerard Manley Hopkins sprung-rhythm metricists and *me*. The Me of Anne's recognition. Says one of the sprung minded to me says he:

All that matters is that a definite number of accents should be observed per line. The number of unaccented syllables between the accented is any you choose to make it. There is plenty of precedent in Gerard Manley Hopkins and the ballads and Crystabel.

Says I to him says I:

Why be bothered with precedent if your whole object is originality. Why not have as many accented syllables in a line as there is room for on the page. But if you are going to keep the rules about accented syllables, you should notice there are equally fixed rules to keep about unaccented. And they be these: You may have one unaccented between every two accented in which case the verse is called iambic or trochaic or you may have two, in which case the verse is called dactylic or anapaestic (sp) (What do I have a secretary for?). On the fringes of these rules is the [possibility] not often taken advantage of to have three unaccented at most or none. The practice and the precedent are just as rigorously found about the unaccented syllables as about the accented. Break the rules about the unaccented and I dont see why you shouldnt break the rules about the accented. Whats the matter with your mind that you shouldnt have noticed that there was anything fixed about the unaccented syllables. There is absolutely no such thing in our English verse as four or more unaccented syllables between two accented. Where have you been the last five hundred years? All at sea? Your folly comes from a fallacy that confuses the words rhythms and meter. As in a College Board examination I must ask you to mark the following line first for its metrical then for its rhythmical accents. This should be your result:

> Shall Í compáre thee tó a súmmers dáy
> Shall I compáre thee to a súmmers dáy

Take another:

> Thou árt more lóvely ánd more témperáte
> Thou art more lóvely and more témperate

What in meter is pentameter in rhythm is in one case trimeter and the other dimeter. You see the conflict between the two, the strain from which arises a third thing to the ear [,] the tune. The line of verse must be said and heard with a sense of both meter and rhythm at once. That is a cultivation known as poetry.

One soon gives up hope of achieving much of any variety from meters. The named varieties are few relatively even in the Latin and Greek. But the escape from monotony is always there in the limitless variety of the rhythms which are largely a matter of expression and meaning. Any methodologist can get up a party on some little violation of the rules of meter. It takes dramatic imagination to vary the speech rhythm the expression rhythm so as to make every poem have a different tune[.]

And there is more to this at points I could mark with an asterisk. I always feel in the young Hopkinsians a bullnecked stupid disposition to butt their hairy young heads against meter to see if it wont yield variety by crumbling down" (unpublished manuscript, Dartmouth College Library).

28.4   The figure is the same as for love] Lawrance Thompson reports a 1959 conversation on this theme: "[Frost] said he remembered saying to F. S. Flint in England, long ago, that there was something wrong with a writer who couldn't get into his subject and screw it to a climax: if you were going to find metaphors for the artistic process in the functions of the body, that was the way you ought to do it. He remembered hearing AE (George Russell) say that all poems were love poems, and he could see how that might be said in the sense that Frost made that remark to Flint, but not otherwise. Of course love was important, but how many different forms love took" (NOTES).

28.4   drinking song] Frost remarks in a 1962 appearance at Kenyon College: "And then let's say this about poetry: that it's just like the college song. It's as common as that. It's about drink, the song is. And it says something about how it will make you happy, make you fat. That's the note of happy sadness. To me it's like a color—a salmon-pink goes by me when I say that. A happy-sad sort of tinge. That's what makes lovely poetry" (for citation see explanatory note 7.5).

28.5   No tears in the writer . . . for somewhere.] Frost remarks in a 1931 lecture at the New School for Social Research: "The best part of observation we do before we are old enough to know we are doing it. When we are old enough to be a newspaper man and observe on purpose it isn't as good as what we do before we know it is of any value. The best part of material is gathered by observation between the ages of 2 yrs old and 18 yrs or 20 yrs. You can drain on that all the rest of your life, and the nice part of that is that you have taken in whole fields without knowing it, without realizing the details, and all you have to do is turn your inward eye on any of those fields, 40 or 60 yrs afterward and pick up what you did not know was there. It is an unconscious observation that takes in whole fields, snapshots, and re-observation that picks up in the act of writing, conversation that picks up unexpected details that are put into little compositions. The delight of those is that they are as surprising to you as they are to the reader. I know that it is possible to say that I am carrying that too high. Some of the observation that one goes out and gets, a story or poem[,] may be pretty good. They say that [Robert] Burns for instance went out with a poem half written and got some more stuff to put in it. There is probably such a thing, but I wouldn't expect it to prosper" (unpublished typescript, Dartmouth College Library).

28.6   We prate of freedom . . . organic.] Frost remarked in a 1927 lecture at Wesleyan College: "The freedom I'd like to give is the freedom I'd like to have. That is much harder than anything else in the world to get—it's the freedom of my material. You might define a school boy as one who could recite to you, if you started him talking, everything he read last night, in the order in which he read it. That's a school boy. That's just the opposite of what I mean by a free person. The person who has the freedom of his material is the person who puts two and two together, and the two and two are anywhere out of space and time, and brought together. One little thing mentioned perhaps, reminds him of something he couldn't have thought of for twenty years. That's the kind of talk I'd rather give; but I'm scared to death, so I don't do it with you here. I'd rather be perfectly free of my material—reach down here in time and off there in space, and here's my two and two put together. Here's my idea, my thought. That's the freedom I'd like to give. It depends so much on the disconnection of things. There's too much sequence and logic all the time, of reciting what we learned over night. There's an attempt in the honor courses to get toward what I mean. I don't know what the honor courses will do toward it. I think what I'm after is free meditation. I don't think anybody gets to it when he's in anybody's company—only when his soul's alone. I do it when I wake up in the morning, when I'm starting an idea, and restarting. Sleep is probably a symbol of the interruption, the disconnection that I want in life. Your whole life can be so logical that it seems to me like a ball of hairs in the stomach of an angora cat. It should be broken up and interrupted, and then be brought together by likeness, free likeness" ("The Manumitted Student," cited above).

29. [Remarks Accepting the Gold Medal of the National Institute of Art and Letters (1939)]

Frost delivered his speech accepting the Gold Medal for poetry awarded by the National Institute of Arts and Letters in New York on January 18, 1939. Frost was the third poet to be awarded the medal, the first two being James Whitcomb Riley in 1911 and E. A. Robinson in 1929. Later that year his acceptance speech appeared in the *National Institute News Bulletin* 5 (1939): 1, 12. A manuscript of the speech is held at the American Academy and Institute of Arts and Letters Library in New York. The Academy Library also holds six typescripts of the address. Three are carbons of one, and a fourth of another, so there are really only two distinct typescript texts. I cannot establish that Frost prepared either of the two original typescripts, which match the published text in all but a few cases. The manuscript seems to represent the last stage to which he brought the essay. According to Lawrance Thompson, Frost wrote it out at the award ceremony itself (*TLY* 377), and I find no reason to doubt him. Frost's manuscript is accordingly the copy-text for the present edition. Following the first appearance, I have corrected misprints and provided apostrophes and periods where they are missing. I have also adopted from the first appearance five commas in two sentences that are consistent with Frost's habits of punctuation in typescripts he brought to completion (see *29.2 and *29.4 in the collation). "Still" is an interjection, not an adverb. The interjection, together with the parenthetical clause which follows the subject of the sentence, makes the grammar complicated enough to require some punctuation. Frost's finished typescripts consistently punctuate for grammar when an absence of punctuation might prove awkward. As for the second sentence: elsewhere in this speech (in the sentence beginning "He has a mind and he has instruments"), Frost uses a comma to coordinate a parallelism, in that case an appositive clause. In the second case noted here (*29.4) it seems likely that he desired commas to support the parallel structure balancing the two "beyonds." I have also adopted from the published text the punctuation of the remark Frost cites at the beginning of the speech. When Frost quotes remarks in his finished typescripts, he typically distinguishes them with such punctuation.

Collation

MS = Frost's manuscript (copy-text for the present edition). 1st = First appearance in *National Institute of Arts and Letters News Bulletin.*

*29.1   "Have you] 1st; Have you MS

*29.1   rewards,"] 1st; rewards MS

*29.1   I don't know] 1st; I dont know MS {Elsewhere in this manuscript Frost includes the apostrophe in contractions (can't) and in possessives ("perturber's," "another's").}

*29.1   self-esteem] self esteem {Elsewhere in the manuscript Frost hyphenates analogous words such as "self-appraisal" and "self-approval."}

*29.1   talk of compromise.] 1st; talk of compromise MS

*29.2   Still, an artist, however well he may fare within and without,] 1st; Still an artist however ~ without MS

29.2   O Time] Oh Time 1st

*29.3   in its orbit.] 1st; ~ orbit MS

*29.3   the extensions of mind] 1st; the extension of mind MS {The plural agrees with "instruments" and with the verb "fit."}

*29.3   Universe.] 1st; Universe MS

*29.4   concede] 1st; conceed MS

29.4   artist had] artist has 1st

*29.4   myself, beyond another's critical opinion of me,] 1st; myself ~ me MS

Explanatory Notes

29.2   Still, an artist . . . absolute judgement.] On this head, see Lawrance Thompson's summary of remarks Frost made in February 1940: "He said that all tied up to the excursions man made outside himself to find himself; trips to the North Pole to see if we could get back. The writer ventures into writing boldly, not to see if he can write, but because he was willing to bet that he could—and when he was recognized, he was back. But nobody else knew for a long time. When did he begin to write well? When *other people* knew that he was writing well? Or when *he* knew? So with him [i.e., Frost], he never grew impatient with others, except that when he read his own poems after reading poems in magazines, he wondered *why* his were too strange to be recognized. We talked more about 'excursions' out of self; of how falling in love was an excursion out of self in search of self in others. And that seems important; to go out of self to find self in others, rather than just to sit at home, secure in self. He thinks people like James Joyce and e. e. cummings make the snobbish mistake of thinking that they need never make excursions outside self to find self. But there must be a common denominator for communication, and we learn that by finding ourselves and recognizing ourselves in others" (NOTES).

29.2   O Time] From Thomas William Parsons (1819–92), "On a Bust of Dante."

29.4   whatever the medal may or may not symbolize] Lawrance Thompson reports the following, from a February 1940 conversation with Frost: "When he received the American Academy Award he felt evil over it, for his only pleasure was in getting it so that [Edna St. Vincent] Millay wouldn't get it" (NOTES).

30. The Last Refinement of Subject Matter: Vocal Imagination (1941)

This essay occupies nine leaves of a notebook held at Dartmouth College Library. I date it 1941 because at that time Frost considered putting together a collection of essays for Henry Holt and Company. A tentative table of contents for such a volume appears in another notebook held at Dartmouth College (see note 4 to the Introduction). Among the essays listed there is one called "Sound as Subject Matter," no doubt a reference to an essay like the one presented herein. It may be that the essay, as it appears in the notebook, was written to be delivered as a talk. But its clarity and finish suggest that it was intended as well to serve at least as a model for an essay to be delivered in print, which is why I include it here.

The document is entirely in Frost's hand. He had difficulty settling on a title, as no fewer than six appear at the top of the first sheet of the essay and in the left-hand margin. "The Sound of Poetry" was apparently the first of the titles. Succeeding it are "A Content of Sound," "The Sound of Sense," "Voice as Subject Matter," and "The Last Refinement of Subject Matter: Vocal Imagination." It is unclear from the manuscript whether the last title is a single title or two separate titles (the colon is imperfectly indicated). In any case, Frost often lectured on the subject of "the sound of sense," using various headings as titles. I have chosen the title that seems most fully descriptive of the essay. (It happens to be a title that recalls the title of the second of Frost's 1936 Charles Eliot Norton Lectures at Harvard, "Vocal Imagination: Merger of Form and Content.") Frost's Dartmouth manuscript provides the copy-text for the present edition. My emendations are limited to the correction of misprints. I have also conventionalized the styling of titles.

On a separate page of the notebook, interleaved with those bearing the essay, appear two remarks: "The sentences must spring from each other and talk to each other even when there is only one character speaking"; and "You mean to say he wants two hundred dollars for that old warhorse?" Plainly, the second is another example of a sentence sound "entrenched" in words. In the margins of other notebook leaves appear a number of additional remarks and fragments. There is no indication as to how these ought to be integrated into the essay, so I reproduce them here in sequence. (1) "Shall I go on? Or have I said enough?" Frost liked to quote this line from Milton's *Comus* in discussions of sentence sounds. (2) "tennis with the net down—tug and breaking—Scotch sword dancer" Frost often said that he would as soon play tennis with the net down as write free verse. The word rendered here as "breaking" is unclear. The reference to the sword dancer is obscure. (3) "recognition and Lowes" Presumably this is a reference to the literary critic John Livingston Lowes. (4) "Bother is the only emotion not poetical."

Much has been written about Frost's theory of "sentence sounds." But there persists in accounts of the theory one misleading idea: namely, that Frost worked it out as a major counterexample to Sidney Lanier's arguments in *The Science of English Verse*, a volume seldom read today but influential when Frost began to publish poetry in the 1890s. (Frost read the book in 1894, when Susan Hayes Ward gave a copy to him as a gift.) We should not confuse Lanier's own practices as a poet—which differ utterly from Frost's—with his theories about where poetry was headed as an art at the turn of the twentieth century; nor should we be misled, here, by the elaborate and eccentric system of musical notation to the explanation of which so much of Lanier's book is devoted. Instead, the curious should consult for themselves the chapter in *The Science of English Verse* titled "Of Tune in

Speech, Its Nature and Office," which contains an exposition of the "sentence sound" theory in all its essentials; and should then read again the letters Frost wrote on the subject in
1913 and 1914 (see *CPPP* 664–86), the essay reprinted herein, and the notes to the essay
given below. Because the relation between the two poets has been consistently misunderstood, I include some further discussion of the matter here.

Several things may be said about the relation of Frost's theory of "sentence sounds" to
Lanier's of "the tunes of speech." First, there is in both theories an emphasis on the distinct role played by the "tunes" of speech in contributing to the meaning of any utterance
(for his part, Frost avoids the word "tune," with its musical implications—his frequent
comparison of "sentence sounds" to birdsong notwithstanding). This role is independent
of that played by the words themselves, by the punctuation, or by the grammar. Frost and
Lanier both maintain that much of what we say would be unintelligible but for the action
of these "tunes" or "sentence sounds." Second, for both men, good poetry has always set
these sentence sounds in a strained, counterpoint relation to the abstractly patterned
rhythms of meter. Third, we find the idea that, though once wedded, poetic composition
and musical composition have been, especially since the Renaissance, diverging in both
technique and theory, with the result that by the late nineteenth century—according to
Lanier—they were well on their way to becoming utterly distinct arts, the one, poetry,
based entirely on the sounds of human speech in animated conversation; the other, music,
based on abstract or "pure" sound.

Lanier writes in his opening chapter: "Our modern speech is made up quite as much of
tunes as of words, and . . . our ability to convey our thoughts depends upon the existence
of a great number of curious melodies which have somehow acquired form and significance. These 'tunes' are not mere vague variations of pitch in successive words,—
which would deserve the name of tune only in the most general sense of that term,—but
they are perfectly definite and organized melodies of the speaking-voice, composed of exact variations of pitch so well marked as to be instantly recognized by the ear. If they were
not thus recognized a large portion of the ideas which we now convey with ease would be
wholly inexpressible" (47). The practical implications of this idea for criticism are set out in
a reading Lanier gives of the ghost scenes in *Hamlet:* "This [idea] the reader may illustrate
by uttering in an absolute monotone the speech of the ghost in *Hamlet,* and contrasting
this monotone with the ever-varying tune in which Hamlet must utter the interjections of
tenderness and horror which occasionally interrupt the ghost's speech. The result will
very clearly prove the point now in hand: the monotone of the ghost, that is, the absence
of tune from his utterance, freezes us with a sense of the unnatural, while the fervent
tunes of Hamlet's brief cries remind us unconsciously of our human kinship with him"
(257). This is hardly conventional criticism. But it is exactly the sort of analysis that Frost's
own thinking about "the brute noises of our human throat" would have us make. See also
in this connection Lanier's vividly Frostian analysis of the scene in *All's Well That Ends Well*
in which the clown explains how many different meanings a courtier may convey with the
single expression "Oh Lord, sir!" simply by varying its "tune." Frost's favorite example of
this sort of thing was the sheer variety of meaning the single syllable "Oh" is susceptible
of in English (see explanatory note 30.5 below). As for annotating Shakespeare, see Frost's
remarks, quoted by Stirling Bowen in the book section of the *Detroit News* on November
27, 1927: "Years ago I came across a volume of Shakespeare's plays. I found that at some
still earlier time I had annotated the pages with directions as to the proper way to read the

lines. But as I studied again my annotations and the plays, I discovered that my annotations were unnecessary and that Shakespeare himself by his way of writing had given or indicated his own directions. There was only one way to read each word. I studied this problem and now in my own poetry I try to make each word serve two purposes; in addition to its own meaning it serves as a guide to the voice in reading preceding and succeeding words. If this is not always true of each word, it is true of each phrase or line. There are only three things, after all, that a poem must reach: the eye, the ear, and what we may call the heart or the mind. It is the most important of all to reach the heart of the reader. And the surest way to reach the heart is through the ear. The visual images thrown up by a poem are important, but it is more important still to choose and arrange words in a sequence so as virtually to control the intonation and pauses of the reader's voice. By the arrangement and choice of words on the part of the poet, the effects of humor, pathos, hysteria, anger, and, in fact, all effects, can be indicated and obtained."

Two more passages from Lanier's treatise make clear Frost's debt to him. In the first, Lanier sums up his argument about the "tunes of speech": "In point of fact, (1) tunes—melodies, distinctly formulated patterns of tones varying in pitch—exist not only in poetic readings, but in all the most commonplace communications between man and man by means of words. (2) Further: every affirmation, every question, has its own peculiar tune; every emotion, every shade of emotion, has its tune; and such tunes are not mere accidents but are absolutely essential elements in fixing the precise signification of words and phrases. (3) Further still: these tunes not only affect the signification of different words, but they greatly modify the meaning of the same words, so that a phrase uttered according to one tune means one thing, according to another tune another thing" (252–54). Frost follows these principles so closely that many paragraphs from his letters and notebooks could be set alongside them. In the second passage, which occurs later in the same chapter, Lanier touches on a point that gets at the very heart of Frost's enterprise as a poet: "If the reader will examine closely the conversation which goes on between daily intimates such as friends, husband and wife, and the like, who have thoroughly learned each other's habitual tunes of speech, it will be found that the words used in their communication to each other, if taken without these tunes, would bear the strangest relations to the matters in hand in the great majority of instances. All the most subtle complexities of passion, of petulance, of satiric under-meaning, of affection, of humor, are expressed in this way" (261). This last paragraph is as good an argument for the kind of poetry Frost writes in *North of Boston* as one might hope to find. And Lanier—whatever he may be like as a poet—saw it coming as early as 1880.

Collation

*30.0   The Last] Last
*30.0   Matter:] Matter
*30.1   Let's hear] Lets hear
*30.1   can't hear it] cant hear to it
*30.1   lenient,] lenient
*30.1   angry,] angry
*30.6   come on one] come one
*30.6   principle uses] principle use
*30.7   over-intellectual] over intellectual

*30.7   two extremes,] two extremes
*30.9   Yeats'] Yates'
*30.9   Browning's] Brownings
*30.9   Kipling's] Kiplings
*30.10 I don't do] I don't do
*30.10 something for] something to for
*30.11 sing-song] singsong
*30.12 chickadee] chicadee
*30.14 ear).] ear.
*30.14 tones of grandeur,] tones of grandeur
*30.14 of sweetness,] of sweetness
*30.16 poetry] poetry?
*30.16 ears?] ears.

Explanatory Notes

30.1   No] Frost used the same example in the second of his six Charles Eliot Norton Lectures, "Vocal Imagination: the Merger of Form and Content," on the evidence of a report of the series prepared by John Holmes for the March 21, 1936, *Boston Evening Transcript*.

30.5   oh-tones] Frost writes in a notebook (*NRF,* 45): "Take six interjected Ohs and write them in a column. They all look alike but I want them all said differently. My best way my only way to get them said differently is to write them as of sentences. (In speaking I can get along very well with the Oh's alone)

Oh / I see now what you mean.
Oh / isn't he lovely.
Oh / you sad fool why would you?
Oh / I slipped. Let me try again.
Oh / murder—help—murder!
Oh / King live forever (This is commonest in poetry—too common)". Another example occurs in the same entry: "I remember trying to show some children . . . exactly what I meant. I told them a 'Primer' story in three sentences about a cat.

> The cat is in the room
> I will put the cat out
> The cat will come back.

All in the tone of statement. Lets see what can be done with them just mechanically to bring them to life and put tones of extra meaning into them. (Extra)

> There's that cat got in.
> Get out you cat!
> No use—she'll be right back."

Incidentally, a variation of the latter exercise was published in *Time* magazine on October 9, 1950, as a part of a long article offering an overview of the poet's career.

30.9   "In a Cloister"] The correct title is "Soliloquy of the Spanish Cloister."

30.9   The fancy I had today] Opening line of Browning's "Prologue" to *Fifine at the Fair*

(1872). Frost knew the poem by heart and often quoted it. In fact, Lawrance Thompson reported having heard Frost recite from memory hundreds of lines of Browning.

30.9 "Put me down somewhere] From Kipling's "Road to Mandalay."

30.10 It has its purpose.] In a 1923 interview with Rose Feld, Frost remarked: "I do not write free verse; I write blank verse. I must have the pulse and beat of the rhythm. I like to hear it beating under the things I write. That does not mean I do not like to read a bit of free verse occasionally. I do. It sometimes succeeds in painting a picture that is very clear and startling. It's good as something created momentarily for its sudden startling effect; it hasn't the qualities, however, of something lastingly beautiful. And sometimes my objection to it is that it's a pose. It's not honest. When a man sets out consciously to tear up forms and rhythms and measures, then he is not interested in giving you poetry. He just wants to perform, he wants to show you his tricks. He will get an effect; nobody will deny that, but it is not a harmonious effect. Sometimes it strikes me that the free verse people got their idea from incorrect proof sheets. I have had stuff come from the printers with lines half left out or positions changed about. I read the poems as they stood, distorted and half-finished, and I confess I get a rather pleasant sensation from them. They make a sort of nightmarish half sense" (*New York Times Book Review,* October 21, 1923).

30.12 they were before words were] Frost explains in another notebook entry: "The brute noises of our human throat that were all our meaning before words stole in. I suppose there is one for every shade of feeling we will ever feel, yes and for every thought we will ever think. Such is the limitation of our throat" (unpublished notebook, Dartmouth College Library). Frost may owe some of these almost anthropological reflections on human speech to Darwin and Herbert Spencer, whom he read in the 1890s, as well as, again, to Sidney Lanier's *Science of English Verse,* which draws heavily on both Spencer and Darwin in discussions of the voice. See in particular Spencer's *The Origin and Function of Music,* which originally appeared in *Fraser's Magazine* in 1857. The outline of Spencer's argument is simple, and it is easy to see how Frost might have been affected by it in his thinking about the human voice: "We have here a principle underlying all vocal phenomena; including those of vocal music, and by consequence of music in general. The muscles that move the chest, larynx, and vocal chords [*sic*], contracting like other muscles in proportion to the intensity of feelings; every different contraction of these muscles involving, as it does, a different adjustment of the vocal organs; every different adjustment of the vocal organs causing a change in the sound emitted;—it follows that the variations of voice are the physiological results of variations in feeling. It follows that each inflection or modulation is the natural outcome of some passing emotion or sensation; and it follows that the explanation of all kinds of vocal expression, must be sought in this general relation between mental and muscular excitements" (404). As I indicate above, Frost did not have to read Spencer's essay to come under its influence. Lanier's *Science of English Verse* draws on it, as does Darwin in a chapter titled "The Means of Expression in Animals" in *The Expression of Emotion in Man and Animals,* where Spencer is prominently cited. The best inquiry into these and related aspects of Frost's thinking is an essential essay by Margery Sabin: "Frost's protests against the anticipated charge of mysticism [in his definition of the sounds of sense] shows that he did want the empirical point to yield ground for faith in a life-force more than personal, more than private, and *more than socially conventional*—a force of human life, transmitted over time from person to person through the intonations of a given language. Frost in 1914 wanted to believe—and wrote poems out of the belief—

that human vitality takes on a suprapersonal existence in the established intonations of speech, intonations which the individual may draw on for personal expression and, perhaps even more important, for the reassuring recognition that his single life is connected to other lives. The connection need not have anything to do with love or sympathy. It invokes, more radically, the shared possession of a repertory of gestures that is the sign of a common range of human experience" ("The Fate of the Frost Speaker," *Raritan* 2 [Fall 1982]: 134–35). The best study of Frost's response to Darwin is Robert Faggen's *Robert Frost and the Challenge of Darwin* (University of Michigan, 1997).

30.12   the imagination of the ear] Frost writes in another notebook: "It is one thing to hear the tones in the minds ear. Another to give them accurately at the mouth. Still another to implicate them in sentences and fasten them printed to the page. The second is the actors gift. The third is the writers" (*NRF,* p. 645).

30.13   the poet's injunction] Ezra Pound, in his essay "A Retrospect."

31. [Preface to a Selection of His Poems (1942)]

Frost's preface, which accompanied a selection of his poems, appeared in *This Is My Best,* edited by Whit Burnett (New York: Dial Press, 1942). Burnett first asked Frost to contribute to the anthology in January 1942. He repeated the request in April and by mid-June had received the list of poems Frost wanted to reprint. Frost waited until late July to submit the preface. In *Robert Frost: Life and Talks Walking* (Norman: University of Omaha Press, 1965), Louis Mertins quotes an August 8, 1942, letter from Frost to the collector Earle J. Bernheimer: "I am enclosing the first draft of a prose preface I have written for a group of poems K.M. [Kathleen Morrison] and I have selected for an anthology of American prose and verse made by Whit Burnett, editor of *Story Magazine.* There are very few of my absolutely first drafts in existence—as I suppose you know" (292). I have been unable to locate the "absolutely first draft" alluded to here. But what appears to be a carbon of the typescript Frost sent to Burnett, with manuscript corrections in Morrison's hand, survives in the collection of Dartmouth College Library. Frost often signed the manuscripts and typescripts he submitted for publication, and though the carbon held at Dartmouth bears no signature, the published text is followed by a printed one: "Ripton, Vt. Robert Frost / July 26, 1942." No doubt this reproduces Frost's signature at the end of the original typescript submitted to Whit Burnett. I reprint the text of the Dartmouth carbon, incorporating into it Frost's signature as printed in the published text. I have also conventionalized the styling of book titles.

Collation

TS = Dartmouth typescript. 1st = First appearance in *This is My Best.*
*31.2   *A Boy's Will*] 1st; A BOY'S WILL TS
*31.2   *North of Boston*] 1st; NORTH OF BOSTON TS
*31.2   *A Boy's Will*] 1st; A BOY'S WILL TS
*31.2   *North of Boston*] 1st; NORTH OF BOSTON TS
*31.2   Ripton {. . .} 1942] 1st; {not present}

Explanatory Notes

31.2   divinity shaping my ends . . . building better than I knew] Frost echoes, respectively, *Hamlet* (5.2.9–10) and Ralph Waldo Emerson's poem "The Problem." As to Emerson, consider RF's remarks in an unpublished talk at Kenyon College in 1950: "[A]ll through the years I've been confronted with the idea . . . whether I say more than I know myself. A poet builds better than he knows. You might say there may be an exactness in the statement but there may be an inexactness in the implication and people can run off in different directions with the implication . . . I'm always re-examining a phrase in some-body's poetry with this idea . . . And then I hear people speak of teen-agers. That comes to me from various quarters, teen-agers. And I think, did the person who gave them that name know what he was saying? Shall I assume that he didn't? Got to be careful about what you assume people don't know. Matthew Arnold uses the word *teen*. He speaks of using our nerves with bliss and teen [in "The Scholar Gypsy"] . . . It means with grief and pain. They're pain-agers. Maybe. Maybe that's in it, I don't know . . . That question's al-ways there and then there's two words if I may bring them out. Two words in Latin that I've turned over in my mind for years with this question in mind, 'Did Catullus know what he was saying when he said that?' And I said that to a Latinist a little while ago and he said, "You may pretty safely say he did." He believed in Catullus, but I rather think Catullus hadn't thought it all out. He said two words, *mens animi,* and . . . I've seen translations of it this way, poetic translations—look out for them. It said "the thoughts of the heart." *Mens*—mind, and *animus*—the spirit, see . . . And it was very arresting to me so I went back to see it again, why I'd been arrested by it—*mens animi.* And I suppose that's what we've been talking about today. The order—*mens* is the order—*mens,* the order of my wildness . . . see that's the way I translate enterprise of the spirit . . . that's the *animus,* that's the enterprise, that's the spirit that breaks the form" (unpublished typescript, Amherst College).

31.2   The group here given] "The Need of Being Versed in Country Things," "Come In," "The Onset," "Stopping by Woods on a Snowy Evening," "On a Tree Fallen across the Road," "The Woodpile," "Willful Homing," "A Blue Ribbon at Amesbury," "Two Tramps in Mud Time," "A Prayer in Spring," "Mowing," "A Drumlin Woodchuck," "Sitting by a Bush in Broad Sunlight," "Sand Dunes," "A Soldier," "The Gift Outright."

31.2   Kossuth] Lajos Kossuth (1802–94), Hungarian patriot and statesman, leader of the 1848 revolution in Hungary.

32. [Essay on the Divine Right of Kings (1943?)]

Dartmouth College Library holds two texts of this brief "essay," which may have been in-tended for inclusion in a personal letter: "We were talking . . ." The first text is a manu-script. The second is a typescript prepared from the manuscript and differing from it in several respects. I reprint here the text of the typescript; the variant readings therein seem authorial. On the back of the typescript Kathleen Morrison has written: "Please consult Larry [Lawrance Thompson] re. This—Has a fine addition—also can show other places where thought occurs." This note may have been addressed to Edward Connery Lathem when he was preparing, with Hyde Cox, *SP.* Another note in Morrison's hand appears at the foot of the manuscript: "In pile round '43." This suggests that the little essay dates from about the year 1943, though Frost made remarks along the same lines some years ear-lier in an informal address called "What Became of New England?" as well as much later in conversation, letters, and poetry. See, for example, his dedication "For John F. Kennedy His Inauguration," in *In the Clearing* (1962). Frost associated his ideas about a "democratic" version of "divine right" with Kennedy's book *Profiles in Courage,* which he sometimes brought up in conversation and in talks. However, I follow Morrison's note in dating this essay. For what it is worth, Lawrance Thompson reports a January 1941 conversation with Frost on the theme of "divine right": "He said that his favorite game was to disperse faulty ideas that were deeply entrenched, such as the idea that democracy had done away with the divine right of kings. Any ruler has an obligation to himself (or to his God) first, and an obligation to his subjects second—and that first obligation was his *divine right* (the categorical imperative). He said that in his own writing he had that same sense of dual obligation—to himself and (incidentally) to his readers. In talking, he knew that his acquaintances and friends had sloped the level and direction of his thinking, and that he was bound to that level by the circumstances of his life. But when he talked or wrote he was not conscious of talking on a level that considered the capacity of his listeners. If some listened and were annoyed, he found himself irked and perplexed to look back and see when first he had strayed from a mutually compatible frame of reference. One of the Dartmouth boys said, 'I am afraid you give me more credit for understanding you than you should.' Actually, he hadn't considered the degree of credit he should or should not give; he had just treated the boy as an equal" (NOTES).

Collation

MS = Frost's manuscript, also held at Dartmouth College Library.
32.1   about] of MS
32.1   first of all to consult] to consult first of all MS

33. [Contribution to 25th Anniversary Bread Loaf Booklet (1944)]

Frost's remarks appeared in the *Bread Loaf School of English Anniversary Bulletin* (Bread Loaf, Vt.: Middlebury College, 1944), a booklet commemorating the twenty-fifth anniversary of the school. Hewette Joyce explains in the introduction to the booklet: "At the suggestion of Lieutenant Owen and with the approval of the President of the College, a number of persons were asked to send brief statements of their recollections and impressions of Bread Loaf for inclusion in a special Twenty-Fifth Anniversary Bulletin." Dartmouth College Library holds a typescript of Frost's remarks with manuscript corrections in his hand and in Kathleen Morrison's. It is the copy-text for the present edition. In the typescript, the second paragraph (where the list of names appears) is unfinished. An instruction precedes it: "insert list of names," and many have indeed been inserted in Morrison's hand at this point, with more following in typing on page two. However, several names are given only in part (with ellipses indicating omissions), and some are misspelled. Also, some present in the published version are missing altogether from the typescript. Doubtless another draft existed with the complete and correct list of names. As published, the list of names given in the second paragraph is surely an authoritative variant, as I am defining "authoritative" in this edition. I have incorporated it into the copy-text.

Collation

TS = Frost's typescript (copy-text for the present edition). 1st = First appearance in *Bread Loaf School of English Anniversary Bulletin*.
*33.1   Bread Loaf] 1st; BreadLoaf TS {Elsewhere the typescript uses two words.}
*33.2   Bread Loaf:] 1st; Bread Loaf:—(insert list of names) TS

*33.2   Wilfred] 1st; Edward TS

*33.2   Walter Prichard Eaton, Burges Johnson] 1st; {not present} TS

*33.2   Sidney] Sydney TS, 1st

*33.2   Colums] Coloms TS, 1st

*33.2   Fred Lewis] Dr. TS; Richard Lewis 1st

*33.2   Conference.] ~ Donald Davidson, the Mirrielees sisters, John Crowe Ransom, Philip Wheelwright, Ted Greene, Hewette Joyce, Bob Gay, Theodore Morrison, Harry Owen, Henry Canby, the Coloms, Marguerite . . . Wilkinson, Elizabeth Drew, Hortense Moore and Raymond Bosworth . . . Pattee, Perry Miller, not to mention my many friends of the Conference. TS {That is to say: TS repeats a number of the names, as well as the last phrase of the paragraph; the ellipses are in the typescript.}

33.3 mountains around] mountains round 1st

*33.3   isn't far] 1st; isnt far TS

Explanatory Notes

33.2   Wilfred Davison . . . Perry Miller] Wilfred Davison, first Dean of the Bread Loaf School of English; Paul Dwight Moody, tenth president of Middlebury College; James Southall Wilson (1880–1958), literary critic, editor, Poe scholar; Walter Pritchard Eaton (1878–1957), editor and drama critic; Burges Johnson (1877–1963), Vermont-born writer, editor, humorist, author of *Beastly Rhymes;* Donald Davidson (1893–1968), poet affiliated with the Southern Fugitive group; Edith Ronald Mirrielees, editor of short-story anthologies; Lucia Bush Mirrielees, author of books about teaching composition; John Crowe Ransom (1888–1974), poet, literary critic, center of the Southern Fugitive group; Philip Wheelwright (1901–70), teacher of philosophy at the Bread Loaf Summer School, 1930, 1942; Theodore Meyer Green (1897–1969), essayist, literary critic, Professor of Philosophy at Yale; Robert Malcolm Gay (1879–1961), literary critic, editor; Theodore Morrison (1901–99), Professor of English at Harvard University, director of the Bread Loaf Writers' Conference 1932–55, husband of Frost's secretary Kathleen Morrison; Henry Seidel Canby (1878–1961), literary critic, educator, editor, chairman of the editorial board of the Book-of-the-Month Club; Padraic Colum (1881–1972), Irish-born poet and playwright; Mary Gunning Maguire [Colum], writer, wife of Padraic Colum; Marguerite Ogden Wilkinson (1883–1928), literary critic; Elizabeth Drew (1887–1965), literary critic, teacher at Bread Loaf School of English 1941–63; Hortense Moore, playwright and editor of *Bread Loaf Book of Plays* (1941); Fred Lewis Pattee (1863–1950), literary critic, novelist, poet, teacher at Bread Loaf School of English 1924–36; Perry Miller (1905–63), literary critic, Professor of English at Harvard University, author of *The New England Mind.*

34. The Four Beliefs (1944)

This brief essay represents a revision of the final paragraph of "Education by Poetry." It was first published separately as *The Four Beliefs* (Hanover, N.H.: Graphic Arts Workshop, 1944) in an edition of 250 copies. One year later *The Four Beliefs* was reprinted, from the same plates, in *Society of Printers; Miscellany 1944, a Cooperative Venture in Wartime Printing Produced by Members for Private Distribution to the Society* (Boston: Society of Printers, 1945). Ray Nash, who prepared the Graphic Arts edition, was a member of the Society of Printers. A copy of *The Four Beliefs* held in the University of Florida Library is described by

John Lancaster in *The Parkman Dexter Howe Library Part VII*: "A gift to Howe from W. A. Jackson, who wrote in an accompanying letter dated February 2, 1945: 'The publisher, Ray Nash, writes [i.e. to Jackson] "Frost wrote it down for me to print last year before Christmas—although, as you know, he has been saying something like this for years and one or two paragraphs are quite similar to what has appeared in print"'"(29). Dartmouth College Library holds a typescript of the essay corrected and revised in Frost's hand. It differs from the published text in three respects, listed in the collation. I have printed the text of that typescript since I cannot determine that Frost is responsible for the changes in wording in the published text.

Collation

1st = First appearance as *The Four Beliefs*.
34.1   There are several beliefs that I know more about from having lived with poetry:]
{not present} 1st
34.4   understand and] understand, 1st
34.6   relationship] relation 1st

Explanatory Notes

34.0   THE FOUR BELIEFS] Frost mentions five beliefs, not four: the self belief, the love belief, the national belief, the art belief, and the God belief. The same discrepancy occurs in the last paragraph of "Education by Poetry." In an uncompleted revision of "Education by Poetry" (held now at Dartmouth College Library) Frost struck out "four" and wrote in "five" in the first sentence of the last paragraph.

35. [Preface to "The Death of the Hired Man" (1945)]

The copy-text for the present edition of Frost's preface to "The Death of the Hired Man" is a signed typescript held in the Barrett Collection of the University of Virginia Library. The preface was printed for the first time in Crane, *Descriptive Catalogue*, 241. Another typescript of the preface is held at Dartmouth College and registers one difference in wording, recorded below. Sometime after he composed it, Frost gave the typescript now held in the Barrett Collection to Earle Bernheimer, with a note appended in his hand: "I dont know whether this was used or not." A further note in Kathleen Morrison's hand reads: "For Whit Burnett / High School Textbook / Preface to / *The Death of the Hired Man* / October 26, 1945." The book in question is *American Authors Today*, edited by Whit Burnett and Charles Slatkin (Boston: Ginn and Company, 1947). Burnett and Slatkin did not in fact use Frost's preface. "The Death of the Hired Man" appears instead with prefatory remarks by the editors themselves.

Collation

35.1   Mr. Burnett's idea] the idea of the editors {Typescript held at Dartmouth College Library.}

36. The Constant Symbol (1946)

"The Constant Symbol" appeared first in *The Atlantic Monthly* 178 (October 1946): 50–52. (Frost reported to Lawrance Thompson that the magazine paid him $500 for the essay.) It was published in November of the same year as the introduction to *The Poems of Robert Frost* (New York: Modern Library), and was later reprinted in booklet form as *The Constant Symbol by Robert Frost; With Christmas Greetings From Cornelia and Waller Barrett* (1962). This third, private edition was limited to 500 copies, and merely reprints the Modern Library text. Barrett first notified Frost (through Kathleen Morrison) of his plans to republish the essay in a September 27, 1962, letter. Morrison conveyed Frost's approval of the project in an October 19 letter to Barrett which makes clear that Frost's involvement extended no farther than the granting of permission.

The relation between the first two of the above-mentioned texts is more complicated. Joseph Blumenthal of the Spiral Press was hired by Random House (publishers of the Modern Library) to design *The Poems of Robert Frost*. The book was well into production by May 1946, as Blumenthal indicates in *Robert Frost and His Printers* (Austin: W. Thomas Taylor, 1985):

> With the typesetting well under way, Frost was late with the promised introduction. Apparently I had made some typographic recommendations which he accepted in a letter, and in which he also promised the preface that finally became the remarkable introductory essay entitled 'The Constant Symbol.' . . . The letter, dated May 7, 1946, follows: 'Decidedlee! Every one of those things you cite should be got out of the design. And maybe some more if you say so. Lucky to have you there as overseer. No dedication at all: which is as it was in the Collected of Henry Holt & Co.
>
> 'And now for the preface. I think I have one in mind. I am waiting for an access of impulse to set me at it. But you mustn't be held up. I shall do it in a day or two now. Kay's orders.' (37–38)

Whether he did it in a day or two is not clear. A manuscript of the essay held in the Barrett Collection at the University of Virginia differs from the published versions in many details and is obviously not a finished draft. Frost dates this manuscript August 1946. But he seems to have added that date some time after he actually finished the essay. In fact, the essay as it appears in the Modern Library edition bears the date "July, 1946" (xxiv). Editorial correspondence between Frost and Robert Linscott of the Modern Library indicates that the essay was received by the publisher in late July. The Jones Library, Amherst, holds a set of galleys for the *Atlantic Monthly* edition of the essay, corrected in Kathleen Morrison's hand and in Frost's, and dated August 15. Dartmouth College Library holds a set of galleys for the Modern Library edition, also corrected in Morrison's hand, which, on the evidence of the associated correspondence, seems to date from mid-August as well. With very few exceptions, the same corrections are indicated on both sets of galleys. Collation of these several documents shows that the *Atlantic Monthly* text most faithfully reflects Frost's intentions. It is the copy-text for the present edition. Below is a table of the variants between the first two published texts of the essay, with reference also to the Modern Library galleys, and the Barrett manuscript. Analysis of them follows (abbreviations are explained in the collation).

36.1   Some knotted riddles tell that] MS, MLG; Some knotted riddles tell what ML

36.3   And there are many other things] MS, MLG; There are many other things ML

36.6   he made choice] MS; he made the choice ML, MLG {The mistaken reading is set in type in MLG and is uncorrected.}

36.8   in my book] in this book ML, MLG, MS

36.11   He has uttered about as much he has] MS; He has uttered about as much as he has ML, MLG {The mistaken reading is set in type in MLG and is uncorrected.}

36.11   *pari passu*] MLG; pari passu ML {the sentence in which this phrase appears is not present in MS}

36.11   had any ambition to be.] MS; ~ be? ML, MLG

36.12   Ode, And] ode and MS; Ode and ML, MLG

36.15   it will be too bad] it will go hard ML, MLG, MS

36.16   that I should have written my verse] MS; that I have written my verse ML, MLG {The mistaken reading is set in type in MLG and is uncorrected.}

36.16   *ly, ing, and ation*] MLG; ly, ing, and ation ML, MS

36.16   something to learn still later.] something to learn later. ML, MLG {This phrase is not present in MS.}

36.16   As much as anything] MS; As much for anything ML, MLG {The Modern Library text misquotes the poem.}

With one exception ("in my book") all the readings listed here from the *Atlantic Monthly* edition are the result of corrections made in manuscript by Morrison (at Frost's direction) on the *Atlantic Monthly* galleys, and, in most cases, on the Modern Library galleys too. Furthermore, six of the nine variants in wording in the *Atlantic Monthly* text listed above agree with the Barrett manuscript against the Modern Library text. Notice that in three of these cases ("riddles tell that," "he made choice," "about as much he") Frost's phrasing is unusual. Perhaps an editor at the Modern Library "rationalized" it, as the editor of the *Atlantic Monthly* galleys apparently did. In fact, a September 5, 1946, letter from Robert Linscott to Frost shows that Linscott refused to make the first of the above corrections, thinking it was a mistake, even though Frost and Morrison clearly indicated the change on the galleys. In short, the manuscript corrections on the *Atlantic Monthly* galleys restore six unauthoritative variant readings—which appear in both the Modern Library text and in the uncorrected *Atlantic Monthly* galleys—to their original form in the Barrett manuscript, though of course the manuscript otherwise differs widely from both published versions. By contrast, variant readings in the Modern Library text agree with the manuscript, and against the *Atlantic Monthly*, in only two cases. One of these is owing simply to the occasion of the Modern Library edition: the reading *"this book"* obviously is meant for the text of the essay which accompanied the collection of poems. The other (at 36.16) is a result of Morrison's manuscript revision of the sentence in the *Atlantic Monthly* galleys, which for the first time established this particular wording ("it will be too bad") against the wording of the manuscript and the Modern Library edition ("it will go hard"). The reading as it stands in the corrected *Atlantic Monthly* galleys is undoubtedly deliberate and authorial. The *Atlantic Monthly* text, then, is clearly to be preferred, though the text of the Modern Library edition has been consistently reprinted in collections of Frost's prose. I have reprinted the text exactly as it appears in *The Atlantic Monthly*. All corrections made on the galleys in Frost's hand and in Morrison's are registered perfectly in the published text. In one case a comma appears in the published text where it is missing in the galleys, owing to a misprint: "The mind is a baby giant who, more provident . . ." (36.15). Though no manuscript correction is present on the galleys, there is a space which indicates that a comma should be there. "The Constant Symbol" has been reprinted since Frost's death without the appended sonnet "To the Right Person." I include it here since he saw to it himself that it appeared with the essay in the Barrett manuscript, as well as in both *The Atlantic*

Monthly and *The Poems of Robert Frost*. Correspondence between Linscott and Frost suggests that Frost considered omitting the sonnet, but then decided to leave it in. The sonnet is integral to the essay in three respects: in "The Constant Symbol" Frost discusses the sonnet form in detail; twice he anticipates the title of his own sonnet in the phrasings of the essay proper; and the last sentence surely welcomes the complement of a poem about an abandoned district schoolhouse.

Collation

ML = Modern Library edition. MS = Early holograph manuscript, Barrett Collection, University of Virginia Library. CP = *Complete Poems of Robert Frost*, 1949.

36.1   implication is] ML; implication being MS

36.7   tell that] MS; tell what ML

36.2   Texture is surely] ML; Texture surely is MS

36.3   And there are many other things I have found myself saying about poetry, but the chiefest of these is that it is metaphor] There are ~ ML; The supreme thing is metaphor MS

36.3   the pleasure of ulteriority.] ML; one of the commonest pleasures of all. Ulteriority. MS

36.3   simply made] ML; simply composed MS

36.20   same old metaphor] ML; same metaphor MS

36.5   is always crying out mind] ML; in the wildness {?} of its {position} breaks out once in so often with an angry Mind MS

36.5   Terence's answer would be all human business is my business.] ML; Terence would reply everything human is my own business MS

36.5   with a rhymester's cleverness] ML; {not present} MS

36.5   unless you made] ML; unless you could make MS

36.5   of the will] ML; of the MS

36.5   alien entanglements] ML; foreign entanglements MS

36.6   Take the] ML; ~ a MS

36.6   made choice] MS; made the choice ML

36.7   the Creed] ML; a Creed MS

36.7   chargeable with] ML; accused of MS

36.7   concerns *us*] ML; matters MS

36.8   my book] MS; this book ML

36.8   on a Snowy Evening.] ML; {not present} MS

36.8   And it was] ML; {not present} MS

36.8   so long] ML; as long MS

36.9   running wild] ML; {An alternate wording is written above this phrase in MS: "aimless".}

36.9   less than its own] ML; but its own MS

36.9   to know it by] ML; about it MS

36.9   shrinks shyly from] ML; {In MS this phrase appears as an alternate reading above the word: "dreads".}

36.9   inner mood] ML; mood MS

36.9   in passing.] ML; ~ No mystery is meant. {I.e., in the MS this phrase is present twice, here in addition to where it appears in the published texts.}

36.11 {On the reverse of the MS page bearing the paragraph beginning "Suppose him to have written . . ." appears a phrase: "Sold his soul to rhyme and meter". It is not clear how this was to have been incorporated into the text.}

36.11 as much he] MS; as much as he ~ ML

36.11 Odd how the two advance into the open *pari passu.*] ML; {not present} MS

36.11 but he has] ML; but he MS

36.11 he will turn] ML; he turns MS

36.11 Up to this point his discipline has been the self-discipline whereof it is written in so great praise. The harsher discipline from without is now well begun. He who knows not both knows neither. His worldly commitments are now three or four deep.] ML; This is the self discipline from within where of so much is written. He goes relatively undisciplined who knows no other whose impulse has not tempted him out into the harsher discipline of the world MS {In MS these sentences are obviously provisional.}

36.11 ambition to be.] MS; ambition to be? ML

36.11 had made most] ML; made all MS

36.11 doesn't even have] ML; hasn't even MS

36.11 bread for the butter or butter for the bread] ML; butter ~ bread ~ bread ~ butter MS

36.12 even to the novel] ML; even the novel MS

36.13 kept to] ML; kept down to MS

36.14 they go again with] ML; we have it—MS

36.14 merciful] ML; kindly MS

36.15 distrust form] ML; distrust any form MS

36.15 all round] ML; {not present} MS

36.16 given—data so-called] ML; {not present} MS

36.16 prosody,] ML; {not present} MS

36.16 be too bad] go hard ML, MS

36.16 should have written] MS; have written ML

36.16 rhyme-set in my "Reluctance"] ML; rhyme MS

36.16 possibilities?] ML; ~. MS

36.16 just] ML; {not present} MS

36.16 something to learn still later.] something to learn later. ML; Live and you learn. MS

36.16 {On the page facing the last page of "The Constant Symbol" in the Barrett manuscript, Frost has written a paragraph which he apparently once considered incorporating into the conclusion: "I have said all this at ease without coming to the point waited for and putting it in so many words that poems together maintain the constant symbol of the confluence of the flow of the spirit of one person with the flow of the spirit of the race. The figure of confluence without compromise. Like walking into an escalator and walking with it. Like entering into the traffic to pass and be passed."}

36.16 *Fourteen Lines*] ML; {not present} MS

36.16 As much as anything] As much for anything ML {That is to say: ML misquotes the poem.}

36.16 there's a tight] ML; there's tight{not present} MS

36.16 knowledge] learning CP

Explanatory Notes

36.0 THE CONSTANT SYMBOL] Frost delivered a talk under the title at Dartmouth on May 20, 1946. Following are some excerpts from Jerry Tallmer's report of it as published in *The Dartmouth* (the college newspaper) for May 22. Some of it is Tallmer's paraphrase, some of it direct quotation: "I always test the other man. I suspect him of having gotten lost in his steadily deepening commitments. Everybody does this . . . We are all always testing each other's sincerity. I do it when I read poetry. I do it when I watch the president of the United States as he gets deeper and deeper into commitments. I watch every marriage that way . . . In this unfolding of the kept or lost intentions within the deepening commitments is the root and basis of all good writing. In everything you write—in a good short story, for example, every single word remembers every other word in it. The last word remembers the first word. That is what we call form. That is what a good short story has . . . for example . . . Hemingway's The Killers . . . A poem is the having of an idea—not an idea put into verse. You drop into whatever you happen to drop into . . . The beauty of them [metaphors] in poetry is that it doesn't stay very well. There's a constant renewal. And that's the first place where you recognize and weigh its originality. In the freshness of the figures. That's where the thinking comes in .°.°. Form—meter, rhyme, verse, stanza, line—the relation of those things are a constant symbol to the world that you and I live in."

36.5 Viennese] Frost alludes to Sigmund Freud. See also a book Frost read some ten years earlier, Herbert Read's *Form in Modern Poetry* (1932): "There are many instincts besides the sex instinct, and if any one instinct is more in question than another, I think it is probably the gregarious instinct" (Vision Press reprint, 21). See also Lawrance Thompson's report of a remark Frost made in 1959: "Frost got going next on Freud and said that he had long ago said that it wasn't SEX which provided the most powerful motivation for human action; it was REX, or the desire within the herd-instinct for the individual to want to sit on top of the pile" (NOTES).

36.5 The beauty of socialism] An interview by Neil Hertz in 1951 records Frost saying: "Socialism? Why every time you get a letter through the mails or talk to a policeman you're taking part in socialism. Just so long as it stays clear of tyranny" (*The Amherst Student*, May 10, 1951: 4).

36.5 Terence's answer] In Terence's play *Heauton Timoroumenos* ("The Self-Tormenter"), line 77: "I am a man: nothing human is alien to me."

36.5 The ultimate commitment . . . alien entanglements.] Frost similarly remarks, in a 1931 lecture at the New School for Social Research: "There is a height, an altitude of the spirit that gets first satisfaction, and can take satisfaction there a long time, in just the works of art that are between the artist and himself. I think anyone would smother in a lifetime. I don't know how long you can stand it in the spiritual. There are examples of people who have gone many, many years, and some you might say a lifetime. Gerard Hopkins . . . held himself in the spirit that way. Emily Dickinson was another. But the natural way seems to be to descend without too much greed . . . from the superior self to the social self. There is the person who from sheer haughtiness likes to take in literature the attitude of being beyond any other person's comprehension or understanding, likes, in other words, to be misunderstood, revels in being misunderstood. There is a book called 'Misunderstood Betsy,' I suppose about a girl . . . who likes to be misunderstood. I didn't know girls were like that but I have known boys who liked being misunderstood. There is a certain cruelty . . . in not letting your fellow man understand you. It sends him to hell, sends him to the devil. Joan of Arc sent many to hell. She didn't do it on purpose, poor child. There are people who have all their lives sent people to hell for misunderstanding them. The most humane thing you can do is to let people know what you are talking about. Let them in. Treat them as if they had something in common with you, as if they were as good as you, as wise as you, as American as you, and other things" (unpublished typescript, Dartmouth College Library). Frost's comment about Dickinson is likely an allusion to her poem "The Soul's Superior instants," though he may, of course, be thinking of any number of poems in which she declines to "descend" into "the social."

36.6   the president in the White House] Lawrance Thompson describes a September 1946 talk at Bread Loaf in which Frost named the president he had in mind: "He talked from (and around) his essay soon to appear in the Atlantic (and Modern Library). Using FDR as the figure about whom he was obviously talking in 'The Constant Metaphor' [sic], he said, 'The emergence of his intention came on rather magnificently'" (NOTES).

36.6   youthfully step-careless] The same "step-carelessness" applies to the poet, it would appear: "Nobody takes up poetry; you drift into it by little things. I wrote verse for twenty-five years, until I was 40, before anybody called me a poet. It was embarrassing. I don't call myself a poet yet. It's for the world to say whether you are a poet or not. I am one-half teacher, one-half poet and one-half farmer: that's three halves" (as quoted in the *New York Times* for Friday March 26, 1954: C23).

36.8   There's an indulgent smile . . . suffer deflection.] What appeals to Frost is the way a poet carries himself, "recklessly" or not, through his formal commitments. He expressed the idea often, as in a 1962 speech at the Choate School. After reading his poem "In winter in the woods alone" two times through, Frost remarked: "Shall I say the poem right through again and just get the action and the beat of the meter the way I play the piece, the way I play it[?] [He repeats the poem a third time.] You wouldn't see from where you are that I kept the end of the line of go, low, afterglow, snow, overthrow and blow. I kept that all through the poem, all three stanzas. And that's what I want you to like if you like me at all . . . Now this—what the critics don't seem to talk enough about—is the performance in the poem—the way the sentences come, the way the lines fit the verse and the way the lines change. They wouldn't know a poem from a hole in the ground" (unpublished typescript, Amherst College Library). See also Frost's short lyric "In a Poem" (*CPPP* 329). Of interest here, too, is a remark Frost made in an appearance at Mt. Holyoke College in October 1937, as reported in the *Springfield Union* for October 16 of that year, in an unsigned article titled "Likens Poem to Polar Trip": "Robert Frost . . . defined the only freedom possible as 'the freedom of your material,' whether it be gardening or writing poetry. You seek to achieve this freedom, said Mr. Frost, in its given form. To illustrate the way this principle works, in his writings and poetry, he read 'Stopping by Woods on a Snowy Evening,' in which, he said, he got himself in and then had to figure how he could get out again without marring the pattern he had set up. Mr. Frost said: 'The fun of a poem is the recklessness with which you plunge in. It is like going to the North Pole so you can prove that you can get back." In its report of the same talk, *The Springfield Republican* (October 16, 1937) wrote: "Discussing the ever disputable relationship of substance and form, Frost suggested that subject matter can carry the poet most of the way, yet 'form is the last assignment of the material. Form exists when one principle is locked in its opposite,' he pointed out, 'not like the clash of good and evil, it is the clash of two goods. I would as soon write verse without form as play tennis with the net down.'" The latter remark is one he often repeated. I quote one further remark toward this same idea, from the report of Frost's April 11, 1950, reading at Yale University: "I never invent a rhyme, in the style of Emily Dickinson. But on the other hand I never let my rhymes change the direction of my poems" (*Yale News* 71:41 [April 12, 1950]: 1).

36.9   like Herrick in "To Daffodils."] The lines in Herrick's poem vary from one to three to four feet in length. Frost mentioned the poem in a June 1946 talk at Bread Loaf, as reported by Lawrance Thompson: "Speaking about poetic intention, he said that Herrick, in 'To Daffodils,' was just as unbothered in his intention when he got to the second verse as he had been in the first. James Russell Lowell, on the other hand, showed a kind of deflection of intention, and escaped from the obligation of his commitment (got out of his intention) too cleverly, so that you felt a certain untrueness, or falseness, in the verse" (NOTES).

36.9   as Blake says] Perhaps in the poem "Love's Secret," which begins: "Never seek to tell thy love."

36.11   When in disgrace] Shakespeare's sonnet 29. Lawrance Thompson reports the following conversation, which took place in June 1946 when Frost was writing "The Constant Symbol": "[Frost] suddenly began to quote Shakespeare's sonnet 'When in disgrace with fortune and men's eyes,' saying that he had to follow that quite a way before he understood it. He continued, checking each line off. If he had ever been in disgrace with fortune and men's eyes, it had not given him any desire to beweep his outcast state, and certainly he had never troubled heaven with his bootless cries, nor looked on himself with that kind of false pity that led some men to curse their fate. As for wishing to be like anyone more rich in hope,

> Featured like him, like him with friends possessed
> Desiring this man's art and that man's scope
> With what I most enjoy contented least

—that was all strange and incomprehensible to him, although he certainly had known enough people who wasted their lives in such stupid talk. 'Yet in these thoughts myself almost despising.' That line pleased him most because it represented the nadir of the downward groping of the poet's mood—and as for the rest, the poem ended with the 'heaven's gate' phrase, so that the weak couplet was a mere nod, an anticlimactic nod to the convention of sonnet writing" (NOTES).

36.11   by what points of jutting rock] See lines 49–51 of Alfred Lord Tennyson's *Morte d'Arthur*: "He, stepping down / By zig-zag paths, and juts of pointed rock, / Came on the shining levels of the lake." I thank Mark Scott for pointing out the echo to me.

36.12   Dobson confesses frankly] In Henry Austin Dobson's (1840–1924) poem "Urceus Exit." "Rose" is a pretty woman who figures in the poem.

36.13   Jeremiah . . . lamentations] "The Lamentations of Jeremiah" follow the Book of Jeremiah. The "Lamentations" comprise five poems, four of which have twenty-two verses. As the Oxford Study Edition of *The New English Bible* points out, four of the poems are alphabetic acrostics in the original Hebrew.

36.14   words of the dictionary] Frost remarked in a 1950 talk at Kenyon College: "They asked me if rhyme wasn't a trammel, a hamper, you know, meter. I said, yes, just the same as words are. And your vocabulary, you haven't got the whole dictionary . . . in your head. And you can't swing any words that aren't in your head. You can't take them out of a dictionary while you're making a poem. So you're hampered to begin with, aren't you, terribly. As someone said today, these emotions we have, these thoughts we have belong to a language we haven't got. That's a poetic way of saying what isn't so. There's no language we haven't got, there's no thoughts that are really thoughts until they [have] begun to pick

up their words, you know, you can't tell me there are; but it's all right. It's one way of saying this. But here you are with a bursting emotion and you're limited to a very small vocabulary [t]hat the teachers have tried to stretch but haven't stretched much for you.
You're so defiant, you don't give a damn for that, you say, 'I don't give a damn if I haven't
got many words. Watch me, watch me take them right out of the air.' The[n] you say,
'Not only that, I'm not scared to limit myself a little more with meter and rhyme.' You
see, it tightens the vocabulary a little bit more, but it just shows that you're alive and
strong and you know you can do it. You know, they can't stop you. I often think about this
question of rhyme. Here's your sincerity, here's your truth, your reality that we've been
talking about today. And is it interfered with? It has one danger . . . your cleverness in
meeting the rhyme problem . . . may spoil the poem, the intention of the poem, the same
as it did for James Russell Lowell. Very often his wit and all that just obscured everything
else he was about. It could do that, it has that danger, like all things" (unpublished typescript, Amherst College Library).

37. Speaking of Loyalty (1948)

Frost delivered "Speaking of Loyalty" at an Alumni Luncheon at Amherst College on June
19, 1948. George Whicher, a colleague of Frost's, prepared a transcript of the talk and submitted it to Frost to be revised for publication. Frost made his revisions directly on the
transcript and the speech appeared in the *Amherst Graduates' Quarterly* 37.4 (August 1948),
with title and notes supplied by Whicher. Frost wrote to Whicher in June:

> The temptation is to go even further than you with this and round it into a real
> piece. But perhaps that wouldn't be fair to those who heard it as a speech or
> talk. They might feel bamboozled. It hurts like everything not to bring my point
> out more sharply. Loyalty is simply to those you have given a right to count on
> you—your country family friends gang church firm or college. The difficult
> thing is to straighten it out with them God and yourself when your fancy falls a
> turning. If it is your country in time of war or if it is your gang you are desert-
> ing you may get yourself shot. Loyalty is as simple a thing as that. It takes a
> lightening [*sic*] change artist to make it out the same thing as disloyalty. The
> transition from an attachment to an attraction would be the interesting thing to
> talk about. The break with England probably distressed every single colonial
> 'patriot' but Tom Paine. It proved too much for Arnold and he repented of his
> unfaithfulness and backed out of the rebellion. But there is a whole article in
> this for another day. I was threatening a dire essay on Traitors and Quislings in
> my travels last year. Robert Bruce was a redeemed Quisling. Then there is
> Smuts. When the British want to hear themselves praised they send for him.
> Dont you think it a little hard on my free rendering of ideas to confront it with
> the studied sophistries of the Commager fellow? You'll notice I stayed pur-
> posely vague about him. But I suppose I mustn't mind. You might enjoy a row
> between him and me if you could get us into one. I listen to the fights myself
> sometimes on the radio.
>
>   I am still dazed with what happened to me in Amherst. I am in no state to
> have to eat my own words like this. Ever Amherst's (and yours) R.F. / Kay

thinks I must be brave and stand by my indiscretions. The only reason I go on the platform at all is to show my bravery. I must remember that. I do it to make up for never having faced bullets like the real hero. I suffer more before and after than during action.

In his July 7 reply, Whicher wrote: "Many thanks for the trouble you have taken to put the speech in order for us. I have copied it off and the Quarterly editor is rejoiced to have it" (unpublished letter, Dartmouth College Library). The corrected transcript of the talk and the manuscript of Frost's letter are held at Amherst College Library. Frost had worked with Whicher once before in preparing "Education by Poetry" for publication in the *Amherst Graduates' Quarterly* and the two texts present similar editorial problems. The punctuation of both was apparently supplied by the transcribers. Frost spoke extemporaneously, leaving no preliminary draft of either speech. Several differences between the two cases are worth noting, however. "Speaking of Loyalty" retains in its published form much more of the character of an extemporaneous talk than does "Education by Poetry," the wording of which was revised heavily for publication. It is necessary in reading "Speaking of Loyalty," for example, to know what poems Frost recited where, since some of his remarks refer specifically to them. Whicher supplies the title of each poem at the point where Frost read it, together with a citation of the page in *The Poems of Robert Frost* (New York: Modern Library, 1947) on which each poem appears. Furthermore, in his notes Whicher condenses rather than quotes fully the remarks that Frost made about the poems he read. In correcting the transcript, Frost chose to let it stand as such, with the result that Whicher's notes are in some cases integral to the meaning of the speech. There is at least the possibility that in preparing the transcript Whicher condensed or otherwise "neatened up" more of Frost's remarks than is apparent from his notes. The published text differs from the corrected transcript in wording and punctuation in a number of minor cases. Because Frost was a friend and correspondent of Whicher, and because Kathleen Morrison, Frost's secretary, wrote to Whicher sometime before the speech appeared in the *Quarterly,* the possibility is strong that Frost and Whicher worked out some further minor revisions not indicated on the corrected transcript, and some of the variant readings in the published form do indeed seem authorial. Accordingly I reprint the published text. The bracketed notes appear within the body of the essay just as they appear in the original; these were supplied by Whicher. Whicher's original footnotes are reprinted below in the explanatory notes.

Collation

MS = The Frost/Whicher corrected transcript, held now at Amherst College Library.
CP = *Complete Poems of Robert Frost, 1949.*
37.3   Law School] {not present} MS
37.4   an oration on "Adventures in Education,"] {not present} MS
37.4   right there] {not present} MS
37.5   The United States is in] The United States is MS
37.5   chemistry, physics, or] chemistry physics MS
37.8   That's loyalty] That's a loyalty
37.8   that? . . .] that . . . MS
37.8   to shut her] to shut MS

37.9   service] war service MS

37.9   That's the] That's MS

37.9   catch him] catch MS

37.11   official in] official of MS

37.11   got out] get out MS

37.13   not to be easy] to be painful to you MS

37.13   To bow] And bow CP

Explanatory Notes

37.0   SPEAKING OF LOYALTY] George Whicher's original footnotes to the first appearance of this essay in the *Amherst Graduates' Quarterly* are given below. I omit those referring to *The Poems of Robert Frost*. Notes not in quotation marks are my own.

37.1   a brand new college] "See Walter Hendricks' article, 'Marlboro College,' in the May, 1948, [*Amherst Graduates'] Quarterly*."

37.2   the obituaries . . .] Lawrance Thompson reports an August 1951 conversation with Frost: "He couldn't get over the difference between the individuals who had something of their own to go on and to 'get up' and those individuals who, having nothing of their own, spent their lives working for others, or working over the ideas of others. He spoke about the number of people who seemed to think that the college determined one's future: if you went to Harvard all would be well with you. But he said that the most interesting part of reading obituaries for him was the discovery that the important people were generally people who started out from nowhere and who had no 'advantages.' It looked, he said, as though there was a major advantage in having no advantage, at the outset" (NOTES).

37.3   Vermont way of life] "Feminine chorus: 'We still do it, and always have done it, everywhere.' According to the tradition cited by Dorothy Canfield, Mrs. Chittenden insisted that her guests should eat at the same table with the farm hands, and this democratic custom shocked her visitors from 'foreign parts.'"

37.5   article in the *Harper's Magazine*] "Henry Steele Commager, 'Who Is Loyal to America?' in *Harper's* for September, 1947." For a discussion of Frost's reaction to Commager's article, see *TLY* 169–72, 414–15. "Loyalty" was much discussed in 1948, of course. In March of the previous year President Truman issued Executive Order 9835, which established the so-called "Loyalty Program," providing for the investigation of all government employees and applicants for federal jobs. In July of the same year the National Security Act reorganized the armed forces under a single Secretary of Defense and established the Central Intelligence Agency; in the same month George Kennan published his watershed article setting out the theory of "containment." As Frost's remarks about loyalty suggest, "containment" was certainly a going concern inside the U.S. within the year. (Whittaker Chambers named Alger Hiss before the House Un-American Activities Committee two months after Frost delivered this address.) In a 1955 tape-recorded conversation with Arthur S. Harris, Frost again took up the question, this time attending to the McCarthyite program of harassment of college and university personnel:

> HARRIS: How do you feel about these teachers who are harassed in the colleges because they—
> FROST: Well, I really don't have any feeling at all about it. They fooled around with those ideas and as far as I am concerned, they ought to stand up to it and

say, 'I did think that' . . . I don't think that anybody molests Max Eastman, for instance, who was an extreme communist—everybody knows he's not one now. They might disparage him maybe for coming clear around the other way. Oh Lord, you've got to expect to be judged. So many of them are cowardly about it. They don't say what they *did* go through. So many sat around and [said,] 'Well of course the capitalist system is washed up,' and of course they say—'we have nothing we believe in in the West. You have to admit the Russians have something.' All that kind of thing went on—so familiar in all the crowd.

HARRIS: The only problem I wonder about is telling on your friends . . . What is a man to do?

FROST: Well, they put you in jail if you don't answer I suppose. I'd go to jail. I don't think I'd like to tell on friends. I wouldn't like that. Of course if you really know somebody who is a member of the party—I think I'd go to jail—take my—I think I would—I've never been caught in such a position. And then taking refuge in the fifth amendment and all that. I was thinking the other day that one of the most liberal governments the world has ever had—the most liberal— is ours, and one of our liberal laws is the fifth amendment. And those radical friends that I had in those days—if they loathed anything it was liberals—they hated liberals—they hated all liberalism. And now, good gracious, they are outraged liberals themselves—they're just taking refuge in the fifth amendment, which I would scorn to do if I had scorned liberalism as much as they did.

HARRIS: I understand.

FROST: I wouldn't do that. But it's more or less of a smile to me. I've lived with them all and I know what that kind of mood—changing mood—all is. I've never, never gone through it. In my own childhood I knew people like Henry George—friends of the family—and I've seen all that sort of thing. My mother read such things as *Looking Backward* [by the socialist Edward Bellamy].

HARRIS: Do you think we are exaggerating this business about the poor instructors who are harassed by communism and witch-hunters, and so forth? I mean—

FROST: Which people do you mean?

HARRIS: Well we had a professor at the University of New Hampshire for instance who is only a mild liberal but certainly not a communist, and the students in his classes when he mentions things that don't agree with their philosophy, begin to catalogue him and peg him, and call him a communist. When he isn't. Don't you think that's—

FROST: Well, that's too bad, but I don't see—you have to expect some of that you know, in any country—the rows going on—everybody is in a foolish state. I know a place where a picture of Jack Reed hangs in one of the college houses, and there'd be a few boys want to take it down because he's buried in the Kremlin with Stalin, Lenin. American boy, Harvard. (unpublished typescript, Amherst College Library)

37.6   Heartily know] From Emerson's poem "Give All to Love." Frost later said, in a November 1951 talk: "Without question, all of us are involved in the political life. Some people try to stay aloof from it but even the most aloof are touched, if only faintly, by the implications of politics. For instance, we are always talking about loyalty. A poet said: 'When half-gods go, you get whole gods.' It was subversive of Emerson to write that. Poets are always thinking about loyalty, which, after all, is the key to politics. There is party loyalty, country loyalty, idea loyalty, or ideal loyalty. Freedom, in a sense, is the breaking away from all attachments. But it is not easy to break away. And you don't do it because you wish to do it. You do it because you have to, almost against your own inclination." A typescript of the talk, titled "Poetry and Society," is held at the University of Michigan Library among a collection of papers, business documents, and printed matter that once belonged to Kathleen Morrison. The occasion for the talk is not known, though Lisa Seale, who has done more work on Frost's public readings and lectures than anyone else, informs me that he spoke at least four times in November of 1951: at West Town, at Tufts, at Dartmouth, and at Simmons. "Poetry and Society" might have been delivered at one or several of these places. The talk was first published by the present editor in *The Robert Frost Review* 12 (Fall 2002): 12–15.

37.8   Astarte] "The episode as recorded by the Carthaginian navigator who first came in contact with pygmies (not anthropoid apes) on the coast of Sierra Leone runs as follows in *The Periplus of Hanno*, translated from the Greek by Wilfred H. Schoff (Philadelphia, 1912), page 5: 'In the recess of this bay there was an island, like the former one, having a lake, in which there was another island full of savage men. There were women, too, in even greater number. They had hairy bodies, and the interpreters called them *Gorrilae*. When we pursued them we were unable to take any of the men; for they all escaped, by climbing the steep places, and defending themselves with stones; but we took three of the women, who bit and scratched their leaders, and would not follow us. So we killed them and flayed them, and brought their skins to Carthage. For we did not voyage further, provisions failing us.'"

37.9   I quote from memory.] "'Diction and sound seem to be dominant; meaning, on the other hand, has been held to be nonessential (and in some few cases even detrimental) to true poetry.' *Columbia Encyclopedia* (New York, 1935), page 1412."

37.10   Merrimack River] "'In 1764 the Connecticut River was established as the western boundary, with the present Vermont belonging to New York. The dispute between Vermont and New Hampshire as to the exact line of demarcation continued into the 20th century.' *Columbia Encyclopedia*, art. 'New Hampshire.'"

38. [Preface to *A Masque of Mercy* (1947)]

Frost's brief preface appeared with his *Masque of Mercy* in *The Atlantic Monthly* 180 (November 1947): 68. Edward Weeks, editor of *The Atlantic Monthly* and a friend of Frost's, wrote to Kathleen Morrison in August 1947, enclosing galleys of the *Masque* and asking her to prepare a brief biographical headnote to accompany it. Frost composed the headnote—his original manuscript draft is held at Dartmouth College—and with Morrison's assistance prepared a clean typescript of it for Weeks. The copy-text for the present edition is that typescript of the preface, also held now at Dartmouth College Library. On September 2, Weeks wrote to Morrison: "The biographical note is just what I wanted. I have tinkered with it to make two small changes, and if it now meets with your approval, it will stand" (unpublished letter, Dartmouth College Library). There are in fact six differences in wording between the typescript and the published text of Frost's brief remarks. No doubt Weeks is responsible for them: except for the addition of the clause about the Pulitzer Prizes and a change in spelling in "belilacked," the revisions are indicated in manuscript on the Dartmouth typescript, but neither in Frost's nor in Morrison's hand. Assuming that they are in Weeks's hand, and that they reflect the changes alluded to in his September 2 letter, I have ignored these revisions, following instead the text as it appears in typing. I have conventionalized the styling of titles. The collation lists all variants in wording between the typing of the typescript (as distinct from the manuscript revisions made on it), the original manuscript, and the published text.

Collation

MS = Frost's manuscript, held now at Dartmouth College Library. TS = Frost/Morrison typescript, held at Dartmouth College Library. 1st = First appearance as headnote to *A Masque of Mercy* in *The Atlantic Monthly*.

38.1   Robert Frost] R.F. MS; Frost, who has four times been awarded the Pulitzer Prize for Poetry, 1st

38.1   Now in] MS; In 1st

*38.1   *Masque of Mercy*] 1st; MASQUE OF MERCY TS

38.1   and] MS; as in 1st

*38.1   *Masque of Reason*] 1st; MASQUE OF REASON TS

38.1   the Bible is taken care of] MS; he pays his respects to the Bible 1st

38.1   some time] MS; in the future 1st

38.1   title] 1st; ~ of MS

39. A Romantic Chasm (1948)

"A Romantic Chasm" first appeared as the preface to an English edition of Frost's works: *A Masque of Reason, by Robert Frost, containing A Masque of Reason, A Masque of Mercy (Two New England Biblicals) together with Steeple Bush and other Poems* (London: Jonathan Cape, 1948). Dartmouth College Library holds two typescripts and one manuscript of the essay. The first typescript bears manuscript corrections in Morrison's hand and in Frost's. This represents an early draft of the essay that differs extensively from the published version. There is also a manuscript in Morrison's hand, with a marginal note in Frost's on page one: "As dictated to Kay." This represents a later version of the essay that differs from the published version in a few minor details. Finally, there is a typescript with a few manuscript corrections in Morrison's hand and one in Frost's; this is based on the Morrison manuscript and represents the final version of the essay. The development of the essay under Frost's care ends with this typescript, which provides the copy-text for the present edition. I have corrected two misprints. Both of them occur in the following sentence, which reads in the copy-text: "I would go to any length short of idolatry to keep great Britain within speaking, or at least shouting distance, of America in the trying times ahead" (39.3 in the present edition). In the earlier typescript and in the manuscript the "g" is, appropriately, capitalized in "Great Britain," as it is also in the first appearance. I have also moved the comma after "distance" to where the grammar seems to demand its placement: after the word "shouting." This emendation follows both the earlier typescript and the first appearance. (No comma appears after either "distance" or "shouting" in the manuscript.)

The differences between the early typescript and the final version are too extensive to be recorded usefully in the collation, so I list only the most striking difference here. Following is a passage (39.4) as it stands, first, in the finished text and, second, in the earlier typescript:

> Suppose American had got as far away from English as present day English is from Chaucerian, or at least Elizabethan; obviously my verse by being in American would automatically, without mental expense on my part, be raised to the rank of having to be annotated. It might be advertised as with glossary. It might be studied.

> Suppose American to have got as far away from present-day English as present-day English has from Elizabethan or even Chaucerian. There would be the compensation that my verse by being in American would be automatically raised to the high rank of having to be annotated. It might be advertised as with glossary. It might have to be translated from American into English. Anyway it would have to be studied. And to be studied is the great thing in life—to be studied at once and not wait for time to make us puzzling. It may be gathered that I would hardly refuse the crown of having to be studied myself if it was pressed on me. But ay me, I fondly dream.

Frost chose to omit the last two sentences from the published text. Perhaps they show too clearly his resentment over the condescension with which he was treated by critics whose tastes ran more to "high modernists" like Pound and Eliot, who had in fact achieved "the high rank of having to be annotated." See also Frost's remarks in the unedited transcript of his talk "On Emerson," likewise omitted from the published version: "It is smart today, you know, to be reading St. John Perse, or T.S. Eliot, or me. No, leave me out. Not smart. 'Cause I'm just the country boy."

Collation

TS = Frost's finished typescript (copy-text for the present edition). 1st = First appearance as the introduction to *A Masque of Reason* (London, 1948). TS-B = Early typescript draft of the essay. MS = Manuscript in Kathleen Morrison's hand, as dictated to her by Frost.
39.2   tired the sun down] MS; tired the sun {not present} 1st
39.2   mansion] 1st; ~ where he lives MS
*39.3   Great Britain] 1st, TS-B, MS; great Britain TS
*39.3   shouting, distance] 1st, TS-B; shouting distance, TS
39.3   only one accent.] 1st; only one accent, and ecdysiast for the artiste who doesn't mind stripping naked so it be of false finery. MS
39.4   the beneficiaries] 1st; beneficiaries MS

Explanatory Notes
  39.1   had it from Kipling] See Kipling's poem "An American":

> Inopportune, shrill-accented,
> The acrid Asiatic mirth
> That leaves him, careless 'mid his dead,

> The scandal of the elder earth.
> How shall he clear himself, how reach
> Your bar or weighed defence prefer—
> A brother hedged with alien speech
> And lacking all interpreter?

39.1   great book] H. L. Mencken's study of American English, *The American Language* (1919; revised 1921, 1923, 1936, with supplementary volumes in 1945, 1948).

39.2   Edward Thomas] Edward Thomas (1878–1917), British poet, essayist, and critic. Frost formed a close friendship with Thomas during his sojourn in England, 1912–15.

39.2   Jack Haines] Frost first met John Haines, an English barrister and amateur botanist, while in England during 1912–15.

39.3   Mark Curtius] *Chambers Biographical Dictionary*: "A noble Roman youth who in 362 B.C. is said to have leapt on horseback into a chasm which had opened in the forum and which the soothsayers said would only be filled by throwing into it the most precious treasure of Rome."

39.3   boustrophedon] "An ancient mode of writing in alternate lines, one from right to left, and the next from left to right, as fields are plowed" (*Webster's New Twentieth Century Dictionary*).

39.3   Ivor Brown] Ivor John Carnegie Brown, philologist, literary historian, and biographer.

39.7   Coleridgian surmise] Frost alludes to the "romantic chasm" of Samuel Taylor Coleridge's poem, "Kubla Kahn," from which he takes this essay's title: "But O, that deep romantic chasm . . ." Frost also likely alludes to the phrase "wild surmise" from Keats's sonnet "On First Looking into Chapman's Homer."

39.7   "entertain her always as a stranger"] Frost adapts line 29 of the anonymous English poem "Preparations." He encountered it first in *The Oxford Book of English Verse*, edited by Sir Arthur Quiller-Couch.

39.7   chapter and verse . . . Saint Mark] See Mark 4:11–12.

40. [Unpublished Contribution to *Understanding Poetry* (1950)]

Frost prepared this essay at the request of Robert Penn Warren, who was, with Cleanth Brooks, one of the authors of the widely used textbook *Understanding Poetry*. The request was conveyed to Frost by Charles A. Madison of the College Department at Henry Holt and Company, Frost's publisher and also the publisher of *Understanding Poetry*. The content of Frost's contribution is in part explained by the letter in which that request was made. Madison writes on January 5, 1950: "In preparing the revision of *Understanding Poetry*, to be published by us in late spring, Robert Penn Warren is eager to make clear to students how good poems are actually written. He wants to show that a poem does not emerge finished and feathered from its creator's brain but sometimes undergoes radical revision in the several drafts. To this end he would like to include several drafts of good poems by Housman and yourself—poems that have undergone fundamental changes in the writing. He already has good specimens of Housman drafts and the permission from Laurence Housman to use them. He is also very eager to get some from you—drafts of perhaps two relatively short poems and, if you will be good enough, your own comments on the writing of the poems. He realized that this would be asking a good deal of you and seemed uneasy about doing so. To make it easier for him I told him I would write you my-self" (unpublished letter, Dartmouth College Library). Frost drafted his response and in-cluded it in the body of a February 26 letter to Madison, written while he was wintering in Florida. He prefaced the text of the essay with the following remark: "Do you suppose a statement like the following (or some part of it) would meet Mr. Warren's requirements? If not why not put him in correspondence with me so we can work out something to-gether. I want to be amenable." Frost appears to have been unsatisfied with his remarks as they then stood. In any case he writes the following before signing the letter to Madison: "It occurs to me that it would have been better if I had a list of the things of mine Mr Warren is using in his book. Then I could have tried my recollections on them. I wish he would speak up." For reasons not clear to me, the contribution was never included in *Un-derstanding Poetry* and is published here for the first time. The Dartmouth typescript was prepared from a manuscript draft that exists in the pages of one of Frost's notebooks (also held now at Dartmouth); that is to say, corrections and excisions indicated interlineally in the manuscript are reflected in typing in the typescript, which forms the basis of the pres-ent edition.

Collation

TS = The Dartmouth typescript.
*40.1   with any poem] with any peom TS
*40.1   "The Song of the Wandering Aengus"] *The Song* of the Wandering Aengus TS
*40.1   tortured himself] tortured hi mself TS
*40.1   sneaking preference] sneaking prefernce TS
*40.1   bear me out in] bear me outin TS
*40.1   "November Days," "The Mountain," "After Apple-Picking," "The Woodpile,"
"Desert Places," "The Gift Outright," "The Lovely Shall Be Choosers," "Directive."] "No-vember Days", "The Mountain", "After Apple-Picking", "The Woodpile", "Desert Places", "The Gift Outright", "The Lovely Shall Be Choosers", "Directive". {Editor's note: No poem titled "November Days" exists amongst Frost's published work, though the phrase appears in "My November Guest," which may be what he here has in mind. There is also, of course, the poem titled simply "November," which appears in *A Witness Tree* (1942).} TS
*40.1   tractability] tractability TS
*40.1   inspired airs] in spired airs TS
*40.2   under head,] under head TS
*40.2   saw it in] saw itin TS
*40.2   disturbed] distrbed TS
*40.2   you in."] you in". TS
*40.2   Rochester, New York] Rochester New York

Explanatory Notes

40.2   a famous poet] Presumably Ezra Pound, whom Frost met in London in 1913.
40.2   lady in Rochester] Unidentified.

41. [Letter to the American Booksellers' Association (1950)]

Frost's letter was apparently solicited by the American Booksellers' Association on the occasion of its fiftieth anniversary. It was published only one time: in facsimile in the *American Booksellers' Association Almanac 1950* (New York: American Booksellers' Association, 1950), 50. I reprint the text of that facsimile exactly. Letters from Carl Sandburg, Christopher Morley, and Franklin Delano Roosevelt (dated 1942) appear alongside Frost's—all of them in facsimile.

42. [Contribution to *The World's Best* (1950)]

Frost's remarks on being anthologized appeared first in *105 Greatest Living Authors Present the World's Best,* edited by Whit Burnett (New York: Dial Press, 1950), 52. I have found no manuscripts or typescripts of his remarks. The copy-text for the present edition is the first appearance. The text there is given in italic type. I have set it in roman.

Explanatory Notes

42.1   a few] Frost chose six poems for inclusion in *The World's Best:* "The Need of Being Versed in Country Things," "The Mountain," "The Road Not Taken," "The Grindstone," "The Gift Outright," "One Step Backward Taken."

43. [Poetry and School (1951)]

These aphorisms appeared together under the title "Poetry and School" in *The Atlantic Monthly* 187 (June 1951): 30–31. A headnote explains: "In his poems he speaks for the country at large; for three decades he has talked and read to college students, and these remarks from his Notebooks show the glint of his philosophy." I have been unable to locate the manuscript of "Poetry and School," though clearly Frost prepared it himself. The only available text is the first appearance, the copy-text for the present edition. Lawrance Thompson reports a June 1951 conversation in which Frost made reference to "Poetry and School": "This year, in teaching the boys, he has used the 'ABC and 123' 'Letters and Numbers' approach on the students, which he says he has summarized in his Atlantic article, each one of those articles being, he says, the key thoughts around which he has built different talks" (NOTES). The "articles" mentioned are actually the separate paragraphs or entries in the "Poetry and School" essay. Reprinted below are several extracts from talks Frost gave on themes sounded in "Poetry and School," as well as similarly relevant extracts from Thompson's "Notes on Conversations with Frost." Together these should give the reader an idea as to what Frost was "teaching the boys" circa 1951.

Explanatory Notes

43.11   Catullus . . . *mens animi*] Frost alludes to a phrase in Catullus's sixty-fifth poem. See note 31.2.

43.12   poetry and prose too regarded as poetry is the renewal of words] In a talk titled "Poetry and Society," Frost has this to say: "Freedom beyond freedom—freedom into the indefinable—that's what we invariably want. Against this, we know all life tends to congeal. Our own blood runs and then congeals. And always we balk against this congealing tendency. We want something that renews and renews. Poetry, to my mind, is the renewal of words, the setting them free. That is what a poet is doing: loosening the words. He has a dread of words become cant, jargon, which is the opposite of poetry. The philosophers come along and say, 'Enough of this jargon. We use a fresh language.' But they arrive soon enough at a technical jargon of their own. So you see, our lives are forever closing, congealing, and then breaking up, and then closing again. Poetry, then, is the breaking up of the congealed." (For details about this talk, see 37.6 above.) Frost also spoke of poetry as the "renewal of words" in a commencement address at Oberlin College in 1937: "I don't know how much of a fight you make to hang onto what's yours," he told the young graduates. "You're younger than I by a good many years, and I suppose the older one is the harder he hangs onto what he's built into his life. When the meaning goes out of anything, as happens, forms crumble, formulae . . . But the whole function of poetry is the renewal of words, is the making of words mean again what they meant. Let me take one or two illustrations, in politics and religion. I heard as I marched in today, ahead of me in the line, two words in the center—I don't know what the rest was. The two words were "divine right." Words with an ancient history, words with a great history, words that too many people too easily give up. They've been laughed out of their meaning. But before I'd give them up I'd . . . In government we have two things: we have the ruler and the ruled. We have two answers . . . Its first answerability is to itself. Its second is the consent of the ruled. Consent? How can there be consent without some guidance to consent to? We've had rulers in this country who had nothing within themselves to which to consent to— one with ear to ground, attempting to find out what people would consent to." For information about this commencement address, see the discussion in the Editorial Principles section of this volume. The text given here is taken from a typescript of the address held at Oberlin College and published in *CPPP* (756).

43. 13   Emotion emoves a word . . . true radical.] See Lawrance Thompson's report of a July 1941 conversation with Frost: "He said that to him poetry could be intelligible if he interpreted the first half of [Theodore] Green's 'emotive-conative' phrase [used in Green's book *The Arts and the Art of Criticism*] as meaning 'moving' a word or words out of their fixed context, as though one should use a word in a poem in such a way that the reader would say, 'On first thought, this word seems to be used incorrectly; but on second thought, this word is being used as it might be used to make sense; to make a new kind of sense out of it.' And it was this elasticity of words which seemed to RF to preserve the potential freshness of words. Any further interest in semantics wearied RF, and he would have none of it; spoke of his chronic hate for semantics. Poetry for him was that playing with words to make meanings sharper, fresher, than they had been before. And he thought of words thus 'moved out' of their old context and then snapping back into the conventional context, to await the coming of someone else who would move the word into a new context and thus renew it" (NOTES). See also Thompson's report of an August 1956 talk Frost gave at Bread Loaf: "Got to talking about observing words that were poetically useful and went briefly into Ogden and [I. A.] Richards as saying that words were useless because we were all caught up in a sea of metaphors, and they mean so much that we are drowned by the multiple meanings. No, says Frost, the function of the writer is to make words mean what he intends them to mean. The intent is of major importance to Frost . . . Of course, the metaphor or symbol can become somehow 'spoiled' for fresh us-

age. Such, for example, is the word 'cross.' That kind of word, for the writer, has become too 'lousy' for usage—'lousy' with meaning. But there are other words which we use daily that are so restricted in meaning that they might be called 'dead end words.' Such words are best suited for fresh poetic usage because they haven't been spoiled. The poetic game is to let them have their 'dead end meaning' and simultaneously to let the context endow them with additional meanings. When you get that double effect you can call it 'double meaning' or ambiguity or double-entendre or metaphor or the part for the whole" (NOTES).

43.17   The escape is to action in words] In its May 21, 1937, edition, *The Christian Science Monitor* reported a talk Frost delivered in Boston on May 10 before the New England Poetry Club, which reads, in part: "Mr. Frost deplores the modern tendency of your people to be so concerned with social and economic problems that they neglect to take any notice of other angles of living. 'That's a form of escape, too—escape from the arts,' he said." Frost had, since the late 1920s, been criticized by left-wing critics as an "escapist" of one sort or another.

44. [Unfinished Preface to an Unpublished Collection of Poems by Hervey Allen (1951)]

This text is prepared from Frost's manuscript preface for a never-published collection of poems by Hervey Allen. Allen, whom Frost knew well, died in 1949. Correspondence regarding the proposed collection of poems, held now at Dartmouth College Library, indicates that Frost was at work on the preface in 1951. His manuscript is now held in the Barrett Collection of the University of Virginia Library. The text of this manuscript was published for the first time in Arnold Grade's *FL* (259–60), and I have relied on his text in interpreting several difficult-to-read words in the manuscript; these are listed in the collation below. However, I do not agree with Grade's conclusion that the two paragraphs of the manuscript represent separate drafts of the preface. It seems to me that they form a single text, the first paragraph being general and theoretical in emphasis, the second being an application of the theory to the particular case of Allen's work. I have corrected several apparent mistakes in the manuscript that seem to derive from slips of the pen on Frost's part. I have also supplied commas in situations where Frost typically employs them in texts prepared for publication. As Grade suggests, the "book heard round the world" mentioned in the second paragraph is Allen's popular novel *Anthony Adverse* (1933).

Collation

MS = holograph manuscript, held at the University of Virginia.
*44.1   ethereal] etherial {Later in the manuscript Frost uses the correct spelling.} MS
*44.1   notion] {Difficult to read in the manuscript.} MS
*44.1   cyclotron] {Difficult to read in the manuscript.} MS
*44.1   wasn't] wasnt MS
*44.1   wicked] {Difficult to read in the manuscript.} MS
*44.1   soul] {Difficult to read in the manuscript.} MS
*44.1   quadruple, none, some, more, most,] {No commas in manuscript.} MS
*44.1   triple, merely some, more,] {No commas in manuscript.} MS
*44.1   burden of] burden MS

*44.2   years to] to to MS
*44.2   all his others,] all his others MS
*44.2   put together,] put together MS
*44.2   if it wasn't] if it wasnt MS

Explanatory Notes

44.1   ethereal] Frost lectured on the topic "What begins more ethereal than substantial in lyric ends more substantial than ethereal in epic" in Gainesville, Fla., in 1951. Mention of the lecture occurs among Frost's annotations in the copy of *Complete Poems of Robert Frost, 1949* that he carried with him during his schedule of readings and talks in the fall and early winter of 1951. This copy of the book is held at the University of Virginia and is described in Crane, *Descriptive Catalogue,* 90–91. An intimation of the way Frost sometimes handled the theme in lectures may be gleaned from a 1956 address at Sarah Lawrence College: "Now there's a word we've had that goes wrong—I don't know whether you've encountered it or not—there's the word, 'the [American] dream.' I wonder about it—how much you've encountered it. I have it thrown in my face every little while, always by somebody who thinks the dream has not come true. And then . . . I wonder what the dream is, or why . . . I wonder who dreamed it. Did Tom Paine dream it, did Thomas Jefferson dream it, did George Washington dream it? Gouverneur Morris? And lately I've decided that the best dreamer of it was Madison. You see I've been reading the Federal[ist] papers. But anyway I am always concerned with it. Is it a dream that's gone by? Each age is a dream that is dying they say, or one that is coming to birth. It depends on what you mean by an age. Is the age over in which that dream had its existence—has it gone by? Can we treat the Constitution as if it were something gone by? Can we interpret it out of existence? By calling it a living document, it means something different every day, something new every day, until it doesn't mean anything that it meant to Madison. And this thought occurred to me the other day when I picked it up. Has the dream, instead of having come true, has it done something that the witches talk about? Has it simply materialized? Young writers that I know, novelists that I know, began as poets, most of them. They began more ethereal than substantial, and have ended up more substantial than ethereal. And is that what's happened to our country—has the ethereal idealism of the founders materialized into something too material? In South America within this last year at a convention I heard everybody regretting or fearing or worrying about our materialism. Not for our own sake, but for their sake because we were misleading them into a material future, see, for the whole world, and anxiety for us. I told them we were anxious about that too. We have scales in all our bathrooms to see how material we are getting" (*A Talk For Students,* New York: Fund for the Republic, 1956). The published text of Frost's address was prepared, without his assistance, from an audio recording.

45. [Contribution to *The Tufts Weekly* (1952)]

This brief article appeared first in *The Tufts Weekly* (October 11, 1952: 1), as part of a supplementary issue celebrating the hundredth anniversary of Tufts College. A facsimile of Frost's manuscript of the article was later printed in *The Tuftonian* (Winter 1957: 4). I have reprinted the text of that manuscript, correcting in one case what is apparently an oversight on Frost's part. The first sentence of the manuscript reads: "Prof Fay invited . . .," with an arrow pointing upward between the first two words indicating that an addition is to be made. The addition is not made in the manuscript, though it is in the text as published in *The Tufts Weekly:* "Professor Charles Fay invited . . ." Also, Professor Blanchard's first name, Harold, is written in the margin of the manuscript, perhaps in Kathleen Morrison's hand. Frost intended that the names of the professors should be given correctly and in full, and I have used "Professor" instead of "Prof" in keeping with Frost's usage of the unabbreviated term later in the article.

Collation

MS = Frost's manuscript (copy-text for the present edition). 1st = First appearance in *The Tufts Weekly.*
*45.1   Professor Charles] 1st; Prof MS
45.1   time and have] time, "Birches," "The Road Not Taken," and "The Sound of Trees," and have 1st {It is not clear who made this addition, which is not indicated, or even suggested, on Frost's manuscript.}

46. The Hear-Say Ballad (1953)

"The Hear-Say Ballad" was first published as the preface to *Ballads Migrant in New England* by Helen Hartness Flanders and Marguerite Olney (New York: Farrar, Straus and Young, 1953). The Frosts were friends of Helen Flanders, and of her husband Senator Ralph E. Flanders of Vermont. Frost had in fact read a manuscript of *Ballads Migrant* some years before it actually went to press. Dartmouth College Library holds two versions of the essay: a fragmentary early draft on two leaves in Frost's hand, and a typescript of the finished essay with several corrections in his hand and two in Kathleen Morrison's. The manuscript has only a few sentences in common with the finished text, and is about one quarter the length. On the other hand, the revisions on the typescript are quite minor. For example, Frost has revised: "We may need" to "We have a right" (46.2). Later in the same paragraph, obviously at Frost's instruction, Morrison has revised the phrase: "they [i e , the ballads] still stay game" to "they have the vitality to stay game" (46.2). In the last paragraph Frost has changed "accompany" to "go with" (46.4) and "She was" to "She has been" (46.4). There are a few more such corrections and revisions.

The text as published in *Ballads Migrant* is corrupt. The most significant of the variant readings introduced into the published text could not have been produced by Frost. Where the typescript reads: "That might be the definition of a true ballad to distinguish it from a true poem," the published text reads: "That might be the definition of a true poem" (46.4). Frost often stressed that the "music of music" and "the music of poetry" are distinct. Consider his remark in a June 27, 1960, lecture at Bread Loaf: "The music of poetry is not like the music of music. And there's a conflict always. There's always a conflict with anything set to music. You are honored by having things set to music. I feel flattered a little but I'm always uncomfortable. The whole thing spoils my fun. It spoils the double thing that is in the poem—it fits the meter but the rhythm is a different thing. The music can't do the double thing in the poem" (Reginald Cook, *Robert Frost: A Living Voice* [Amherst: University of Massachusetts Press, 1974], 154). In keeping with this belief, he is distinguishing, in "The Hear-Say Ballad," the "true ballad" from the "true poem," not offering a definition of "the true poem" which *includes* the ballad, as the published text suggests. The copy-text for the present edition is the typescript as corrected by Frost and Morrison. There, Frost misprints Francis James Child's name "Childe." I have given the correct spelling.

I include here Frost's commentary on an English ballad called "Thomas the Rhymer," which he knew by heart: "Some people think that beauty is truth. They aren't ineffable enough though to know that that isn't so. Keats didn't pretend to be ineffable when he said that: 'Beauty is truth, truth beauty . . .' No. One of the poets a long time ago wrote like this: he got up a story about a fellow called True Thomas; it's in an old ballad: 'True Thomas lay on Huntley bank, / And a wonder came riding by,' something supernatural came riding by, a beautiful lady. And he rose up from where he was, and 'louted low down,' it says, 'to his knee.' And she says: 'Rise up, Thomas! Who do you think I am?' He says: 'You're so beautiful, you must be the Queen of Heaven!' And she says: 'Oh, you couldn't make a greater mistake! I'm only the Queen of Fairyland!' You see, she was the Queen of Beauty, but not of Truth." The comments are taken from Frost's "Remarks on the Occasion of the Tagore Centenary." John Frederick Nims transcribed Frost's remarks from a tape recording and published them in *Poetry* 99 (November 1961): 106–19. Frost did not assist in preparing the published text. He later told Lawrance Thompson that the Asia Society paid him $1000 to deliver the address.

Collation

1st = First appearance of the essay as the preface to *Ballads Migrant in New England*. TS = Frost's finished typescript.

46.2   in and brought to book] to book 1st

*46.2   Child] 1st; Childe TS

46.4   till] until 1st

46.4   ballad to distinguish it from a true poem.] poem. 1st

46.4   of music] {not present} 1st

46.4   as the] the 1st

Explanatory Notes

46.2   Thus Addison] In Addison's essay "On Popular Poetry; the Ballad of Chevy Chase," number 70 in his series for *The Spectator*.

44.2   Child] Francis James Child, American scholar and professor at Harvard University. Child published *English and Scottish Ballads* (8 volumes, 1857–58) and *English and Scottish Popular Ballads* (5 volumes, 1883–98).

47. The Prerequisites (1954)

"The Prerequisites" appeared first under the title (not supplied by Frost) "A Poet, Too, Must Learn the Magic Way of Poetry" in the *New York Times Book Review* (March 21, 1954): 1. It next appeared under the title "The Prerequisites" as the preface to a selection of Frost's poetry, *Aforesaid* (New York: Holt, 1954), published on March 25 in celebration of its author's eightieth birthday. An early manuscript draft of the preface is held at Dartmouth College Library. It is a fragment, extremely difficult to read at some points, and represents an early, distinct version of the essay: much of what it contains is not present in the finished text, and much that is present in the finished text is not present in the manuscript. I have been unable to find the finished manuscript or typescript that served as copy-text for the two published texts. Between those two published texts there are several differences in punctuation and one in wording. None of the variants in the *New York Times* seems authoritative. The copy-text for the present edition is the second appearance in *Aforesaid*.

Lawrance Thompson reports in some detail a 1953 conversation he had with Frost about Emerson's poem "Brahma." As the poem seems to have been much on his mind in the months before he published "The Prerequisites," I reprint Thompson's report here: "That got him started, and he reflected that if you left the Hebraic-Christian tradition and turned to the oriental religions, you could find that the word 'sin' did not assume the same prominence. For example, he said, in Emerson's poem 'Brahma,' you got an entirely different picture:

> The strong gods pine for my abode,
> And pine in vain the sacred Seven;
> But thou, meek lover of the good!
> Find me and turn thy back on heaven.

Frost thought 'the sacred seven' was a deliberate error made for the sake of the rhyme; that the reference was to the seven stages of life, the highest stage being Nirvana, where all values were lost in a complete state of peace and rest, without tension and conflict between values. Heaven was a state which might be attained; but Heaven was not the highest, and the great fear was that the individual might get stuck in Heaven without ever reaching the perfect state, Nirvana. There, in Brahmin thought, Frost said, you did not find the word 'sin' employed as either fortunate or unfortunate; the emphasis was on something else. By contrast, the Hebraic-Christian concept started out with a fairy-tale about how God had started man off with the most extreme form of in-breeding that could be imagined: According to the Bible, said Frost, Eden was not the first habitation of man and woman; instead, it was an Experimental Station, made perfect merely for purposes of experiment. God might have permitted Adam to go out and find himself a wife among the daughters of men; but no, God in-bred Adam by forming a new woman out of Adam himself—out of Adam's rib—and then punished Adam for misbehaving with himself. Later on, Frost said, God got impatient with the whole shooting match, and decided to drown all mankind. You might have thought he would start over again; but no, he permitted Noah and Noah's family to start over with further in-breeding. And, said Frost, the next big gesture made by God came when he sent his own son down to earth to take on himself the sins of the world. And, said Frost, this amounted to another kind of deluge, flood, drowning, because ever since that event, the Western World had been practically drowned again in Christianity" (NOTES).

Collation

47.2   the Bering Strait] Bering Straits {First appearance of the essay in the *New York Times Book Review*.}

Explanatory Notes

47.3   "Brahma"] By Emerson.

47.9   Titans . . . Yidags] Categories of being in Buddhism. Frost explains in a talk delivered at Bread Loaf in 1953: "There are three things, called the three poisons which keep us from attaining Nirvana and so getting out of the round of existence. And the round of existence? You have to be careful about that. In translation, it's often translated as 'the wheel' of existence. Wheel isn't good. That's been chucked. The round of existence. And you want to get out of that: your object is to get out of that, you get dizzy getting born into so many beautiful things. The things you can be born into, you know, are angels, human beings, animals, purgatorians, titans, and yidags. That's all. Even when you're an angel, you haven't got out. The three poisons that keep you out are the pig, the cock, the snake. Can you make anything of them? Probably not . . . Pig? It just means ignorance. Now the cock means ambition, desire. And it has to do more with desire than anything else. The snake? It's anger. Those are the three poisons that keep you from becoming the only nothing that's something" (unpublished typescript, Alderman Library, University of Virginia).

47.9   deceptively Christian] Frost had some interesting, if tantalizingly incomplete, things to say about Asian religion—specifically, Buddhism—and its possibly "deceptive" relation to certain aspects of Christianity. He often touched the topic in his readings, as in a 1950 talk at Kenyon College: "Another thing that I have been thinking as I listen here. It is a great joke—it is one of the great jokes of history that we Westerners should have picked up an Asiatic religion and gone back peddling it in Asia. We call it Christianity, but it's Asiatic and I'm going to say too that I don't believe that it ever really belonged to us anyway. We are not very good if you test us by the Sermon on the Mount. It's a very pacifist Asiatic sort of thing . . . [T]here is the separateness . . . of our thinking—we'll say the Asiatic and the European[,] the Northwestern[—]that will always be mixing together, mixing and mixing for the next billion years. And I shall always be a little anxious for the next billion years, wherever I am—a little anxious for the spiritual side, the Asiatic side, I can see that. I don't think myself[—]privately I probably don't think that this world was ever meant to be a place where your soul would automatically be saved. You see, that is Asiatic, not European" ("The Separateness of the Parts," unpublished typescript, Dartmouth College).

47.9   He was a confirmed symbolist.] Perhaps the better to set himself apart from the emerging "archetypal" criticism soon to be associated with such writers as Northrop Frye, Frost remarked in a talk at Amherst College on November 11, 1953: "Different symbols mean different things in different places . . . Whenever people talk about set symbols they're not talking about poetry. Poetry is loose, free" (*The Amherst Student,* November 16, 1953: 1). And the *New York Herald Tribune* quotes him as saying: "Like Aaron Burr when someone asked him, 'Burr, how is it with your soul?' I am a little coy about that. I am a little coy about where the human race is headed. As a matter of fact, whenever you can't pin me down on some specific point, it's due to my quality of uncatchability" (March 26, 1954).

48. [Message to the Poets of Japan (1954)]

This brief "message" bears no title. Dartmouth College Library holds a typescript with manuscript corrections in Frost's hand and in Kathleen Morrison's. I have found no other versions of it. Frost's reference to his age (eighty) dates the message to 1954; the occasion may have been a greeting sent to him by some Japanese poets. I have been unable to determine whether this "message" was published. The Dartmouth typescript is typed all in capital letters, perhaps by Frost himself. Some of the manuscript corrections are ambiguous. Above the sentence beginning "There must first be" (48.1) the clause "I must be personal before I can hope to be interestingly interpersonal" is inserted interlinearly, and it is not clear where it is to be placed. Frost has also inserted handwritten brackets around the clause "An instinct told me long ago" (48.1), though their meaning is not clear. I have chosen the placement of the interlinear revisions that seems to me to require the least accommodation on the part of the sentences already in type. I have also printed the text in regular upper- and lowercase typography.

Explanatory Notes

48.1   An instinct told me] Frost often sounded the theme, as in his "Remarks on the Occasion of the Tagore Centenary": "I'm a terrible nationalist myself—formidable. And I can't see how one can be international unless there are some nations to be *inter* with. And the clearer and distincter the better. I can deal with them well even when I'm more or less at variance with them; if they're clear and sharp and all. And I don't care how far it goes into what you might call some sort of noble antagonism, if we can stand off and look each other in the eye. We can come to whatever we come to; blows or not blows, and we needn't blackguard each other. We needn't be ignoble. I've always felt that, all my life" (for a full citation see the notes to "The Hear-Say Ballad").

49. [Caveat Poeta (1955?)]

"Caveat Poeta" was not published during Frost's lifetime. The typescript from which the present edition derives is held at Dartmouth College Library and is, apparently, the only surviving text of the essay. The date of composition is unknown, though it dates from after 1938, when Kathleen Morrison first became associated with Frost, as it bears manuscript corrections in her hand. On the basis of its themes and tone I place the essay in the mid 1950s. I have adopted the essay's refrain—"caveat poeta"—as a title since no title is given in the typescript. A cover sheet to the typescript includes a paragraph, perhaps introductory to the essay, dictated by Frost to Morrison: "It should be amusing to people that I should be the one asked to answer for the harm done by the educational system to the fine arts—I who never went to school and college more than six years of my life and have nothing to do with them except as a teacher in them now and then and the object of their lavish patronage. Very extraordinary, nothing like it in the world's history." There also appears in Morrison's hand an underlined word printed at the top of the cover sheet which appears to read: "Karsh." The only Karsh I know of in connection with Frost is the Armenian-born Canadian photographer Yousuf Karsh, who once took a portrait of him.

Collation

*49.2   initiative of] initiative of of

Explanatory Notes

49.1   Much goes on in college that is against the spirit] Frost remarks in a 1962 lecture at the Choate School, referring to a man who approached him on a train: "He asked me if I didn't think education spoiled poetry. It's a queer thing after all[,] that idea about education. And I asked him 'Why did you stand it? Didn't you care for the poetry enough to get out, same as I did?['] You know it's a curious notion that people have that the academic world lives on poetry, with all the stuff you translate, about all of it is verse. And then in the English it isn't so much that way[,] the proportion is a little lower, still largely the greater names, Shakespeare and all. I myself have [ever] had that feeling about it that it was inimical . . . the way poetry was handled in school and college. That was why I ran away [i.e., from Dartmouth College in 1892]. I ran away because I was a restless boy and I wanted to try myself. I didn't want to be considered a pretty good writer considering I was a freshman, a pretty good writer considering I was a sophomore, a pretty good writer considering I was a junior, a pretty good writer considering I was an undergraduate. I wanted to find out whether I could write or not. And I had that perhaps too young, that feeling of wanting to do it" (unpublished typescript, Amherst College Library). And the *New York Herald Tribune* for January 17, 1958, reports Frost as saying, in an article titled "Robert Frost: An Appreciation": "I would much rather receive a degree from a university than an education. I was looking into the new Oxford Dictionary and there were the 800 words of Basic English and a couple of rules of grammar. That's all anybody needs. It shows that there's not much sense in getting an education."

49.2 Meccano] "An instructional game played with miniature metal parts from which engineering models are constructed" (*Concise Oxford Dictionary*).

49.3 The conventions have to be locked horns with] Lawrance Thompson reports a conversation he had with Frost in the early 1960s: "The Jesus story is a very pretty story if you take it as a story of the crucifixion of 'the spirit' by 'respectability,' or by orthodoxy. But that kind of crucifixion is what always happens: of necessity, the spirit is always harnessed into conventions. We have to have the conventions; we want a doctor with a doctor's certificate, and those without certificates are likely to be fakers or quacks or crooks. But: the best of everything is always outside convention. Frost went on to remind me that he had said it another way, long ago: 'There is more poetry outside of verse than in; more religion outside of church than in; more love outside of marriage than in.' This time, he went on to say that he himself had lived a life in which he had chosen to stay outside, and he had gotten away with it; he hadn't been crucified for it. But lots of people had tried to write him off because of the way he took" (NOTES). An interesting variation on this theme occurs later in Thompson's "Notes" (this time he is quoting Frost directly): "There is more wisdom outside philosophy than in; more religion outside the church than in; more love outside of marriage than in; more poetry outside of verse than in, and you see where all that leaves me: I'm inside the conventions of poetry, and believe in the necessity of all conventions" (NOTES). The meaning of the last remark seems to be: "You see where all that leaves me—namely, in a tough position: I am inside the conventions of poetry and believe in conventions, and yet I know that there is, in a sense, more poetry outside of verse," etc.

50. [Perfect Day—A Day of Prowess (1956)]

"A Perfect Day—A Day of Prowess" appeared first in *Sports Illustrated* (July 23, 1956): 51–53. An editorial headnote explains the occasion: "The All-Star Game is an All-American affair. Appropriately, SPORTS ILLUSTRATED invited America's greatest living poet to sit in the grandstand as guest columnist. Herewith, his impressions, which he sums up happily as a 'Perfect Day—a Day of Prowess.'" As Frost's remarks in the essay indicate, the 1956 All-Star game was played in Washington, D.C. No manuscripts or typescripts of "A Perfect Day" are known to survive. My query to the magazine disclosed that they do not retain editorial files for more than a few years; any documents pertaining to Frost's article were long ago disposed of. The copy-text for the present edition is the first appearance in *Sports Illustrated.* I have corrected one obvious misprint.

Collation

*50.8   American League] American Leagur or 1st

Explanatory Notes

50.1   Boyer] Ken Boyer, third baseman for the St. Louis Cardinals; with three hits, Boyer led the National League team to a 7–3 victory.

50.3   Ed Lewis] Edward Morgan Lewis, National League pitcher; afterward President of the University of New Hampshire and a friend of Frost's. Frost spoke at a memorial service for Lewis in 1936. The text of his remarks was later reprinted in *The Services of the University of New Hampshire in Memory of Edward Morgan Lewis A.M., Litt.D., LL.D. Eighth President of the University of New Hampshire and the New Hampshire College of Agricultural and the Mechanic Arts 1927–1936* (Durham: University of New Hampshire, 1936). There, he anticipates the themes of his essay for *Sports Illustrated:* "I first knew 'Ted' Lewis twenty years ago and the first time I saw him, he was reading in public the poetry of a new poet. When a teacher, he was a teacher of literature and chiefly of poetry. He told me once—I was afraid that the story might not be left for me to tell—that he began his interest in poetry as he might have begun his interest in baseball—with the idea of victory—the 'Will to Win.' He was at an Eisteddfod in Utica, an American-Welsh Eisteddfod, where the contest was in poetry, and a bard had been brought from Wales to give judgment and to pick the winner; and the bard, after announcing the winner and making the compliments which judges make, said he wished the unknown victor would rise and make himself known and let himself be seen. (I believe the poems were read anonymously.) The little 'Ted' Lewis sitting there beside his father looked up and saw his father rise as the victor. So poetry to him was prowess from that time on, just as baseball was prowess, as running was prowess. And it was our common ground. I have always thought of poetry as prowess—something to achieve, something to win or lose."

50.3   Edward Thomas] See explanatory note 39.2.

50.3   Anson] Adrian Constantine "Cap" Anson, first baseman for Chicago's National League club from 1876 to 1897. He had a .334 lifetime batting average.

50.4   Kreymborg] Alfred Kreymborg (1883–1966), American poet.

50.6   Clark Griffith's gem of a field] Clark Griffith (1869–1955), pitcher, manager, and owner of the Washington, D.C., Senators. Griffith Stadium, where the Senators played from 1911 to 1960, was named for him.

50.6   Walter Johnson] Walter Perry "The Big Train" Johnson, pitcher for the Washington, D.C., Senators from 1907 to 1927.

50.6   here Gabby Street] Charles Edward "Gabby" Street (1882–1951), a catcher.

50.6   Howard Schmitt] A friend of Frost's from Hamburg, N.Y. (*TLY* 214).

50.6   Temple of the Redlegs] John Ellis Temple, second baseman for the Cincinnati Reds (during the McCarthy years renamed the "Redlegs").

50.7   Musial, Williams, Mays, and Mantle] Stan Musial, first baseman for the St. Louis Cardinals; Ted Williams, outfielder for the Boston Red Sox; Willie Mays, outfielder for the New York and San Francisco Giants; Mickey Mantle, outfielder for the New York Yankees.

50.9   Prowess of course comes first] See Kenneth Burke's etymological meditation in *A Grammar of Motives* (New York: Prentice-Hall, 1945): "Consider, for instance, the Greek word for 'virtue' (*arete*), and the corresponding Latin, *virtus*. Originally, these words had intensely active meanings. Indeed, *arete* is from the same root as *Ares*, the god of war, and as the Latin words for *art* and military *arms*. 'Prowess' would be a good translation for the word in its origins" (42).

51. [Message to the Poets of Korea (1957)]

Frost's "Message to the Poets of Korea" first appeared in *Korea Times* (March 21, 1957: 3), an English-language paper published at Seoul. It was subsequently reprinted in *The Voice of Korea* 14.228 (May 24, 1957: 4), published by the Korean Affairs Institute in Washington. Both publications of this brief essay include a note from Frost to the Korean poet Moh Youn-Sook explaining the occasion for the essay: "Dear Miss Moh: Nothing but the charm of your visit could have inspired me to so much of a message as the enclosed to people I have never met and know so little about. I can't name names and I can't quote poems. My sympathy has to be very general. You may see how much more political than literary it is likely to be under the circumstances. Wouldn't it be great if we could have an era of peace all over the world so that we could come and go with each other on nothing but errands like yours to America. / Robert Frost." Her errand had been a five-month tour in the United States at the invitation of the State Department, during which she visited Frost in Boston. The texts of the published versions of Frost's "message" are identical, with one exception: the *Times* spells the name Moh Youn-sook, whereas the *Voice* spells it Moh Youn Sook. However, both published versions differ in several respects from a typescript of the "message" held at Dartmouth College Library. Obviously, the typescript is not simply a copy of the published version prepared after the fact by a third party. It must have been prepared beforehand by Frost and Morrison, and is therefore the best text since the variants in the *Korea Times* are not apparently authoritative. The Dartmouth typescript is the copy-text for the present edition.

Collation

1st = First appearance in *The Korea Times*.
51.1   poetess Youn-Sook Moh] poetess, Moh Youn-Sook, 1st
51.1   the more] more 1st
51.1   apparently that] apparently than 1st
51.1   individuality and originality that we wouldn't want to see it removed.] individuality. 1st
51.1   Youn-Sook Moh's] Moh Youn-Sook's 1st

Explanatory Notes

51.1   Youn-Sook Moh] Moh Youn-sook, Korean poet, author of *The Bright Zone* (1933), *Wren's Elegy* (1938), *A Jade Hairpin* (1947), and other volumes. She often represented the Republic of Korea at international conferences of writers.

51.1   We must remember] For related remarks on poetry and nationality, see Frost's letter to the editor of *Poetry* in praise of its issue devoted to the poets of Israel (60.1).

52. Maturity No Object (1957)

"Maturity No Object" appeared first as the introduction to *New Poets of England and America* (New York: Meridian Books, 1957), edited by Donald Hall, Robert Pack, and Louis Simpson. Hall asked Frost to write the preface in July 1956. Frost replied with a September 18 letter from Ripton, Vt.:

> Dear Don Hall:
>
> There would be no excuse in the world for my not writing you juniors a preface to your poetry unless it were the poor one that I try to keep a rule of not writing prefaces. But rules aren't meant to be kept. They're meant to break on impulse when you have any impulse left in you; before the evil days when fun ceases. So if you will let me see some of the poems to take off from I'm your cheerful victim. I'll be down in Cambridge in a week or two now where I can see you to talk the matter over. I've been hoping to see you anyway.
>
> Mind you I'm roused up to do this con amore and I'm not so lazy that I can't do it. (Quoted in Edward Connery Lathem, *Robert Frost 100*, 91.)

Dartmouth College Library holds two versions of the complete essay: a typescript with frequent manuscript corrections, revisions, and additions; and a second, neat typescript. Frost appends a brief note to the end of the former: "KM / This must be my letter to you for the moment. Make a careful copy of it in a hurry for Donald Hall. He is after me with his anxiety. / Oh my oh me oh my / Me." Kathleen Morrison ("KM") prepared the second typescript of the essay. It registers a few revisions in punctuation and wording not indicated by Frost on the first, but which nevertheless seem authoritative. (Frost often dictated corrections to Morrison.) The copy-text for the present edition is the second, finished typescript. "Maturity No Object" was later reprinted in *Writing Poetry*, edited by John Holmes (Boston: The Writer, Inc., 1960), with five commas added to the text.

Collation

TS = Frost's finished typescript (copy-text for the present edition). 1st = First appearance as the introduction to *New Poets of England And America*. TS1 = Frost's penultimate typescript, held now at Dartmouth.

52.1   great concern] 1st; great concerns TS1
52.2   I have ever heard] 1st; ever I heard TS1
*52.3   at best irrelevant.] 1st; at best irrevelant. TS
52.4   himself without] 1st; himself with out TS1
52.4   the excitement of the morning from the autointoxication of midnight.] 1st; inspiration from animus, the exhilaration of the morning from the autointoxication of midnight. TS1
52.4   out of doors] 1st; out of door TS1
52.5   poetry poetry] TS1; poetry 1st

Explanatory Notes

52.1   Shakespeare says] In *As You Like It* (3.2.120).
52.2   Landor has set an example] See explanatory note 13.2.

53. [Preface to *A Swinger of Birches,* by Sidney Cox (First Version and Published Version, 1957)]

The first version of this preface presents the text of Frost's original typescript, as submitted to Wilson Follet of New York University Press on June 28, 1956, and now held at Dartmouth College Library. I have reprinted the text of that typescript exactly. (This draft of the preface was published for the first time in *Robert Frost and Sidney Cox,* edited by William R. Evans, 278–80.) Follet's invitation to write the introduction had been pending since October 1954 and it was only after considerable prodding from him that Frost agreed to comply. The poet's irritation is evident in the first version of the preface, which casts the book and the critical acumen of its author in an unflattering light. Nevertheless, Follet accepted the preface just as Frost wrote it. (The full details of their engagement, and the surviving correspondence, are, again, given in Evans, 278–80.) However, after consulting Cox's widow, who wanted him to preface the book for the increased sales his name would bring, Frost decided quite on his own to rewrite the preface, and asked Follet to return the manuscript. He wrote to Follet on September 14: "A letter from Alice Cox puts our situation in an entirely new light. She doesn't share my hesitation about the preface at all. She wants it and is sure Sidney would want it. That's all I ask and should have asked from the first. It doesn't matter to me now about this slight discomfort I may still feel in prefacing my own praises. If it is not too late I should like another chance at the preface to touch it up a little and perhaps make it sound a little less grudging. This is partly for my own sake; if I've got to do the unusual thing I don't want to be ungraceful or ungenerous" (*Robert Frost and Sidney Cox,* 283).

The revised, and much more politic, version of the preface finally reached Follet's office in December 1956. This second version is also reprinted in the present edition. Dartmouth College Library holds two typescripts of it: one is crudely typed and bears a few manuscript corrections in Frost's hand; the other is corrected in Kathleen Morrison's hand. The latter typescript is neatly typed, and differs from the first in several details. It incorporates in type all but one of the revisions made in manuscript on the first. The exception occurs in this sentence: "But we stood up to each other to support each other as two playing cards may be made to in building" (53.2). An alternative wording—"could stand up" for "stood up"—appears in Frost's hand in the margin and interlinearly. Apparently he decided to reject it. The second typescript also bears a note in Morrison's hand: "NYU Press is publishing 'A Swinger of Birches' very soon. Somehow they got Robert to write this introduction." Morrison seems to have given this particular copy of the preface to someone—probably Lawrance Thompson or Edward Connery Lathem. In any event, her note dates the second typescript as contemporary with the preparation of the book, and it is almost certainly the final typescript of the preface prepared by Frost and Morrison for submission to the publisher. It matches the text of the published version exactly, with the sole exception that, there, the title "New Republic" is given in italics. The copy-text for the present edition is the second typescript. I have conventionalized the styling of titles in both versions.

Collation

TS1 = Frost's finished typescript for the first version. TS2 = Frost's finished typescript of the second version (copy-text for the present edition). 1st = First appearance as preface to *A Swinger of Birches*. TSA = Penultimate typescript of the second version, held at Dartmouth.

*53.1   *The New Republic*] the "New Republic" TS1
*53.2   *The New Republic*] the New Republic TS2
53.2   but we stood] 1st; but we could stand TSA
*53.2   He disdained] 1st; He diddanined TS

Explanatory Notes

53.1   He once wrote an article] "The Sincerity of Robert Frost," *The New Republic* (August 25, 1917): 109–11.

54. [Contribution to *Esquire*'s Symposium on "What Worries You Most about America Today?" (1958)]

Frost's remarks appeared as part of a symposium in *Esquire* 51.2 (February 1958): 47–53: "Top Brass of America's intellectual capital give answers to a key question of our time / What Worries You Most About America Today?" Dean Brelis explains in a headnote to the symposium: "The challenges facing the United States are ones which apparently cannot be solved by armies alone. In a time when brain power measures the rise and fall of a nation, the lasting strength of a people is its capacity to think, to plan for the future. In the average-sized American city of Cambridge, Massachusetts, the thinking that is taking place now may well determine the survival of the United States . . . With this in mind, Esquire has asked some of the great minds in America's intellectual center to tell what worries them most about America—to help chart the course of national survival." Arthur M. Schlesinger, Jr., Arthur M. Schlesinger, Sr., H. A. Wolfson, Henry Kissinger, John K. Galbraith, Al Capp, Archibald Macleish, and Paul Tillich also contributed. It is unclear whether their remarks were taken in interview, or whether each man submitted written statements. The copy-text for the present edition is the first appearance in *Esquire*. Apparently no other text of Frost's remarks has been preserved. I am grateful to John Lancaster for bringing this item to my attention.

Frost was an advocate, in his way, for publicly funded secondary schools. He remarks in a 1962 reading at the Choate School: "I go around talking to the high schools. I am envious for the high schools that they don't have quite what our great prep schools have. Somebody has to sit around speeding them up, hardening them up. I have no interest in that. It's all right. But all I am interested in is toning them up—giving them the quality of the right tone about faith and unfaith and all that" (unpublished typescript, Amherst College Library). That "right tone," apparently, is something learned only through an education by poetry.

55. Merrill Moore (1958)

Frost's tribute to his longtime friend, the poet and psychiatrist Merrill Moore, was first published in the *Harvard Medical Alumni Bulletin* 32 (February 1958): 25. Dartmouth College Library holds a typescript of the essay, corrected in Frost's hand and in Morrison's. This represents the last stage to which Frost brought the essay, and therefore forms the copy-text for the present edition. Five variants in punctuation occur in the first appearance, none of which seem authoritative.

Collation

TS = Frost's finished typescript (copy-text for the present edition). 1st = First appearance of the essay in the *Harvard Medical Alumni Bulletin.*
*55.1 was saying] 1st; was aying TS
*55.1 Ransom] 1st; Ransome TS
*55.1 Theodore] 1st; Theodre TS
*55.1 Ransom's] 1st; Ransome's TS
*55.3 and shipping] 1st; ans shipping TS
*55.4 Revenge."] 1st; Revenge" . . TS
*55.4 accompaniment] 1st; accompanimentt TS
*55.4 South Sea] 1st; Sout Sea TS
*55.4 troubadour.] 1st; troubador. TS

Explanatory Notes

55.1 hundred thousand pieces] Moore composed thousands of sonnets.

55.1 Fitts . . . Morrison] Dudley Fitts, American educator, translator of Aristophanes and Sophocles. For Morrison, see explanatory note 33.2.

55.4 "L'Allegro" and "Il Penseroso"] Poems by Milton.

55.4 laws of Petrillo] James Caesar Petrillo (1892–1984), American labor leader and president of the American Federation of Musicians from 1940 until 1958.

55.5 Squantum] A peninsular projection into Boston Harbor at the mouth of the Neponset River.

55.5 Tyrtaeus] Greek poet of the middle seventh century B.C. Tradition holds that his martial verses inspired the Spartans in their victory over the Messenians.

56. [Statement of Robert Frost in the Case of the United States of America versus Ezra Pound (1958)]

Frost's statement was read by Thurman Arnold, counsel for Pound, before the United States District Court for the District of Columbia on April 18, 1958, as a part of the hearings determining whether Pound should be released from St. Elizabeth's Hospital in Washington, D.C., where he was confined on charges of treason. (Frost himself was not present.) On November 16, William Van O'Connor wrote Frost, asking his permission to reprint the statement in *A Casebook on Ezra Pound,* which he was editing with Edward Stone (New York: Thomas Y. Crowell Company, 1959). In his reply, Frost agreed but referred O'Connor to Arnold for the text of the statement. A notarized copy of the statement, signed by Frost, is held at the Jones Library, Amherst. That text is identical to the text published in *A Casebook on Ezra Pound* and is the copy-text for the present edition. Additional typescripts of Frost's statement, of unknown origin, are held at Dartmouth College Library and at Trinity College's Watkinson Library. The text of each is identical to the Jones Library document. Incidentally, Bess Furman reports the following remark Frost made about Pound's *Cantos* in an October 16, 1957, article in the *New York Times:* "The Cantos, those lengthy things, I don't say I'm not up to them. I say they're not up to me.

Nobody ought to like them, but some do, and I let them. That's my tolerance." However, when asked by Richard Gillman for the *Daily Hampshire* (Northampton, Mass.) whether he thought that poets like Pound ought to be held "morally responsible" for their actions, Frost replied: "Yes. They have to take their medicine along with the others. Writing poetry is no excuse for crime. But, I didn't like seeing Pound ending his years ignominiously. Some people have asked me, 'Would you have done the same thing [i.e., advocate Pound's release] for a nobody?' I tell them: I don't hear about nobodies. I heard about Pound" (October 25, 1958, in an article titled "Grand Old Man of Poetry Producing Another Volume").

Explanatory Notes

56.1 I append a page or so] See *A Casebook on Ezra Pound* for the statements of the other writers. These had been compiled by Archibald MacLeish. A full account of Frost's efforts on behalf of Pound is given in *TLY* 247ff.

56.1 Dr. Overholser] Winfred Overholser, Head of St. Elizabeths Hospital in Washington, where Pound was being held.

57. [Remarks on Being Appointed Consultant to the Library of Congress (1958?)]

The copy-text for this edition of Frost's remarks is a typescript held at Dartmouth College Library, revised and corrected in his hand. A note at the head of the first sheet in Kathleen Morrison's hand reads: "Letter / drafted but / never sent." A note at the end in Frost's reads: "R.F. 1962 / I must have said or written this / for them at the Library of Congress last / year or the year before." So far as I have been able to determine, these remarks were never published during Frost's lifetime. In the typescript, Frost misspells the name of General William Starke Rosecrans, the subject of a political biography written by his father. I have given the correct spelling. Frost's first appointment as Consultant in Poetry to the Library of Congress was announced at a press conference held on May 21, 1958, at the Library. (He succeeded Randall Jarrell in the position.) The term was from fall 1958 through spring 1959. However, in June 1959 Quincy Mumford of the Library of Congress proposed that Frost continue serving for an additional three years, this time under the title Honorary Consultant in the Humanities. The remarks here reprinted date from Frost's initial appointment, confirmed by his reference to Senator Ralph Edward Flanders from Vermont. Flanders did not run for reelection in November 1958 and so was no longer Vermont's senator when Frost was reappointed to the consultancy in 1959. It is worth mentioning here that Frost, who dubbed himself "Poet in Waiting" as he assumed his new office, singled out four paintings that he would like to have hanging in his office: Winslow Homer's *Four Bells,* Andrew Wyeth's *Wind from the Sea,* James Chapin's *Ruby Green Singing,* and one from Thomas Eakins's series of paintings of the Schuylkill (title unidentified). See Bess Furman's article in the *New York Times* for October 16, 1958. I add here one further remark for what light it may shed on Frost's use of the office of Consultant in Poetry, and on his thoughts regarding integration: "I once said to [Supreme Court Justice Benjamin] Cardozo—I said to him that the Supreme court will bear watching because it might lose the distinction between being a referee and being a handicapper." Insofar as this bore on the great question of integration, Frost grew, according to this interviewer, Andrew Tully, quite "heated." Frost, it seems, felt that the legislative branch of government had been "delinquent" in this matter: "It should have tended to the things the Supreme Court was driven to in desperation. There. That's telling 'em" (*Petersburg Press*, November 12, 1958, "Poet Frost Ices Up on White House Art").

Collation

*57.1   Rosecrans] Rosencrantz
*57.2   Platonist to] Platonist to to

Explanatory Notes

57.1   the honor of being appointed] See *TLY* 258ff for an account of Frost's years at the Library of Congress.

57.1   Flanders and Aiken] Ralph Edward Flanders, Senator from Vermont 1946–58. George David Aiken, Senator from Vermont 1940–50, 1956–75.

57.1   a small book . . . General Rosecrans] Frost's father, William Prescott Frost, Jr. (1850–1885), wrote the political biography *William Starke Rosecrans, His Life and Public Services* (San Francisco: Democratic Congressional Committee, 1880). Rosecrans (1819–98) had been a brigadier general in the Union army, involved, most famously, in leading Union troops to defeat at Chickamauga. He served in the California delegation to the U.S. House of Representatives from 1881 to 1885.

57.4   consultant to everybody in general] In a reading at the Choate School in 1962 Frost said: "I have just become in the last two or three years the consultant at the Library of Congress. And it's partly a jest, partly a joke. I was invited down there to be a consultant in Poetry. And I complained all the time that I had come under a misunderstanding. I thought I was to be the Poetry Consultant in everything, politics, science, religion, and I avoided my job all the time because as for being consulted in poetry—I was willing to be partly that along with other things. And they asked me what I would like to be and I said Consultant to Congress and to the world in everything. They said that sounded a little too much like my informal style" (unpublished typescript, Amherst College Library).

58. The Way There (1958?)

"The Way There" is a preface to a proposed but never published selection of Frost's poems for younger readers. Dartmouth College Library holds a June 25, 1958, letter from Frost to his editor Alfred Edwards in which the book is discussed: "We are talking it over now which should come next, the volume of selected poems to be called AFORESAID and to supersede COME IN and THE ROAD NOT TAKEN or the definitive NORTH OF BOSTON about doubled in size and with one of my inimitable prefaces. Either one of these might make the gate ahead of THE WAY THERE if it [is] going to take too much time to get it illustrated. What a lot of pleasure we'll have in writing and telephoning to each other over it all this summer." Filed with the letter at Dartmouth College Library are a proposed table of contents for "The Way There" (given below) and a dedication page. Four versions of this unpublished preface are held at Dartmouth, two being somewhat shorter than the others. The two longer versions are clearly related as rough draft to finished draft. Both of these are typescripts, and manuscript revisions on the first are incorporated in typing in the second, which in addition registers two variant readings—one in wording, one in punctuation. This second typescript is signed by Frost and bears a few corrections in Kathleen Morrison's hand. I reprint this second typescript since it includes, with variant readings, all of the matter contained in the shorter texts of the essay. Frost's proposed table of contents for "The Way There" is as follows: "Preface," "Questioning Faces," "Birches," "The Pasture," "Last Word of a Bluebird," "Locked Out," "Going for Water," "A Tuft of Flowers," "Dust of Snow," "Gathering Leaves," "Stopping by Woods on a Snowy Evening," "Looking for a Sunset Bird in Winter," "Spring Pools," "Blue Butterfly Day," "A Drumlin Woodchuck," "The Runaway," "A Peck of Gold," "A Time to Talk," "Blueberries," "A Minor Bird," "Lodged," "Christmas Trees," "Good Hours," "A Record Stride," "The Need of Being Versed in Country Things," "A Young Birch," "Wild Grapes," "Morning." No poem titled "Morning" appears in Frost's *Complete Poems 1949* or in *In the Clearing;* it is possible that "Mowing" is the poem intended.

Collation

TS1 = First complete typescript, with manuscript additions and corrections.

58.3   touching the ground] touching ground TS1

Explanatory Notes

58.1   Jog on, jog on] From a song in Shakespeare's *Winter's Tale* (4.3.133–356).

58.1   the days of your Godmother Goose] At the Choate School in 1962, Frost remarked: "Any one is lucky who has come to poetry before he has to study his way into it. He may study his way through it but his way *into* it[,—]he is lucky if he has it before he starts to study it: sing-song, Mother Goose. The beginning of it for me was [. . .] I was unaware that I ought to like it or dislike it or anything else. I remember that I saw a line once, 'ran through caverns measureless to man down to a sunless sea.' That sunless sea, caverns 'measureless to man.' Nobody told me to like that . . . Then I saw under a picture 'Ye secret black and midnight hags, what do ye here?' And they said 'A deed without an end.' You know where that comes from. It lifted me out of my boots" (unpublished typescript, Amherst College Library). The first quotation is from Coleridge's "Kubla Khan," the second from *Macbeth* 4.1.46–48, where the reading is "a deed without a name." Frost puts the matter a different way, again with reference to Mother Goose, in another 1962 talk, at Kenyon College: "I might say just a little bit more about poetry. One of the great problems that you have to deal with if you care for poetry at all, or care for literature at all, is whether you can desiccate poetry, then soak it in water and make it come alive. You have to decide that—and I decided you couldn't. My approach would be different. Mine was by singsong play, catchiness, the catchiness of street songs, Mother Goose, and all that. That's the approach, my approach, all the way and however the way. It goes with something in science that I've been thinking lately. Scientists seem sure that if they analyze matter and put the right parts of it together it'll come to life. It won't. I know what's wrong about it. Life itself is, as it were, one element, and it puts things together. It isn't a resultant, it's a cause. And that's what poetry is. It isn't a resultant of formulae, it's a cause. Let them make the formulae if they want to, but it doesn't have much to do with me" (for citation see explanatory note 7.5).

58.3   Susan Hayes Ward . . . Ernest Jewell] Susan Hayes Ward was literary editor of *The Independent* when it published, in the 1890s, several of Frost's early poems. Ernest Jewell, Frost's classmate at Lawrence High School, was editor of the High School *Bulletin* when Frost's first published poem, "La Noche Triste," appeared there in 1890.

58.4   Nicasio . . . Ripton] Towns in, respectively, California and Vermont.

59. [Unpublished Preface to an Expanded *North of Boston* (1958?)]

Frost's typescript of this preface, apparently the only version, is held now at Dartmouth College Library. A note appears at the foot of the sheet in Kathleen Morrison's hand: "Trial flight / for proposed revised / 'North of Boston' / KM." This may have been addressed to Edward Connery Lathem, to whom she apparently gave a number of Frost's manuscripts to assist him in preparing, with Hyde Cox, *SP.* (Lathem quotes most of Frost's preface in his own preface to a new edition of *North of Boston* prepared after the poet's death.) The preface was intended for an expanded edition of *North of Boston* that was never published. The idea first arose in Frost's correspondence with his publisher, Henry Holt and Company. In February 1949, Frost wrote to Glen Gosling, an editor at the firm: "Kay tells me you might consider the possibility of having a new and more inclusive *North of Boston* with a few pictures not too illustrative some holiday. That's long been a dream of mine. I tried to make [Robert] Linscott do it in the Modern Library. But he was bent on more. It would bring in The Witch of Coos, Paul's Wife, Two Look at Two, West-Running Brook, An Old Man's Winter Night, Snow, The Grindstone to spread in variety, have the same old frontis poem and for a new end piece symbolically Closed For Good. I could roll up my sleeves and write a small preface to go desperately to posterity with" (*TLY* 178–9). Gosling expressed interest, but at the time the firm was reluctant to embark on new and expensive projects. It is not clear whether Frost actually wrote the preface before the project was canceled. In any event, the expanded *North of Boston* came up again in May 1953 when Frost approached Andrew Wyeth about illustrating the volume (*TLY* 203). Wyeth agreed, but the plan was once again scuttled by Holt. Frost's hopes for an expanded *North of Boston* were revived one more time in 1958. In a June 25 letter to Alfred Edwards, his editor at Holt, Frost writes: "We are talking it over now which should come next, the volume of selected poems to be called AFORESAID and to supersede COME IN and THE ROAD NOT TAKEN or the definitive NORTH OF BOSTON about doubled in size and with one of my inimitable prefaces." The "inimitable" *North of Boston* preface may date, then, from as late as 1958, or from as early as 1949. I place it in 1958, since plans for the publication of the volume seem to have progressed furthest at that point. The copy-text for the present edition is the Dartmouth typescript. It appears to have been typed by Frost himself, contrary to his usual practice, and the few manuscript markings on it—a line indicating the addition of a phrase typed in the margins—are surely in his by this time unsteady hand. I have corrected one misprint, which occurs at *59.1 in the present edition. I have also conventionalized the styling of titles.

Collation

*59.1   Aeneas] Aenius
*59.1   luckily] luckily,
*59.1   *The Boston Globe*] the Boston Globe
*59.1   *North of Boston*] North of Boston

Explanatory Notes

59.1   one about Julius Caesar] Frost's early blank verse poem, "A Dream of Julius Caesar," originally published in the Lawrence, Mass., High School *Bulletin*. See *CPPP* 490–92.

59.1 Aeneas and Meliboeus] Meliboeus, a shepherd, appears in Virgil's first eclogue, Aeneas in *The Aeniad*.

59.1 I like its being locative.] Apropos of location and poetry, Frost remarks in a 1950 reading at Kenyon College: "Out of the ground, out of the parish, out of the family, out of the neighborhood, you know, and out of all this rises everything. The only source of sane originality is in the subject matter of the ground around you, that's for sure. But where that is I don't talk too definitely. They say I'm a Vermonter, they say, 'You're a Vermonter and you would say that'" (unpublished typescript, Amherst College Library).

60. [Letter to the Editor of *Poetry* (1958)]

Frost's letter to Henry Rago appeared in *Poetry* 92 (September 1958): 398. He wrote in praise of a special number of *Poetry* (July 1958) that published work by a number of young Israeli poets and which was edited by the Israeli poet and novelist Simon Halkin. Rago, editor of *Poetry*, apparently copied Frost's letter, keeping the original for himself. Only the copy, which matches the published text exactly, remains in the *Poetry* archives at the Regenstein Library, University of Chicago. (I thank Caroline Coven of the Library for calling this fact to my attention.) The copy-text for the present edition is the first appearance.

Explanatory Notes

60.1 the last paragraph] See Simon Halkin's essay in the July number, which concludes: "But it is important to notice that several of these poets are beginning to sense this danger of constant beating against the confines of their own private startled and frightened worlds, and to sense a larger range and a more secure direction in one or other of our local party programs. Yet within the limits of this essay it is impossible to consider whether they will reveal the 'dominant idea' by this means; that idea for which their verse cries out for redemption from the confines of their inner selves. One thing seems clear: the 'dominant idea' which may at some time in the future come to prevail in the young poetry will not come about in accordance with wholesale excogitation. The poetry has a multi-colored individuality both in its achievements so far and in its potentialities for the future, and those who produce it will succeed in leading it onward only if each one continues to see his own path, and aims to expand it in response to the cry of his own soul. The very wish to reveal the 'dominant idea' by dint of group effort is the opposite of self-deepening and of hearkening faithfully to the creative forces of the soul. Only in accordance with those forces can this poetry with all its manifold possibilities drive its broad highway onward in the life of the Jewish people in their own land in these 'lofty' and wondrous days." Halkins's rather high diction is quite remote from Frost's, but Frost found congenial the idea that a poet must strike a balance between individual and collective identity. See the variant paragraph omitted from the published text of "The Constant Symbol" given in collation 36.17 above.

61. Dorothy Canfield (1958)

Frost's tribute was published in *Dorothy Canfield Fisher: In Memoriam* (New York: Book-of-the-Month Club, 1958). Dartmouth College Library holds a manuscript of the essay written and corrected in Kathleen Morrison's hand (dictated by Frost), and a typescript based on the earlier manuscript bearing a number of additional corrections in Frost's hand. His corrections are in one respect incomplete. He has written an alternative, and tentative, wording of part of the last sentence in paragraph two at the foot of the page (see *61.2 in the collation). There are also some tentative manuscript revisions to that sentence made interlinearly and in the right margin next to where the sentence appears in typing, and still a third alternative wording in the left margin. Clearly, there once existed another typescript reflecting Frost's final decisions as to how that sentence should read. That must have been the printer's copy, but I have been unable to locate it. In any event, the sentence in question, as published, is virtually identical to the alternative wording Frost wrote at the bottom of the typescript, which is no doubt the one he adopted. The Dartmouth typescript is the copy-text for the present edition. I have incorporated into it the reading for the sentence (at *61.2) as it stands in the first appearance. No other variants in the published text seem authorial. I have conventionalized the styling of book titles.

Collation

TS = Frost's typescript (copy-text for the present edition). 1st = First appearance of the essay in *Dorothy Canfield Fisher: In Memoriam*. MS = Manuscript in Kathleen Morrison's hand, as dictated to her by Frost and held at Dartmouth College Library.

*61.1   great lady] 1st; great ladt TS
*61.1   *Hillsboro People*] "Hillsboro People" TS
61.1   than story telling] MS; than storytelling 1st
*61.2   her work with] 1st; he work with TS
61.2   of course they were] 1st; they were of course MS
*61.2   ancestry, Episcopalian, among the other sects non-conformist that came up from Connecticut and Rhode Island to settle the state.] 1st; ancestry Episcopalian among all {?} the other sects nonconformist that came up from Con and RI to settle the state TS; ancestry that made her an Episcopalian among the non-conforming sects that came up from Connecticut and Rhode Island to settle Vermont. MS
*61.3   Canfield?"] 1st; Canfield?". TS; Canfield. MS

Explanatory Notes

61.1   *Hillsboro People*] Published in 1915.
61.1   the Basques] Canfield did relief work in the Basque region of Spain during the First World War; she later drew on the experience in *Basque People* (1931).
61.2   Book of the Month Club] Canfield served on the Editorial Board of the Book-of-the-Month Club from 1926 until her death in 1957. Frost's 1936 volume *A Further Range* was a selection of the Club.

62. [List of Five Favorite Books (1958)]

Frost's list of the five books "that meant . . . the most to [him] in [his] lifetime" appeared in the *Chicago Tribune* "Magazine of Books" (November 30, 1958, part 4: 28). His list was part of a cluster of articles on Christmas book gift ideas. A great many authors and politicians were asked to contribute, among them Richard Nixon, John F. Kennedy, Hemingway, and Carl Sandburg. I am grateful to John Lancaster of Amherst College Library for bringing this item to my attention. The copy-text for the present edition is the first appearance in the *Chicago Tribune.* Lawrance Thompson reports a Thanksgiving Day 1946 conversation with Frost about the "great books" fetish of the 1940s: "As for the 100 great books, he disapproved because 60% of them were in translation and who wanted to soak in a 'bath' of translators for four years. He would give his students four books to buy—not to read now, but at their leisure: Emerson's *Poems,* Thoreau's *Walden,* Darwin's *Voyage of the Beagle,* and St. Thomas's *Summa*" (NOTES).

Explanatory Notes

62.4 Catullus] Lawrance Thompson reports a June 1946 conversation in which "Frost said he didn't care for Catullus, 'who wrote the loveliest of lovely things—and also the loathesomest.' Frost thinks Ezra Pound is influenced by Catullus in his dirty talk" (NOTES). But see Frost's remarks below in the notes to item 71.

62.6 "Incidents of Travel in Yucatan"] John Lloyd Stevens (1805–52), American explorer and railroad and steamship executive, wrote several volumes about his archeological investigations into Maya culture.

63. [On Emerson (1959)]

"On Emerson" was published first in *Daedalus* 88 (Fall 1959): 712–18. It was originally delivered as a speech on October 8, 1958, before the American Academy of Arts and Sciences. The occasion was the Academy's award of the Emerson-Thoreau Medal to Frost. Dartmouth College Library holds three texts of "On Emerson." The first—which I refer to here as text 1—is a transcript of the talk as delivered. It bears some corrections in Kathleen Morrison's hand. Text 2 is Frost's much-revised version. It was distilled from the transcript, apparently by Frost himself, with a great many additions, cuts, and revisions. The first three pages of text 2 are typed, with Frost's manuscript corrections; the remaining nine pages are entirely in his hand. There are also some corrections and annotations in Morrison's hand. Apparently the two of them went over this draft together before preparing a final typescript. Text 3, a typescript, is ten pages long, with a few corrections of misprints in Morrison's hand and instructions to the printer to set off one of the longer quotations from Emerson in a block. This is apparently a carbon. The original, I assume, was sent to *Daedalus.* There are a number of minor differences in punctuation and wording between texts 2 and 3. I have reprinted text 3 since, as I have indicated elsewhere, it was Morrison's habit to work closely with Frost in preparing typescripts of his essays, sometimes taking corrections and revisions by dictation. The version as published registers a number of variants in punctuation and two in wording. They are not of a character to suggest Frost himself made them. In addition to correcting typographical errors, I have made two emendations in editing the finished typescript for publication. The first (*63.15 below) corrects an apparent typographical error in text 3, which is sustained in the published text. Text 2 begins the quotation at "There," and indeed the subsequent remark "I agreed with him that there wasn't a philosopher in his university" implies that the quotation of Frost's friend should begin at "There." As for the second (*63.15): in text 2 these sentences appear in Frost's hand. They are not enclosed in quotation marks, and no question mark appears after "Does it." However, he begins the report of this conversation in text 2 by quoting the speech "There wasn't a philosopher in it," which suggests that he meant to enclose the speech of his young friend in quotation marks. Accordingly I have supplied them here, as did also the editors of *Daedalus*. I have also conventionalized the styling of titles.

Collation

TS = Frost's finished typescript (copy-text for the present edition). 1st = First appearance of the essay in *Daedalus*. TS1 = Penultimate typescript, two-thirds of which is in Frost's hand; identified as #2 in the notes above. PRWE = *Poems of Ralph Waldo Emerson* (New York: Oxford University Press, 1914).

63.1   the proud occasion] TSA; this proud occasion 1st

*63.4   *Representative Men*] "Representative Men" TS

63.4   came to me] 1st; came in on me TSA

63.5   a follower] 1st; anyone's follower TSA

63.5   The God who] 1st; The God that TSA

63.6   now to return to the speech that was his admiration and mine] 1st; to the speech was his admiration TSA

63.6   wouldst thou] will you PRWE

63.6   that can teach] who can teach PRWE

63.6   Yet they turn] But they turn PRWE

63.6   the statesman's art and] clerks' or statesmen's art or PRWE {Following this line are six lines that Frost omits in his quotation.}

63.6   That keeps the ground] Which keeps the ground PRWE

63.6   the mark] its mark PRWE

63.6   And the solid] While the solid PRWE

*63.7   Richards'] Richard'd

63.8   it is dramatic] 1st; is that dramatic TSA

63.9   In a recent preface to show my aversion to being interrupted with notes in reading a poem, I find myself resorting to Emerson again.] 1st; I find myself resorting to Emerson again in a recent preface to show my aversion to being interrupted with notes in reading a poem. TSA

63.10   won freedom] 1st; freedom TSA

*63.12   *Harper's Magazine*] Harper's Magazine

63.12   transcended] 1st; transcendent TSA

63.12   socialism] 1st; incipient socialism TSA

63.12   shards and flints] shard and flint PRWE

63.12   of all freedoms is ours to insist on meaning.] TSA; is ours to insist on meaning. 1st

*63.13   hater of tyranny] hater of tyrrany

*63.15   "There wasn't a philosopher in it. I can't stand it."] There wasn't a philosopher in it. "I can't stand it." TS

*63.15   "Does it," he said. "Where would I go?"] 1st; "Does it?", he said. Where would I go? TS; Does it he said. Where would I go? TSA

63.19   a story teller] 1st; of a story teller TSA

63.20   April] April's PRWE

Explanatory Notes

63.1   Fred Melcher] Frederic Gresham Melcher (1879–1963), co-editor of *Publishers' Weekly*, 1918–58.

63.4   St. John Perse] Pseudonym of Alexis Saint-Léger (1887–1975), French diplomat and poet. Saint-Léger lived in America from 1940 to 1958, working at the Library of Congress and teaching at Harvard University.

63.5   "Cut these sentences and they bleed."] See Emerson, "Montaigne": "Cut these words, and they would bleed; they are vascular and alive" (*EL* 700).

63.5   The God who made] From Emerson's poem "Ode, Inscribed to W. H. Channing."

63.5   the days of Franklin Pierce] Franklin Pierce (1804–1869), a Democrat, became the fourteenth president of the U.S. (1853–57); he supported states' rights, a policy that was, in those days, associated with the interests of slavery, and he defended the infamous (or so it was considered by many New England circles) Fugitive Slave Bill of 1850. Nathaniel Hawthorne wrote his campaign biography.

63.7   Ivor Richards' basic eight hundred] English literary critic I. A. Richards (1893–1979) helped develop "BASIC English" (short for "British, American, Scientific, International, Commercial English"). A theoretical universal language, it draws on a fundamental list of 850 English words. See Richards's *Basic English and Its Uses* (1943).

63.8   Erskine] John Erskine (1879–1951), Professor of English at Columbia University, and author of a number of volumes of literary criticism.

63.9   In a recent preface] "The Prerequisites," which prefaced *Aforesaid* (New York: Holt, 1954), a selection of Frost's poems.

63.9   "Whose worth's unknown] See Shakespeare's sonnet 116.

63.10   "Would take the sun] From Emerson's "Ode Sung in the Town Hall, Concord, July 4, 1857."

63.12   "Heartily know] From Emerson's poem "Give All to Love."

63.12   invoked in *Harper's Magazine*] See explanatory note 37.5.

63.12   "Musketaquit, a goblin strong] From Emerson's poem "Two Rivers."

63.15   the Bible says] 1 Samuel 4:9.

63.17   a mere Τὸ Μὴ ὄν A mere "that which is not"; a nonentity.

63.17   "Unit and universe] From Emerson's poem "Uriel."

63.19   scandal story] Namely, that Joseph was a cuckold. See Frost's jeu d'esprit, "Mary Had a Little Lamb" (NOTES, entry for May 1946):

> Mary had a little lamb,
> His name was Jesus Christ;
> Joseph was her legal ram,
> But he took it nice.

Another version of the poem is printed in *RFLU*. More than once Frost spoke of the "scandal" at the heart of Christianity. Lawrance Thompson reports the following conversation with him, which took place at Ripton, Vt., in August 1959: "Then we got going on pornography, and Frost told about how he had gone to Baltimore to talk, recently (probably as much as two years ago) and with nuns in the audience had begun to wonder whether you got better results by crossing a god with a woman or a goddess with a man: if you stopped to think of it, you got Julius Caesar by the latter, but that took a long time. Yet in the other case, you got Jesus Christ right off the bat. The point of all that becomes a typically Frostean ridicule of the miraculous virgin birth" (NOTES). I include here further remarks

Frost made on the subject of Christianity, also as reported by Thompson: "So he had read through the book of John again, had been particularly disappointed because John seemed to place faith entirely on belief or acceptance of belief without proofs; that the story itself provided no evidence except for unsupported assertions. Believe or be damned. And worse than that, the lofty moralizations were undermined with some very ugly anecdotes. For example, the story of the betrayal. John said that when Christ had been asked who would betray him, he had said, 'The one to whom I next give a sop of wine.' And then he turned and gave it to Judas. Then the text says, 'After he had given him the sop, the devil entered into Judas.' And Christ said, 'What you do, go and do immediately.' And Judas left the room and betrayed Christ. Here, says Frost, the wording makes it sound as though Judas were all right until Christ betrayed Judas, and here was a quaint conflict between good and evil, the motivating evil being Christ's. That in turn got Frost going on the whole question as to why Christ had so obviously kept making references to Old Testament prophecies. It was Frost's notion that Christ, human and not divine, had early become obsessed with the psychopathic notion that he was the Messiah: at the age of twelve, he was mingling with the rabbis, and confounding them with his talk: 'Wist ye not that I must be about my father's business?' He assumed the role of messiah, and acted out the part by dramatizing the prophecies. And Frost was particularly charmed by the fact that in one of the old prophets, perhaps Zachariah, there had been the prophecy that the Messiah would ride into Jerusalem on an ass with a foal alongside; that when Christ finally got around to make his entry, he not only got an ass but also a foal, 'that it might be fulfilled.' All the way through, that phrase, 'That it might be fulfilled.' . . . It would be easier for me to become a Jew [Frost said] than a Christian" (NOTES).

63.20   By the rude bridge] From Emerson's "Hymn Sung at the Completion of the Concord Monument."

63.20   the tall shaft] The Washington Monument.

64. The Future of Man (1959)

This essay was Frost's contribution to a symposium on "the future of man" sponsored by Joseph E. Seagram and Sons, Inc. The occasion was the dedication of the Seagram Building at 375 Park Avenue. With Frost on the panel were Bertrand Russell (1872–1970, mathematician and philosopher), Julian Huxley (1887–1975, biologist and cofounder of UNESCO), Ashley Montagu (1905–1999, anthropologist and author of the UNESCO *Statement on Race*), and Hermann J. Muller (1890–1967, Nobel Prize–winning geneticist). Apparently a list of suggested topics was circulated beforehand, as nearly all panelists touch on the same themes: national rivalry, internationalism, war, evolution, and eugenics. The symposium was published by Seagram and Sons in booklet form as *The Future of Man* (New York, 1959). Dartmouth College Library holds a copy of the transcript of the symposium—prepared by A. A. Schechter Associates of New York—that was sent to Frost to be corrected for publication. They hold also a number of typescript and manuscript drafts of different versions of the essay (described in the textual notes to the next item). The published version differs from the corrected Schechter transcript in a number of respects, chiefly as to how the penultimate paragraph should read. Frost's manuscript corrections there are difficult to construe, particularly for anyone not used to his handwriting, and they are perhaps incomplete. The variants in wording in the published text, however, appear to be authorial. Since the paragraph in which they occur differs significantly from the paragraph as revised by Frost on the transcript, I can only conclude that they derived from a finished, authoritative typescript, now lost, or perhaps from another revised copy of the transcript itself. I reprint the published version of the text.

Collation

1st = First appearance of the essay in *The Future of Man* (copy-text for the present edition). TS = Frost's corrected transcript.

64.2   ahead into the future with my eyes shut—] ahead, with my eyes shut—TS

*64.3   be an intelligible] an intelligible 1st

64.5   growth is not] it isn't TS

64.5   the doubleness, I foresee,] this doubleness I foresee, TS

64.5   and in itself] but in itself it TS

64.7   another thing about the god who provides the great issues. He's a god of waste, magnificent waste. And waste is another name for generosity of not always being intent on our own advantage, nor too importunate even for a better world. We pour out a libation to him as a symbol of the waste we share in—participate in. Pour it on the ground and you've wasted it; pour it into yourself and you've doubly wasted it. But all in the cause of generosity and relaxation of self interest.] about God who provides the great issues he's a god of waste, magnificent waste. And waste is another name for generosity. Lavish—it's a lavish god. And we must share in that—we pour out a libation to him as a symbol of his waste—participating in the waste. Pour it on the ground and you've wasted it; pour it into yourself and you've doubly wasted it. And it's all in the cause of generosity and relaxed self interest, relaxed importunity for a better world even. TS

Explanatory Notes

64.0   The Future of Man] During the question period following the panelists' speeches at the "Future of Man" symposium, Frost made the following remarks, as quoted in the published text.

> Well, the balance is between our being members of each other and being individuals. You see, we're members of each other, that's what you're all talking about, insisting on, and civilized society is a society that tolerates all sorts of divergences, to the point of eccentricity and to the point, even, of doubtful sanity. (51)
>
> But let me say something about science—I'm lost among scientists here, you know. I don't want to seem at variance with them. I am lost in admiration for science. It's the plunge of the mind, the spirit, into the material universe. It can't go too far or too deep for me. But you have to stop and think who owns it. It's a property. Science says, "It belongs to me." No, it's a property of the race. It belongs to us. And who are we? Science can't describe us; it contributes very little to our description, a very little bit in all this newness wonder of science that they talk about—it's very slight. The wonderful description of us is the humanities, the book of the worthies and unworthies through the ages, and anything you talk about in the future must be a projection from that. (52–53)
>
> The chief guide in the world for us in the long way we've come is some more

or less intelligent handling of that inexorable thing in us, Biblical thing, you know—passionate preference for something we can't help wishing were so, wishing were true. All your guidance in politics, religion, and love is something way in the middle of your heart that you can't help wishing was so. All the time. That's what we're talking about here, what we can't help wishing were so. (53–54)

Well, I was just going to say that these philosophers, you know—they have always wanted to be rulers—they always wanted to be philosopher-kings. And they have been once or twice. And one or two college presidents have been. And in these philosopher-kings philosophy has once or twice got as formidable as science. We have had to give some thinkers hemlock or burn 'em at the stake. And I hope Lord [Bertrand] Russell feels as if he'd lived a formidable enough life to have been burned at the stake. (56)

The certainty of conflict is originality, that's all, the bursting power, the bursting energy and daring of man and it's always there, always there. You can't hope for anything that doesn't include that. (56)

One more question to Lord Russell. Since we all agree that we're now smart enough to go on with what we are in an evolutionary way, we ought to be smart enough to stop where we are. And I am in favor of stopping where we are because I like all this uncertainty that we live in between being members and being individuals. That's the daily problem—how much I am a member, how much I am an individual, how comfortable I am in my memberships. It's an endless problem that you can hire psychiatrists about—and they can't help you. I like the layout. Do you, Lord Russell? LORD RUSSELL: Yes, very much. (58)

288.5   Yggdrasill] In Norse mythology, the ash tree whose branches hold the universe together.

65. The Future of Man (Unpublished Version [1959])

In preparing his contribution to the Future of Man symposium Frost worked through a number of manuscript and typescript drafts, with Kathleen Morrison's assistance. The occasion seemed to stimulate in him an uncommon industry. Few of his essays survive in as many different forms as does "The Future of Man." Frost dictated several pages of an early draft to Morrison, and after that worked from typescripts which bear corrections in both his hand and hers. Dartmouth College Library holds four typescripts of the essay, each with variant readings; Amherst College holds still another. (One of the Dartmouth typescripts is a carbon of the Amherst typescript, but manuscript markings on them vary.) Two typescripts among these five seem to be finished products, both of which are held at Dartmouth. They register in clean typing revisions indicated on other typescripts in manuscript and interlinear type. And yet these two are really distinct versions: one is shorter than the other by about half, though the two agree almost exactly in the text they have in common. The shorter of these two "finished" texts bears a note in Morrison's hand at the head of page one: "PROSE." I do not know whether Morrison considered the shorter text Frost's final version, or, if she did, what her reasons may have been. Furthermore, both it and the version from which it is condensed are quite different from the address Frost actually delivered at the symposium and published in *The Future of Man* (reprinted above). I reprint here the longer of the two "finished" versions for the following reasons: the shorter contains no new material; the longer one contains much interesting material not included in the shorter text; and in any event, Frost's own preferences are not evident. The collation describes all differences in wording between the short and long versions, as well as between those two texts and one earlier typescript draft. I have made several emendations in the wording and punctuation of the copy-text. These are to correct obvious misprints, and also to correct what were apparently accidental omissions of words present in other versions of the essay. All are described in the collation. I have adopted the spelling "Yggdrasill" for the ash-tree of Norse mythology. The word is spelled variously throughout Frost's "Future of Man" documents. I have conventionalized the styling of titles.

Collation

TS = Frost's typescript (copy-text for the present edition). TS2 = Another typescript of the essay, held at Dartmouth. STS = Shortened version of this finished typescript, held at Dartmouth. Unless otherwise indicated TS2 agrees in wording with TS and the present edition.

65.1 There is {. . .} guess me.] {not present} STS

65.1 His speed {. . .} refreshment.] {not present} STS; {"His speed . . . police" not present in TS2}

65.1–2 The party {. . .} do the same.] {not present} STS

*65.2 suppress it,] suppress, it TS; suppress it TS2

*65.3 What are you going] what are you going TS

*65.3 for you to be] TS2; you to be TS

65.3 It must {. . .} Melbourne.] {not present} STS

65.3 But I suppose . . . commentators.] {not present} STS

65.3 was change] was to change STS, TS2

*65.4 taking in hand] TS2; takibg in hand TS

*65.4 left-over] TS2, STS; left-over left-over TS {Where this passage appears in other typescript versions of the essay only one "left-over" is used.}

65.5 6 But while {. . .} colonization.] {not present} STS

65.5 There never was] There was never TS2

65.5 VIII] the eighth TS2

*65.5 Talleyrand] Tallyrand TS

*65.5 *Moby Dick*] Moby Dick TS

65.6 The one the mystic] What the mystic STS

65.6 trusted in to] trusted to STS

65.7 The free-for-all {. . .} nation.] {not present} STS

65.7 that in the tree] like the tree STS

*65.7 Yggdrasill that] Ygdrasil that TS; Yggdrasill—the great ash tree symbolizing the Universe—that STS

65.7 self-stopped] self stop STS

65.7 are like its] are its STS, TS2

65.7 waste is double] waste is doubled STS

*65.7 burnt to] STS, TS2; to TS

Explanatory Notes

65.1 The great challenge] In a 1950 lecture at Kenyon College, Frost had this to say about wildness and order: "I have said to myself that there ought to be on every table as well as a pepper shaker and a salt shaker a chaos shaker, so there'd be a sprinkle of chaos in everything. We mustn't forget that we came from chaos. That's the wildness I'm talking about. When Reed Powell talked the way he did today against the Supreme Court of the United States of America, what was, shall I say, eating him? It was this[:] he was thinking that he'd learned to think since the Nineties that there's something in man that runs out ahead of the law for the law to catch up with him if it can. And when you think of the big interests as criminal[—]some people do, you know[—]it just means . . . that they're the ablest of us who are not trying to outwit the law but . . . running out ahead of it for the law to overtake them when it can. And that's the *animus,* that's the enterprise, that's the spirit that breaks the form . . . I remember Kipling . . . said 'There's a spirit in the American . . . that bids him flout the law he makes and bids him make the law he flouts.' In those two lines he says . . . just what I'm saying, that the spirit of man bids him flout the law he makes and bids him . . . go right on making the law he's going to flout. He thinks that's characteristically American. It's characteristically human and that's what we mean by the wildness in poetry . . . the thoughts that come from this spirit of enterprise are the only thoughts that belong to poetry" (unpublished typescript, Amherst College Library). See also Lawrance Thompson's account of a February 21, 1940, conversation with Frost: "In his ideas on politics he thinks of civilization as giving us a right to indulge our individualities, our eccentricities, even our perversions. A government is like a great breathing monster—giving out greater freedom, liberty, license—and then at times taking it in. A communal state is a taking in. A democracy is a letting out. But even a democracy, in time of war, calls all its liberties in, temporarily, for the communal good. Capital in Wall Street indulges its liberties to the extent of perversion and then is checked" (NOTES). And see as well the following, from Frost's 1951 talk "Poetry and Society": "I take it that is what happened to Luther. His difference came out of his nature. 'I could do no other,' he said. That is the essence of the very individuality in art. I could do no other. Macbeth put it another way: 'Bid my will avouch it.' I did it because I did it, is what Macbeth is saying. The spirit of man looks criminal because it is constantly reaching out for freedom, it is just kind of running out ahead of the law—and, of course, after awhile, the law catches up. The will first, the law second. That may not be the way it ought to be, but it is the way it is. First the strength, then the control. Punch your fist against your hand and this act expresses the strength and the control." (For information about this talk, see 37.6 above.)

65.1   this conclave] The "Future of Man" symposium.

65.2   The challenge of science to government . . . we will do the same] Frost probably has in mind Robert Oppenheimer's words after the explosions at Hiroshima and Nagasaki: "A scientist cannot hold back progress because of fears of what the world will do with his discoveries" (quoted in Lansing Lamont, *Day of Trinity* [New York: Athenaeum, 1965], 261).

65.3   Darwin, Spencer, and Huxley] Lawrance Thompson reports a June 1948 conversation with Frost about evolution: "And Frost remembered one other thing about [William Jennings] Bryan which had aroused Frost's sympathy. When the famous Tennessee [Scopes "Monkey"] trial came off, and Bryan went down to defend the fundamentalists, Frost said his sympathies were with Bryan because he saw him as the under dog. And what annoyed him most was the cock-sureness of the evolutionists, who could no more prove their assumption than the fundamentalists could prove Genesis. But they went on the assumption that because they could follow natural history a little way back, that gave them authority for following back all the way to the beginning. Of course they couldn't. Their 'pourquoi' story had to be as much of a guess as Genesis" (NOTES). It is difficult to tell whether or not Frost was merely provoking Thompson with this reference to the "pourquoi" story of modern science, for which he had a great deal of respect. But see his poem "Too Anxious for Rivers" (*CPPP* 342–43).

    65.5   Critias] Critias, Athenian orator and statesman; pupil of Socrates.

    65.6   Ararat] See Genesis 8:4.

    65.6   where ignorant armies clash] See the last line of Matthew Arnold's poem "Dover Beach."

66. [Talk and Reading, 25th Anniversary Dinner of the Academy of American Poets (1959)]

Frost delivered this talk and reading at the Waldorf Astoria Hotel in New York before the Academy of American Poets on November 4, 1959. The talk was transcribed and given to Frost to be revised for publication in the booklet *Twenty-Fifth Anniversary Dinner of the Academy of American Poets* (New York: Academy of American Poets, 1959). A copy of the transcript with minor revisions in Kathleen Morrison's hand is held at Dartmouth College Library. It seems clear that she worked under Frost's direct supervision since her corrections are not limited to misprints. In one case, for example, she adds a sentence: "A great occasion, profoundly moving" (66.1). A number of variants appear in the published text, but I find no evidence that they are authorial. (All variants in wording are given in the collation.) Frost's role in preparing the text apparently ends with the corrected transcript, copy-text for the present edition. I have made several emendations. The transcript does not include the texts of the three longer poems Frost read, but instead has the instructions: "INSERT POEM," or "INSERT POEM—see 'Collected Poems,'" and so on. Only the short poem "Away" and the couplet "Forgive, oh Lord" are printed in the transcript, though the text of "Away"—the lineation of which is mistaken—has been struck out by Frost and Morrison. Following the instructions given in the transcript, I have supplied the texts of all of the poems. I have followed the text of the first appearance of "One More Brevity" as Frost's Christmas card for 1953; the poem was later collected in *In the Clearing* (1962), some two years after Frost gave the reading under discussion here. When he collected the poem Frost made several alterations in the wording; to print the later version here might be anachronistic. "Away" also remained uncollected until *In the Clearing* was published. It had appeared first as Frost's Christmas card for 1958. For *In the Clearing* Frost made one change in the wording of "Away": the phrase "words of a song" became "urge of a song." The latter wording is given in the improperly lineated text of the poem that is struck out on the typescript of the talk. This suggests that Frost had already made the revision at this time, and so for "Away" I have followed the revised text as it appears in *In the Clearing*. The texts of "The Tuft of Flowers" and "Birches" are taken from *Complete Poems of Robert Frost, 1949*, the book Frost customarily carried with him to talks and readings.

Collation

TS = Frost's corrected transcript (copy-text for the present edition). 1st = First appearance in *Twenty-Fifth Anniversary Dinner of the Academy of American Poets*.

*66.2   Nineveh] 1st; Ninevah TS

*66.2   ruined Nineveh] 1st; ruined Ninevah TS

66.2   There is a lot of] A lot of 1st

66.3   earth. Nor is it] earth, nor 1st

66.5   It was some years] It was years 1st

66.5   following me around] followed ~ 1st

*66.5   all sciences"] all sciences," 1st, TS

66.5   one of all,] one of all is 1st

*66.6   ONE MORE BREVITY {followed by text of poem}] 1st; INSERT POEM TS

66.6   {In its first appearance, and in *In the Clearing,* the poem comes with a footnote at the word "song," toward the end of the poem: "But see *The Great Overdog* and *Choose Something Like a Star,* in which latter the star could hardly have been a planet since fixity is of the essence of the piece."}

66.7   very early ones] early ones 1st

66.7   "A Tuft] 1st; "The Tuft TS

*66.7   {Text of "The Tuft of Flowers"}] 1st; INSERT POEM—see "Collected Poems" TS

66.8 urge of a song] words of a song 1st

*66.8   {Text of "Away!"}] 1st; REPEAT "Away" TS

66.9   urge of a song] words of a song 1st

*66.10   {Text of "Birches"}] 1st; INSERT—See "Collected Poems" TS

Explanatory Notes

66.2   "We in the ages] From Arthur William Edgar O'Shaughnessy's (1844–1881) poem "Ode."

67. [A Poet's Boyhood (1960)]

"A Poet's Boyhood"—the title is not Frost's—appeared in a brochure announcing a reading held at the Berkeley Community Theatre in Berkeley, California, on November 6, 1960: *Dana Attractions Inc. Presents in Person America's Poet Laureate Robert Frost Reading from His Own Works* (Berkeley: Dana Attractions, 1960). Dartmouth College Library holds a manuscript draft of the article in Kathleen Morrison's hand, as dictated to her by Frost. There are also corrections and revisions in Morrison's hand; doubtless these were dictated by Frost as well. Dartmouth College also holds a neat typescript of the essay, which registers the corrections indicated on the manuscript, but which also introduces a number of changes in wording. Apparently Morrison prepared this typescript under Frost's oversight. This final typescript seems to be a carbon: two ink smudges have been clarified in Morrison's hand in the margins. The original was probably sent to Dana Attractions. The Dartmouth typescript matches the published text exactly, with the exception that Frost's signature appears at the end of the essay in the brochure. He must have signed the original typescript of the Dartmouth College carbon. The published text also corrects one misprint: at 67.4 of the present edition the typescript mistakenly reads "out history" for "our history." The copy-text for the present edition is the published text, since it reproduces accurately the text of the signed document submitted by Frost and Morrison.

Collation

TS = Frost's typescript. MS = Manuscript in Kathleen Morrison's hand, as dictated to her by Frost.

67.1   political, of crossing] TS; political. I remember crossing MS

67.1   on a train] TS; on the train MS

67.1   as delegate] TS; ~ as a delegate MS

67.1   and very intense] TS; very intense MS

67.1   ones] TS; ~ in those days MS

67.1   of Garfield's] TS; {not present} MS

67.2   I was taken] TS; they made me come MS

67.2   to carry] TS; and carry MS

67.2   on foot] TS; walking MS

67.2   either way] TS; {not present} MS

67.3   my health not being] TS; since my health wasn't MS

67.3   and taken] TS; to go MS

67.3   to his office] TS; {not present} MS

67.3   in a buggy] TS; {not present} MS

67.3   in a buggy and] TS; in a buggy MS

67.3   tack hammer] TS; hammer MS

67.3   acted as his] TS; acted as MS

67.3   who was my kind friend] TS; {not present} MS

67.3   my lunches free] TS; free lunches MS

67.4   I got away before the big one. And there was] TS; {not present} MS

67.4   Gardens with] TS; Gardens and MS

67.4   both these] TS; both MS

67.4   I could get you to] TS; you'd all MS

67.4   to yourself] TS; {not present} MS

67.4   before I have to] TS; Before I MS

67.4   our history] MS; out history TS

67.4   (My father, William {. . .} "The Bulletin.")] TS; {not present} MS

67.4   like these:] TS; like this: (I have lost all but a fragment, the beginning. I never published it.) MS

67.4   The rest is lost. I wish I could recapture it. It was never published.] TS; {not present} MS

67.5   Nothing but] TS; All MS

67.5   Corruption may have been in it.] TS; There may have been corruption. MS

67.5   Cambridge {. . .} Frost] {not present} TS, MS

Explanatory Notes

67.1   Hancock] Winfield Scott Hancock (1824–86), major general in the Union army and nominee of the Democratic party for President of the U.S. in 1880.

67.2   I thought elected Grover Cleveland] As to political affiliation, Frost often described himself as a Democrat who had been unhappy since Grover Cleveland left office. He remarks, as reported by James Reston in the *New York Times* for October 27, 1957: "I keep reading about old Grover and after sixty years I have to admit there were one or two things that could be said against him, but I concede it reluctantly. As Mencken said, Cleveland got on in American politics, not by knuckling to politicians but scorning and defying them. He didn't go around spouting McGuffy Reader slogans or wanting to be liked." William Holmes McGuffey (1800–1873) was the author of what by some accounts is the single most important text in the history of American pedagogy, his celebrated (and famously pious) *Reader,* which through its many editions profoundly influenced generations of American primary-school students.

67.3 Buckley] Chris Buckley was the Democratic Party boss of San Francisco in the days when the Frosts lived there; he was blind. Frost later recalled how his father became involved with Buckley: "He had become embittered with life, having been disappointed in everything he tried to accomplish. Such a condition made him an easy mark for a fellow like Buckley. He wanted to be treasurer of San Francisco, county or city—for no other reason I can explain except to have access to the money. How he planned to get any of it I have never figured out. All I know is that he soon became the willing slave of the blind boss, rushing to do his every bidding without question" (quoted in Mertins, *Robert Frost: Life and Talks-Walking,* 23). It was no doubt on these errands with his father that the young Frost met Buckley.

67.4 Have I not written] See "At Woodward's Gardens" and "Once by the Pacific."

67.4 Europe might sink] Frost also inscribed these lines of poetry on the flyleaf of a copy of *A Masque of Mercy* (1947) given to William Meredith following a trip the two men took together to California in the fall of 1960; it was on this trip that Frost gave the reading at the Berkeley Community Theatre.

67.5 Steffens . . . come in.] Lincoln Steffens (1866–1936), pre-eminent American journalist of the "muckraking" school and author of *The Shame of the Cities* (1904), an exposé of corruption in city government. In a 1950 talk at Kenyon College, Frost said this about his San Francisco boyhood: "I've often thought that some day I'd do a companion piece to a longish one I wrote called 'New Hampshire' and I would call the companion piece 'San Francisco' and it would be a strange medley of politics and political corruption. I took part in it at the age of ten. I marched in the Democratic processions in those days. Not so innocently as you might think" (unpublished typescript, Amherst College Library).

68. [A New England Tribute (1961)]

"A New England Tribute" appeared in the *Official Program of the Inaugural Ceremonies of John F. Kennedy and Lyndon B. Johnson* (Washington: Kennedy-Johnson Inaugural Committee, 1961). The title was suggested to Frost by the Committee. It complements an article by Walter Prescott Webb titled "A Southwestern Tribute," which also appears in the program. Frost changed the last line of "The Gift Outright," which follows his tribute, at Kennedy's request: the original reads "would become" for "will become" (68.3). Dartmouth College Library holds a number of documents pertaining to this "Tribute." Among them are four drafts of two very similar versions: an early, incomplete manuscript draft in Kathleen Morrison's hand, as dictated to her by Frost, together with a typescript of the same with a few corrections in her hand; and another manuscript draft in her hand of the text more or less as published, together with a typescript of the same with a few corrections in Frost's hand and in hers. The corrections on this second typescript are tentative, and another manuscript fragment in Morrison's hand contains finished versions of the revised sentences, albeit in a somewhat abbreviated form (see collation 68.1). Her instructions on the fragment leave no question as to how they should be incorporated into the essay. I have reconstructed the text from the typescript and the manuscript fragment, following the published text at 67.1 ("four of them . . ." etc.) as a guide to how Morrison's abbreviations are to be expanded. The text as published doubtless reproduces a final Frost-Morrison typescript which is now lost, but it also introduces three typographical errors; otherwise it matches the present edition exactly.

Collation

MSA = Manuscript draft in Morrison's hand, as dictated to her by Frost. TSA = Typescript prepared from MSA, and corrected in Frost's hand and Morrison's (copy-text for the present edition). TSB = Typescript of an earlier, variant version of the article. (I have not recorded variant readings from the manuscript, also held at Dartmouth, that served as the basis for TSB; it is incomplete, and any further record of variants would over-complicate an already complicated list.) CP = *Complete Poems of Robert Frost, 1949.*

68.1   Hard of course to judge of the importance of an event at the time of it, but an] MSA; An TSB

68.1   may well be looked back on] MSA; might be something we should like to look back at TSB

68.1   turning point] MSA; ~ not only TSB

68.1   even perhaps] MSA; but even perhaps TSB

68.1   forward toward] forward towards MSA, TSB

68.1   had been accomplished; the old agonies and antagonisms were over; it was tacitly conceded that our founders were not far wrong;] MSA; was accomplished in a sort of tacit admission that our founders were right; our TSB

*68.1   four of them who are on record to this effect, Washington, Jefferson, Adams, and Madison, enshrined in a temple on the North Shore of Massachusetts.] 1st; ~ effect, Washing. Jeff Ad & Mad, enshrined in a temple on the N. Shore of Mass TSA; our four greats, Washington, Jefferson, Adams, and Madison, in what I choose to call a temple on the North Shore of Massachusetts, all of them on record I believe for the separation of church and state. We hope to stay separate. But as I say it is hard to foresee the future. MSA; the four great founders, Washington, Jefferson, Adams, and Madison in what I will call a temple on the North Shore of Massachusetts, all of them on record for keeping the hands of church and state off each other. I like to put it this way but of course it is hard to judge of the importance of events at the time of them. TSB

68.1   "How still a moment may precede / One that may thrill the world forever. / To that still moment none would heed / Man's doom was linked no more to sever."] TSB; "How still a moment / 4 lines" MSA; How calm ~ / One that shall ~ OBEV

68.1–2   Such was our gift for Christmas confirmed by vote one hundred and eighty years after the first election. ¶ For New Year's the inauguration might be another gift, a more than New Year's resolution, to make sure of the more than social security of us all in a] {The typing of TSA follows MSA here; manuscript corrections in Frost's and Morrison's hand match the present edition.}; Such was our gift for Christmas. For New Year's, the inauguration might be like a more than New Year's resolution to make sure of the more than social security of us all in our MSA {The reading is tentative: the first of these sentences is struck out, with no substitute indicated}; So much for the Christmas of it. For New Years the inauguration might be like taking more than a New Year's resolution to make sure of the more than social security of us all in our TSB

68.2   A little] MSA; ~ more physical elan, a little TSB

68.2   decision, we] MSA; decision. We TSB

68.2   where or how. We] MSA; where or how but TSB
68.2   the sports to the sciences and arts] MSA; science to sports TSB
68.2   Olympic games as yet] MSA; Pyrrhic dance as yet TSB
68.2   Olympic spirit] MSA; Pyrric phalanx TSB
68.2   manlier one?] TSB; manlier one. MSA
68.3   heard the despairers] heard despairers MSA, TSB
68.3   Our Revolution was:] MSA; {not present} TSB
68.3   OUR GIFT] TSA, MSA; The Gift TSB
68.3   found it was] found out that it was CP
68.1   will become] would become CP

Explanatory Notes

68.1   a turning point . . . Christendom] Kennedy was the first Roman Catholic to be elected President.

68.1   portraits by Stuart] Gilbert Charles Stuart (1755–1828), American portrait painter.

68.1   "How still a moment] From Alfred Domett's (1811–87) "A Christmas Hymn, 1837."

69. [Shakespeare Festival of Washington (1961)]

Frost's remarks appeared as part of an advertisement taken out by The Hecht Company in the *Washington Post* (June 12, 1961): B-20. However, they do not appear in newsprint. Instead, a typed card bearing the remarks with Frost's manuscript corrections and signature is reproduced in facsimile. I have found no other documents pertaining to, or reprinting, Frost's remarks. The copy-text for the present edition is the first appearance in the *Post*. The occasion for the advertisement was the opening of the Washington, D.C., Shakespeare Festival with a production of *Twelfth Night*, directed by Ellie Chamberlain.

70. [Tribute to Ernest Hemingway (1961)]

Frost's tribute to Hemingway appeared along with a number of similar tributes from other writers in a *New York Times* obituary notice titled "Authors and Critics Appraise Works" (July 3, 1961: 6). The copy-text for the present edition is a manuscript of Frost's tribute in Kathleen Morrison's hand, held now at Dartmouth College Library. Frost dictated it to her. It is identical to the published text, with the exception that the *Times* prints the title "'The Killers'" inside quotation marks, not underlined or in italics.

Explanatory Notes

70.1   die by accident] "For some time [after Hemingway's suicide Frost] could talk and think of nothing else, and he felt sure that he knew just why Hemingway had done what he had done: he had become convinced that he had lost the ability to write. Frost would not tolerate any criticism of Hemingway's action. He insisted that he had shown great courage in killing himself when the thing he had lived for was gone" (*TLY* 294).

71. [Comments on "Choose Something Like a Star" (1962)]

Frost's comments were published together with his poem "Choose Something Like a Star" in *Poet's Choice*, edited by Paul Engle and Joseph Langland (New York: Dial Press, 1962), 1–

2. I have found no manuscripts or typescripts of his contribution to the volume. The copy-text for the present edition is the first appearance in *Poet's Choice*. Frost often recited "Choose Something Like a Star" at readings and lectures during the last months of his life. He remarked after reading it in Detroit on November 14, 1962: "I don't have to explain that [poem] to you. I meant by that a poet or somebody in the distance, a star or something, a text in the Bible . . . I happened to be—when I wrote that I was thinking of Catullus. See, when I'm bothered by . . . having voted the wrong way, you see, I put my mind on Catullus, something distant . . . It's a rather Horatian ending . . . 'So when at times the mob is swayed to carry praise or blame too far, we may take something like a star to stay our minds on and be staid.' Good night" (unpublished typescript, Amherst College Library). In a talk given on May 18, 1962, at Wooster College, he remarked: "I have a poem or a line in the Bible or some saying to guide me. I often say this takes the bite out of the confusion of things. I sometimes use a star as a symbol to guide me out of the mess of the day's news, a star brings me back to the straight line, when I've been way off on one side or another" (one of a series of extracts from the talk printed in the *Wooster Alumni Bulletin*, for June 1962). Of the line in "Choose Something Like a Star," "Some mystery becomes the proud," Frost had this to say in a reading at the Library of Congress in October 1962, on the occasion of the National Poetry Festival: "Now take this one. My sympathy with all the poets I know—and I know a lot of them—is often tried, and I say naughty things; and then sometimes I say things of reconciliation. When they puzzle me, and I don't know what they're talking about, I finally find myself saying, right in the middle of a poem, something you may notice here. Shall I call your attention to it first or will you notice it for me?" After reading the poem he explained: "Now that's preaching to myself, but the line I'm going to call your attention to is wrung out of me from many years of trying to understand poetry I couldn't understand. I just said to myself, 'One line and all is forgiven, all is nice between us': 'Some mystery becomes the proud.' That's something of magnanimity, too, you see—giving in, but coming out on top, too. I'm triumphant." See also Frost's lecture "On Extravagance" (*CPPP* 926).

Explanatory Notes

71.2   my new book] *In the Clearing* (New York: Holt, Rinehart and Winston, 1962), Frost's last volume of poetry.

72. [Tribute to William Faulkner (1962)]

I reprint Frost's tribute to Faulkner, who died June 6, 1962, from Kathleen Morrison's manuscript, held in Dartmouth College Library. It was dictated to her by Frost. I have corrected one misprint: the manuscript reads "Rio de Janeira" for "Rio de Janeiro." So far as I can determine, these remarks were never published.

Collation

*72.1   Janeiro] Janeira

Explanatory Notes

72.1   "Tale Told by an Idiot"] Faulkner's novel *The Sound and the Fury* (1929), whose title is taken from *Macbeth*: "It is a tale / Told by an idiot, full of sound and fury, / Signifying nothing" (5.5.24–28). In referring to the novel as a "tale told by an idiot" Frost has in mind the portion of *The Sound and the Fury* told from the point of view of Benjy, who is mentally retarded.

72.1   Rio de Janeiro] Frost met Faulkner in 1954 while both were attending the World Congress of Writers in Sao Paulo, Brazil. I include here part of a talk that has, regrettably, nothing to do with Faulkner, but which was occasioned by Frost's visit to Brazil, and bears considerable intrinsic interest. Frost delivered the following remarks in English; they were subsequently translated into Portuguese for publication in the official proceedings of the Congress, *Congresso International de Escritores e Encontros Inteletuais* (Sau Paulo, 1957). Robert Johnson of the University of Massachusetts then translated them back into English at the request of G. Stanley Koehler of the Department of English at Amherst. The text of Johnson's translation is held both at Amherst College and at the Jones Library, Amherst. I reprint it here with a few emendations suggested by Barbara Joels of Rutgers University, who kindly agreed to check-read Johnson's translation against the original Portuguese. Johnson, in passing his translation along to Koehler, adds in passing that Frost's remarks "must have left quite a few delegates with mouths ajar," and one can readily see why he said so. Following, then, is the "heart" of Frost's speech at the Congress, as refracted through Portuguese and back into English:

> Before getting at the heart of my few remarks, I wish to inform all of you that I did not come here to this assembly to instruct you, but rather to make a few rapid comments. At times, thinking about these events, I become partly sad and somewhat apprehensive because I see that there are people who have a sort of fear of my country. Our basic principle—that of Americans I mean—is somewhat complex. But note: John Adams was the man who decided upon our separation from the Old World, Europe. He imagined, for example, that there scarcely existed between us a degree of kinship. Afterward, Tom Paine noted that the war was not so much a war of separation but rather one for liberty and the inspiration of the French Revolution. Now, that man almost had his head chopped off, having escaped because he fled from his prison thanks to a fortunate accident. But our world did not revolt struggling for equality; scarcely anything was done in equality's name. The great realization, the real consequence of the revolution was the separation, and I should be greatly troubled if we remained separate from Europe—the Old World—without demonstrating some originality to the world. Because I always want to have the hope and satisfaction of knowing that we possess something new and fresh to contribute to the future of humanity.
>
> I want everyone to know that I am speaking in my own name.
>
> I should like to mention here the name of George Washington, who represents something basic for my nation because of his dignity and reserve. George Washington might have had much more power than he did; but he preferred to hold back and did not act as other personalities have acted in the history of my country. He was able to maintain his dignity and reserve and, above all, knew how to discipline himself. That is our land, that is our country. And now, after many years, we are reminded by some poets who referred to this.
>
> The enthusiasm for equality, for the distribution of land wealth, finally, the enthusiasm for humanity—that enthusiasm disappeared from our earth, and I

can see nothing through the Iron Curtain. The truth of the matter is that everything disappeared with the disappearance of Tom Paine.

    Another point that we must observe is the following. We must avoid a great
danger that threatens us: big capitalism that never remembers to hold back, to
restrict itself. It is necessary that big capitalism remain constantly under observation, principally by other countries. The saving grace is that our army never
adhered to big capitalism, for, if this were to happen, it would be our end.

And with that, Frost made his obligatory remarks of gratitude to his hosts and left the
stage.

73. [Comments on "The Cold War Is Being Won" (1962)]

Frost's remarks appeared as part of an informal symposium on the theme "The Cold War
Is Being Won" in *County Government Magazine* (December 1962: 13), an official publication
of the State of New York. Other contributors to the symposium included then Vice-Presi-
dent Lyndon B. Johnson; Walter Von Hallstein, President of the European Economic
Community; former Secretary of State Christian A. Herter; and Lucius D. Clay, United
States Army General, Retired. James H. Heineman, editor of *County Government*, explained the project to Frost in an October 8, 1962, letter: "We earnestly invite you to state
your opinion on where you feel we stand today in the Cold War, and how you believe
leading poets can contribute in the fight to achieve victory . . . Because of the important
part you have played in the world as a poet and as a humanitarian, your answers to our
questions will contribute directly to current history by influencing our audience of leading
government officials to create closer understanding between people. May we hear from
you as soon as possible?" Frost dictated a reply to Kathleen Morrison; this appears on the
reverse of Heineman's letter, held now in the Dartmouth College Library. Morrison prepared a typescript of the letter for Frost's signature, which was sent to *County Government*,
though I do not know whether it still exists. The copy-text for the present edition is the
Morrison manuscript, as dictated by Frost. The published text introduces two variant
wordings; the first is a misprint, the second a change in style. The published text also omits
Frost's signature and his address to Heineman. I have made one emendation to the copy-
text. In taking the dictation, Morrison abbreviated the phrase "Sin yrs / RF"; I have given
the full form.

Collation

73.1   Dear Mr. Heineman:] {not present in 1st}
73.1   running the county] running the country 1st
73.1   till we find] until we find 1st
*73.1   Sincerely yours, ¶ Robert Frost] Sin yrs ¶ RF MS; {not present in 1st}

Explanatory Notes

73.1   My limit seems to be verse and talk.] Actually, Frost has a very great deal to say in
verse with regard to the Cold War and its associated problems. See "Frost and the Cold
War: A Look at the Later Poetry," by the present editor, in *Roads Not Taken: Rereading Robert Frost*, ed. Earl Wilcox and Jonathan N. Barron (Columbia: University of Missouri Press,

2000). I would cite here as well a remark Frost made in a talk delivered at Wooster College on May 18, 1962: "Some people don't realize that there is a doubt going through our country as to who we are, where we are, and what we are, or whether we amount to anything or not. That's one I am going to write someday" (quoted in *The Wooster Alumni Bulletin* for June 1962). In fact, he had already written this cold war theme up, and quite well, too: see "Cabin in the Clearing," collected in his last book of poetry, *In the Clearing* (1962). As to the question of a nuclear apocalypse, Frost could be quite cavalier, as in the following interview with Inez Robb published in the *New York World Telegram* for March 30, 1954, under the title "Frost on the Trees": "There'll be a few of us left in the crevices after the explosions are over." Or as in this one with Ray Josephs, which appeared in *This Week Magazine* (a section of the *New York Herald Tribune*) on September 5, 1954: "In three words I can sum up everything I have learned about life. *It goes on.* In all the confusions of today, with all our troubles . . . with politicians and people slinging the word fear around, all of us become discouraged . . . tempted to say this is the end, the finish. But life—*it goes on.* It always has. It always will. Don't forget that" (2). Or, to take yet another example, consider these remarks in the *New York Times* for October 27, 1957, as reported by James Reston: "We ought to enjoy a standoff [with the Soviet Union]. Let it stand and deepen in meaning. Let's not be hasty about showdowns. Let's be patient and confident in our country . . . The question for every man and every nation is to be clear about where the first answerability lies. Are we as individuals to be answerable first only to others or to ourselves and some ideal beyond ourselves? Is the United States to be answerable first to the United Nations or to its own concept of what is right?"

74. [Statement Concerning the Beginning of His Career (1963)]

Frost prepared this statement for inclusion in a brief book edited by Edward Connery Lathem, *Robert Frost: His American 'Send-off'—1915* (Lunenburg, Vt., 1963). In the statement he refers to a June 12, 1915, letter he wrote to the English critic Edward Garnett who, as the statement implies, wrote a laudatory article about Frost for *The Atlantic Monthly*, then edited by Ellery Sedgwick. (Frost's letter to Garnett is reprinted in *SL* 178–80.) Garnett's article, "A New American Poet," and the three poems listed in Frost's statement, appeared in *The Atlantic Monthly* 116 (August 1915): 214–24. Frost's signed typescript statement, with manuscript corrections in his hand, appears in facsimile in *Robert Frost: His American 'Send-off.'* That typescript, now held at Dartmouth College Library, is the copy-text for the present edition. I have conventionalized the styling of titles.

Collation

*74.3 *The Atlantic*] The Atlantic

Explanatory Notes

74.2 Edward Garnett] Edward Garnett (1868–1937), English writer and literary critic.

74.2 Ellery Sedgwick] Ellery Sedgwick (1872–1960), American writer and editor of *The Atlantic Monthly* from 1908 to 1938.

75. [Press Release on Being Awarded the Bollingen Prize (1963)]

On January 5, 1963, the Bollingen Prize Committee announced that Frost had been awarded the Bollingen Prize for Poetry for his last collection, *In the Clearing* (New York: Holt, Rinehart, Winston, 1962). He was then in Peter Bent Brigham Hospital in Boston, where he dictated to Kathleen Morrison the press release reprinted here. I have reprinted the text of the original manuscript in Morrison's hand, signed by Frost, and held now in the Dartmouth College Library.

76. [Statement Written for the 53rd Annual Dinner of the Poetry Society of America (January 17, 1963)]

Frost dictated this statement to Kathleen Morrison from his bed at Peter Bent Brigham Hospital. It was printed first in *The Poetry Society of America Bulletin* (February 1963) with the following note: "This is the message Robert Frost sent from his hospital bed in Boston, by the hand of his daughter Lesley, the early afternoon of January 17, for transmission the same evening to The Poetry Society of America, on the occasion of its 53rd Annual Dinner at the Hotel Astor in New York. It proved to be the last greeting Robert Frost was to send to a public gathering of poets." Frost died twelve days later. The copy-text for the present edition is a typescript held at Dartmouth College Library, apparently prepared by Kathleen Morrison. It bears the heading: "Dictated the day of the Poetry Society Dinner for Lesley to read there." Lesley Frost did in fact deliver the statement, and when it was printed in the *Poetry Society Bulletin* a number of variants (chiefly in punctuation) were introduced. I assume that these variants are owing to the (possibly) oral transmission of the document at the dinner itself. The collation lists the sole difference in wording between the typescript and the published text.

Collation

76.1 over the whole country] throughout the whole country 1st

Line-End Hyphenation

1. Copy-text List

The following are editorially established forms of compounds that are hyphenated at line-ends in the copy-texts:

1.17	subjoin
1.80	venturesome
1.80	curbstone
1.89	Today
1.93	undertone
1.59	eyebrows
3.81	offspring
3.231	overhead
14.1	fellowships
22.14	praise-word
24.10	northward

2. Critical-text List

In quotations from the present edition, no line-end hyphens in ambiguously broken compounds should be retained except these:

1.119	after-thought
1.123	after-thought
1.130	bell-toned
4.232	over-head
21.6	man-made
23.8	best-sellers
46.2	hear-say

Acknowledgments

Grateful acknowledgement is due the Estate of Robert Frost, Peter Gilbert, Executor, for permission to reprint and quote from Frost's published and unpublished works, and to Henry Holt and Company for permission to quote from Frost's poems. Special thanks are due to Philip Cronenwett and the staff of the Dartmouth College Library; to John Lancaster, Daria D'Areinzo, and the staff at Amherst College's Robert Frost Memorial Library; and to the staff at the Alderman Library, University of Virginia, for generously making available to scholars their great collections of Frost's books and manuscripts. In addition, I would like to acknowledge the following libraries for their help: University of Florida Library; New York Public Library; Oberlin College Library; American Academy and Institute of Arts and Letters Library, New York; Firestone Library, Princeton University; Middlebury College Library; Lawrence, Massachusetts, Public Library; Immigrant City Archives, Lawrence; Derry, New Hampshire, Public Library; The Jones Library, Amherst; National Agricultural Library, Beltsville, Maryland; Regenstein Library, University of Chicago; Houghton Library, Harvard University; and the Nils Yngve Library, Tufts University. For help in tracking down Frost's contributions to the Pinkerton Academy *Catalogue*, I am grateful to Olive Abbott, Alumni Office Historian, Pinkerton Academy, Derry, New Hampshire. I remember many helpful conversations with J. M. Thomas about the business of editing. I am further indebted to Mark Scott for help in tracking down the sources of a number of Frost's quotations. And I thank Richard Poirier, Thomas R. Edwards, and G. Thomas Tanselle—the committee that oversaw a by now much earlier version of this edition when it was part of my doctoral dissertation—for sound advice.

General Index

References are by item and paragraph number, followed by "n" if to a note or headnote. Roman numerals refer to page numbers in the Introduction; entries followed by "ep" refer to the Editorial Principles by page number. Frost's immediate family members are indexed under "Frost," even where names were later changed by marriage. Persons mentioned in Frost's texts and in a note keyed to the same item and paragraph number are indexed by text reference only.

Heineman, James H., 73n
Hemingway, Ernest, 56.1, 70.1, 36.0n, 62n;
    death of, 70.1n; "The Killers," 70.1,
    36.0n
Hendricks, Walter, 37.4
Henry VIII (King of England), 65.5
Herrick, Robert, 36.9; "To Daffodils," 36.9,
    36.9n
Herter, Christian A., 73n
Hertz, Neil, 2n, 36.5n
Hickler, Roger, 75.1
Hitler, Adolf, 32.1
Holden, Raymond, 50.3
Holmes, John, 45.1, 52n
Holmes, Oliver Wendell, 1.41
Homer, 62.2, 66.1; *Odyssey*, 5.13, 18.41–42,
    23.1, 36.1, 62.3
Hopkins, Gerard Manley, 28.2n, 36.5n
Hopkins, Mark, 12.5
Horace (Quintus Horatius Flaccus), 71.3
Huxley, Julian, xxvii, 64n
Huxley, Thomas Henry, 65.3

Imagism, 13.2

Jackson, Gardner, 2n
James, William, xxiii; *Pragmatism*, xxiv;
    Talks to Teachers, xxiii, xxxii n20;
    "What Makes a Life Significant,"
    xxiii, xxiv, xxxii n20
Jarrell, Randall, 57n
Jefferson, Thomas, 63.2, 68.1
Jewell, Ernest, 58.3
Jewett, William, 2n
Joels, Barbara, 72.1n
Johnson, Burges, 33.2
Johnson, Lyndon B., 73n
Johnson, Robert, 72.1n
Johnson, Walter Perry ("The Big Train"),
    50.6
Joson, Benjamin, 5.26; *Silent Woman, The*,
    5.26

Karsh, Yousuf, 49n
Keats, John, 18.47
Kennedy, John Fitzgerald, xxvi, 32n, 62n;
    Profiles in Courage, 32n
Kipling, Rudyard, 5.21, 30.9, 39.1, 39.1n;
    "American, An," 39.1n; *Jungle Book*,
    23.9; "Road to Mandalay," 30.12n
Kissinger, Henry, 54n
Koehler, G. Stanley, 72.1n
Kohn, John S. Van E., 18n
Kossuth, Lajos, 31.2

Kreymborg, Alfred, 50.4
Krushchev, Nikita, xxvii, 75.1

Lamb, Charles, 16.1
Lancaster, John, 8n, 18n, 34n, 62n
Landor, Walter Savage, 13.2, 52.2
Langland, Joseph, 71n
Lanier, Sidney: *Science of English Verse*, 30n
Lathem, Edward Connery, x, 237ep, 1n, 4n,
    18n, 21n, 32n, 53n, 59n
Lawrence, T. E., 23.1
Ledoux, Louis, 22n
Lee, Robert E., 37.16
Lewis, Edward Morgan, 50.3
Lincoln, Abraham, 63.2
Linscott, Robert, 36n
Lloyd, Alfred, 12n
Longfellow, Henry Wadsworth, xxxii n17,
    9.3n, 19.6n
Lowell, James Russell, 36.9n
Lowell, Robert, 75.1
Lowes, John Livingston, 30n
Luther, Martin, 22.2

Macaulay, Thomas Babington: "Horatio at
    the Bridge," 5.13
Mackaye, Percy, xxi–xviii, 14.1–3
MacLeish, Archibald, 56.1, 54n
MacVeagh, Lincoln, 10n
Madison, Charles A., 40n
Madison, James, 68.1
Maeterlink, Maurice: *The Blue Bird*, 5.26
Mantle, Mickey, 50.7
Markham, Edwin, 22.25n
Marlowe, Christopher, 5.8, 5.21; *Doctor Faustus*, 5.8–10
Marx, Karl, 65.4, 65.6
Masefield, William, 13.2
Mays, Willie, 50.7
McGuffey, William Holmes, 67.2n; *Reader*,
    67.2n
Meiklejohn, Alexander, 7.4
Melcher, Frederic Gersham, 63.1
Melville, Herman: *Moby Dick*, 65.5
Mencken, Henry Louis: *The American Language*, 39.1
Meredith, William, 67.4n
Mertins, Louis, 31n
Millay, Edna St. Vincent, 29.4
Miller, Perry, 33.2
Milton, John, 5.8, 5.25, 19.6n; *Comus*, 5.8–10,
    10.6; "Il Penseroso," 55.4; "L'Allegro,"
    55.4
Mirrielees, Edith Ronald, 33.2

Index of Items by Title